CLIMATE
CHANGE

TURNING UP THE HEAT

A. BARRIE PITTOCK

EARTHSCAN

CSIRO
PUBLISHING

National Library of Australia Cataloguing-in-Publication entry

Pittock, A. Barrie, 1938– .
Climate change: turning up the heat.

Bibliography.
Includes index.
ISBN 0 643 06934 3.

1. Global warming. 2. Climatic changes. I. Title.

363.73874

A catalogue record for this book is available from the British Library

Library of Congress Cataloging-in-Publication Data

Pittock, A. Barrie, 1938–
Climate change: turning up the heat / A. Barrie Pittock.
p. cm.

Includes bibliographical references and index.

ISBN 1-84407-300-9
1. Climatic changes. I. Title.
QC981.8.C5P58 2005
363.738'74-dc22
2005 18167

Published exclusively in Australia, New Zealand and the Americas, and non-exclusively in other territories of the world (excluding Europe, the Middle East, Asia and Africa), by:

CSIRO PUBLISHING
PO Box 1139 (150 Oxford St)
Collingwood VIC 3066
Australia

Tel: (03) 9662 7666   Int: +(613) 9662 7666
Fax: (03) 9662 7555   Int: +(613) 9662 7555
Email: publishing.sales@csiro.au
Website: www.publish.csiro.au

Published exclusively in Europe, the Middle East, Asia (including India, Japan, China, and South-East Asia) and Africa, and non-exclusively in other territories of the world (excluding Australia, New Zealand and the Americas) by Earthscan, with the ISBN 1-84407-300-9.

Earthscan
8-12 Camden High Street
London, NW1 0JH, UK

Tel: +44 (0)20 7387 8558
Fax: +44 (0)20 7387 8998
Email: earthinfo@earthscan.co.uk
Website: www.earthscan.co.uk

22883 Quicksilver Drive, Sterling, VA 20166-2012, USA

Earthscan is an imprint of James & James (Science Publishers) Ltd and publishes in association with the International Institute for Environment and Development

Front cover photo by Robert Kerton, Scienceimage

Set in Times New Roman PS and Stone Sans
Cover and text design by James Kelly
Typeset by Desktop Concepts Pty Ltd, Melbourne
Printed in Australia by BPA Print Group

Disclaimer: The views expressed in this work are the author's own and do not necessarily reflect those of his employer, referees, editors or publisher.

Contents

Foreword

Barrie Pittock has been a leading researcher of considerable standing worldwide on various aspects of climate change. The quality and content of research carried out by him has established a benchmark that sets the standard for several of his peers and provides a model for young researchers.

In this book he has provided a comprehensive analysis of various aspects of climate change, which he begins by examining the physical and biological aspects of climate change and a detailed analysis of the science of the climate system. The book assumes great topical interest for the reader because of several questions that the author has posed and attempted to answer, such as the recent heatwave that took place in Paris in the summer of 2003, the frequency of closure of the Thames barrier, and the melting of glaciers which affects not only parts of Europe but even the high mountain glaciers in the Himalayas.

A study of paleoclimate is an important component of present day climate change research, and the book goes through a lucid and useful assessment of the evidence that is available to us today in understanding and quantifying the nature and extent of climate change in the past. Also presented in considerable detail are projections of climate change in the future including a discussion of the emissions scenarios developed and used by the IPCC and projections obtained from it as well as from other sources.

An extremely eloquent statement is conveyed in the title of Chapter 4, which states 'Uncertainty is inevitable, but risk is certain'. This really is the key message in this book particularly as it goes on to describe the impacts of climate change, the seriousness with which these should be considered and the imperative need for adaptation. In Chapter 8 a comprehensive and detailed assessment is provided on several mitigation actions. The volume ends by making a logical transition into political issues that have national as well as international dimensions.

For sheer breadth and comprehensiveness of coverage, Barrie Pittock's book fills a unique void in the literature in this field. Coming as it does from an author who knows the scientific and technical complexities of the whole subject, this book should be seen as a valuable reference for scientists and policymakers alike.

In my view, which is shared by a growing body of concerned citizens worldwide, climate change is a challenge faced by the global community that will require unprecedented resolve and increasing ingenuity to tackle in the years ahead. Efforts to be made would need to be based on knowledge and informed assessment of the future. Barrie Pittock's book provides information and analysis that will greatly assist and guide decision makers on what needs to be done.

Dr Rajendra K Pachauri
Director-General, The Energy and Resources Institute, India
and Chairman, Intergovernmental Panel on Climate Change

Acknowledgements

This book is the result of many years working on climate change, nearly all based in CSIRO Atmospheric Research (now part of CSIRO Marine and Atmospheric Research) in Australia and especially with the Intergovernmental Panel on Climate Change (IPCC). I therefore thank many colleagues in CSIRO and many others from numerous countries whom I met through IPCC or other forums. My views have been influenced by their collective research and arguments, as well as my own research, and I owe them all a debt of gratitude.

A book such as this inevitably draws from and builds on the work that has gone before it. Since subtle changes in wording can easily lead to misinterpretation in this field, some content in this book has been carefully paraphrased from, or closely follows the original sources to ensure accuracy. Some sections in the present book are drawn from the following: parts of the *IPCC Third Assessment Report* (IPCC 2001a, b, c and d); a book that I edited for the Australian Greenhouse Office (AGO) in 2003 *Climate Change: An Australian Guide to the Science and Potential Impacts*; and a paper I wrote for the journal *Climatic Change* in 2002 'What we know and don't know about climate change: reflections on the IPCC TAR' (*Climatic Change* vol. 53, pp. 393–411). (See bibliography for full details of all these publications.) This applies particularly to parts of Chapter 3 on projecting the future, Chapter 5 on projected climate changes, Chapter 6 on impacts and Chapter 7 on adaptation concepts. I thank the AGO, the IPCC and Springer (publishers of *Climatic Change*) for permission to use some common wording. I have endeavoured to acknowledge all sources, however, if any have been overlooked I apologise to the original authors and/or publishers.

The following Figures come from other sources, who granted permission to use them, for which I am grateful. Some have been modified, and the original sources are not responsible for my changes. These are: Figures 1, 7, 10, 15, 16, 23 and 25 from IPCC; Figure 4 from UK Environment Agency; Figure 5 from INVS, France; Figure 9 from David Etheridge, CSIRO; Figures 13, 14 and 21, Roger Jones, CSIRO; Figure 17, US National Snow and Ice Data Center; Figure 18, T. Coleman, Insurance Group Australia; Figure 20, Water Corporation, Western Australia; Figure 27, CSIRO Climate Impacts Group and Government of New South Wales; Figures 28 and 29, Greg Bourne, now at WWF Australia; Figure 30, Kathy McInnes, CSIRO and Chalapan Kaluwin, AMSAT, Fiji.

The views expressed in this work are my own and do not necessarily represent the views of CSIRO, the AGO, the IPCC or other affiliated parties.

Particular people I want to thank are:

From CSIRO: Tom Beer, Willem Bouma, John Church, Kevin Hennessy, Paul Holper, Roger Jones, Kathy McInnes, Simon Torok, Penny Whetton, and

John Wright. Also Rachel Anning (UK Environment Agency), Martin Beniston (Universite de Fribourg, Switzerland), Andre Berger (Université Catholique de Louvain, Belgium), Greg Bourne (WWF, Australia), Pascal Empereur-Bisson-net (INVS, France), Dale Hess (BoM, Australia), William Howard (U. Tasmania), Murari Lal (Uni. South Pacific, Fiji), Mark Maslin (U. College London, UK), Tony McMichael (ANU, Australia), Bettina Menne (WHO, Italy), Neville Nicholls (BoM, Australia), Martin Parry (Jackson Institute, UK), Jamie Pittock (WWF, Australia), Thomas W. Pogge (Columbia University, USA), Brian Sadler (IOCI, Australia), and Christopher Thomas (NSW GH Office, Australia). Probably I have omitted some people who helped, and apologise to them for my oversight.

Special thanks goes to Graeme Pearman and Greg Ayers, successive Chiefs of CSIRO Atmospheric Research, for my position as a Post-Retirement Fellow, and more recently as an Honorary Fellow. Special thanks also to Paul Durack and Roger Jones for help with Figures, and to Ann Crabb and colleagues at CSIRO Publishing. Ann's insightful and helpful editing comments and discussions have greatly improved the book.

Finally, I want to thank my partner Diana Pittock, for her support and forbearance during the writing of this book.

Introduction

Back in 1972 I wrote a paper entitled 'How important are climatic changes?' It concluded that human dependence on a stable climate might be more critical than is generally believed. This dependence, I argued, is readily seen in the relationship between rainfall patterns and patterns of land and water use, including use for industrial and urban purposes. The paper argued that the severity of the economic adjustments required by a change in climate depend on the relation between the existing economy and its climatic environment, and the rapidity of climate change.

My first projections of possible future patterns of climate change were published in 1980, based on the early findings of relatively crude computer models of climate, combined with a look at the contrasts between individual warm and cold years, paleo-climatic reconstructions of earlier warm epochs, and some theoretical arguments.

In 1988 I became the founder of the Climate Impact Group in CSIRO Atmospheric Research in Melbourne, Australia. This group sought to bridge the gap between climate modellers, with their projections of climate change and sea-level rise, and people interested in the potential effects on crops, water resources, coastal zones and other parts of the natural and social systems and environment. Despite reservations from some colleagues who wanted greater certainty before going public on scientific findings that identify risk, the Climate Impact Group approach of publicly quantifying risk won wide respect, culminating in the award in 2003 of the Sherman Eureka Prize for Environmental Research, one of Australia's most prestigious national awards for environmental science.

The object of the Climate Impact Group's endeavours was never to make exact predictions of what will happen, because we recognised that there are inevitable uncertainties about both the science and socio-economic conditions resulting from human behaviour. Rather, we sought to provide the best possible advice as to what might happen, its impacts on society, and on the consequences of various policy choices, so that decision-makers could make informed risk assessments and choices that would influence future outcomes.

These days, writing a book on a 'hot topic' like climate change is a bit of a wild ride. Lots of things keep happening during the process. Two developments have stood out in the case of this book.

The first was the release of the fictional disaster film *The Day After Tomorrow* in May 2004. My draft already included a discussion of possible abrupt changes in climate, thresholds, instabilities and large-scale changes to the climate system. This included possible slowdown or cessation of the circulation in the ocean that transports heat from the tropics to Western Europe, which is the scientific underpinning of the film. Such possibilities were discussed in the 2001 report of the Intergovernmental Panel on Climate Change, and indeed much earlier, so they are hardly new.

In the plot of *The Day After Tomorrow* the scientist hero warns politicians of the possibility of such disasters occurring within the next century or so, but the onset of large cooling in the northern hemisphere actually happens in the film in a matter of 10 days. This is quite unrealistic, as are quite a few parts of the plot – but then it is only a story for entertainment, not a prediction or a scientific treatise.

Nevertheless, it seems to me important to set the record straight for all those who were scared, or at least challenged, by the film, and to put the situation in a more hopeful perspective. As someone who has spent the last two decades working on climate change science, I want to say that there is still hope of avoiding the worst consequences if we act now. Yes, the matter is serious, and yes, there is a small risk of drastic climate changes occurring in the next few decades. But there is hope. It is not yet too late.

Then came the second big development. This was a scientific paper in August 2004, rapidly followed by another in January 2005 (in *Nature*, 27 January) refining estimates of the range of uncertainty in what is known as the 'climate sensitivity'. The climate sensitivity is the amount of global surface warming which would occur if the carbon dioxide concentration in the atmosphere were to double, as is likely during this century. Climate models, and other lines of evidence, suggested in 1979 that the likely range was somewhere between 1.5 and 4.5°C, with a middle estimate of about 3.0°C. This figure was used in all three major reports of the Intergovernmental Panel on Climate Change, including the latest in 2001.

The new results in 2004 suggest that in fact the likely range is more like 2.4 to 5.4°C, while the 2005 paper by a UK team of scientists headed by D. A. Stainforth of Oxford University, puts the range at 2 to 11°C. These results have strong implications for the risk of large warmings during the twenty-first century, and greatly reduce the probability that global warmings by 2100 will be less than the 2 or 3°C identified by many scientists as liable to lead to dangerous impacts. We are now forced to consider whether in order to avoid dangerous climate change we must keep greenhouse gas concentrations below something like 400 to 500 ppm carbon dioxide equivalent. This is a 'big ask', as we are already at about 380 ppm and rising at a rate of 1 or 2 ppm each year. These new results therefore heighten the urgency of reducing emissions well below present levels in the next decade, rather than several decades down the track.

So maybe it is too late after all. This is especially so if we take the advice of some politicians and fossil-fuel advocates, who deny, at least by their actions, that there is a need for immediate action. Such people often raise genuine but exaggerated uncertainties to justify continuing with business as usual.

I prefer to follow a risk management strategy, and the advice and examples of the technological optimists and entrepreneurs who argue and demonstrate that we can rapidly develop a prosperous future with low carbon dioxide emissions. That way we can improve living standards both in the industrialised and developing countries, while minimising the risks of climate change.

While acknowledged uncertainties mean we are dealing with risks rather than certainties, the chance of drastic climate change in the next couple of decades still seems small, at least on a global scale. But the risks will certainly increase rapidly over coming decades, and drastic global changes may become inevitable due to lags in the climate system. We can reduce these risks by urgently setting about reducing emissions of greenhouse gases now. If we sit back and say to ourselves that the risks are too small to worry about, and too costly to prevent, they are likely to catch up with us, if not this decade then the next or the one after. We, as consumers, business people and members of the public can turn things around by our choices and our opinions made known now. We do not have to wait for national governments to act, or for laws and taxes to compel us. Individual choices, initiatives, ingenuity, innovation and action can achieve wonders.

However, our individual actions would be more effective if we could persuade governments to recognise the urgency and act now to really push for a reduction in greenhouse emissions this decade. Climate change, abrupt or not, is a real risk. It is also a challenge and an opportunity for innovative thinking and action. With a bit of luck and a lot of skill, we can transform the challenge of climate change into a positive. Reducing emissions will also help avoid other environmental damages and promote sustainable development and greater equity between peoples and countries, so it is well worth doing.

My intention with this book is to answer, in readily understood terms, frequently asked questions about climate change, such as:

- What is the relationship between natural climate variations and human-induced climate change?

- What are the major concerns regarding climate change?

- Why are there arguments about the reality of climate change, and its policy implications?

- How does climate change relate to other problems like population growth, poverty, pollution and land degradation?

- How urgent is the problem? What can we do about it, and how much will it cost?

This book is meant, in a concise and understandable manner, to sort fact from fiction. It recognises that uncertainties are inevitable, and sets climate change in a framework of assessing climate risk alongside all the other human problems about which we have imperfect knowledge. It should help readers to choose a sensible course between the head-in-the-sand reaction of some contrarians and the doom-and-gloom view of some alarmists. It builds on the scientific base of the well-tested and accepted reports of the Intergovernmental Panel on

Climate Change, putting the findings in the context of other human concerns. The book suggests that it is possible, with help from ordinary people, for the international community to deal constructively with the problem of climate change and in the process move society towards a more just and sustainable future. However, it also suggests that the necessary sense of urgency is missing. Without early action, costly emergency measures may be necessary when the full extent of the problem becomes obvious.

We must look beyond the doom and gloom. Projections of rapid climate change with severe consequences are a prophecy, not in the sense that they are bound to come true, but in the sense of a prophetic warning that if we continue on our present course these could be the logical consequences. Modern scientific 'prophets of doom' follow in the tradition of the Old Testament prophets. The Biblical prophets were not preaching damnation, but appealing for a change of direction, so that damnation could be avoided. Similarly, climate scientists who warn about potentially dangerous climate change hope that such forebodings will motivate people to act to avoid the danger.

Hope lies not in science, but in going beyond the science to examine the policy questions and the moral imperatives that the scientific projections throw into stark relief. In this book I go some way down this road, making direct links between the science and the consequences, which I regard as important for policy. If this encourages you to address the issues, to make your own assessment of the risk, and to act accordingly, this book will have achieved its purpose.

Scientific books are often replete with footnotes, or references to the literature in parentheses. This can be off-putting to the general reader, so I have avoided these options. Instead, at the end of the book there is a short bibliography of the more important or accessible books, reports and articles (sometimes with references to websites where they can be obtained), and an annotated list of useful websites. Some extensive notes and references arranged by chapter under various subject headings can be found on the publisher's website (see p. 296).

Finally, I want to dedicate this book to my two granddaughters, Jenny and Ella, whose future is at stake, along with that of all future generations. It is for them that we must meet the challenge of climate change.

1

Climate change matters

*Today, global climate change is a fact. The climate has changed
visibly, tangibly, measurably. An additional increase in average
temperatures is not only possible, but very probable, while human
intervention in the natural climate system plays an important, if not
decisive role.*

Bruno Porro, Chief Risk Officer, Swiss Reinsurance, 2002.

*Climate change is a major concern in relation to the minerals sector
and sustainable development. It is, potentially, one of the greatest of
all threats to the environment, to biodiversity and ultimately to our
quality of life.*

***Facing the Future,* Report of the Mining Minerals and
Sustainable Development Australia project, 2002.**

Climate is critical to the world as we know it. The landscape, and the plants and
animals in it, are all determined to a large extent by climate acting over long
intervals of time. Over geological time, climate has helped to shape mountains,
build up the soil, determine the nature of the rivers, and build flood plains and
deltas. At least until the advent of irrigation and industrialisation, climate determined food supplies and where human beings could live.

Today, with modern technology, humans can indeed live in places where it was
impossible before. This is achieved by the provision of buildings and complex
infrastructure tuned to the existing climate, such as urban and rural water supplies,
drainage, bridges, roads and other communications. These involve huge investments of time and money. Trade, particularly of food and fibre for manufactured
goods, has also been strongly influenced by climate. Roads, buildings and towns
are designed taking local climate into consideration. Design rules, both formal and
informal, zoning and safety standards are developed to cope not just with average

climate but also with climatic extremes such as floods and droughts. If the climate changes, human society must adapt by changing its designs, rules and infrastructure – often at great expense.

In broad terms, 'climate' is the typical range of weather, including its variability, experienced at a particular place. It is often expressed statistically in terms of averages over a season or number of years of temperature or rainfall and sometimes in terms of other variables such as wind, humidity, and so on. Variability is an important factor. 'Climate variability' is variability in the average weather behaviour at a particular location from one year to another, or one decade to another. Changes in the behaviour of the weather over longer timescales, such as one century to another, are usually referred to as 'climate change'.

Conventionally, 30-year intervals have been used for calculating averages and estimating weather variability. However, natural climate varies on time scales from year-to-year, through decade-to-decade to longer-term fluctuations over centuries and millennia.

Extreme weather events are part of climate. Their impact is reflected in the design of human settlements and activities (such as farming) so as to be able to survive floods, droughts, severe storms and other weather-related stresses or catastrophes. Because climate can vary from decade to decade, reliable averages of the frequency and magnitudes of extreme events require weather observations over longer periods than the conventional 30 years. Engineers design infrastructure (buildings, bridges, dams, drains, etc.) to cope with extreme weather events that occur on average only once in every 50, 100 or 1000 years. The more serious the consequence of design failure under extreme weather conditions, the longer the time interval considered, for example for a large dam as opposed to a street drain.

Turning up the heat

Climate has changed greatly over geological timescales, as we shall see in Chapter 2. But what is of immediate concern is that climate has shown an almost unprecedented rapid global warming trend in the last few decades.

Since the start of reliable observations in the nineteenth century, scientists from weather services and research laboratories in many countries have examined local, regional and global average surface air and water temperatures, on land and from ships.

The World Meteorological Organization, which coordinates weather services around the globe, has declared that 2004 was the fourth warmest year since reliable weather records began in 1861, and just warmer than 2003. The warmest year remains 1998, while each of the last 10 years (1995–2004), with the

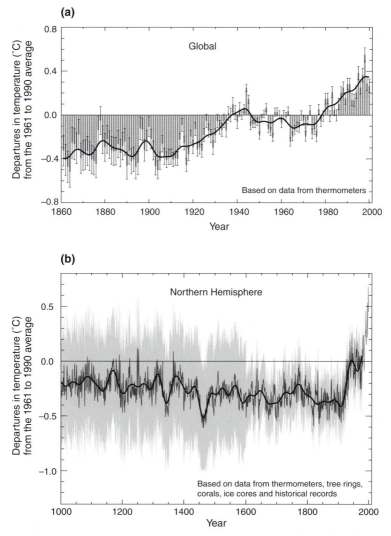

Figure 1: Variations of the Earth's surface temperature. Variations (a) for the last 140 years (global) and (b) the past 1000 years (Northern Hemisphere). (Adapted with permission from IPCC 2001a, Figure 1 of Summary for Policymakers.)

exception of 1996, is one of the warmest 10 years on record. Indirect evidence from tree rings, ice cores, boreholes, and other climate–sensitive indicators (see Chapter 2) indicates that the late twentieth century warming is unprecedented for at least the last 1000 years (see Chapter 2 for a later discussion). Variations of the Earth's surface temperature for the last 140 years (thermometer measure-ments), and the last 1000 years (data from thermometers, tree rings, corals, ice cores and historical records) are shown in **Figure 1**.

Based on these observations, a critical review by the Intergovernmental Panel on Climate Change (IPCC) in 2001 concluded that the global average surface temperature has increased over the twentieth century by $0.6 \pm 0.2°C$.

Note that when scientists give such estimates they usually include a range of uncertainty, which in this case is plus or minus 0.2°C – that is, the increase could be as low as 0.4°C or as high as 0.8°C. Such uncertainties allow for possible inaccuracies in individual measurements, and how well the average from the limited number of individual measurement stations represents the average from all locations.

Two things are notable about this IPCC conclusion. First, it shows that a warming of at least 0.4°C (that is, 0.6 minus 0.2°C) almost certainly occurred. Second, the value of 0.6°C, while it may appear to be small, is already a sizeable fraction of the global warming of about 5°C that took place from the last glaciation around 20,000 years ago to the present inter-glacial period (which commenced some 10,000 years ago). Prehistoric global warming led to a complete transformation of the Earth's surface, with the disappearance of ice sheets, and massive changes in vegetation cover, regional extinctions and a sea-level rise of about 120 metres.

Some critics have questioned the IPCC's estimated warming figures on the following main grounds. First, there are questions of uncertainties due to changes in instruments. Instrumental changes include changes in the housing of thermometers ('meteorological screens') which affect the ventilation and radiant heat reaching the thermometers, and changes in ships' observations from measuring the temperature of water obtained from buckets dropped over the side of ships to measurements of the temperature of sea water pumped in to cool the ships' engines. These changes are well recognised by scientists and have been allowed for. They contribute to the estimate of uncertainty.

Second, there are concerns that estimates are biased by observations from stations where local warming is caused by the growth of cities (an effect known as 'urban heat islands').

The heat island effect is due to the heat absorbed or given out by buildings and roads (especially at night). However, this effect works both ways on observed trends. In many large cities, observing sites, which were originally near city centres (and thus subject to warming as the cities grew) were replaced by observing sites at airports outside the cities. This led to a temporary observed cooling until urbanisation reached as far as the airports. Observations from sites affected by urban heat islands have, in general, been either corrected for this effect or excluded from the averages. A recent study of temperature trends on windy nights versus all nights shows similar warming trends, even though wind disperses locally generated heat and eliminates any heat island effect.

One of the strengths of the surface observations is that those from land surface meteorological stations tend to agree well with nearby ship observations, despite different sources of possible errors. Also average sea surface temperatures show similar trends to land-based observations for the same regions. Airborne observations from balloon-borne radio-sondes at near-ground levels also tend to support the land-based observational trends.

Another issue often raised is the apparent difference between the trends in temperature found in surface observations and those from satellites, which began in 1979. The satellite observations are not straightforward, as corrections are needed for instrumental changes and satellite orbital changes. Moreover, they record average temperatures over the lowest several kilometres of the atmosphere (including the lower stratosphere at mid- to high-latitudes) rather than at the surface, so they do not measure the same thing as surface observations. A recent correction to the satellite estimates to take account of the simultaneous cooling of the lower stratosphere has removed the discrepancy and confirms that surface warming is occurring.

Supporting evidence for recent global warming comes from many different regions and types of phenomena. For example, there is now ample evidence of retreat of alpine and continental glaciers in response to the twentieth century warming (there are exceptions in some mid- to high-latitude coastal locations where snowfall has increased). This retreat has accelerated in the last couple of decades as global warming has accelerated. **Figure 2** shows dramatic evidence of this for the Trient Glacier in the Valais region of southern Switzerland. The surviving glacier is in the upper centre, extending right to the skyline. Measured retreat of the terminus of the glacier since 1986–87 is roughly 500 metres. Early twentieth century terminal and lateral moraines (where rock and earth are dumped by the glacier) are evident, free of trees, indicating recent ice retreat, and the present terminus of the glacier is slumped, indicating rapid melting.

Changes in other aspects of climate, broadly consistent with global warming, have also occurred over the last century. These include decreases of about 10% in snow cover as observed by satellites since the 1960s, and a 10 to 15% decrease in spring and summer sea-ice since the 1950s in the northern hemisphere. Warming has also been rapid near the Antarctic Peninsula, although not around mainland Antarctica.

Observed melting of permafrost is documented, especially for Alaska, by the US Arctic Research Commission in its *Permafrost Task Force Report* in 2003, along with recommendations for further observations and research. Similarly, the NASA Earth Observatory has documented increased summer melting of ice on the Greenland Ice Cap, which shows a melting trend since 1979, only interrupted in 1992 by the effects of the volcanic eruption of Mt Pinatubo. Extreme

recent lateral moraine

Trient glacier

Rapidly melting terminus

recent terminal moraine

Figure 2: The Trient Glacier near Forclaz in the Valais region of southern Switzerland in 2000. Rapid retreat has occurred during the latter part of the twentieth century. (Photograph by A.B. Pittock.)

melt years were 1991, 1995 and 2002. Observed changes in the Arctic are summarised in **Box 1**.

Other changes include rapid recession of the ice cap on Mt Kilimanjaro in Kenya and other tropical glaciers in Africa, New Guinea and South America, as well as glaciers in Canada, the United States and China. Permafrost is melting in Siberia (where it has caused problems with roads, pipelines and buildings) and in the European Alps (where it has threatened the stability of some mountain peaks and cable car stations due to repeated melting and freezing of water in crevices in the rocks, forcing them apart). Catastrophic release of water dammed behind the terminal moraines of retreating glaciers in high valleys is of increasing concern in part of the Himalayas, notably Bhutan and Nepal, according to a United Nations Environment Program report. All of these phenomena have accelerated in recent decades.

Measurements of the Southern Patagonian ice sheet in South America indicate accelerated melting by a factor of two since 1995, with the current rate of melting being about 42 cubic km per year, which is equivalent to 1 mm per decade rise in global average sea level.

A decrease in sea-ice extent in the Arctic spring and summer of 10 to 15% since the 1950s is consistent with an increase in spring and, to a lesser extent, summer temperatures at high northern latitudes. There is little indication of

Box 1: Observed changes in the Arctic

Highlights of presentations at the final conference on the Arctic Climate System Study, in St. Petersberg, November 2003, included:

- The Arctic experienced very strong warming during the last 30 years in concert with global trends.

- Some evidence suggests that a recent freshening of the sub-Artic seas might be a local expression of a change in the global water cycle.

- Satellite microwave data reveal that Arctic sea ice extent has decreased by 2.5% per decade since 1972, with September (the seasonal minimum) showing the largest decrease.

- Arctic sea ice has thinned substantially over the last 20–40 years in most deep-water areas, especially in summer.

- In 2002, the Greenland ice sheet experienced the most extensive melt since satellite observations began in 1980.

- River runoff into the Arctic Ocean has increased significantly during recent decades and the river ice season has shortened.

- There has been a northward movement of the Arctic tree line since the late 1950s, particularly in north-west Canada and eastern and coastal Siberia.

Source: Thierry Fichefet and others, *EOS*, Vol.85, 20 April, 2004.

reduced Arctic sea-ice extent during winter despite warming in the surrounding regions. Antarctic sea-ice extent has fluctuated in recent decades but remained fairly stable, apart from the area around the Antarctic Peninsula where rapid regional warming has led to sea-ice retreat and the disintegration of several large semi-permanent ice shelves attached to the mainland (see **Figure 17**).

Global warming has led to thermal expansion of the ocean waters as well as melting of mountain glaciers. John Church, from CSIRO in Australia, and colleagues recently compared model calculations of regional sea-level rise with observations from tide gauge and satellite altimeter records. They concluded that the best estimate of average sea-level rise globally for the period 1950 to 2000 is about 1.8 to 1.9 ± 0.2 mm per year (that is just under 10 cm), and that sea-level rise is greatest (about 3 mm per year or 30 cm per century) in the eastern equatorial Pacific and western equatorial Indian Ocean. Observed rates of rise are smallest (about 1 mm per year) in the western equatorial Pacific and eastern Indian Ocean, particularly the north-west coast of Australia. Regional variations are weaker for much of the rest of the global oceans, and are due to different rates of warming in different parts of the oceans, and changes in winds, currents and atmospheric pressure.

Evidence for a strengthening of the global hydrological cycle, in which more rapid evaporation takes place in low latitudes, and more rain and snowfall occurs at high latitudes, comes from observations of salinity increases in the tropical and sub-tropical surface waters of the Atlantic Ocean over the last 50 years. This is accompanied by a freshening of surface waters in the high latitudes of the North and South Atlantic. Estimates indicate that net evaporation rates over the tropical Atlantic must have increased by 5–10% over the past four decades, with an accelerated trend since 1990.

Other regional changes are also evident in rainfall, cloud cover and extreme temperature events, but due to large natural variability these are not yet well established. Many regional climate variables have variations on timescales of several decades. These are difficult to distinguish from longer-term changes without records longer than those presently available from modern instruments.

Analyses of indirect evidence of climate changes ('proxy data' – see Chapter 2) for the Northern Hemisphere indicate that the increase in temperature in the twentieth century is likely to have been the largest of any comparable period in the past 1000 years (**Figure 1b**). It is also likely that, in the Northern Hemisphere, the 1990s was the warmest decade and 1998 the warmest year of the millennium. Because fewer data are available, less is known about annual averages in the 1000 years prior to the present and for conditions prevailing in most of the Southern Hemisphere prior to 1861.

The result in **Figure 1b**, referred to as the 'hockey stick' because of the long 'handle' from 1000 AD to about 1900, and the relatively sharp rise thereafter, has been hotly contested by various sceptics. The way in which various proxy data sets were combined and the way they were adjusted for various effects have been debated. This is discussed further in Chapter 2, but the upshot is that, while the handle of the hockey stick may not have been as smooth as depicted in **Figure 1b**, the temperature rise after about 1970 remains unprecedented over the period of record.

Why is the present rapid warming happening?

Scientists believe the rapid warming in the last several decades is due mostly to human-induced changes to the atmosphere, on top of some natural variations. Climate change induced by human activity may occur due to changes in the composition of the Earth's atmosphere from waste gases due to industry, farm animals and land clearing, or changes in the land surface reflectivity caused by land clearing, cropping and irrigation. These gases include several, such as carbon dioxide, methane and oxides of nitrogen, that can absorb heat radiation from the Sun or the Earth. When warmed by the Sun or the Earth they give off heat radiation both upwards into space and downwards to the Earth. These gases are called greenhouse gases and act like a thick blanket surrounding the Earth. In effect, the Earth's surface has to warm up to give off as much energy as heat radiation as is being absorbed from the Sun. Soot particles from fires can also lead to local surface warming by absorbing sunlight, but reflective particles, such as those formed from sulfurous fumes (sulfate aerosols) can lead to local cooling by preventing sunlight reaching the Earth's surface.

Natural greenhouse gases include carbon dioxide, methane and water vapour. These help to keep Earth some 33°C warmer than if there were no greenhouse gases and clouds in the atmosphere.

Human activities have increased the concentrations of several greenhouse gases in the atmosphere, leading to what is termed the 'enhanced greenhouse effect'. These gases include carbon dioxide, methane and several other artificial chemicals. The Kyoto Protocol, set up to begin the task of reducing greenhouse gas emissions (see Chapter 11), includes a package or 'basket' of six main gases to be regulated. Besides carbon dioxide (CO_2) and methane (CH_4), these are nitrous oxide (N_2O), hydrofluorocarbons (HFCs), perfluorocarbons (PFCs) and sulfur hexafluoride (SF_6).

Anthropogenic, or human-caused increases in carbon dioxide, come mainly from the burning of fossil fuels such as coal, oil and natural gas, the destruction of forests and carbon rich soil and the manufacture of cement from limestone. The concentration of carbon dioxide before major land-clearing and industrialisation in the eighteenth century was about 265 parts per million (ppm). Methane comes from decaying vegetable matter in rice paddies, digestive processes in sheep and cattle, burning and decay of biological matter and from fossil fuel production. HFCs are gases once widely used in refrigerants and other industries, but which are largely being phased out of use because of their potential to destroy atmospheric ozone. PFCs and SF_6 are industrial gases used in the electronic and electrical industries, fire fighting, solvents and other industries.

Water vapour concentrations in the atmosphere are closely controlled by the surface temperature. These can act as an amplifier of warming due to increases in other greenhouse gases or indeed warming due to Earth's orbital variations. Similarly clouds can act as an amplifier by absorbing heat radiation, or as a reducer of warming by reflecting incoming sunlight. The net result of clouds on the Earth's temperature depends on their height, latitude and droplet size.

Amplifying effects are called positive feedbacks (as in electronic circuitry). Loss of snow cover due to warming is another positive feedback, and leads to greater absorption of sunlight at the Earth's surface and thus more warming. On the time-scale of the glacial-inter-glacial cycles of thousands of years, carbon dioxide concentrations in the atmosphere also act as a positive feedback. This is because warmer oceans can hold less carbon dioxide in solution, and thus increase the natural warming due to the greenhouse effect.

As early as the nineteenth century some scientists noted that increased emissions of carbon dioxide might lead to global warming (see Chapter 11). Present estimates of future climate change are based on projections of future emissions of greenhouse gases and resulting concentrations of these gases in the atmosphere. These estimates also depend on factors such as the sensitivity of global climate to increases in greenhouse gas concentrations; the simultaneous warming or cooling effects of natural climate fluctuations; and changes in dust and other particles in the atmosphere, from volcanoes, dust storms and industry. Such projections are discussed in more detail in Chapter 3 ('Projecting the future') and Chapter 5 ('What climate changes are likely?').

Given that climate has changed during the twentieth century, the key question is how much of this is due to human-induced increased greenhouse gas emissions, and how much to other more natural causes. This has great relevance to policy because, if the changes are due to human activity, they are likely to continue and even accelerate unless we change human behaviour and limit our emissions of greenhouse gases.

In 2001 the IPCC concluded: 'There is new and stronger evidence [since an earlier IPCC report in 1996] that most of the warming observed over the last 50 years is attributable to human activities.' Points made by the exhaustive IPCC study include:

- there is a longer and more closely scrutinised temperature record as well as new model estimates of variability;
- the warming we have seen over the past 100 years is very unlikely to be due to natural variability of the climate alone, as estimated by current models;
- reconstructions of climate data for the past 1000 years indicate that the observed warming over the last three decades or so is unusual and unlikely to be entirely natural.

A paper by William Ruddiman of the University of Virginia, in *Climatic Change* in 2003, raises the possibility that human influence on the climate has been significant since well before the industrial revolution, due to the cutting down of primeval forests to make way for agriculture, and irrigated rice farming in Asia. Ruddiman claims that the Earth's orbital changes should have led to a decline in carbon dioxide and methane concentrations in the atmosphere from 8000 years ago. Instead there was a rise of 100 parts per billion in methane concentrations, and of 20 to 25 ppm in carbon dioxide by the start of the industrial era. He calculates that this has led to the Earth being 0.8°C warmer than if humans had not been active, an effect hidden because it has cancelled out a natural cooling due to orbital variations.

Simulations of the response to natural forcings alone (that is, natural changes causing the climate to change), such as variability in energy from the Sun and the effects of volcanic dust, do not explain the warming experienced in the second half of the twentieth century. However, they may have contributed to the observed warming in the previous 50 years (see Chapter 2). The sulfate aerosol effect, while uncertain, would have caused cooling over the last half century.

The best agreement between model simulations of climate and observations over the last 140 years has been found when all the above human-induced and natural forcing factors are combined. These results show that the factors included are sufficient to explain the observed changes, but do not exclude the possibility of other factors contributing. Several studies since the IPCC 2001 report support these conclusions globally and regionally (see notes on the web; see p. 296).

Furthermore, it is very likely that the twentieth century warming has contributed significantly to the observed sea-level rise of some 10 to 20 cm, through the expansion of sea water as it gets warmer, and widespread melting of land-based ice. Observed sea-level rise and model estimates are in agreement, within the uncertainties, with a lack of significant acceleration of sea-level rise detected during the twentieth century. The lack of an observed acceleration is due to long time lags in warming the deep oceans, although there is some evidence for accelerated (although still relatively small) contributions from melting of land-based ice in Alaska and Patagonia.

Studies by US scientists of twentieth century drying trends in the Mediterranean and African monsoon regions suggest that the observed warming trend in the Indian Ocean, which is related to the enhanced greenhouse effect, is the most important feature driving these dryings, through its dynamic effects on atmospheric circulation. Another study shows a tendency for more severe droughts in Australia, related to higher temperatures and increased surface evaporation. Both studies see tentative attribution of drying trends to the enhanced greenhouse effect, and are pointers to future regional climate changes.

A deepening and poleward shift of the belts of low atmospheric pressure surrounding each pole, known technically as an increase in the 'annular mode' of the atmospheric circulation, has been observed in the last several decades. It is also found in model simulations of climate with increasing greenhouse gas concentrations. However, the observed shift is greater than the simulated projections. Model simulations have now resolved this difference by including the effect of reductions in ozone in the upper atmosphere, which have occurred especially in the high latitude winter, since the 1970s (see Chapter 9). Both enhanced greenhouse gases and ozone reductions in the upper atmosphere increase the equator-to-pole temperature difference, leading to a strengthening of the westerly winds at high latitudes. These changes help explain decreasing rainfall in southern Australia, and a stronger North Atlantic Oscillation, which affects storm tracks and climate in Europe.

Climate models suggest a slowdown of the ocean circulation driven by differences in temperature and salinity (known as the 'thermo-haline circulation') in response to warming, increased rainfall and runoff at high latitudes, and reduced sea-ice formation. The reality of a slowdown of the thermo-haline circulation is supported by a variety of recent observations from several areas, as well as paleo-climatic evidence that it has occurred before (see Chapter 2). This could lead to rapid climate changes in the North Atlantic region, and has prompted the setting up of a monitoring and research program called Rapid Climate Change Programme (RAPID) by the UK Natural Environment Research Council and the US National Science Foundation. The aim is to improve the ability to quantify the chances and magnitude of future rapid climate change. Its main focus is the Atlantic Ocean's circulation, including the possibility of a slow-down in the Gulf Stream and cooling in Western Europe.

The importance of delayed climate responses

Delayed climate responses to greenhouse gas emissions require early action. At present there is a large imbalance between present and past emissions of carbon dioxide into the atmosphere and their slow removal into the deep ocean. Even if we stopped emitting greenhouse gases tomorrow, the increase in atmospheric concentration of carbon dioxide as a result of the burning of fossil fuels and destruction of forests since the industrial revolution would persist for centuries. This is due to the slow rate at which carbon dioxide from these human 'sources' can be reabsorbed into the large reservoirs on the ocean floor and in the solid earth (called 'sinks'). It is as if we are pouring a large amount of water into three connected bowls, from which there is only one small outlet drain.

This is illustrated schematically in **Figure 3**. The relative magnitude and rapidity of carbon dioxide flows are indicated approximately by the width of the arrows. Fossil fuel emissions of carbon dioxide into the atmosphere (large upwards arrow) reach equilibrium with carbon in the land and soil biota and in the shallow oceans ('CO$_2$ exchange' arrows) in only one to ten years. Carbon dioxide is only slowly removed into the deep ocean, taking hundreds to thousands of years ('natural CO$_2$ removal').

Rapid exchanges take place between the biosphere (plants, animals and soil) and the atmosphere, but due to limitations of climate and soil fertility, the biosphere cannot expand enough to take up the huge increase in carbon dioxide from fossil carbon. Most of the former fossil carbon stays as carbon dioxide in the atmosphere, where it changes the climate, or is absorbed into the surface layers of the oceans, where it changes the chemistry of the oceans. The portion that stays in the atmosphere is known as the 'airborne fraction' and is currently about 50% of all emitted carbon dioxide. This airborne fraction is limited by the

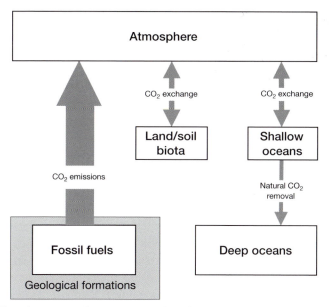

Figure 3: Flows between carbon reservoirs. This schematic diagram illustrates the present imbalance between emissions of carbon dioxide into the atmosphere, soil and land biota and shallow oceans, and its eventual removal into the deep oceans.

solubility of carbon dioxide in the surface waters of the oceans and the rate of downward penetration of the carbon dioxide. Moreover, the airborne fraction will decrease, as the shallow oceans get warmer, because warmer water can hold less dissolved carbon dioxide, and there will be less mixing of the warmer water into the relatively cold deep oceans. The resulting atmospheric carbon dioxide concentration will remain for centuries near the highest levels reached, since natural processes can only return carbon to its natural sinks in the deep oceans over geological time-scales.

More or less permanent natural sinks for carbon include carbon-rich detritus from marine organisms, mainly microscopic algae and plankton, but also larger creatures, which fall to the ocean floor. Carbon is also transported to the oceans by rivers and wind-borne organic particles, and some of this also ends up on the ocean floor in sediment layers. Carbon is also stored in plants and the soil on land, but this can be returned to the atmosphere rapidly by fire or decomposition. The possibility of increasing sinks artificially is discussed in Chapter 8, which deals with mitigation.

Emissions of carbon dioxide from the burning of fossil fuels (oil, coal and natural gas) and deforestation will have to be reduced eventually by 70 or 80% relative to present emissions to stop concentrations increasing in the atmosphere (Chapter 8). This will take many decades to achieve without disrupting human society. The more we delay in reducing greenhouse gas emissions, the larger the inevitable magnitude of climate change will be, and the more drastic will be the reductions in emissions needed later to avoid dangerous levels of climate change. To use the water-into-bowls analogy again, it is as if we wanted to stop the water rising above a certain level, but were slow to reduce the rate at which we kept adding water – the slower we are to reduce the input, the more drastically we will need to reduce it later.

Carbon dioxide concentrations in the atmosphere will stabilise only when the rate of emissions is reduced to the rate of deposition or sequestration into the deep oceans (or, as represented in **Figure 3**, not until the left hand emissions arrow and the lower right removal arrow become the same size). Alternatively, there is the possibility of artificially increasing the rate of sequestration of carbon or carbon dioxide into the deep ocean or into subterranean storages (artificially widening the downwards arrow). Artificial sequestration into the oceans is controversial, while subterranean sequestration is less controversial and is already happening in some cases (Chapter 8). Balancing the inflows and outflows of carbon dioxide into the atmosphere will take many decades or even centuries.

Furthermore, because of the slow mixing and overturning of the oceans, surface temperatures will continue to rise slowly for centuries, even after concentrations of carbon dioxide in the atmosphere have stabilised, and the deep oceans will continue to warm. This will lead to continuing thermal expansion, and thus rising sea levels, for centuries after stabilisation of greenhouse gas concentrations. Our children and grandchildren will be seeing the inevitable results of our continuing greenhouse gas emissions long after we have gone.

Observed impacts

While the 0.6°C increase in global average surface temperature in the twentieth century may seem small, observational evidence indicates that climate changes have already affected a variety of physical and biological systems. As well as shrinkage of glaciers and thawing of permafrost mentioned above, examples of observed changes linked to climate include: shifts in ice freeze and break-up dates on rivers and lakes; increases in rainfall and rainfall intensity in most mid- and high latitudes of the Northern Hemisphere; lengthening of growing seasons; and earlier dates of flowering of trees, emergence of insects, and egg-laying in birds. Statistically significant associations between changes in regional climate and observed changes in physical and biological systems have been documented in freshwater, terrestrial and marine environments on all continents.

The investigations reported by the IPCC in 2001 were based on possible links between observed changes in regional climate and biological or physical processes in ecosystems. The authors gathered more than 2500 articles on cli-

---

Box 2: Delayed climate system responses matter

Slow or delayed responses are widespread (but not universal) characteristics of the interacting climate, ecological, and socio-economic systems. This means that some impacts of human-induced climate change may be slow to become apparent, and some could be irreversible if climate change is not limited in both rate and magnitude before crossing thresholds at which critical changes may occur. The positions of such thresholds are poorly known.

Several important policy-relevant considerations follow from these delayed response effects.

- Stabilisation of the climate and climate-impacted systems will only be achieved long after human-induced emissions of greenhouse gases have been reduced.

- Stabilisation at any level of greenhouse gas concentrations requires ultimate reduction of global net emissions to a small fraction of the current emissions, and it will likely take centuries to reduce carbon dioxide concentrations much below the highest levels reached.

- Social and economic time scales for change are not fixed. They can be changed by policies, and by choices made by individuals, or by reaching critical thresholds where change may become rapid and traumatic (for example, emergency programs, policy revolutions, technological breakthroughs, famine or war).

- Higher rates of warming and multiple stresses increase the likelihood of crossing critical thresholds of change in climatic, ecological, and socio-economic systems (see Chapter 6).

- Delays and uncertainty in the climate, ecological, and socio-economic systems mean that safety margins should be considered in setting strategies, targets and timetables for avoiding dangerous levels of climate change.

- Inevitable delays in slowing down climate change makes some adaptation essential, and affect the optimal mix of adaptation and mitigation strategies.

- Slow responses in the climate system, and the possibility of reaching critical thresholds in the interacting climate, ecological and socio-economic systems, make anticipatory adaptation and mitigation actions desirable.

Source: Based on IPCC *Synthesis Report* (2001d), pp. 87–96.

---

mate in conjunction with one of the following: animals, plants, glaciers, sea ice and ice on lakes or streams. To determine if these have been influenced by changing climate, only studies meeting at least two of the following criteria were included:

- a trait of these entities (for example, range boundary, melting date) shows a change over time,

- the trait is correlated with changes in local temperature,

- local temperature changed over time.

At least two of these three criteria had to exhibit a statistically significant correlation. Only temperature was considered because how it influences the entities examined is well established and because temperature trends are more globally uniform than other locally varying climatic factors, such as changes in rainfall. Selected studies also had to have examined at least 10 years of data; with more than 90% having a time span of more than 20 years.

Since the IPCC 2001 report, several papers published by some of the IPCC authors, and others, further discuss this evidence. While there is some discussion about levels of confidence, both reviews published in 2003 find a 'systematic trend' or 'fingerprint' in changes in the distribution and behaviour of wild animals and plants. They report an average range shift polewards due to global warming of 6.1 km per decade, and events in spring occurring an average of 2.3 days earlier per decade. Such trends, combined with other stresses such as habitat destruction, could lead to disruption of the connectedness of species within ecosystems, and to numerous local losses and possible extinctions of species.

Other recent analyses supporting such observed trends discuss crustaceans in the North Atlantic; an extension of range northward of southern fish species in the North Atlantic; modelled and satellite observations of high northern latitude greening and spring budburst; spring flowering of British plants; and upwards movement of plant species in Norwegian mountains. A study of breeding behaviour in a red squirrel population in the Yukon, Canada, found that the timing of breeding has advanced by 18 days over the last 10 years (six days per generation). This is attributed both to changing behaviour within generations, and to selective breeding favouring early breeders.

While most of these observations are for Northern Hemisphere plants and animals, where long datasets are available, shorter data sets in Australia suggest similar shifts toward the south (bats, birds), upward in elevation (alpine mammals) or along changing rainfall contours (birds, semi-arid reptiles).

Attribution of changes in crop production is complex, with climate change being only one factor along with changes in crop varieties, application of fertilisers, effects of pollutants such as ozone and nitrogen fallout, and direct effects of increasing carbon dioxide concentrations affecting water use efficiency and photosynthesis. Nevertheless, two papers claim to have detected yield trends due to climate change.

In a 1997 paper, Neville Nicholls of the Bureau of Meteorology in Australia, removed the long-term trends in Australian wheat yield and climate data to obtain a relationship between climate variability and yield. He then used this relationship, and the observed climatic trends to estimate the proportion of the yield increases that might be due to climate change. Over the period 1952 to 1992 he found that climate change accounted for some 30–50% of the yield increase. This was mainly due to increasing temperatures, including reduced frost frequency, and may not hold for much greater warmings. Lobell and Asner analysed data for yields of corn and soybeans in the Midwestern United States for 1982–1998, and corresponding local climate. They found a strong negative relationship between year-to-year yield data and temperature, and that local temperatures had in fact fallen over this period (contrary to the global average). Their study suggested that, with an increasing temperature trend in the future, yields might fall. Both these studies are open to debate, but they do suggest a detectable influence of temperature trends on crop yield in the real world.

Attributing these observed changes to climate change is complicated by possible multiple causes. This is strikingly illustrated by the increasing use of the Thames Barrier in the UK, a moveable gate-like structure designed to control flooding in the lower Thames River, which became operational in 1983. The number of times the Thames Barrier has been closed each year since 1983 is shown in **Figure 4** by the black columns; theoretical closures from 1930 based on tidal and river flow data are denoted by the grey columns. The increase in the frequency of closure since 1983 could readily be taken as evidence of rising sea level or storminess. However, these closures could be occurring due to a combination of several effects, including relative sea-level rise (part of which may be due to land subsidence), increased storminess and changing operational procedures.

According to a review of this data in 2003, the barrier is now sometimes used to retain water in the Thames River at low tide during drought, as well as to reduce the risk of flooding from the sea at high tide. Increased relative sea-level rise and increased storminess are both likely, at least in part, to be due to the enhanced greenhouse effect, and increased drought may also be related to climate change, but sorting out the relative importance of these possible causes requires a more detailed analysis.

Another recent example of a climate impact that is at least a forerunner of what may be expected with continued global warming is the series of extreme high temperatures experienced in Europe during the northern summer of 2003. Maximum temperatures were up to 5°C above the long-term averages for the same dates between 1961 and 1990, and the French Health Ministry reported 14,802 more deaths in August than would be expected on the basis of recent summers. Thousands more excess deaths were reported in Germany, Spain and the UK. Drought conditions, low river flows and wild fires were widespread across Europe during this summer period. The World Monitoring Glaciers

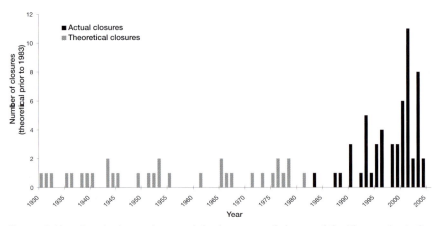

Figure 4: Has climatic change increased the frequency of closure of the Thames Barrier? (Figure courtesy of Environment Agency, UK.)

Service in Zurich reported an average loss of ice in Alpine glaciers in Europe equivalent to a 5 to 10% reduction of the total volume of all Alpine glaciers.

Daily maximum and minimum temperatures in Paris at the height of the heat wave, with the corresponding deaths recorded in major Parisian hospitals are shown in **Figure 5**. The top graph (triangles) shows daily maximum temperatures, and the middle graph (squares) show daily minimum temperatures (scale on right). Vertical bars are the daily number of deaths recorded in Paris (scale on left). Maximum deaths occur near the end of the heat wave on 13 August. The excess death rate was due largely to the aged and infirm in non-air-conditioned apartments. A longer-term warming might lead to adaptations such as the installation of air conditioners, but this would be costly and energy-intensive.

Martin Beniston, of the University of Fribourg (Switzerland) and Henry Diaz cite the 2003 heat wave in Europe as an example of what to expect in future warmer summers, while Gerry Meehl of NCAR (USA) and colleague show that more frequent and intense heatwaves are to be expected, especially in Europe and North America, in the second half of the twenty-first century. Peter Stott of the UK Meteorological Office and others estimate that human influence has at least doubled the risk of a heatwave in Europe exceeding the magnitude of that in 2003 and that the likelihood of such events may increase 100-fold over the next 40 years.

Trends in human vulnerability

It is often argued that as human societies become richer and more technologically advanced, they become less dependent on nature and more able to adapt to climatic change. Poorer societies are likely to be more adversely affected by cli-

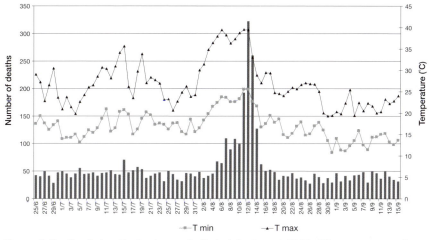

Figure 5: Deaths during the heat wave in Paris, July–August 2003. (Figure courtesy of Institut de Veille Sanitaire, InVS, France, per Pascal Empereur-Bissonnet.)

mate change than richer ones, so the capacity of a society to adapt, it is said, will inevitably increase with economic development. In terms of the number of deaths from weather and climatic disasters, such as storms, floods and droughts, this appears to be borne out by common observations and statistics. However, the same statistics show that monetary damages from such disasters are greater in many richer developed countries, and that, irrespective of climate change, there is a rising trend in such damages.

Even in rich countries, it appears, there are trends towards greater exposure to weather and climatic hazards, such as flooding by rivers and along low-lying coasts, drought, hail and windstorms. Examples include the increasing population and investments along the hurricane-prone Atlantic Coast of the United States, and the cyclone-prone coasts of northern Australia. These developments lead to greater economic losses. Reductions in loss of life are only achieved through large expenditures, for example on cyclone-proof buildings, early warning systems, evacuation, and rescue services.

Trends that make matters worse ('counter-adaptive' trends) are widely in evidence. These include population growth in general, increases in per capita consumption of water and energy, preferential growth in climatically hazardous areas, increased barriers to migration of people and natural ecosystems, the spread of new monoculture crop cultivars, and increasing reliance on limited technological fixes. The last include flood levee banks and sea walls, which encourage investment in hazard zones as they provide protection from small hazards, but fail when larger hazards occur. This was evidenced in the case of the major floods in the upper Mississippi Valley in the United States in 1993,

Table 1: Increase in disasters since 1960. Comparison, decade by decade, of the number and costs (US$ billion) of catastrophic weather-related and non-weather-related events since the 1960s. Note the marked increase in weather-related disasters and their costs, but only a small increase in non-weather related disasters. Data comes from the International Federation of Red Cross and Red Crescent Societies annual *World Disasters Report*.

	1960–69	1970–79	1980–89	1990–99	Ratio 90s/60s
Number of weather-related disasters	16	29	44	72	4.5
Number of non-weather-related disasters	11	18	19	17	1.5
Economic losses	50.8	74.5	118.4	399.0	7.9
Insured losses	6.7	10.8	21.6	91.9	13.6

when major levees were breached causing millions of dollars damage. Reversing such counter-adaptive trends is not easy.

Evidence of increasing vulnerability comes from the observed rapid increase in damages from climatic hazards in the last several decades of the twentieth century. **Table 1** summarises some of the evidence.

While part of this increase in the number of weather-related disasters and damages may have been due to an increase in the frequency of climatic hazards, this has not been clearly established. Most of the increase is attributable to increased exposure of populations and investments in locations subject to climatic hazards, such as low-lying coastal zones, riverine floodplains, and areas subject to tropical cyclones and storm surges. It is possible, as the Mississippi flood example suggests, that societal changes may in some cases have more influence on vulnerability and resilience to climatic variability and extremes than climate change, and that they either compound or reduce the effects of climate change. Much more attention needs to be paid to such questions, which have strong policy implications through the identification of developmental trends that may make exposure, adaptive capacity and mitigation potential better or worse.

Climate change adds to the impact of these counter-adaptive societal trends.

Projections of future climate change

In 2001 the IPCC developed a new set of climate change projections, based on plausible scenarios for future greenhouse gas emissions. These were based on 'story lines' about future development affecting greenhouse gas emissions, as an update on earlier scenarios used in 1992 and 1996 (see Chapter 3 for details). Using models of the carbon cycle, that is, of how carbon is moved around between the atmosphere, the biosphere, the soil and the oceans, the IPCC estimated that by the year 2100, atmospheric carbon dioxide concentrations would range in total anywhere from 490 to 1260 ppm. Such concentrations are 75 to 350% higher than the pre-industrial estimate of 280 ppm in 1750. Carbon dioxide concentrations in 2005 are already about 378 ppm, or 35% above the pre-industrial value.

These projected concentrations of carbon dioxide led to estimates that by 2100 average global surface temperatures are likely to be between 1.4 and 5.8°C warmer than in the IPCC baseline year of 1990 (see Chapter 5). The IPCC did not say what the probabilities of the various increases were within this range because estimates of probability are difficult and depend on how society changes its use of fossil fuels in the future. The IPCC also estimated sea-level rise by 2100 to be in the range of 9 to 88 cm, mostly from thermal expansion of the oceans as they warm up.

The projected warming in the twenty-first century is likely to be between two and 10 times as large as the observed warming in the twentieth century, and larger than any since the large and abrupt Younger Dryas event 11,000 years ago (see Chapter 2). Projected temperatures would be much warmer than during the so-called Medieval Warm Period, which was most evident in the North Atlantic region around 800 to 1300 AD. Warming as large and rapid as that projected for the twenty-first century might be expected to create severe problems for natural ecosystems and human societies. Indeed evidence from past climate changes of similar magnitude point to major impacts, which, if humans had been present in numbers like today, would have been disastrous.

Facing the challenge

Scientific research in the latter half of the twentieth century led many climate scientists to alert governments to the issue of climate change. This was done individually and through conferences and policy statements. This led to the setting up of the Intergovernmental Panel on Climate Change to provide policy-relevant scientific advice, and it led to discussion in the United Nations General Assembly.

The General Assembly called for a United Nations Framework Convention on Climate Change (UNFCCC) in 1990. The Convention was finally adopted in New York in May 1992, and was opened for signatures at the Intergovernmental Conference on Sustainable Development, held in Rio de Janeiro in 1992. Framework conventions are general agreements that leave the details of implementation to be worked out later via a series of protocols, legal devices or agreements to be adopted by the countries that signed the Convention. Up to 24 May 2005, 189 countries have ratified the UNFCCC.

The objective of the UNFCCC is stated in Article 2 to be:

...the stabilisation of greenhouse gas concentrations in the atmosphere at a level that would prevent dangerous anthropogenic interference with the climate system. Such a level should be achieved within a timeframe sufficient to allow ecosystems to adapt naturally to climate change, to ensure that food production is not threatened, and to enable economic development to proceed in a sustainable manner.

The UNFCCC contains no binding commitments on emissions levels, but it does lay down some general principles and objectives to shape future negotiations on these commitments. These include that:

- Developed countries (most members of the Organisation for Economic Cooperation and Development (OECD)) plus former communist states undergoing transition to a market economy, collectively known as 'Annex I' countries, should take the lead with abatement measures.

- The climatic and economic vulnerabilities of developing countries should be recognised.

- Abatement, or emissions reductions, should be consistent with sustainable development and not infringe the goals of an open and supportive international economy.

These provisions, and negotiations towards their implementation, have led to much argument between the countries that are parties to the Convention (and who meet as the 'Conference of Parties', or COP), especially over the contents and implementation of the Kyoto Protocol adopted in 1997. The Kyoto Protocol is a first agreement to start the process of reducing greenhouse gas emissions, with very modest targets set for reductions in Annex I countries averaging 5.2% relative to 1990 emissions, to be achieved by 2008–12. These arguments have been compounded by uncertainties as to the actual risk from climate change, and regarding the costs of impacts and abatement measures. There has also been a clash of various national and corporate interests, ideological positions, and economic advantages. These political matters are discussed more fully in Chapters 10 and 11.

Conclusion

This discussion strongly suggests that climate change is happening, and is projected to increase due to the ongoing and increasing release of greenhouse gases into the atmosphere. The main greenhouse gas (other than water vapour) is carbon dioxide, and its concentration in the atmosphere has increased from the pre-industrial value of about 280 ppm to more than 378 ppm today. It will take centuries to reduce this concentration, and probably more than a century even to stop it increasing. Meanwhile this increase in greenhouse gases has already had impacts on the climate, and on natural ecosystems and human societies.

The impacts of climate change will become more serious as global warming continues over the coming decades, with an increasing risk of drastic changes to the climate system. Whether this is disastrous will depend on how rapidly greenhouse gas concentrations increase and on our ability to adapt to a changing climate. Our capacity to adapt is limited and adaptation is costly, so it is imperative that humans reduce their emissions of greenhouse gases as soon as possible to limit the rate and magnitude of climate change. Globally, most countries – including Australia and the United States, two developed countries that have not ratified the Kyoto Protocol – have already agreed that there is a problem and, despite differences, through the UNFCCC and other channels they are trying to work towards a solution.

In the following chapters we look in more detail at the complexities of climate change and its potential impacts. We will also examine potential policy responses, namely adaptation and mitigation in the context of other environmental and developmental problems and the varying interests of different countries. My own position is that, despite some costs, there are realistic solutions, which can be reached with some effort and cooperation. Our task is to see that this happens, and that it starts now.

2

Learning from the past

Time present and time past
Are both perhaps present in time future.
And time future contained in time past.

T.S. Eliot (1888–1965), *Four Quartets*, Burnt Norton.

We recommend that scientists from many disciplines be encouraged to
undertake systematic studies of past climates, particularly of climates
in epochs when the Arctic Ocean was free of ice...

Report of the Study of Man's Impact on Climate, Massachusetts Institute of
Technology, 1971.

Given all the fuss about climate change, it is important that we understand the
Earth's climate and how it works. We base this knowledge on two things:

- knowledge of how the climate has behaved in the past, and

- our ability to explain past climate changes.

If we can explain the past, we can build conceptual and then detailed computer models. These will enable us to make predictions about future climate
changes, given the likelihood of future changes in those factors which drive the
climate system. As a general rule, if something happened once, the system is
such that it could happen again, given similar preconditions. But we only truly
understand the system if we can explain what happened before. If we have that
understanding, we have some ability to predict what may happen from now on,
especially if we see similar preconditions occurring.

Life has existed on the Earth for 3.5 thousand million years, so potentially
we have a very long record to examine for climatic behaviour, although it is only
since the start of the Cenozoic period, about 65 million years ago, that we have
a useful climatic record. This record plus theories based on the laws of physics,
chemistry and mathematics, can tell us what sort of things influence climate.

Ideally this helps us to develop a 'model' of the climate system, that is, how the solid earth, water and atmosphere interact with the energy from the Sun to produce climate. Such a model may be merely a set of qualitative ideas, or a set of quantitative mathematical representations of those ideas, which can be used to make calculations on a computer.

Once we have such a model of the climate system, detailed knowledge of past conditions and climatic behaviour enables us to test how well the model works. Such testing can be done by looking at episodes of climatic change in the distant past, or by looking at what has happened over the last century or so, for which we have much more detailed observations.

Accordingly, we can use two main types of climatic data for analysing past climatic variations.

- Direct or instrumental measurements. These generally started up to about two hundred years ago with the advent of modern instruments such as thermometers, rain gauges and anemometers, and were discussed in Chapter 1. They provide a fairly accurate record, but the record is too short to sample the whole range of climate changes that have occurred before and may occur again.

- 'Proxy' or indirect data. Such data can provide a much longer time perspective, and are obtained from natural or human archives that in some way record past climate variations. Proxy data includes written records of harvests, or other properties of artefacts or substances that have been influenced by climate in the past. Notable examples are geological formations such as glacial moraines (soil and rocks left behind by retreating glaciers), the annual growth rings in trees, layers of sediment deposited on the beds of lakes or oceans, or the radioactive isotopes of various chemical elements deposited in ice cores, tree rings or sediments. Proxy data is vitally important to our understanding of past climatic variations and changes, so it merits further explanation.

Proxy data: clues from the past

Dramatic evidence of past climates comes from landscape features such as U-shaped valleys (see **Figure 6**) and large and small lakes dammed behind glacial moraines. These are evidence that glaciers and ice caps once covered far more of the Earth's surface than today. The Great Lakes in North America are a striking example: they were formed at the southern edge of huge ice caps covering Canada and the northern parts of what is now the United States. When we map such features and make inferences about climate from them, we are using

Figure 6: The glacial valley above Lautenbrunnen, Switzerland, in 1999. This characteristically U-shaped valley was carved out by a large glacier during the last glacial period some 20,000 years ago. The glacier, visible in the distance, has now receded many kilometres up the valley in response to a global average warming of only some 4 or 5°C in the last 20,000 to 10,000 years. The glacier is retreating further now due to warming in the twentieth century. This is dramatic evidence of past natural climatic change, and of the potential impacts of future climate changes that may be due to human influence. (Photograph by A.B. Pittock.)

'proxy' evidence or data to make scientific deductions about past or paleo-climates ('paleo-' means old or ancient).

There are many types of proxy data used by climatologists (**Table 2**), and they are often used in combination to build up a reliable picture of the past. Each has its merits and limitations. The interpretations made from them depend on sometimes-complex models or understandings of what caused the proxy data and under what conditions. For example, glaciers result from snow that has accumulated in higher elevations compacting into ice and gradually flowing downwards along valleys, until it reaches lower elevations where it melts or evaporates. Relationships between the length of a glacier and the temperature and snowfall can be deduced from observations, or from first principles from the mathematical relationships between snowfall, depth of ice or snow, volume, evaporation, melting, bottom friction, elasticity of the ice, and so on. This can all be put in a mathematical model and the changes with time calculated on a computer.

Proxy data must be calibrated against instrumental data for a meaningful cli-mate interpretation to be made, and they vary in usefulness according to how closely related they are to climate, and how well the dates can be determined.

The dating and time resolution (the ability to separate adjacent time intervals) is especially important where attempts are made to look at spatial patterns of change, or to see whether one event preceded another, as may be necessary to establish cause and effect.

Dating of glaciers can be done from fragments of plant material in the terminal moraines, or found under where the glacier was after it has receded again. Such dates can come from radioactive carbon concentrations, since short-lived isotopes such as ^{14}C (formed in the atmosphere by cosmic rays striking air molecules) gradually disappear after the plant material dies. Dates from radiocarbon are useful for material up to about 50,000 years old, but only accurate to within a few per cent of the age from the present. Dating for much older material comes from other isotopes with longer decay times. An example is Uranium isotope 238, which decays to Uranium 234, and which in turn decays to Thorium 230. Ratios of ^{230}Th to ^{234}U can be used for dating back millions of years. Time resolution with these methods is coarse.

Estimates of spatial patterns of decadal, annual or seasonal climate variations in past centuries, however, must rely on proxy evidence having finer time resolution. That is, it needs to resolve annual or seasonal variations. This evidence includes the width or density of annual growth rings in trees; layer thickness and particle size in annual layers in sediment cores from the bottom of lakes or the oceans; the isotopic composition, chemistry and thickness of annual layers in ice cores; isotopes from coral growth layers; and scattered historical information from human documentation of things like crop yields, floods, frosts and the break-up of frozen rivers.

Annual growth rings in trees are a good example. These can often be counted back from the present using samples from many different trees. In some cases, for example, with Oak in Western Europe, Kauri in New Zealand, and Bristlecone Pine in the western United States, this record can be taken back thousands of years. Similar dating is possible from annual layers of silt in lakes, although in longer time series from the floor of the ocean where sediment layers may be disturbed by burrowing creatures, radioactive dating is necessary. Sediment records may go back many thousands or millions of years using much longer-lived isotopes than ^{14}C.

The record of the ice ages

By studying many different proxy data records from places around the globe scientists have found evidence of global-scale climate changes. Climate has varied from times known loosely as 'ice ages' or 'glacial periods', when huge ice sheets covered large areas that are now ice-free, to periods like now when ice sheets are largely confined to Antarctica, Greenland and the floating Arctic sea ice. Records indicate that climate changes occurred over the last two million

Table 2: Proxy indicators of climate-related variables

Indicator	Property measured	Time resolution	Time span	Climate-related information obtained
Tree rings	Width, density, isotopic ratios, trace elements	Annual	Centuries to millennia	Temperature, rainfall, fire
Lake and bog sediments	Deposition rates, species assemblages from shells and pollen, macrofossils, charcoal	Annual	Millennia	Rainfall, atmospheric water balance, vegetation type, fire
Coral growth rings	Density, isotope ratios, fluorescence	Annual	Centuries	Temperature, salinity, river outflows
Ice cores	Isotopes, fractional melting, annual layer thickness, dust grain size, gas bubbles	Annual	Millennia	Temperature, snow accumulation rate, windiness, gas concentrations
Ocean sediment cores	Species assemblages from shells and pollens, deposition rates, isotopic ratios, air-borne dust, pollen	Usually multi-decadal or centuries	Millennia	Sea temperatures, salinity, acidity, ice volumes and sea level, river outflows, aridity, land vegetation
Boreholes	Temperature profile	Decades	Centuries	Surface air temperature
Old groundwater	Isotopes, noble gases	Centuries	Millennia	Temperature
Glacial moraines	Maximum glacier length	Decades	Centuries to millennia	Temperature and precipitation
Sand dunes	Orientation, grain size	Centuries	Millennia	Wind direction and speed, aridity
Coastal landforms	Ledges, former beach lines, debris lines	Decades to centuries	Decades to millennia	Former sea-level, tropical cyclones
Documentary evidence	Reports of extremes, harvests, dates of break-up of river or lake ice	Annual	Centuries to millennia	Temperature, precipitation

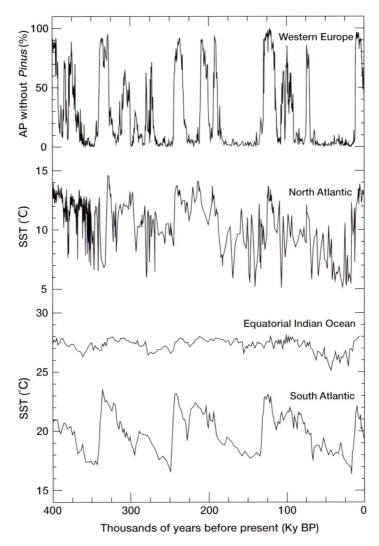

Figure 7: Climate variations over the last 400 thousand years. The top graph shows percentage variations in tree pollen amount, excluding pine tree species. High percentages correspond to warm climates. The lower three curves show estimated sea surface temperatures in the North Atlantic, equatorial Indian Ocean and the South Atlantic, based on deep-sea cores. Variations between glacial and inter-glacial periods were large in high latitude regions, but much less in low latitudes. Variability was much greater in the North Atlantic region. (Graphs are from Figure 2.23 in the IPCC 2001a report.)

years in a rather regular cyclic manner, with glacial periods lasting roughly 100,000 years, and warmer inter-glacial periods occurring in between. The latter lasted much shorter time intervals of around 10,000 years (see **Figure 7**). These climatic fluctuations were accompanied by large variations in global average sea level, of up to about 120 metres, and resulted in dramatic changes in vegetation cover, lakes, rivers and wetlands, and the distribution of plants and animals.

Huge areas of the continental shelves were exposed during the glacial periods, joining Alaska to Siberia, the Australian mainland to New Guinea and Tasmania, Britain and Ireland to Western Europe, and many South-east Asian islands to the Asian mainland. At the end of the last glaciation some 18,000 years ago, the ice sheets melted over Canada, northern Europe and elsewhere, and the Greenland and Antarctic ice sheets contracted. This again flooded the above areas of the continental shelves, taking thousands of years to do so.

Smaller changes in relative sea levels are still occurring regionally due to the continental plates slowly rebounding and flexing. This happens because of the removal of the weight of the ice sheets from the continental interiors and the increased weight of sea water along the continental margins. Thus much of Scandinavia is still rising relative to the sea, while parts of the east coast of the United States are gradually subsiding. Sea-level changes are thus not uniform, and estimates of actual global average sea-level rise must come from combining measurements from many parts of the world.

Life survived, and indeed flourished, despite these huge climatically forced variations in the environment, but many individual species of plants and animals became extinct, and others had to migrate large distances to more congenial regions. The latter included our human ancestors, who skirted around ice sheets to migrate from Asia to North America, and crossed small straits to migrate from South-east Asia to Australia. Rising sea levels between 20,000 and 10,000 years ago forced people to move from land that is now under the Black Sea, and many to move inland from coastal plains in North America, Europe and Australasia. Such mass migrations would be much more difficult now, with six billion people and rigid national boundaries, than at the end of the last ice age when the Earth was only sparsely populated by humans.

The causes of past climate change

There are many contributory causes of past climate change, including continental drift, variations in the Earth's orbit around the Sun, changes in solar output, volcanic emissions, cosmic collisions and particulate matter in the atmosphere, commonly referred to as 'aerosols'.

Variations in the Earth's orbit

The remarkable history of more or less regular fluctuations in the Earth's climate, as evidenced by the sea level and temperature records over the last two million years, suggests a strong periodic influence on the climate. The series of

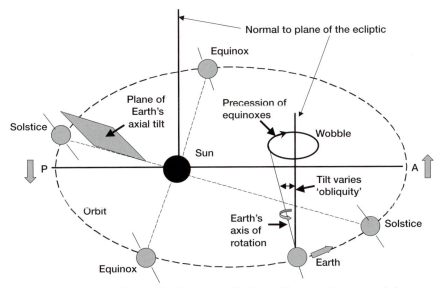

Figure 8: Geometry of the Sun–Earth system. This Figure illustrates the origin of changes in solar radiation reaching the Earth at particular latitudes and seasons associated with variations in the Earth's orbit around the Sun. (P = perihelion, A = aphelion.)

periodicities, or regular variations, associated with the Earth's orbit around the Sun is the obvious candidate for this, since the periods involved are similar. These orbital characteristics are shown schematically in **Figure 8.**

During the course of a year, the Earth moves in a slightly elliptical orbit around the Sun, which is at present at a distance of about 147.1 million km at its point of closest approach ('perihelion', P), and 152.1 million km at its furthest distance ('aphelion', A). This causes the solar radiation reaching the Earth to vary by about 3.5% above or below the average 'solar constant' during each year. At present the strongest radiation reaches the earth in January, during the Southern Hemisphere summer.

But the long axis (A–P in the Figure) of the elliptical orbit also revolves slowly around the Sun. It completes one revolution after an irregular interval that averages 96,600 years and so the time of year at which the Earth is closest to the Sun changes very gradually with that timescale. To complicate matters, the eccentricity of the orbit (the degree to which it departs from being circular) varies as the orbit revolves in space, with the same period of 96,000 years.

Also, the Earth's axis of rotation is not upright ('normal') with respect to the plane of its orbit (called the 'ecliptic'). This spin axis wobbles like that of a spinning top, so that it marks out a cone in space completing one revolution in about 26,000 years, a phenomenon known as the precession of the equinoxes. Because the precession is in the opposite direction to the rotation of the Earth in its orbit, the perihelion recurs at the same time of the year after a period of less than 26,000 years, about 20,600 years. The tilt of the Earth's axis of rotation, and the Earth's annual journey around the Sun, means that first the northern hemisphere, and six months later the southern hemisphere, is more full-on to the Sun and receives more solar energy, causing the progression of the seasons.

Finally, the tilt of the Earth's axis of rotation from the normal to the ecliptic (known as the obliquity of the ecliptic) itself varies, undergoing a slow oscillation, with a period of about 40,000 years, between 24°36' and 21°59'. At present the angle is 23°27' and decreasing. This is why the Tropics of Cancer and Capricorn (where the Sun is overhead in mid-summer) are at about 23°27' north and south, respectively.

How do these astronomical periodicities help to explain the glacial-interglacial record? That question occurred to the Serbian climatologist Milutin Milankovitch in the 1930s. Milankovitch theorised that variations in solar energy received over the northern continents at about 65°N due to these orbital variations, particularly in the northern summer, would have driven the growth and decay of the continental ice sheets. He argued that a span of cool summers, caused by relatively large Earth-Sun distances, would result in winter snow accumulating from year to year as it failed to completely melt, whereas warm summers would cause winter snow to melt and glaciers and ice sheets to recede. In 1938 Milankovitch published tables of how solar radiation varied with time at key latitudes, notably 65°N. These tables have been recalculated more accurately since, and the original theory seems to hold true.

On the much longer timescales (hundreds of millions of years) associated with large tectonic changes like continental drift and uplift, changes in the distribution of land and sea and in elevation of the continents play a large part in climate, and vary the effect of the astronomical cycles. Milankovitch's focus on 65°N was reasonable because during the Pleistocene and Holocene epochs (the last two million years) large continental areas where snow could accumulate existed at these latitudes.

With the advent of more powerful computers and mathematical techniques, the association between the astronomical cycles and the climatic record has been refined. Hays and others in 1976 demonstrated excellent time correspondence between the cycle of the eccentricity of the orbit at about 96,000 years and the main observed glacial-interglacial cycle. About half the total variation in the climatic record is contained in the periodicity due to eccentricity, with some 25% due to the obliquity cycle (about 40,000 years) and 10% due to precession.

Variations in greenhouse gas concentrations

Computer models of climate can now be used to calculate quantitatively the effects of the various drivers of climatic change. Use of climate models shows

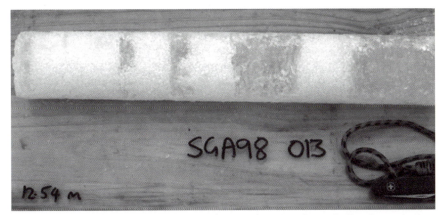

Figure 9: Ice core drilled from Antarctica. This core from Law Dome in East Antarctica is shallow and only about 50 years old. Ice layers formed from refrozen melt water during summer months alternate with winter snow layers. Water isotopes are measured and used as proxies of temperature. Incorporated impurities from marine emissions, volcanic eruptions, atmospheric chemistry and so on provide information on conditions in the past. When the ice becomes deeper and denser, the air inclusions are sealed off and represent samples of the past atmosphere from which past concentrations of carbon dioxide and methane can be measured. (Photo courtesy of David Etheridge, CSIRO Atmospheric Research.)

that variations in solar energy at the Earth associated with the astronomical cycles cannot by themselves explain the relative strength of the observed periodicities in the climatic record. According to these models the effects of the orbital eccentricity cycle must have been amplified or enhanced by some other factor. That additional factor has now been identified as variations in the greenhouse gas concentrations present in the atmosphere. Most notable are the concentrations of carbon dioxide and methane, both of which are stored in large quantities in peat, tundra and ocean sediments during colder climates, and are released into the atmosphere in warmer climates. Any warming due to orbital changes results in more carbon dioxide and methane being released into the atmosphere, leading to greater warming.

This explanation is supported by paleo-evidence for varying concentrations of these gases in the atmosphere, notably from measured concentrations in gas bubbles stored in ice cores from Antarctica and Greenland (see **Figure 9**). Recent work by William Ruddiman at the University of Virginia confirms the Milankovitch theory and the crucial role of amplification by methane and carbon dioxide variations.

Comparing modelled changes over the astronomical cycles with observed paleo-climatic changes enables an independent estimate to be made of the sensitivity of the climate to changes in greenhouse gas concentrations. This suggests a climate sensitivity (global warming for a stabilised doubling of carbon dioxide concentrations) in the upper part of the range adopted by the Intergovernmental Panel on Climate Change (IPCC) in its 2001 report, of 1.5 to 4.5°C. These results provide strong support for the role of greenhouse gases in changing past climate, and confirm that any changes to greenhouse gas concentrations in this century are very likely to affect future climate.

Variations in solar output

The basic source of all energy for driving the climate system on Earth is radiation from the Sun. Thus any variations in solar output would drive changes in the climate. There is a long history of claims to have detected effects of solar variations on surface weather and climate, but many of these claims have been based on poor statistics (as I demonstrated in critical reviews of the scientific literature more than 20 years ago). It is only in recent decades that accurate measurements of solar variations have been made. These have been used to extrapolate estimates of variations in solar radiation back in time using correlations with sunspot numbers, which have been observed since the 1700s.

The IPCC in its *Third Assessment Report* in 2001 adopted a best estimate of the increase in solar radiation since 1750 of about 0.3 Watts per square metre, with an uncertainty range from 0.1 to 0.5 Watts per square metre. Various suggestions have been made as to how this small change (about 0.02% of the solar output) may be amplified in the atmosphere, for example by effects on ozone or clouds. The effect on ozone has been modelled, and is taken into account, while the other mechanisms remain highly speculative.

Climate models have been run with various types of forcing including changes in greenhouse gases, volcanic particles, ozone, solar variations and the effects of air pollution particles. When used to simulate the observed temperature variations over the twentieth century, the climate models tend to give a better reproduction of the observations if they do include solar variations. This is especially so for the first half of the twentieth century, when solar radiation was increasing and increases in greenhouse gases were relatively small. However, solar radiation did not increase much during the second half of the twentieth century, but both temperature and greenhouse gases did.

All reconstructions of solar radiation changes over the twentieth century due to solar variability indicate that it was only about 20 to 25% of the total change in radiation at the Earth's surface. The bulk of the changes in radiation were due to increased greenhouse gases. Changes in solar radiation cannot explain the rapid global warming in the 1980s and 1990s, and future warming is likely to be increasingly dominated by increases in greenhouse gases, unless substantial greenhouse gas emission reductions are achieved in the next few decades.

Volcanoes, cosmic collisions and aerosols

After Mt Tambora in Indonesia exploded in 1815, the northern hemisphere experienced what became known as the 'year without a summer' in 1816. This inspired Lord Byron to write his poem *Darkness*, which included the lines:

I had a dream, which was not all a dream.
The bright sun was extinguish'd, and the stars
Did wander darkling in the eternal space,
Rayless, and pathless, and the icy earth
Swung blind and blackening in the moonless air...

While Byron's poem rather exaggerated the situation, there were many crop failures in the summer of 1816.

The most recent major explosive volcanic eruption was Mt Pinatubo in the Philippines in 1991. Such eruptions inject large quantities of dust particles and reactive gases (mainly sulfur dioxide and hydrogen sulfide) into the lower and upper atmosphere. If the particles and sulfurous gases remain in the troposphere (the well-mixed lower atmosphere where clouds and rain occur), they can be washed out in a matter of days to weeks, and so have little climatic effect. However, if the dust and reactive gases enter the more stable region of the stratosphere, which is free from water clouds and precipitation, the dust and gases can remain for longer periods. The heavier large particles still fall out due to gravity, but finer particles, mostly formed in the atmosphere by chemical reactions between gases, may stay in the stratosphere for many years.

The most long-lasting effects come from small sulfate particles that form in the stratosphere due to reactions between the sulphurous gases and ozone. These generally remain in the stratosphere until the lower stratospheric air is exchanged with the troposphere, when they can be washed out. This can take several years for the larger ones, and the finest particles can remain in the middle and upper stratosphere for decades.

Observations suggest that for the few years following a major explosive volcanic eruption regional effects on climate are quite likely, with warming in the stratosphere, and cooling at the surface, due to the particles absorbing some sunlight and reflecting more back into space. Regional surface cooling of about 1°C has been observed, along with warming in the stratosphere by a few degrees. Both these effects are well reproduced by recent climate models. Effects are greatly reduced by the second year after such eruptions, and are quite minor after several years. So unless there are a series of major eruptions in quick succession, no major climatic effects are to be expected. Projections of future climate changes usually have an implicit reservation that volcanic eruptions may provide a temporary interruption to any warming trend.

Collisions of Earth with a major meteor or asteroid could be far more disastrous, and there is geological evidence for such events in the past. None having major effects has been recorded in human history. However in the 1980s, they did provide some inspiration and an analogy in considerations of the possible climatic effects of a nuclear war (via the release of large clouds of smoke from burning cities) – an effect known as 'nuclear winter'. Major cosmic collisions are far less likely than major volcanic eruptions in the next few centuries, and are ignored in current climatic projections.

More relevant to current projections are the presence of large quantities of small particles in the lower atmosphere commonly referred to as 'aerosols'. These arise mainly from the emission of sulfurous gases and soot particles, from the burning of fossil fuels, as well as more natural dust particles from arid windy surfaces. All of these particles have only short lifetimes in the lower atmosphere before they fall out or are washed out. However, they are quickly replaced as more fossil fuels are burnt, or by wind erosion in arid areas.

Measurements from the ground and satellites indicate the large presence of such particles regionally, and that they have significant effects on regional climate. Aerosols directly absorb or reflect incoming solar energy, and also to absorb some outgoing heat radiation. Absorption of solar energy will cause local heating in the lower atmosphere, which may in turn heat the surface. Thus soot particles add to global warming. Absorption of heat radiation from the surface also tends to heat the surface. However, reflection of incoming solar radiation has a cooling effect at the surface. This is thought to have dominated in recent decades, leading to some polluted regions downwind of major industrial areas experiencing less warming than would have otherwise occurred.

A recent dramatic example of how aerosols effect the daily temperature cycle was observed in the United States when commercial aircraft were grounded following the terrorist attack on 11 September 2001. As reported in *Nature* on 8 August 2002, this led to less vapour trails from aircraft, with a statistically significant increase in the difference between daily maximum and minimum temperatures.

There are also indirect effects of aerosols on clouds, first suggested by Sean Twomey of the University of Arizona in 1977, that is, a reduction in cloud droplet size due to the particles acting as condensation nuclei. This increases the reflectivity of the clouds, and decreases precipitation efficiency, which increases cloud water content and cloud lifetime, leading to further surface cooling.

Recent excitement about so-called 'global dimming' (for example a paper by G. Stanhill in *Weather*, January 2005, and various media reports) is in fact a rediscovery and measurement of these effects of aerosols, which have long been held responsible in part for the global cooling experienced in the 1950s and 1960s. The direct effects of aerosols have been included in most recent global climate model simulations, and some simulations have also included estimates of the indirect effects.

Aerosol amounts due to industrial activity are now decreasing in some regions, especially in Europe and North America, due to efforts to clean up emissions of sulfurous gases because of acid rain and urban pollution effects. Thus, while greenhouse gas emissions continue to increase, the particles that were having a cooling effect are decreasing, leading to a greater dominance of increased greenhouse warming on the observed climate. This is part of the explanation for the increased rate of global average warming in the last two decades. When aerosol effects are added to global climate model simulations, they better account for the temperature variations observed over the twentieth century.

Past records from sedimentary layers offshore of the continents (notably China, north Africa and Australia), and in ice cores from Greenland and Antarctica, indicate that increases in wind-blown dust have occurred in previous more arid climates. Depending on the size and radiation absorptive qualities of these particles, they may have locally contributed to warming or cooling. They certainly testify to the ability of climate change to alter the frequency and severity of dust storms and soil erosion.

Rapid climate changes in the past

Despite the slowly varying nature of the astronomical variations, the paleo-climatic record is replete with examples of surprisingly rapid climatic changes. The extreme rapidity of some of these changes has only become apparent in recent decades as improved analysis, sampling and dating techniques have enabled changes to be observed on timescales of years to decades rather than centuries and millennia. Older analyses had smoothed out very rapid changes that can now be seen clearly.

Richard Alley, Chair of the Committee on Abrupt Climate Change of the US National Research Council (NRC), wrote in the preface to its 2002 report:

> *'Large, abrupt climate changes have repeatedly affected much or all of the earth, locally reaching as much as 10°C change in 10 years. Available evidence suggests that abrupt climate changes are not only possible but likely in the future, potentially with large impacts on ecosystems and societies.'*

Alley is not talking about abrupt external causes of change such as large meteor impacts or nuclear war, but rather abrupt climate changes that can occur when variables that are gradually changing push the earth system across some instability threshold. He likens this to how the slowly increasing pressure of a finger can flip a light switch from off to on. Gradual changes in the Earth's orbit, or drifting of the continents, can switch the Earth to a new and very different climatic state. When orbital changes and rising greenhouse gas concentrations warmed the Earth after the last glaciation, paleo-records show that the smooth changes were punctuated by abrupt global or regional coolings and warmings, wettings and dryings.

It should be added that such a switch cannot readily be turned off again, due to large delays or inertia in the climate system: it is more like one of those sensor switches used for lighting, which can be turned on by some sudden movement but only turn themselves off in their own good time.

The best known of these large and abrupt past changes was the Younger Dryas event, indicated, along with two other lesser events, by the shading in **Figure 10**. The Younger Dryas was a sudden interruption of a gradual global warming after the end of the last glaciation, and began about 12,800 years ago. This sudden return to a cold global climate lasted for 1200 years, and was followed by a very rapid warming of about 8°C in 10 years, taking the climate to interglacial conditions not much different from today. Proxy data for the Younger Dryas event is especially prominent in the ice core records from Greenland (top curve), where there is evidence of cooling, reduced snow accumulation, and changes in windiness and dust accumulation. Within about 30 years of this final warming, atmospheric methane concentration rose about 50%, reflecting changes in wetlands in both the tropics and high latitudes.

Evidence for a similar late-glacial reversal comes from ice cores on Baffin Island in Canada, and glaciers in Peru and Bolivia, and this is probably also the Younger Dryas. However in Antarctica the evidence is mixed, with records from Byrd showing relative warmth at the time of the cold conditions in Greenland.

Pollen evidence for changes in vegetation, however, provides a wider geographical coverage. During the Younger Dryas cooling occurred throughout Europe, from Norway to Spain and Italy, with the strongest effects near the western coast. Average July temperatures in Norway were 7–9°C lower than today, and as much as 8°C lower than today in Spain. Evidence also comes from North America that the Younger Dryas had significant effects there. Fossil pollens show that in the southern New England region of the United States July temperatures were 3–4°C cooler, and in the eastern maritime provinces of Canada they were 6–7°C cooler. Evidence of somewhat weaker effects is also found in the US Midwest, coastal British Columbia and Alaska, Costa Rica and Guatemala. In the Southern Hemisphere evidence is more confusing, with some cooling, but some areas where warming may have occurred, and others where no effects are found in the records. Glaciers advanced during the Younger Dryas in many European regions, notably in Norway, Finland and Scotland, and also in Canada, Wyoming in the US and Ecuador. Ice retreated in Peru, probably due to reduced precipitation, but the Franz Joseph glacier advanced in New Zealand.

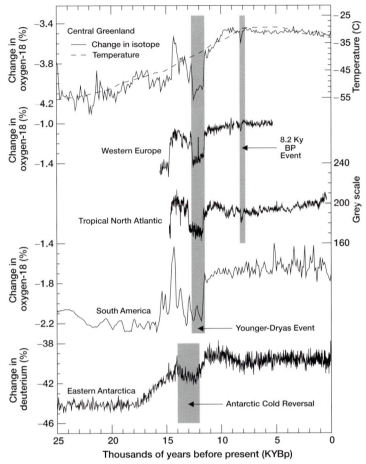

Figure 10: Records of climatic variations from the height of the last glaciation until the present. This includes three rapid climate change events (shaded), namely the Younger Dryas, the Antarctic Cold Reversal and the 8.2 thousand years before present event. (Source: IPCC 2001a, Figure 2.24, with permission.)

Marine sediment cores from the North Atlantic during the Younger Dryas show an increased abundance of polar planktonic species, which suggests that the formation of deep water, by the sinking of surface water, was reduced in the region. Other oceanic evidence supports this and provides evidence for the origin of the Younger Dryas event in the waters of the North Atlantic. Marine records from many other parts of the world, including the Caribbean, the North Pacific, the Indian Ocean and the Arabian Sea point to a global scale phenomenon, although some regions show little effect.

Despite the need for more data, the picture emerges of the Younger Dryas as cold, dry and windy in many regions at least of the northern hemisphere. However, there are locally wetter regions, possibly associated with changes in the tracks of storms. At the same time, the far South Atlantic, the southern Indian Ocean and Antarctica were relatively warm. Changes were largest around the North Atlantic, and appear to have been associated with reduced deep water formation and related changes in ocean circulation. Deep water formation results from the sinking of cold, high salinity and thus more dense surface waters. Slowing or cessation of deep water formation was due to warming or freshening of the surface waters.

Events similar in size, rate and extent to the Younger Dryas event occurred some 24 times during the 110,000 year record derived from the ice cores of central Greenland. They all show gradual cooling from a warm interval, then more abrupt cooling, a cold interval, and finally an abrupt warming. The warm times have been termed Dansgaard/Oeschger events, and the sequences Dansgaard/Oeschger oscillations. The colder phases were marked by increased rafting by icebergs of glacial debris (rocks and dirt scraped up by glaciers) into colder, fresher surface water, and by a reduction in the strength of North Atlantic deep water formation. Changes in material such as dust and methane from outside Greenland, trapped in the ice cores, demonstrate that these events affected large areas of the earth simultaneously.

Despite only gradual changes in driving forces, these observed rapid climate changes appear to have occurred because the drivers reached some sort of tipping point or threshold at which climate flips into a new state. Such mechanisms suggest that similar rapid climate changes could happen again, even when driven by only gradual increases in greenhouse gases. We will return to the significance of these past events for climate change risk in the twenty-first century and beyond in Chapter 5, which deals with what climate changes are likely, and in Chapter 6, on climate change impacts.

The last 10,000 years

Climatic changes since the Younger Dryas event more than 10,000 years ago have generally been much smaller in amplitude, but nevertheless sometimes rapid, with sudden increases in the frequency and severity of extreme events such as droughts and floods. Even these relatively small changes evidently had large impacts on ecosystems and human societies, although usually at a regional rather than global scale.

In relation to human impacts, it is sometimes difficult to pin down exactly what was cause and what was effect, due to variations in factors other than climate. Population pressures, diseases, wars, economic forces, technological changes and resource substitutions can all affect human societies in ways that may or may not be related to climate. However, in some cases the climatic influence is clear and well documented. A case in point is the settlement of Greenland by the Vikings in the twelfth century during what is known as the Medieval Warm Period, and the abandonment of these settlements during the fifteenth century as conditions in the North Atlantic region became cooler, agriculture became more marginal, sea ice extended and the settlements became more isolated.

The extent to which human history has been influenced by climate has been long debated by historians and climatologists. The US historian-geographer Huntington in 1915 famously advocated a form of climatic determinism, that is, that climate determined human racial differences and levels of civilisation. Carpenter and Lamb in the 1960s argue for the influence of climate on Greek civilisation, and Le Roy Ladurie, in his seminal book in 1971, for a wider influence especially on European history. Dansgaard and colleagues in 1975 argued for a strong influence on Norse culture, especially in regard to the settlement of Iceland and Greenland, and Singh in 1971 for a determining climatic impact on the civilisation of the Indus valley in north-west India, which collapsed following droughts in the eighteenth century BC. Climatic fluctuations are also argued to have influenced the migrations of peoples in the South Pacific, including the settlement of New Zealand by the Maori peoples around 800 AD. The Zhou Dynasty in China was affected by increasing aridity around 1150 AD.

Climatic fluctuations such as extended drought are thought to have played a major part in the abandonment of American Indian settlements in the south-western United States around 1090 AD, and again in the thirteenth century AD, and the fall of the Mayan civilisation in Central America around 850 AD. Extensive analysis of tree ring data, lake levels and sand dunes in the Great Plains of the United States indicates that over the last 2000 years extended drought conditions comparable with, or more severe than, that of the 1930s dust bowl occurred on several occasions. It was concluded that if such large scale droughts were to occur in future they would have a significant impact on North American society, with a reduction in water supply, crop failure, rangeland stress, suspension of recreational and tourist activity and heat-related deaths.

Perhaps most importantly, large areas of the African and European continents underwent massive changes in their vegetation cover and ecosystems in the early and mid-Holocene periods, some ten to five thousand years ago. This must have had enormous impacts on the lives of the scattered human inhabitants at those times, forcing large-scale population movements or population losses.

In Africa, the Sahara went from a largely grassy area, populated by hunter-gathering peoples who left artefacts and records of the animals they hunted in rock paintings, to desert rather suddenly around 6000 years ago. Evidence for this is found in lake sediments and estimated levels, and in marine and land pollen records. This change is thought to be related to the Earth's orbital variations and an amplification of the effect of changing solar radiation by the interaction of the vegetation with climate, possibly passing some critical threshold. This sudden drying may have spurred migration into the Nile Valley and the start of the Egyptian civilisation. Climate models have partly simulated these rapid climate changes, although results differ from one model to another.

And in East Africa, lake levels and salinity fluctuations in Lake Naivasha (Kenya) indicate that the era from 1000 to 1270 AD, (during the Medieval Warm Period in Europe) was significantly drier than today, while the era 1270–1850 AD was relatively wet (corresponding at least in part to the cool period in Europe known as the Little Ice Age). Moreover, three shorter periods of drought, in 1390–1420, 1560–1625 and 1760–1840 correspond to periods of political unrest and large-scale migration, according to oral traditions, with periods of prosperity in between.

Evidence for a Little Ice Age and a Medieval Warm Period is fairly widespread across Europe and parts of North America, to a lesser extent elsewhere in the northern hemisphere, and much less evident in the southern hemisphere. Pollen and charcoal analyses from sediments in parts of the north-western United States, and from Yellowstone Park and central Idaho point to greater fire frequency during the Medieval Warm Period, and lesser fire frequency during the Little Ice Age. However, in Alberta, Canada, the same sort of analyses point to the opposite tendency. This local effect has been related to declining groundwater levels at one site in Alberta, leading to a change from fire-prone shrub Birch trees to less fire-prone Aspen.

Records of prehistoric tropical cyclones occur in the form of ridges of coral rubble, sand, shell and pumice; erosional terraces in raised gravel beaches; barrier washover deposits; and various other sediments. Such records for a number of sites around the world suggest that the frequency and possibly the intensity of tropical cyclones have varied in the past. However, the number of events analysed is small and statistical significance is therefore not great.

Changes in sea level since the end of the last glaciation are dominated by the slow but massive rise of some 120 metres due to the melting of the huge continental ice sheets in the northern hemisphere between about 20,000 and 8000 years ago. This was not entirely regular, but was punctuated by pauses and sudden rises of a few metres due to temporary glacial re-advances and sudden outbursts of melt-water stored by huge glacial dams or surges in glacial motion and iceberg formation.

Sea-level rise in the last 8000 years or so has tended to be small and regional, with rises in some regions and relative falls in others, mainly due to earth movements and rebound of the continental plates. The majority of the Earth's coastlines are at present subject to relative sea-level rise and erosion. Local consolidation of sediments, either due to slow natural adjustments, earthquakes, or withdrawal of groundwater, oil or natural gas, has contributed to coastal problems. Notable is the loss of some ancient cities around the Mediterranean coast, such as ancient Alexandria, Menouthis and Heraklion in Egypt, and others around Greece, Italy and Turkey. Growing subsidence problems also exist in other cities such as Bangkok, London and Venice, and in the Chesapeake Bay region in the United States. These problems would be accentuated by any systematic sea-level rise due to the enhanced greenhouse effect, especially if sea-level rise accelerates, as now seems likely.

There is also clear evidence that melting of ice caps has led to the underlying land slowly rising as the weight of ice was removed. This is called 'glacial rebound', and as well as causing local sea-level falls (with compensating rises elsewhere as the water is displaced), it adds stress to tectonic faultlines, leading to local increases in earthquake activity.

As regards proxy evidence for temperature variations, we saw in Chapter 1 that the proxy record over the last thousand years suggests that the twentieth century saw the largest temperature rise, at least in the Northern Hemisphere, with the sharpest rise occurring since the 1970s. This claim was challenged by Soon and Baliunas in a paper in 2003 claiming that 'Across the world, many records reveal that the twentieth century is probably not the warmest nor a uniquely extreme climatic period of the last millennium.' However, this is very misleading, since the paper does not compare estimates of past *global* or *hemispheric* average temperatures with those of the twentieth century, but merely *non-synchronous* (that is, not occurring at the same time) and unquantified temperature (and rainfall) 'anomalies' in each local record. Local anomalies can occur for many reasons, and often cancel out across larger regions, so the number of occurrences of short warm periods in long records from many different regions is not comparable to hemispheric average warming such as has occurred in the twentieth century.

Michael Mann and others published replies to the Soon and Baliunas paper. However, a paper by Hans von Storch of the German Institute for Coastal Research and others in *Science*, 22 October 2004, did find that discrepancies arise in analyses of the proxy-record of climate over the last 1000 years due to the statistical methods used. They found that methods used to derive **Figure 1b** (the 'hockey stick'), underestimated the past variations by a factor of two or more. Another paper by Anders Moberg from Stockholm University and others in *Nature*, 10 February 2005, also found larger variations than in the Mann and others' curves. However, neither of these new analyses leads to estimated temperatures during the Medieval Warm Period as high as those reached in the 1990s. Moreover, as pointed out by Tim Osborn and Keith Briffa of the Climatic Research Unit in the UK (see *Science*, 22 October 2004), the larger estimated temperature variations in the 1000-year record suggest a greater climate sensitivity to small changes in forcing factors and this would also apply to greenhouse gases. This is consistent with the claims for human influences over this period, via changes in land cover, made by William Ruddiman.

Ruddiman suggests that the cool period before the Medieval Warm Period and the Little Ice Age may both have been due to bubonic plague-induced depopulation in western Asia and Europe, which led to regrowth of forest on abandoned farmlands. This theory has caused wide discussion in the scientific community. If true, it suggests high climate sensitivity to relatively small changes in greenhouse gas concentrations and that humans are capable of achieving these changes. Moreover, it means that while past human activity may have helped to avoid prolonged conditions like the Little Ice Age by widespread land clearing, projected increases in greenhouse gas concentrations at a rate at least ten times faster than our ancestors achieved means that we will see much larger warmings in the twenty-first century and beyond.

Conclusions from the past record

Past climatic changes are relevant because they demonstrate what is possible in the natural climate system, when forces occur such as volcanic eruptions or variations in the Earth's orbit around the Sun. Orbital variations act slowly, on timescales of thousands of years, while volcanic eruptions act in a matter of days or weeks. Now we are forcing changes on the climate system due to large greenhouse gas emissions on a timescale of decades to a century. These are equivalent to changes which occurred previously over thousands of years. Therefore we might well expect similar impacts on natural systems to those which occurred in the past over thousands of years, but telescoped into a much faster time frame, leading to rapid and possibly catastrophic changes.

Climate change has occurred naturally in the past due to internal fluctuations in the climate system consisting of the atmosphere (air, water vapour, constituent gases, clouds and particles), the hydrosphere (oceans, lakes, rivers and groundwater), and the cryosphere (continental ice sheets, mountain glaciers, sea ice and surface snow cover). External changes such as volcanic eruptions, variations in the Sun's output and the Earth's orbital variations and changes in the solid Earth (continental drift, mountain building, erosion and siltation) have also driven changes in climate.

At the end of the last glaciation, average global warming occurred at a rate of about 1°C or less per thousand years, although there were short periods during which warming was much faster. The last of these was at the end of the so-called 'Younger Dryas' reversal, about 11,500 years ago. Since then, and certainly since the dawn of civilisation, rates of warming have never exceeded about 0.5°C per century (0.05°C per decade) for periods of more than a few decades.

Our interest in the past is not only in what sorts of climate changes can happen, but also in what sort of impacts they had on natural systems such as plants, animals and landscapes. However, in interpreting paleo-climate induced changes, we must think carefully about rates of change, rates of adaptation, and changed circumstances as regards human populations and societies.

Pollen records show that in response to warming after the end of the last glaciation around 15,000 to 10,000 years ago, forests migrated at rates of, at most, tens of metres per century. Over the next century we can expect climate to change so rapidly that forests would need to migrate at rates of hundreds of kilometres per century to remain in their optimal climatic zones. This is clearly unlikely. What is far more likely is that forests that no longer are located in their correct climatic zones will die from heat stress, drought, disease and fire. Similarly, many crops will no longer yield well in their present locations, and will have to be re-located hundreds of kilometres away to provide equivalent climate conditions. But often the crops will be on different soils, on land owned by other people, and even in different countries. Dislocations to society will therefore be large, far larger than was the case for the small numbers of hunters and gatherers who existed tens of thousands of years ago.

Paleo-climatic analogies to our present predicament confuse many people. They argue that if large climate changes occurred before, and humans and other species survived, then life, and even humans, can survive today, so there is not much to be concerned about. This fails to consider the different time scales, the very different place of humanity in the ecosystems then compared to now, and the many restrictions that exist today which limit our ability to adapt to such large and rapid changes. These include national boundaries, mass reliance on relatively few crops for food, and other environmental stresses caused by some six billion people. Human beings and their societies may well be threatened, not with extinction, but with severe disruption, and possibly catastrophic economic and social effects. This is especially so if we happen to cross a threshold which leads to rapid climate change of a magnitude and speed unparalleled since the Younger Dryas event, and one which cannot be quickly reversed.

The upshot of all these studies is that climate change of the magnitude we are expecting in the next 100 years and beyond has happened before, although usually at a much slower rate and from a cooler starting point. Projected changes in climate by 2100 are comparable to those from the last glaciation (20,000 years ago) to the present, which led to large rises in sea level, massive changes in plant and animal numbers and distribution, and changes in the land-sea borders. Some places changed from tundra to temperate forests, and others from forests to desert. Today we face similar change, but much faster, and from a base climate which is already as warm as any experienced since human societies began.

3

Projecting the future

Foresight provides the ability to influence the future rather than to predict it.

Richard Freeman

As we know, there are known knowns. There are things we know we know. We also know there are known unknowns. That is to say we know there are some things we do not know. But there are also unknown unknowns, the ones we don't know we don't know.

Donald Rumsfeld, US Secretary of Defense, news briefing 12 February 2002

The need for, and nature of, foresight

While I am not a fan of Donald Rumsfeld, I think the quote above from one of his news briefings drew some rather unfair lambasting. It summarises, if one concentrates on its meaning and applies it to climate change, some important aspects of the science of climate change as well as defence policy questions. That is, there is a whole range of aspects of climate change, with some much more certain than others. There are also uncertainties and possibilities we are aware of, and may even be able to quantify in terms of risk. But, there is also a possibility that there are things about climate that we simply do not know, and which may totally surprise us.

The Intergovernmental Panel on Climate Change (IPCC) was formed to provide foresight in relation to the possible human impacts on climate, with a view to helping governments formulate wiser policy options and decisions in relation to climate change. Foresight is the act or power of seeing into the future, a perception gained by looking forward, and care or provision for the future. It is an everyday occurrence. Prudent people use foresight to decide or plan their actions so as to improve their future prospects. In this spirit governments around the world have recognised that human societies, through their use of resources and waste products are capable of changing the environment, including the climate.

Foresight requires some estimate of future conditions. In the case of climate change this includes projections of future emissions of greenhouse gases and particulates into the atmosphere, consequent concentrations of these pollutants in the atmosphere, and their effects on the climate. In addition, so as to understand how serious this might be, estimates are also needed of the consequences for society in terms of potential impacts on areas such as agriculture, water supply, health and building safety and comfort. This is complicated by the fact that impacts depend not just on the stresses applied by climate, but also on the strength and adaptability of society. This requires an understanding of how changes in society will affect its capacity to absorb or adapt to climatic stress.

There are, as viewed from the present, many possible futures. How we foresee the future possibilities, and the conscious or unconscious choices we make that will influence development of society, will help determine which of the possible futures will actually occur. The purpose, from a policy perspective, is not to predict which of the possible futures will occur, but rather to inform us so that we might choose which one we would prefer and attempt to bring to reality.

Predictions, scenarios and projections

People are often confused by various terms used to characterise future climate changes, namely 'predictions', 'scenarios' and 'projections'. A prediction is a statement that something *will* happen in the future, based on known conditions at the time the prediction is made, and assumptions as to the physical or other processes that will lead to change. Such predictions are seldom certain because present conditions are often not known precisely, and the processes affecting the future are not perfectly understood. Predictions are thus best expressed with probabilities attached. Daily weather forecasts are 'predictions' in this sense – they are predictions of what the weather will be like, but have uncertainties due to inexact observations and weather models. They are often expressed in probabilistic terms, such as 'There is a 60% chance of rain today'.

A scenario is a plausible description of some future state, with no statement of probability. It is used to enable people to explore the question 'What if such and such were to happen?' Scenarios are often used in literature to stretch the imagination, and increasingly in businesses and government to help to develop a range of strategies or contingency plans to cope with possible changes in business or other conditions. Scenarios are alternative pictures of how the future might develop. They are used to assess consequences, and thus to provide a basis for policies that might influence future developments, or enable businesses or governments to cope with the future situation if and when it occurs. Examples might include businesses planning for various possible future developments like a new competitor, a fire, or a failure of the electricity supply. No one knows when or if these contingencies or scenarios may happen, but the business needs plans in place to ensure survival if they happen.

Projections are sets of future conditions, or consequences, based on explicit assumptions, such as scenarios. For example, in the case of a business faced with loss of production due to a fire, how much production would be lost, how soon can it be recovered, and how will it affect contracts and the solvency of the company? Even for a given scenario or set of assumptions, projections introduce further uncertainties due to the use of inexact rules or 'models' connecting the scenario conditions to the projected outcomes. Thus, a climate model can project the future climate based on a given scenario for future greenhouse gas emissions, and a crop model may project how this would affect yield. Such projections are conditional on the scenario and the models used.

A key issue in projecting the future on the basis of a scenario is the plausibility of the scenario. If a scenario is not plausible it is not worth worrying about in setting policy, but if it is plausible we may need to take its possibility into account. Scenario plausibility has several elements: that the scenario must be logically, physically, biologically, and historically possible.

Plausible scenarios are useful for asking 'What if...' questions, and thus for helping to make policy choices that may influence which of the 'what ifs' actually comes to pass. In the climate change context they are useful for influencing policy regarding the need to reduce greenhouse gas emissions. If reducing greenhouse gas emissions is costly, the urgency and extent of such reductions depends not just on the possibility of a scenario, but also on its probability. The probability of projections based on given scenarios is therefore a legitimate issue.

Even in the absence of estimated probabilities, scenarios are of some use in relation to adaptation policy (that is, how to cope with unavoidable climate change) in that they suggest what conditions we might need to adapt to in future. Scenarios help us to anticipate what sort of adaptations might be needed, and to identify the need for increased resilience (capacity to bounce back) and adaptive capacity (capacity to adapt to change). However, in order to answer specific planning questions like 'How large should the spillway of a new dam at location x be in order to cope with the maximum possible flood at that location in 2070?' it is necessary to know more than that a given change in rainfall is *possible*. Rather, the *probability* of such a change needs to be known, since expensive engineering design needs to be based on cost-effective risk minimisation.

As suggested in the Introduction to this book, climate change projections based on high-emission scenarios for greenhouse gases may, hopefully, be seen in retrospect as self-denying prophecies: if high emissions demonstrably lead to disastrous impacts, they may well be avoided through policy settings aimed at lowering emissions.

The emissions scenarios used by the IPCC

In order to provide policy-relevant advice on the consequences of human-induced climate change in the twenty-first century, the IPCC commissioned a range of scenarios of greenhouse gas and sulfate aerosol emissions up to the year 2100. These emission scenarios were developed by a panel of authors, with wide consultation, and an open process of review and comment by experts and governments, followed by subsequent revisions. The scenarios were reported in the *Special Report on Emissions Scenarios* (SRES), published in 2000. They were intended to feed into projections of climate change in the *Third Assessment Report* in 2001, and to enable a discussion of the potential impacts, adaptations and vulnerability of sectors, regions and countries.

Future emissions are the product of complex interacting systems driven by population change, socio-economic development, and technological change. All of which are highly uncertain, especially when extended as far as the year 2100.

The original 40 SRES scenarios were based on four different 'storylines' of internally consistent developments across different driving forces (see **Box 3**), and multiple modelling approaches. This led to a reduced total of 35 scenarios containing data on all gases required to force climate models. Resulting accumulated emissions by 2100, expressed in units of thousands of millions of tonnes of carbon equivalent (GtC) range from a low of 770 GtC to approximately 2540 GtC. This range compares with previous IPCC projections from 1992 and 1995 (based on what is known as the IS92 scenarios), which range from 770 to 2140 GtC, so the upper end of the projected range is now greater than before. Accumulated emissions are an important indicator of eventual climatic effects because the effective lifetime of carbon dioxide in the atmosphere is so long that this figure largely determines eventual carbon dioxide concentrations and the resulting global warming.

Corresponding projected carbon dioxide concentrations for the illustrative scenarios in the year 2100 range from 540 to 970 ppm, that is, roughly 2 to 3.5 times the pre-industrial levels. As the scenarios only went to 2100 and concentrations had not stabilised by then, stabilised concentrations are likely to be well in excess of these numbers.

The SRES scenarios include estimated emissions of carbon dioxide, methane, nitrous oxide and sulfur dioxide. Generally, the SRES emission scenarios contain higher upper limits on carbon dioxide emissions, but lower emissions of sulfur dioxide than the previous IS92 scenarios. The higher upper limit carbon dioxide emissions would increase the upper limits of global warming due to increased infrared absorption, but a large part of the increase in warming relative to earlier scenarios comes from the lower sulfur dioxide emissions, which lead to reduced regional cooling by sulfate aerosols in highly industrialised regions such as Europe, the United States and southern and eastern Asia.

Explicit policy options to reduce greenhouse emissions, such as might be adopted under the United Nations Framework Convention on Climate Change (UNFCCC), were excluded from the scenarios. However, other socio-economic and technological trends considered by the SRES lead in some cases to consid-

---

Box 3: The SRES emissions scenarios

A1. The A1 storyline and group of related scenarios describe a future world of very rapid economic growth, global population that peaks in mid-century and declines thereafter, and the rapid introduction of new and more efficient technologies. Major underlying themes are convergence among regions, capacity building and increased cultural and social interactions, with a substantial reduction in regional differences in per capita income. The A1 group scenario is split into three groups that describe alternative directions of technological change in the energy system. The three A1 groups are distinguished by their technological emphasis: fossil intensive (A1FI), non-fossil energy sources (A1T), or a balance across all sources (A1B) (where balanced is defined as not relying too heavily on one particular energy source, on the assumption that similar improvement rates apply to all energy supply and end-use technologies).

A2. The A2 storyline and group of scenarios describe a very heterogeneous world. The underlying theme is self-reliance and preservation of local identities. Fertility patterns across regions converge very slowly, which results in continuously increasing population. Economic development is primarily oriented to particular regions and per capita economic growth and technological change more fragmented and slower than other storylines.

B1. The B1 storyline and group of scenarios describe a convergent world with the same global population that peaks in mid-century and declines thereafter, as in the A1 storyline but with rapid change in economic structures toward a service and information economy, with reductions in material intensity and the introduction of clean and resource-efficient technologies. The emphasis is on global solutions to economic, social and environmental sustainability, including improved equity, but without additional climate initiatives.

B2. The B2 storyline and group of scenarios describe a world in which the emphasis is on local solutions to economic, social and environmental sustainability. It is a world with continuously increasing global population, at a rate lower than A2, intermediate levels of economic development, and less rapid and more diverse technological change than in the A1 and B1 storylines. While the scenario is also oriented toward environmental protection and social equity, it focuses on local and regional levels.

Source: IPCC 2001a, Box 4 of Technical Summary

erable reductions in greenhouse gas and/or sulfur emissions. These scenarios were characterised by the SRES as 'plausible', but no further estimates of probability were attached, and indeed estimates of probability would be difficult to derive with any confidence. They are clearly not predictions, and do not have equal probability of occurrence in the real world.

Some critics have argued on technical grounds, related to how currency exchange rates between countries are calculated, that the high emissions scenarios are unrealistic. However, carbon dioxide emissions are related, in the final analysis, simply to population, energy use per capita and carbon dioxide emissions per unit energy. Thus the use of different exchange rates in measuring gross domestic product makes no difference to calculated emissions in each individual country. Whether or not it makes any difference globally depends on how the national figures are combined to get global ones, that is, whether the addition is done before or after emissions are calculated. National emissions depend on national energy use and the carbon per unit energy, not on how the national economy is measured.

In any case, the critics miss the real point, which is that the SRES scenarios are not predictions, but merely a plausible range of emissions, used to bound discussion of climate change impacts. Moreover, the climate models used to produce the projections of climate change that underlie the IPCC assessment are developed and validated separately from the emissions scenarios. Any reassessment of the range of the SRES scenarios may affect the upper and/or lower bounds of the projected climate change over the next 100 years, but are most unlikely to alter the main conclusions that significant climate change is likely to occur, with significant impacts. The SRES emissions projections are drawn from, and consistent with, the published literature, including several recent US studies that use more sophisticated models than were available at the time the SRES scenarios were developed.

Moreover, due to their late publication, the SRES scenarios were not applied in any detailed studies of impacts globally or regionally in time for inclusion in the IPCC report in 2001. Rather, estimated impacts globally and regionally resulting from earlier and generally lower emissions scenarios were put in an interpretive framework in the 2001 report in which the possibility of larger emission scenarios was considered. Details of the SRES scenarios are thus immaterial to the main conclusions from the 2001 IPCC report, which do not focus on projected impacts for the most extreme scenarios.

Emissions of chemicals, mainly sulfur dioxide and hydrogen sulfide from the burning of fossil fuels, lead to the formation of sulfate aerosols, which have a localised cooling effect and also cause urban air pollution and acid rain. Historically, such emissions have been concentrated in the large industrial regions of the United States, Europe and southern and eastern Asia. The resulting localised cooling has counteracted or masked some of the warming due to increasing greenhouse gas concentrations in and immediately downwind of these regions. However, it has been relatively easy to reduce these aerosol-forming emissions by the use of low-sulfur fuels and scrubbing of the combustion fumes. This is well under way in the United States and Europe, but not to the same extent in southern and eastern Asia. SRES scenarios project continuing reductions in aerosols in North America and Europe, and also in Asia in coming decades.

The result of these changes in sulfur emissions and aerosol levels is that the masking effect on enhanced greenhouse warming is rapidly disappearing over North America and Europe, as seen in recent record warmth in these regions. A similar effect is expected to occur later over Asia, and is one reason for a projected increase in the rate of global warming. This is one reason why the resulting projected global warming in the IPCC *Third Assessment Report* in 2001 is larger than that in the *Second Assessment Report* in 1995, when a less rapid reduction in sulfur emissions was expected.

Several other factors that may impact on projections have not been taken into account in the SRES scenarios. One is the emission of carbon black particles, largely from open fires such as wildfires, land clearing and burning of stubble. Such emissions have short lifetimes in the atmosphere, but seasonally they can be large and may have significant regional surface warming effects.

Another is the effect of land clearing, farming and irrigation on absorption or reflection of sunlight at the land surface. Again, this varies regionally, but is in general only important in limited areas of the continents. Its main effect is on local surface heating and the effect of this on cumulus convection, although this can have downwind effects on the weather if the area concerned is large. Climate model calculations have found that this effect may be important where large forest areas are being cleared, such as in the Amazon Basin, and ideally it should be included in climate change simulations. Land clearing can in general be reversed in most areas, and indeed some farmlands in developed countries have recently reverted to forests. Scenarios of land-use change are being developed in consultation with the IPCC.

Irrigation also affects surface climate via the cooling effect of evaporation, and also by injecting moisture into the atmosphere. But again, the areas are relatively small, especially in comparison with the area of the oceans, so they have little effect on large area and global water budgets. Climatic effects of irrigation are essentially local.

Projections of socio-economic futures

An important consideration in estimating potential impacts of climate change is the future exposure of populations, human systems and ecosystems to climatically induced stresses, and the capacity of those so exposed to adapt to the stresses. With the notable exception of the UK Fast Track project (see *Global Environmental Change*, Vol. 14, pp. 53–67), this has been largely neglected, with only the most general comments on likely changes in exposure and the capacity of societies to absorb or adapt to climate changes. For example, sea-level rise and storm surges are likely to cause more damage in particular low-lying coastal zones where populations and investments are increasing.

As stated by Edward Parsons and colleagues in reference to the 2001 US National Assessment of Potential Consequences of Climate Variability and Change, constructing socio-economic scenarios for impact assessment is more complex and challenging than constructing scenarios of future emissions. Emissions scenarios require only a few national-level characteristics such as population, economic growth, total energy use, and carbon emissions per unit economic output. However, socio-economic determinants of vulnerability and adaptation to climate change can be very localised, may not be obvious, and interact strongly with other factors such as social organisation and technological progress. Local vulnerability may be linked with international competition and commodity prices, which in turn may be affected by changes elsewhere.

Ideally, socio-economic scenarios used to estimate future emissions of greenhouse gases should be used at the local or regional scale as the basis for consistent estimates of exposure and adaptive capacity. The SRES scenarios contain such data at a broad regional level, for example in 13 world regions for scenarios A1, B1 and A2 and 11 regions for scenario B2, although these data have not been widely used in impact studies. It is complicated, however, by the fact that different global socio-economic scenarios may lead to similar magnitudes of climate change globally and regionally but with different regional exposures and adaptive capacities.

The global SRES socio-economic scenarios have been reduced to a national scale by Stuart Gaffin for the United States and Wolfgang Lutz for Austria. Additionally, the UK 'Fast Track' project went on to produce finer resolution data at a sub-national scale in order to estimate and map global impacts of climate change on a number of industrial and societal sectors. However, downscaling was often based on assumed uniform behaviour across each nation. Generally, the socio-economic data have not been provided at the space scales appropriate to specific regions that may be at risk, for example, estimates of vulnerability and adaptability to sea-level rise on rapidly developing coastal strips in the south-eastern US, south-eastern China or north-eastern Australia.

In the case of coastal exposure to sea-level rise and storm surges, existing trends make it reasonable to assume greater growth rates in population and investment in coastal areas than in national averages. This affects not only the exposure, but also the rate of localised sea-level rise, since greater coastal populations tend to withdraw more ground water, leading to greater local subsidence.

Scenarios of future population changes are well documented by both the United Nations and the International Institute of Applied Systems Analysis (IIASA), although the UN studies tend to be broad scale. They were downscaled to the national level by IIASA. There is a convenient discussion entitled 'The end of world population growth' by Wolfgang Lutz of IIASA, which suggests that global population is likely to peak in the twenty-first century, with early declines in many developed countries, but continued growth mainly in the poorest countries of Africa and southern Asia until later in the century. Joel Cohen of Rockefeller University also projects population trends until 2050, and emphasises the importance of migration from the poorer to the richer countries. Migration is discussed again in Chapters 6 and 10, where we consider the potential impacts of climate change, and especially sea-level rise, on migration for economic and environmental reasons.

The United Nations Environment Programme has published a series of Global Environment Outlooks. The latest, published in 2002, looks at environmental change and related policies since 1972, and goes on to provide an outlook up to 2032. It takes four contrasting socio-economic scenarios:

- markets first, in which most of the world adopts the values and expectations prevailing in today's industrialised countries,

- policy first, where decisive initiatives are taken by governments trying to reach specific social and environmental goals,

- security first, in which there is a world of striking disparities, where inequality and conflict prevail, and

- sustainability first, in which a new environment and development paradigm emerges in response to the challenge of sustainability.

As might be expected, the effect in relation to greenhouse gas emissions is that the first and third scenarios, lacking effective environmental policies, lead to significant increases in greenhouse gases over the next 30 years. The policy first scenario leads to actual reductions in emissions starting around 2030, while the sustainability first scenario leads to a decline by the mid-2020s. Different environmental outcomes in other areas will also clearly affect societal capacity to adapt. But one of the most significant lessons drawn from the scenario exercise by the authors is that 'much of the environmental change that will occur over the next 30 years has already been set in motion by past and current actions', and that 'many of the effects of environmentally relevant polices put in place over the next 30 years will not be apparent until long afterwards'.

Some idea of future exposure and adaptive capacity could be based on various scenarios of regional population growth and socio-economic conditions contained in various foresighting studies already undertaken. Nevertheless, the broad storylines of the global SRES scenarios need to be borne in mind when assessing likely exposure and adaptive capacity at the local level.

An alternative, which may be more relevant for many local or national studies, is to use local scenarios for socio-economic development in that country. These may capture some of the relevant detail about internal shifts in growth patterns, and community dependence on local industries, which may be affected by technological change or global commodity prices. Some of these local scenarios also have policy relevance, although their consistency with global scenarios is problematic. This may not be critical, however, since any global scenario, such as the SRES scenarios, will not apply uniformly in regard to socio-economic changes, so that local departures from the broad-scale scenarios may not greatly affect global emissions and resulting climate changes.

For example, in Australia several scenario exercises have been performed by business related groups, such as the Business Council of Australia, looking at alternative futures, with an eye to influencing government policies in the area of business, population growth, globalisation and the environment.

Another ongoing Australian study by the Resources Futures Program of CSIRO Sustainable Ecosystems has an integrated approach where interactions between the environment and population are simulated. This study aims essentially at providing insight into options for Australia's population, technology, resources and environment to 2050. It looks at the consequences of low, medium and high population growth rates, and explores the consequences for people, urban infrastructure, the natural environment, energy, water and a range of other issues. Among the conclusions of their 2002 report was a need to recognise that:

- Australia's social, economic and physical systems are linked over very long time scales,

- short-term decisions have long-term consequences, and

- there is inbuilt inertia in our institutional systems, requiring time for change to take effect.

These conclusions apply in many places besides Australia, and are themes reflected in the IPCC *Third Assessment Report*. They suggest that any realistic assessment of the overall impacts of climate change on any local or national community, and of its capacity to cope with or adapt to climate change, will need to integrate studies of socio-economic futures with climate change studies. They are all part of an interconnected future.

Unfortunately, to date very few international climate impacts studies have taken different possible socio-economic futures into account. One that did is the UK 'Fast Track' project, discussed above.

Forecasting the weather

Foresight is routinely used in regard to the weather, and affects many of our day-to-day decisions. It is therefore useful to compare the basis for weather forecasting with that for climate projections, in order to understand both what they have in common and what the differences are.

Weather forecasting used to be based on experience with past situations, which developed into changed weather patterns that experts could either remember or look up from past records. This was called 'analogue forecasting', that is using the past as an analogue for the future. During and after the Second World War, things started to change with the use of growing theoretical understanding of how weather disturbances grow, move and decay. Quantitative calculations of how the atmosphere changes were pioneered by Lewis Richardson, an English schoolteacher and scientist who, by hand, calculated solutions to the governing equations of motion and continuity of matter to produce the first numerical weather forecast. His work, done in the trenches as an ambulance worker in the First World War, was published in 1922.

However, Richardson's calculation was not very accurate, and application of his methods had to wait for the development of larger electronic computers. John von Neumann and Jules Charney took up the challenge at Princeton University just after the Second World War, using one of the first electronic computers. The first computer-based weather forecasts were issued in 1955.

It quickly became apparent that the skill of numerical weather forecasting decreases rapidly with time into the future. Mathematical theory, developed by Edward Lorenz of Massachusetts Institute of Technology demonstrated that the accuracy of forecasts declines due to the growth of errors present in the initial input data. Known as 'chaos theory', this shows that small differences in initial conditions, such as those that arise from imperfect observations of the present weather, lead to larger and larger errors with time. Lorenz used the analogy of a pinball machine to explain what happens.

In a pinball machine, a rolling ball hits a post (or pin) and bounces off in a straight line until it strikes a second pin, then a third and so on. Lorenz considered that if the ball, in its initial motion, ran over a small piece of dust it would be slightly deflected, striking the pin at a slightly different angle. After several such strikes the ball would be travelling in a sufficiently different direction to miss a pin that it would have hit in the no-dust case, so that the predictability of which pins it would strike later on would rapidly decrease. The predictability is critically dependent on knowing exactly what path the ball takes in its first encounter, and the more accurately that is known the more strikes could be accurately predicted. However, if the experiment were repeated many times, an average path could be found, and it would be possible to say how probable it was that the ball would strike a particular pin. Thus it would not be possible to predict with complete confidence which pin would be hit, but from repeated observations the probabilities of striking various pins could be determined.

Weather forecasting is a similar type of initial value problem, that is, one in which the eventual outcome depends on how accurately the initial conditions are known. Any error in specifying the initial conditions is amplified and eventually leads to a breakdown in predictability of the exact outcome, although it may result in the ability to predict the probability of various outcomes, that is, to predict the statistics of the weather. Lorenz and others showed that the limit of predictability of particular weather is about three weeks.

Progress towards improved weather forecasts is partly due to better observations of initial conditions, and more accurate calculations that minimise any rounding off errors. Thus numerical weather models calculate properties of the atmosphere to many decimal places, to slow down the propagation of errors. Repeated model calculations of the same situation can also provide multiple forecasts, with the average usually being more reliable than a single forecast.

Other improvements in weather forecasting have come from the incorporation of heat and moisture exchange between the atmosphere and the oceans, assisted by satellite observations of sea surface temperatures. The fact that the skill of numerical weather prediction has improved over the years is testimony to the growing understanding of how the atmosphere and oceans combine to produce weather, and to how this is incorporated into computer models.

Why climate projections are different

Numerical prediction of climate is a different problem, even though it starts with the same equations governing atmospheric motion and continuity of matter (the amount of air and water in the atmosphere). There are two main differences:

- First, climate projections are not about predicting the exact weather at any time in the future, but rather about projecting the statistics (average behaviour and variability) of the future weather. This reduces the relevance of short-term chaotic behaviour in the atmosphere.

- Second, because climate projections are about the statistics of weather many months, years or even centuries into the future, much slower influences on the weather or climate must be taken into account.

Thus the propagation of errors in initial conditions is not important, but rather the knowledge of slower internal variations in the climate system, and so-called 'boundary conditions'. Slower internal variations include exchanges of heat, salt and chemicals such as carbon dioxide with the deep ocean, and the growth and decay of ice sheets and glaciers. **Figure 11** shows some of the components that are included in the internal part of a climate model. Others, not shown, include interactive soil and vegetation, atmospheric chemistry, and cloud interactions with particles (aerosols).

External factors include changes in atmospheric and land surface properties, variations in the orbit of the Earth around the Sun, solar variability and volcanic eruptions (which put gases and particles into the atmosphere). Some of these external factors can be specified as inputs or boundary conditions to the climate models, rather than calculated. However, they can be calculated internally in an enlarged climate system, if they can be predicted and the equations can be added to the model. As computers become bigger, faster and cheaper, more and more that used to be external to the climate models can now be incorporated into the models and thus predicted rather than given as external boundary conditions.

How good are climate models?

Two or three decades ago most climate models considered the oceans to be external and used prescribed sea surface temperatures at the bottom of the atmosphere. Results were conditional on the assumed sea surface temperatures. Today, faster computers enable nearly all climate models to have an interactive ocean, and indeed deep water temperatures are calculated, as are ocean currents. Historically, the scientific literature is full of papers describing simulations of climate using models of varying complexity and detail, and it is important in reading these papers to understand just what is calculated and what is given as assumed input. It is also important not to rely on outdated assessments of the skill of climate models, which tends to occur in the critiques of climate modelling by some who question climate change. Citing out-of-date assessments of climate models ignores recent improvements in modelling and shows a lack of appreciation of how much work has gone into improving their accuracy.

A range of different types of climate models are available, and various names or abbreviations are used to indicate differences in their complexity. For example, there are very simple 'energy balance models' which calculate only the incoming and outgoing energy into the climate system to determine the Earth's global average surface temperature, or that in latitude bands. These ignore lots of internal processes and do not give outputs useful at particular locations on Earth, but they are quick and cheap to use and are often used to study a wide range of conditions.

Next there are 'atmospheric general circulation models' or AGCMs. These calculate what goes on in the atmosphere, including changes to cloud cover and properties, but have prescribed or given sea surface temperatures. Thus, they do not allow for changes in the ocean climate (currents, and temperature and salinity with location and depth).

ATMOSPHERE

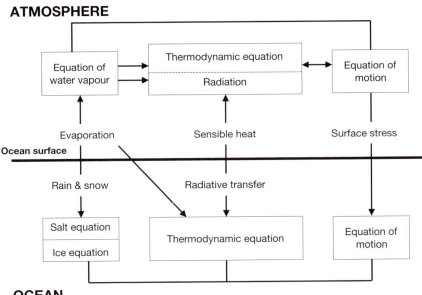

OCEAN

Figure 11: Some internal components of a climate model. Some of these components can be changed by external forces (such as variations in the Earth's orbit around the Sun, or in solar radiation), or changes in the composition and radiative properties of the atmosphere (such as the addition of more greenhouse gases or particles of dust). (After John Mitchell, UK Meteorological Office, 2003.)

Today nearly all climate models used for climate projections have fully interactive oceans. These are called 'coupled atmosphere-ocean general circulation models' or AOGCMs, and usually include calculations of sea-ice cover. Even so, there are still many external components of the climate system that are only gradually being internalised into climate models, even where these components act on, and are changed by the climate. These components include glaciers, continental ice sheets, and surface properties determined by vegetation.

Climate models have been tested and improved quite systematically over time. There are many ways of doing this. One is to closely compare simulated present climates with observations. Climate modellers often judge models by how well they do in reproducing observations, but until recently this has mainly been by testing outputs from models against observations for simple variables such as surface temperature and rainfall. However, this process can be circular in that climate models, with all their simplifications (for example in how they represent complex processes like cumulus convection, sea-ice distribution or air-sea exchange of heat and moisture) can be adjusted, or 'tuned', to give the right answers, sometimes by making compensating errors. Such errors might then lead to serious differences from reality in some other variable not included in the tests. Comparing simulated outputs for many more variables, some of which were not used to tune the models, now checks this.

Other tests used include how well the climate models simulate variations in climate over the daily cycle, for example daily maximum and minimum temperatures, or depth of the well-mixed surface layer of the atmosphere. Changes in average cloud cover and rainfall with time of day are other more sophisticated variables that are sometimes tested.

Related tests involve calculating in the models variables that can be compared with satellite observations, such as cloud cover and energy radiated back to space from the top of the atmosphere. Until recently many climate models have not done very well on some of these tests, but they are improving.

To test longer time-scale variations, tests are made of how well climate models simulate the annual cycle of the seasons. Different test locations from those the model builders may have looked at when building their models are often used. For example, how well does an Australian climate model perform over Europe, or a European model perform over Africa?

A popular test is to use a climate model with observed boundary layer conditions, for example sea-surface temperatures in an atmospheric global climate model, to simulate year-to-year variations such as a year with a strong monsoon over India versus a year with a weak monsoon. Similarly, tests are made of how well a climate model reproduces the natural variations in a complex weather pattern such as the El Niño-Southern Oscillation (ENSO), which is important in year-to-year variations in climate. ENSO is a variation in oceanic and atmospheric circulation, mainly across the tropical Pacific Ocean, but has effects in many other parts of the world. Getting ENSO right is an important test, and it is only recently that some AOGCMs have done well with this test.

At even longer time scales, tests can be made as to how well climate models can reproduce paleo-climatic variations. This is only possible where changes in external conditions can be well specified, such as changes in solar energy input, atmospheric composition, land-sea distribution and surface properties. It is also necessary to have lots of paleo-evidence for climate patterns at the time being simulated to see if the climate models reproduce it well. This is a tall order, but nevertheless paleo-modelling is useful as a test of climate models, and also helps us to understand and test theories of what cause climate fluctuations and what is possible.

In order to provide climate change projections relevant to many local and regional climate change impacts, climate models need to provide output at finer and finer spatial scales. That is, where global climate models a decade back only gave output data on climate changes at distances several hundred kilometres apart, for many purposes the need is for data at locations only a few tens of kilometres apart. The limitation was essentially computer capacity, since the number of calculations increases roughly by a factor of eight for every halving of the distance between data points.

There are three ways in which this finer spatial resolution can be achieved:

- running global climate models at finer and finer spatial scales,
- statistical downscaling,
- running local or regional climate models driven by output from global models.

Rapid improvements in computer speed and capacity have enabled global climate models to be run at finer and finer spatial resolutions. Some models now routinely produce output at spatial scales as fine as 100 or even 50 kilometres, although this still cannot be done for many different scenarios. There has also been a technical development using variable spatial resolution in global models, whereby it is possible to run a global model with coarse resolution over most of the globe, but fine resolution over an area of interest. This latter option is fine if you only want detailed information about one region, for example if you are in a national laboratory modelling for information relevant to one region, such as the UK or Japan. However, while it is important to get detailed information for your own region, many countries will also want to know what may happen in detail in other parts of the world, at least for broad policy reasons, and maybe even for telling what the impacts of climate change may be on trade partners and competitors.

The need for truly global simulations at fine spatial scales thus remains important. Japan has recognised this, and has built the Earth Simulator supercomputer, capable of modelling the climate at fine scales for the whole globe. It contains the equivalent of many hundreds of ordinary supercomputers (circa 2004), and currently is running a climate model with 100 levels and a horizontal resolution of 10 kilometres, compared to most AOGCMs that have a resolution of around 100 or more kilometres. So far they have only carried out short simulations.

The second way of getting finer spatial detail for particular locations is to use statistical relationships between the observed large-scale climate patterns and local climate to derive estimates of local changes from model-simulated large-scale changes. This is called statistical downscaling, and requires a lot of detailed climate observations for the region of interest. It is also important that the statistical relationships between the large-scale changes and local change will be valid under conditions of climate change as opposed to present observed climate variability. That is not the case with all large-scale variables and must be tested.

The third method for obtaining detailed local output is to use a local or regional fine-scale climate model driven by the output of a global coarse-resolution model. The easy way to do this is to use output from the global model at the boundaries of the regional model domain to determine the model values at the boundaries of the regional model, and force the regional model to adjust its values inside the boundaries to be consistent with this. This is termed 'one-way nesting'.

However, local changes within the region may in reality force changes at a larger scale, for example if the region includes a large lake from which the atmosphere may pick up additional moisture. To account for this possibility, ideally the output from the regional model should be fed back into the global model and thus modify the large-scale climate. This is termed 'two-way nesting'. Many climate-modelling groups have performed one-way nesting, but so far two-way nesting is less common, and has revealed sometimes-significant differences in results for the same region.

The performance of fine spatial resolution modelling has also been carefully tested by comparing different models over the same regions, and by trying to reproduce particular historical situations using regional models forced at their boundaries by observations. Results have been mixed, and in general it is conceded that regional detail is not as reliable as the large-scale output. This applies particularly to rainfall patterns, although regional detail is necessary especially for rainfall because it can vary greatly over small distances due to topography and land-sea boundaries.

Overall, model performance and verification is complex, but is being actively tested and improved. Climate models provide projections that are far more sophisticated and reliable than simple extrapolations from observed climate trends. Moreover, the IPCC and other bodies studying climate change have taken the uncertainties into account. These uncertainties are being progressively decreased to provide more reliable and policy-relevant information.

The IPCC 2001 report summarises its conclusions regarding the state of coupled atmosphere-ocean climate models as follows:

> *Coupled models have evolved and improved significantly since [1995]. In general, they provide credible simulations of climate, at least down to sub-continental scales and over temporal scales from seasonal to decadal. The varying sets of strengths and weaknesses that models display lead us to conclude that no single model can be considered 'best' and it is important to utilise results from a range of coupled models. We consider coupled models, as a class, to be suitable tools to provide useful projections of future climates.*

The state of climate projections

Projecting the future is an everyday procedure for providing insight into what may happen. It forms the basis of many decisions about what to do. In relation to climate it is made more difficult by the complexity of the climate system, the long time-scales and the possible human influences on climate through future human behaviour.

Projecting future climate is not just a matter of extrapolating from recent trends, but of using computer models that take many different processes into account. While climate models are based on weather prediction models, they involve longer time-scales and include slower processes. They are less dependent than weather forecast models on getting the initial conditions correct. The performance of modern climate models is tested in many ways and they are rapidly becoming more reliable.

Prediction of human behaviour, and thus of future greenhouse gas emissions, is probably less reliable than predicting climate on the basis of a particular scenario of human behaviour. Therefore any climate projections based on climate models is conditional on scenarios of human behaviour. The SRES scenarios for future greenhouse gas emissions, used by the IPCC in its 2001 report, cover a wide range of possibilities, which was not influenced by climate policy. What is more relevant for climate policy are projections for a range of policy-driven scenarios. These will be discussed later in this book.

4

Uncertainty is inevitable, but risk is certain

... it would be wrong to completely ignore possible developments simply because they are regarded as not very probable – or not sufficiently probable to justify an examination of their possible consequences. Probability itself should not be the criterion for deciding whether or not to prepare ourselves for an event, but only for how we prepare ourselves.

Swiss Reinsurance Company, *Opportunities and Risks of Climate Change*, 2002.

Where there are threats of serious or irreversible damage, lack of full scientific certainty shall not be used as a reason for postponing cost-effective measures to prevent environmental degradation.

The Precautionary Principle, as stated in the Rio Declaration at the Earth Summit, June 1992.

Despite uncertainties, decisions have to be made

Many years ago, when I supervised first year physics students at Melbourne University, we used to give them a steel ball and a micrometer to measure its diameter. We asked them to measure it ten times and see what values they got. Many of them were surprised to find that the answers were not all the same, for example, 53.1, 52.8, 53.2, 52.9, 53.1, 53.5, 53.0, 52.9, 53.2, and 53.3 mm. Why did they get such a range of answers to a simple measurement of a clear physical quantity? And what then was the actual diameter? Well there are several reasons for a range of answers, for example, no ball is exactly spherical, it changes its diameter as it expands or contracts due to changes in temperature, and the measurement depends on how hard the micrometer is tightened. The 'actual diameter' cannot be known exactly: the measurements range from 52.8 to 53.5, the average is 53.1, and the 'standard error' (root mean square deviation from the average) is about 0.14. The exact numbers will depend on who did the measurements, under what conditions they did them, and on the number of measurements made.

As this example illustrates, contrary to a widely held belief, no measurement of a continuous quantity is absolutely exact.

Moreover, nothing is absolutely certain in science. It is common in the physical sciences to say that something is 'true', 'certain' or 'well-established' if the evidence suggests that there is less than a 5 per cent chance (1 in 20) of it being wrong. If you want to be even more cautious, you might insist on less than a 1% chance (1 in 100), or even a 0.1% chance (1 in 1000). Such a low probability of being wrong applies to such common expectations as the Sun rising tomorrow morning, something that would only fail if something extreme like a cosmic collision were to happen. It also applies to many practical engineering matters, that is, matters of applied science, like the design of a bridge or dam to ensure that it will not collapse. Here the design standard is set to ensure that there is only a very small chance of failure, because failure would be catastrophic.

However, even in the case of engineering design, there is a choice of safety level or risk level, which may depend on expected frequency and duration of use, expense and urgency – for example lesser safety levels may be legitimately applied to a temporary bridge built in war time than for a permanent structure in peace time. Such choices are a matter of circumstance, purpose and values.

There are many circumstances where a less exacting standard of certainty is sufficient to find a proposition, prediction or theory useful. For example, we find weather forecasts useful even if the chances of their being wrong are ten per cent (1 in 10) or even 33% (1 in 3). This is because, in most cases, the consequences of being wrong are not disastrous, for example if we would only get wet if we did not take an umbrella. Given that we know that weather forecasts are not entirely accurate, we might hedge our bets and take an umbrella anyway.

Even where losses may be incurred if a forecast is wrong, we will gain on average by acting repeatedly on imperfect forecasts, if they have some skill, than by ignoring them. For instance, if forecasts are wrong one time in three, we may still gain on average by acting many times on them, because we will have acted correctly two times in every three. This might apply, for instance, to a farmer acting on seasonal rainfall forecasts as he or she decides how much to plant: good harvests two years in three may well make up for a crop failure one year in three.

How we react to uncertainty depends on what is hanging on the results. For example, forecasts of tropical cyclone landings on the coast are serious – if we are prudent we take precautions even if we are only near the possible path of a tropical cyclone, because we know that there is a margin for error in the predictions. In such cases, we take precautions *because* we know that, even if the exact prediction is that it will miss us, the exact prediction is uncertain. Even a small chance of a disaster makes it worthwhile to take precautions.

In a more extreme case, most of us prudently insure our house against loss by fire, even though we believe that it is very unlikely that our house will burn down. We know that the total loss of our house would be disastrous, and the premium we pay the insurance company is relatively small, so we insure against the low probability of a fire. Whether we insure depends on the relative size of the premium versus the size of the potential loss, as well as on the probability of a fire.

When it comes to so-called 'laws' about, or predictions of human behaviour (as opposed to the behaviour of the physical world), uncertainty is usually much greater. This applies in many of the social sciences, for example economics. Economic forecasts are made based on various theories (often just simple extrapolations) of human behaviour and various assumptions. These assumptions may not hold in the future as human behaviour may change or be influenced by factors not considered.

As the case of insurance demonstrates, uncertainty does not prevent decisions being made. Indeed, in any practical situation passive or active decisions are inevitably made all the time, despite uncertainty. We either decide to take out insurance, or we decide (perhaps unconsciously) not to do so. Investors and policy makers make decisions every day despite uncertainties – they assess probabilities and risks and then take decisions, because without these decisions nothing would be done.

Uncertainty in climate change projections

In any estimates of future climate change there are a number of sources of uncertainty. Some of these arise from the science itself, and some from uncertainty about future human behaviour – especially future emissions of greenhouse gases. As it happens, these two major sources of uncertainty each account for about half the total uncertainty. This is fortunate, since it means that, despite the total uncertainty, different assumptions about future human behaviour can be used to test the effect of such behaviour on climate. This can give us useful information about what sort of human behaviour is desirable to avoid the worst possible climate changes. In other words, it is useful for developing policy.

In the case of future climate impacts, there are a number of different assumptions, and a number of models of different parts of the climate system. These range from models of human society leading to future greenhouse gas emissions (socio-economic models), through models of how much of the emitted greenhouse gases stay in the atmosphere (carbon cycle models), to their effects on global climate (climate models), local or regional climatic changes (downscaling models), and eventually to the effects of climate change on biological and human systems (sectoral impact models). Uncertainties at each stage in this chain of reasoning lead to what some authors have called a 'cascade of uncertainty', as shown in **Figure 12**.

There is a long list of uncertainties relating to possible future climate change and its impacts. To start with the causes of climate change, we need to know future greenhouse gas emissions, and any other effects such as emissions leading to more particles in the atmosphere, or natural climatic variability and change. Human emissions will depend on world population growth, the rate of growth in energy use per person, the mix of energy sources (for example coal and oil versus sun and wind) and energy efficiency (that is, emissions per unit energy produced, and economic production per unit energy used), rates of deforestation or reforestation, and industrial emissions such as for fertiliser manufacture. Most of these factors are a product of human behaviour, which may change with attitudes to quality of life and wealth. Many depend on rates of technological change, including research and development, and rates of penetration or adoption of new technologies. Nearly all of these factors can be influenced by policy, which may depend on the understanding policy makers have of the consequences of alternative policies.

Other uncertainties relating to the causes of climate change include natural climate fluctuations due to internal processes in the climate system (for example changes in vegetation or deep ocean circulation), or natural external forces operating on the climate system (including periodic variations in the Earth's orbit around the Sun, variations in solar energy output, and volcanic eruptions). There are possible further effects on climate due to human activities such as land clearing, irrigation, and atmospheric pollution (for example, carbon black from fires or increased dust from desertification).

There are also uncertainties about how much of the emissions into the atmosphere stay there. This requires modelling of the chemical processes in the atmosphere for methane and nitrous oxide, and modelling of removal processes for particulates such as washout or gravitational settling over the oceans and land surfaces. Removal processes for the main greenhouse gas, carbon dioxide, largely depend on biological interactions. Growth rates of vegetation and plankton, the effects of forest fires, and interactions between climate itself and the rates of these processes are all factors.

Given the emissions and how much stays in the atmosphere, climate models are needed to calculate what effect the changed concentrations of greenhouse gases will have on the climate. While these models are based on the well-established laws of motion, atmospheric radiation, and thermodynamics (transfer of heat), there are many uncertainties. Some of the main areas of concern are

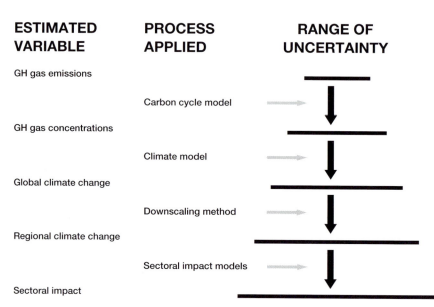

ESTIMATED VARIABLE   **PROCESS APPLIED**   **RANGE OF UNCERTAINTY**

GH gas emissions

Carbon cycle model

GH gas concentrations

Climate model

Global climate change

Downscaling method

Regional climate change

Sectoral impact models

Sectoral impact

Figure 12: The 'cascade of uncertainty'. Schematic representation of the growth of the range of uncertainties in the chain of reasoning associated with climate change and its potential impacts. New uncertainties at each step expand the total range of uncertainty at the previous step. However, the individual ranges are not additive since the extremes will become progressively less likely as different ranges of uncertainty are combined. (After Henderson-Sellers, 1993; Jones, 2000.)

the behaviour of clouds that absorb and reflect both heat and light radiation, interactions at the land and ocean surfaces, and the effect of small spatial scale and very rapid processes in the atmosphere that are not well modelled. These include rainfall variations in regions of varying topography (mountains and coastlines), and extreme events such as heavy rain, tropical cyclones, thunderstorms, peak winds and hail. Confidence in the simulation of these sorts of events in global climate models is low. It is higher, however, in models that calculate what is happening on finer spatial scales, especially in finer scale regional models, which can be driven by the global models at their boundaries.

Then there are the uncertainties in models that calculate the impacts of climate change, for example on crop production, river flow, flooding, coastal storm surges, and damages. How well do crop models treat the effects of different soils, of increasing atmospheric concentrations of carbon dioxide on plant growth, and of pests and diseases? Costing is a vexed question (discussed in Chapters 6, 7 and 8), that includes assessment of the costs and benefits of various adaptations to climate change and of measures to reduce emissions

The first rule in assessing uncertainty, and particularly arguments based on results of assessments, is that we should understand what uncertainties have been taken into account and what assumptions have been made. This applies especially in areas where ranges of uncertainty are often not given, such as estimates of costs of climate change impacts or of mitigation or adaptation measures. Too often results of such assessments seem to be biased, intentionally or not, towards the outcomes wanted by special interests that commission or fund the studies. This often takes the form of choices as to what is included, what scenarios are used, what values are assumed, and what alternatives are considered.

The important thing with all these uncertainties is that we should be aware of them and take them into account, both in our own estimates, and in assessing those of others. We should examine assessments to see how clearly (or 'transparently') they state assumptions and uncertainties. Further, we should not regard results as of no use at all if they have large uncertainties attached to them – after all, admitted uncertainty implies a degree of understanding and honesty, and such results still limit the possibilities. Moreover, the most likely results are probably somewhere near the middle of the range of uncertainty, unless the study is biased by its assumptions. Some knowledge is better than none, provided we use it wisely in full awareness of its limitations. Obviously, where uncertainties are large we should try to reduce them, but in the mean time we need to make the best of what we have to guide both adaptation and mitigation policy.

When it comes to estimating how uncertain projections of future climate change and climate change impacts may be, we need to distinguish between two types of uncertainty. One is the uncertainty about something that can be measured repeatedly. This can in principle be reduced by taking more measurements: the best answer is likely to be the average derived from the most measurements and is in most cases the most frequent answer. Statisticians call this a 'frequentist' problem. The example at the start of this chapter, of measuring the diameter of a steel ball illustrates this.

The other sort of uncertainty arises when there cannot be repeated measurements. This is usually because we are dealing with some prediction of the future based on a theory or model, often with assumptions about future behaviour or influences. Future climate cannot be measured now, and there will only be one future climate. Here uncertainty can be estimated by calculating the effects of different assumptions in the input data, the theory and the models. In this case we need to use additional knowledge about the assumptions and models, such as how uncertain they are, and then explore the range of results arising from the range of plausible assumptions or models. Estimation of uncertainty of future climate or its impacts requires us to look at the results of all the possible combinations of assumptions, which may number in the thousands. This sort of uncertainty estimate requires complex computations. It is known as 'Bayesian statistics' after the eighteenth century Reverend Thomas Bayes, who first suggested the method, but did not have a computer to carry out the calculations.

People working on climate impacts, including the scientists and policy advisors associated with the Intergovernmental Panel on Climate Change (IPCC), have only recently started to come to grips with this complex problem, and there was a new emphasis on quantifying uncertainty in the IPCC's *Third Assessment Report* in 2001. Thus, many of the estimates of uncertainty given in this book are preliminary, and may not cover the full range of uncertainty in some cases. In particular, there may be unexpected developments and 'surprises', which may well lead to larger, as well as smaller, climate changes and impacts.

From polarisation to probability and risk

People respond in different ways to uncertainty. Sometimes they get confused and see it as a reason for concluding that they know nothing useful on the subject, and therefore see no reason to act. This is especially the case if action would have obvious costs, and is the position taken by many who challenge the reality of human-induced climate change. These people in denial tend to focus on the uncertainties rather than on what is known. Some (but not all) may have a vested interest (financial or ideological) in doing nothing, and use the uncertainty as an excuse for delaying meaningful action.

In other situations, however, people may conclude that although there is uncertainty, it is worth taking a gamble and doing something even if the odds are only marginally favourable. We all do this to a certain extent. Farmers do this as part of their everyday coping with the uncertainties of the weather. Some people even gamble when the odds are stacked against them, as in gambling casinos or lotteries. In other cases, people may decide that even a small chance of a damaging outcome makes it worthwhile to take some form of insurance, even at some expense.

How we react to uncertainty depends in large part on how well we understand the odds, and on what is at stake. Consider a weather forecast of a 30% chance of rain in a rather large district (typically 100 km by 100 km). What that usually means is a 30% chance that it will rain somewhere in the district (but not necessarily at our particular location) some time in the next 24 hours. If all that is at issue is whether we should walk the dog we may accept the risk and go anyway. But if we were thinking of pouring a large slab of concrete that might be ruined by heavy rain and cost us thousands of dollars, we may well hesitate to do it. We would want to know what sort of rain was expected, and certainly look into providing covers to go over the slab.

So we need to understand what the uncertainty means for our particular situation, and to weigh the possible consequences of either taking the risk or avoiding it. It is not only the probability that matters, but also the consequences.

Consider a simple example of a climate change prediction, such as that which arose from a study of future climate change impacts on the Macquarie River in New South Wales, Australia. Here the projected rainfall changes in all four seasons spanned a range from increase to decrease, with slightly more chance of an increase in summer and a stronger chance of a decrease in winter. To the uninformed or the sceptic this might well signal that the change could be zero, so there is nothing to worry about. Two things argue against this superficial conclusion, first the real probability of negative changes in rainfall, and second the combined effects of rainfall changes and warming on water supply and demand. In this case the projected rainfall change by 2070 in winter (which is the wettest season, with most runoff into the rivers) ranged from a decrease of 25% to an increase of 8%. While this still spans zero, it means that the most likely change is a decrease of around 8%, with about a 50% chance that the decrease will be more than 8% (the middle of the range of uncertainty). Moreover, the warming was projected to be between 1.0 and 6.0°C by 2070, which would increase evaporative losses of water, thereby reducing runoff, and increasing water consumption by crops and towns in the valley. Using runoff models, the projected change in runoff into the main water storage dam was in fact between no change (zero) and a decrease of 35% by 2070, which means a 50% chance of water supply decreasing by more than 17%. It is this figure that needs to be considered in calculating what is at stake in the Macquarie River basin for irrigation farmers, town water supply, and the economy of the region. So an apparently very uncertain projection of rainfall changes translates, when all things are considered, into a result that has important implications for planning and policy.

To put this in more general terms, what matters is not the probability of a particular numerical outcome coming to pass, which is usually very uncertain, but the cumulative probability of getting a range of outcomes that is of practical importance. It is not a matter of the accuracy of a particular prediction, but of the probability of a range of outcomes with serious consequences. This is usually expressed as a risk assessment, where risk is understood as the probability of an outcome multiplied by its consequences. Thus a likely outcome having large consequences is a large risk, while a small probability of a low-consequence outcome is a small risk. A high probability of a small but non-negligible effect may also be worth worrying about, as would be a low, but not negligible, probability of a very serious effect.

In the case of climate change, natural and human systems have been forced by past natural climate variability to evolve or adapt so that most of the time they operate within a 'comfortable' range in which they operate well. Sometimes systems exist outside that range in climatic conditions in which they survive, but not well. This is sometimes called the 'coping' range. Occasionally natural and human systems experience extreme climatic events that are damaging, sometimes fatally. These events are called 'natural disasters' and include droughts, floods, storm surges and wildfires. Climate change moves the average climate so that comfortable conditions become less common, and extreme events, which can be defined as those falling outside the previous coping range, become more common or of greater severity. What is of concern in climate change is therefore the risk associated with changes that take us more frequently into more extreme conditions that are damaging or disastrous. What we are concerned about is the risk of changes that take us above the threshold of these extremes.

Figure 13 illustrates how normal climate variability, with no climate change, covers a range of values that may be OK for a given activity, but sometimes goes outside that range to cause loss or other problems. Even if we cannot say when exactly the threshold will be exceeded, we can estimate, from a long record of observations of the variable, how frequently on average the threshold is exceeded. This enables us to calculate the risk to our enterprise.

The case of climate change is shown in **Figure 14**. Here an unchanging climate is shown at the left, and a changing climate at the right. Again, the coping range and thresholds for vulnerability are shown by the horizontal lines. In the upper graph we see how climate change can cause the variable (such as rainfall) to rapidly increase the frequency with which it exceeds the threshold for vulnerability, and thus the risk to the enterprise. The lower graph includes an extension

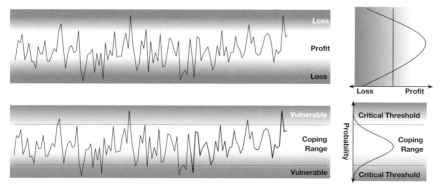

Figure 13: The concept of exceeding a threshold. This schematic illustrates at lower left a coping range under an unchanging but variable climate for a variable such as rainfall (with time increasing towards the right), and an output such as profit from a crop (upper right). Vulnerability is assumed not to change over time. The upper time series and chart shows a relationship between climate and profit and loss. The lower time series and chart shows the same time series divided into a coping range using critical thresholds to separate the coping range from a state of vulnerability. The upper critical threshold might represent the onset of dangerous flooding, while the lower threshold might represent the onset of drought. Darker shading represents more severe consequences. (Figure courtesy of R.N. Jones, CSIRO.)

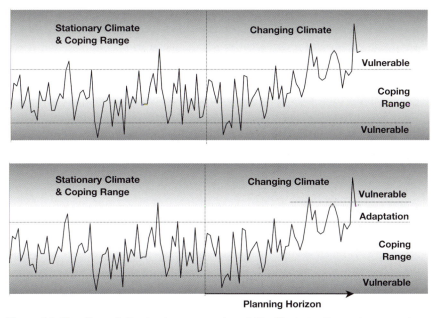

Figure 14: The effect of climate change on vulnerability. Illustrates the coping range for a variable such as rainfall, showing how climate change can rapidly lead to exceeding the threshold for vulnerability more frequently (upper curve), and how adaptation to change can reduce that vulnerability (lower curve). (Figure courtesy of R N Jones, CSIRO.)

of the coping range due to improving our ability to cope (called 'adaptation'), which reduces the vulnerability to climate change and thus the risk.

Fortunately, the probability of exceeding a particular impact threshold of, say, temperature or rainfall at some time in the future can be determined more confidently than the probability that the temperature or rainfall will have a particular value at that time.

To understand why this is so, we need to know what a *probability distribution* is, and what it looks like. This is the way in which the probability of a particular variable having a particular value varies with the value of the variable. For instance, the temperature at some place x at some time y could be anywhere between 5.0°C and 10.0°C, with a very small chance (say less than one in 20) of it being either less than 5.0°C or greater than 10.0°C, but a large chance of it being between those two values, and probably greatest of being about 7.5°C. The probability is usually assumed to vary according to a 'normal distribution', in which case the distribution graph is bell-shaped and we can assign probabilities of the variable lying in any given range, with the most likely being the middle value (see lower right of **Figure 13**). But not all variables follow a normal distribution (particularly ones like daily rainfall that can have positive values or be zero, but never a negative value). An assumption that a variable is normally distributed is convenient because it allows us to apply simple statistics to its behaviour, but it is not always appropriate.

Assigning a *normal distribution* to a variable is an assumption, and if we really have no idea what the probability distribution looks like, apart from its limiting values, a more conservative (that is, cautious) assumption is to assume that any value within the range has an equal probability. Arguably that is what the IPCC report in 2001 did by failing to discuss different probabilities for different scenarios of future carbon dioxide emissions, and of resulting global warming estimates. An assumption of equal probability gives a much greater probability to the extremes of the range than in a normal distribution.

In the above example, if we assume the variable is normally distributed, and the threshold is 7.5°C, then we find the probability of exceeding this threshold is 50%. If we make the very different assumption of a flat or equal probability distribution over the range, then, although the probability of the temperature being exactly 7.5°C is much smaller, the probability of the temperature exceeding this value is still 50%. This is because the probability of exceeding a threshold integrates (or adds up) all the values below the threshold.

Such a result is even more robust when we consider the result of combining two or more ranges of uncertainty. This is because the probability of exceeding a particular threshold is the result of a number of different individual *probability distributions* for a number of different variables all of which contribute to the uncertainty. While any one of these probability distributions may be difficult to quantify, the probability distribution of the combination is often less uncertain, and in general more likely to be peaked, and for combinations of more variables becomes in general closer to being normally distributed. This is because when any two probability distributions are combined, the probability of combining extreme values of the two variables to produce a new extreme of the combination is less than the probability of multiple combinations of the two variables leading to the same intermediate value of the product.

What this means in practice is that the probability distribution of any variable influenced by multiple uncertainties is likely to be bell shaped, with the most likely value near the middle of the combined uncertainty range, and the cumulative probability of exceeding the mid-range value is likely to be around 50%. While this is a good rule of thumb, there are exceptions, especially where the combined variable (for example, runoff in a river) cannot be negative. In the latter case, the probability distribution is likely to be skewed, with more small values and a few large values.

Estimating risk

The IPCC, in its report in 2001, was reluctant to attach probabilities to particular magnitudes of warmings within the large range of 1.4 to 5.8°C that it estimated for the year 2100. This was due to the great difficulty of assigning probabilities to the relevant population, socio-economic and technological factors that would determine greenhouse gas emissions decades ahead. This difficulty was accentuated by the likely influence of future policies on these factors that determine emissions. Moreover, multiple scenarios of the future are useful to decision-makers, even without likelihoods, if they help decision-makers choose between policies that may lead to desirable or undesirable outcomes.

Nevertheless, the lack of probability estimates presents problems in developing policy for reducing greenhouse gas emissions and in planning for adaptation to climate changes. Decision-makers need to base decisions on some risk assessment both in mitigation and adaptation policies, since such policies involve costs.

The United Nations Framework Convention on Climate Change (UNFCCC) states that the central objective must be to avoid concentrations of greenhouse gases that may lead to 'dangerous interference with the climate system'. Therefore, developing appropriate mitigation policy requires an understanding not only of the impacts of any given concentration of greenhouse gases in the atmosphere (which has a range of uncertainty), but also of the *likelihood* of reaching a critical level of greenhouse gas concentrations (a dangerous threshold) at some time in the future. The urgency and severity of any mitigation measures needed to avoid reaching a critical threshold depends on the *risk* (probability multiplied by consequence) of what may happen if such measures are not taken.

Similarly, appropriate adaptation policy is related to the rate and magnitude of climate change that affects design parameters or critical thresholds for particular infrastructure (buildings, dams, drains, sea walls, etc.) and activities (farming, water supply etc.). For example, engineers designing a dam required to last 100 years or more, need to know the likely maximum flood flows for which a spillway will need to cope to avoid possible collapse of the dam. Engineers and planners require similar estimates for the height of bridges, size of drains, or setbacks from rivers or coastlines subject to possible flooding or coastal storms. It is relatively easy to establish the sensitivity of systems to climate change, and to suggest measures for increasing adaptability and resilience, such as higher bridges, larger spillways and stronger buildings. But the extent and urgency of the measures that should be taken depends on the probability of a given change and its consequences. Such measures incur costs, so a risk assessment is needed.

Risk cannot be managed or treated efficiently unless it is properly assessed. This requires an estimate of both the probability of an event occurring and an assessment of its consequences. The risk of exceeding some critical level of consequences (defined by collective global value judgements in the case of the UNFCCC) is central to deciding the urgency and extent of reduction in greenhouse gas emissions (that is, mitigation) that is needed.

Some scientists have argued that it is too difficult to assign probabilities to future climate change. However, Steve Schneider of Stanford University has argued that, in the absence of better expert advice, decision-makers will make their own formal or informal estimates of probability, and that this is worse than using informed estimates provided by relevant experts. That such probability estimates for global warming are possible is illustrated by a number of estimates in the scientific literature, although they get varying answers. Most find single-peaked probability distributions (that is, a single most probable outcome), but a study by Gritsevskyi and Nakicenovik of the International Institute of Applied Systems Analysis found a double-peaked distribution (that is, two very different but more or less equally likely outcomes). They attributed this to a split in technological development pathways towards either a low-carbon emissions technology or a high-carbon emissions technology, rather than some mixture of the two. This suggests that an early and deliberate choice of emissions technology pathways may be crucial to the future.

Although probability estimates are needed, and in principle possible, methods for deriving probabilities require further development and cannot be said to be well-established at present. In fact, a risk management approach requires not an assessment of the probability of a particular emission amount or global warming at some future time, but rather, as Roger Jones of CSIRO (Australia) has pointed out, an estimate of the likelihood of exceeding an identified critical impact threshold. This integrates the probabilities from the greatest or upper limit warming down to some critical level, and is much less dependent on the underlying assumptions.

However, the relatively low but not negligible probability of large or catastrophic changes, sometimes called 'surprises', must also be considered, since these may contribute appreciably to the overall risk. Indeed, even if such catastrophic changes occur many decades or even centuries into the future, they may dominate any risk assessment because of their very high costs (see discussion in Chapter 6). The importance of these potentially high-risk events means that high priority must be placed on better understanding them, especially their likelihood, potential impacts, and any precursors that may enable them to be detected in advance and avoided. Those who argue that the risk from climate change is small often ignore these uncertainties on the high-impact end of the range of possibilities.

It is interesting to note that a joint US–European project called 'Rapid' is now focussing on one possibly catastrophic possibility, a slow-down of certain North Atlantic currents including the Gulf Stream. Early detection of any change is seen as a high priority.

If probabilities are not attached to possible climate change impacts, the present wide range of IPCC projected warmings suggests that engineers and planners, as they adapt design standards and zoning to climate change, will need, for the time being, to foster resilience and adaptive capacity, hedge their bets, and delay their investment decisions, or gamble on whether humanity will go down high or low emissions development pathways. Probabilities will allow proper risk assessments and the costs and benefits of specific adaptation policies to be calculated. This is a high priority for further research to assist in policy development.

Uncertainty and the role of sceptics

Genuine questioning and scepticism in science is good: it is one of the ways that science progresses, leading to the critical examination of assumptions and conclusions, and eventually the substitution of newer and more reliable theories for older ones that are less robust. This is the scientific method of hypothesis testing and development of new paradigms. However, challengers need to apply their critical faculties to both sides of an argument, and to admit uncertainties that may work for or against any particular proposition.

It is a safe generalisation that in a world of many uncertainties, one test of whether a scientist, or scientific challenger, is open to all the evidence and therefore unprejudiced is whether they say 'on the one hand this, and on the other hand that'. While such admissions of uncertainty are often used to put down scientists, genuine scientists seldom make statements without some qualification or caveat because there are usually at least two sides to any complex argument. People who admit to only one side are usually either biased or taking a 'devil's advocate' role.

Some genuine sceptics (often academic scientists) take the 'devil's advocate' position to stimulate debate and test propositions. This is bolstered by one traditional academic view of science as a process leading to a body of tested propositions or theories that can be regarded as truths (at least until subsequently disproved). This view, in statistical terms, traditionally requires that a proposition be established at the 95 or 99% probability level (that is, 95 or 99 chances out of 100 that it is true, respectively) before it can be regarded as established. On this basis one or two pieces of contrary evidence is usually enough to discredit a proposition. Such a view protects the limited body of 'truth' from any falsehood, but may end up denying as unproven many propositions that might be true. For example, if a proposition has been shown to have an 80% chance of being true, this view would reject it as unproven, when in fact it may well be true and could have serious consequences.

This academic view of science takes little account of the relative consequences of whether a proposition is true or false, and fails to acknowledge that decisions on practical matters may require us to act despite uncertainty. If this view were adopted in daily life we would seldom insure against accidents because they are not certain to happen to us. It ignores the concept of risk, that is, that in making practical decisions we weigh the probability of an event against its consequences. Policy-relevant or applied scientific advice must take account of risk even when it is not a 95% certainty.

Another problem with this view that 'it must be proven beyond reasonable doubt' is that in practical matters outside the laboratory it is often difficult to find counter-evidence of a proposition that is any more certain than each individual line of evidence for the proposition. We cannot then automatically use a single apparently inconsistent 'observation' or published paper to 'disprove' a proposition: we need to test the contrary line of evidence at least as rigorously as the supporting evidence, and decide on a balance of evidence, considering all the uncertainties. For example, if we have ten sets of observations pointing to global warming (land temperatures, ocean temperatures, sea ice, glaciers, snow cover, plant flowering dates, bird distributions, dates of river ice break-up, bore hole temperatures, melting permafrost), and one which does not (some satellite data), do we simply conclude that the ten sets are wrong, or do we look critically at the reliability of all the evidence and decide which is more likely?

The devil's advocate position is legitimate in a purely scientific debate, where there is plenty of time for contending arguments to be put and an eventual decision reached by the scientific community as a whole. However, where critical policy issues or urgent decisions are at stake, responsible scientists will give balanced advice, admitting any uncertainties on either side of the debate.

In the current debate about the reality, seriousness and urgency of climate change, governments, through the IPCC, requested a pro tem consensus position, based on the balance of evidence. The conclusions from the IPCC have always been subject to uncertainty, always subject to revision, and as the science has progressed the conclusions have been expressed more and more explicitly in terms of estimated ranges and probabilities.

A number of people have emerged who deny there is significant human-induced global warming and treat science like a debate in which they apparently see their job as to selectively use any possible argument against a proposition to which they are opposed, instead of looking at the balance of evidence. In adversarial politics, where 'point-scoring' is common, and often accepted as legitimate, such selective use of evidence is often condoned, even if its source is dubious and its veracity in doubt. However, in a debate affecting world affairs, economies and human welfare, debate should be responsibly directed at finding the balance of evidence, the testing of all statements, and the free admittance of all doubts and uncertainties, whether they favour a particular proposition or not. In this context, one-sided challengers should more accurately be labelled 'contrarians' rather than sceptics, since they are sceptical of one position but do not also question the contrary.

Examining the projection of global warming by 2100 in the range of 1.4 to 5.8°C, made by the IPCC in its *Third Assessment Report*, a genuine sceptic may well say that the range of uncertainty has been underestimated. But what some contrarians argue is that the warming may be (or is definitely) less than 1.4°C because of some selected uncertainty. How often do you hear these same contrarians argue that due to uncertainty it might equally well be greater than 5.8°C?

It is invidious to ascribe motives to particular individuals, and in most cases I will not do that here. However, we can think of a number of possible underlying positions or interests, related to the enhanced greenhouse effect and its impacts, which may motivate or explain the positions held and arguments used by some contrarians.

One such prejudice comes from people, often scientists in disciplines other than climatology, who are not convinced of the value of predictive modelling in the physical and mathematical sciences. Sometimes such people think of a 'model' as merely a theoretical framework to explain a set of observations, rather than a set of well-tested mathematical non-linear equations that can be used to project behaviour of physical and chemical systems forward in time. Such people may be deeply suspicious of any claim to use a 'model' to predict future behaviour, even of a purely physical phenomenon, however simple or complex. The fact is, of course, that such predictive models do exist and are used routinely for many practical purposes such as daily weather forecasting, predicting the tides, and predicting the motions of the planets. Climate projections are just more complex, and admittedly more uncertain, than some of these examples. Climatologists are well aware and open about the uncertainties. If climatologists are doing their job well, they build their models carefully, test the model's components and overall performance, and carefully estimate their reliability and possible errors. This is part of a climatologist's job description.

Another question raised by some contrarians comes from those familiar with the geological and other paleo-evidence of past natural changes in climate, which clearly were large, and not the result of human influence. These contrarians say that if such changes happened naturally in the past, why should any changes occurring now be due to human influence? Or else they argue that, since life survived such changes in the past, it will survive similar changes in the future, so why worry about it? However, while natural climate change has happened before and can happen again, this does not rule out the simultaneous occurrence of human-induced climate change. Moreover, human-induced climate change may be more immediate and rapid than past changes, and it would happen at a time when there are an unprecedented six billion human beings alive on Earth. Considering the consequences to such a human population if it had existed during the last glacial cycle should dispel any equanimity about the consequences of imminent rapid climate change.

Another class of contrarian is those who are driven by economic and political judgements. A case in point is the best-selling book *The Skeptical Environmentalist* by the Danish statistician Bjørn Lomberg, whose reasoning is quite explicit. Lomberg takes the position that many environmental issues have been exaggerated and proceeds selectively to produce statistics pointing to environmental improvements in recent decades (many the result of agitation by the environmental movement). Considering the enhanced greenhouse effect, Lomberg, while tending to downplay the risks from climate change, concedes that it is a reality. His argument is not that human-induced climate change is not happening, but rather that it is manageable, and that reducing greenhouse gas emissions would be prohibitively expensive. This is a value-judgement based on discounting the more severe possible impacts, technological optimism regarding our adaptive capacity, and technological pessimism regarding our ability to reduce greenhouse gas emissions at low cost. He argues that other issues such as world hunger and water supplies are more important than climate change, but fails to recognise how climate change impacts on these issues. These matters are discussed in Chapters 6 (impacts), 7 (adaptation), 8 (mitigation) and 9 (climate change in context).

Contrarians sometimes characterise 'environmentalism' as a new religion or ideology, or as some new form of totalitarianism. Variously, such contrarians may hold beliefs about 'environmentalists' whom they see as wishing to halt 'progress' or 'development' for ideological reasons. They tend to ascribe ulterior motives to proponents with a genuine concern about human-induced climate change, and do not accept the need to consider the supporting evidence on its merits. It is true that some environmental alarmists do highlight as fact extreme disaster scenarios that are unlikely (and thus suffer from some of the same selective characteristics as 'contrarians'). However, this does not excuse the selective denial by contrarians of more likely possibilities.

Some contrarians are deeply suspicious of the motives and integrity of climate scientists. Allied with this is often a deep suspicion of international climate science as too much influenced by funding and government (despite there being no concensus amongst governments on many matters). They especially suspect the IPCC as deeply biased and flawed and accuse it of censoring or doctoring its reports. This is quite contrary to the rigorous open reviews and other procedures adopted by the IPCC to safeguard against bias, and the fact that its reports have to be approved by a whole range of governments with many different views and interests.

Beyond all these possible motivations for prejudice are those who have a real or perceived economic interest in denying that human-induced climate change is a reality. Some of these genuinely believe the enhanced greenhouse effect is not so, while others fail to see any urgency and seek to delay action for their own (and possible others') economic benefit.

Occasionally individual contrarians are accused of arguing the way they do purely for their own economic benefit, in order to receive payments from fossil fuel industries or other interests and lobbies. In many individual cases I know, it seems to me that such contrarians do not seek out payments; rather, such economic lobbies seek out contrarians who may fit into any of the categories described above, and pay to promote their contrarian views through grants, paid tours, publications, testimonies and so forth. These sponsored contrarians may in a sense be hired guns, but they were often contrarians, or even genuine sceptics, first, and are usually genuine in their beliefs. This makes them more convincing through their sincerity, but no more correct.

The economic self interest argument is often used against those scientists who believe there is a real problem of human-induced climate change, namely that scientists say these things because it gets them grants or pays their salaries. This is the charge of lack of integrity and ascribing of ulterior motives to do bad science that most offends the contrarians when applied to them. In the case of the climatologists engaged in the science it is an ironic argument for scientists in countries such as the United States and Australia, where governments have not welcomed explicit policy-related conclusions and recommendations that question government inaction.

The public perception of the debate over climate change is shaped by the media's adherence to a doctrine of 'balanced reporting'. This tends to give equal space to the considered judgements of the scientific community, expressed in peer-reviewed publications such as the IPCC reports, and the often completely un-refereed opinions or advocacy of a contrarian minority. Although this is changing in some cases, there has been a media tendency for giving equal space to unequal scientific arguments, which often misrepresents the balance of evidence and plays into the hands of vested interests opposed to any real action to limit climate change.

Peer review is the process in which scientists normally submit their research findings to a journal, which sends the draft paper out to be assessed for competence, significance and originality by independent experts in the relevant field. These experts do not necessarily agree with the conclusions, but if they agree that the conclusions are worthy of consideration, then the paper is published. The peer review system means that statements based on such papers tend to be more reliable than other kinds of statements or claims. Claims made by politicians, newspaper columnists, special interest think tanks and campaign groups are not normally subject to such quality review beforehand.

Peer review is not perfect and does not guarantee correctness. It is just the first stage: a hypothesis or argument that survives this first test is still subject to further testing by other scientists. However, peer-reviewed papers and reports can be considered to be more than an opinion, and should not be lightly dismissed in favour of untested opinions. An awareness of the peer-review system and the sources of information can help the media, the public and decision-makers to distinguish between arguments derived from well-based scientific judgements and those arising from un-checked personal opinions.

Application of the 'precautionary principle'

Uncertainty in regard to the rate and magnitude of climate change, and in relation to its effects, operates in both directions: it can mean that effects may be less than the current best estimates, or more. This raises the problem, common to most human endeavours, of how to make decisions in the face of uncertainty. The problem is even more acute, in the case of climate change, because decisions made now may determine consequences many decades into the future.

Clearly there are a number of strategies, which are used consciously or unconsciously in everyday life. Essentially these amount to weighing the potential consequences in terms of the probabilities and what is at stake (that is, in formal terms, we do a risk assessment). If the consequences of a particular course of action may be disastrous, we tend to avoid that eventuality by cautious action, taking out some form of insurance, or working to prevent the worst potential consequences from occurring. And if we believe that we can reduce the uncertainty by seeking better information we tend to delay the decisions or take a bet each way until we become better informed. This is called hedging our bets. We may make a tentative or pro tem decision, to avoid the worst happening, and then review the decision in the light of developments. This is called adaptive decision making. The whole process is one of risk management.

The *Precautionary Principle*, as included in the Rio Declaration at the Earth Summit in June 1992, and assented to by representatives of most of the nations of the world, states

> *Where there are threats of serious or irreversible damage, lack of full scientific certainty shall not be used as a reason for postponing cost-effective measures to prevent environmental degradation.*

This principle has been incorporated into many environmental agreements and regulatory regimes, including Article 3 of the UNFCCC, where it is expressed as follows

The parties should take precautionary measures to anticipate, prevent or minimize the causes of climate change and mitigate against its adverse affects. Where there are threats of serious or irreversible damage, lack of full certainty should not be used as a reason for postponing such measures, taking into account that policies and measures to deal with climate change should be cost-effective so as to ensure global benefits at the lowest possible cost.

This is the type of reasoning that, in a broader context, has long governed engineering design, safety regulations, the insurance industry, and indeed foreign policy and military planning. It is normal to consider worst case scenarios and to consider what action is appropriate either to avoid such scenarios coming to fruition, or to deal with them if they do occur

Uncertainty should be seen, not as a reason for inaction on climate change, but as a reason for proceeding cautiously, with a readiness to adapt policies to changing insights and circumstances, as we continue to conduct what the Toronto Conference on climate change in 1988 called an uncontrolled global experiment.

This leads to two key questions: what counts as serious environmental damage that should be avoided, and what measures are justified as reasonable and cost-effective responses? The answers to these questions are really what successive IPCC reports, and the UNFCCC are all about: they are complex and multi-faceted, combining scientific information and human values. Differing human values and different self-interests will inevitably lead to controversy, debate, and the exercise of political power in deciding what action is actually taken by governments, businesses and ordinary people.

In what follows, this book will explore the above questions, with a view to suggesting what a creative and adaptive policy response might entail, and how we might help it along.

5

What climate changes are likely?

In terms of key environmental parameters, the Earth system has recently moved well outside the range of natural variability exhibited over at least the last half million years. The nature of changes now occurring simultaneously in the Earth System, their magnitude and rates of change are unprecedented and unsustainable.

Paul Crutzen (Nobel Laureate) and Will Steffen (International Geosphere-Biosphere Programme, Executive Director), 2003.

The complexity of the climate system makes it difficult to predict some aspects of human-induced climate change: exactly how fast it will occur, exactly how much it will change, and exactly where those changes will take place. In contrast, scientists are confident of other predictions. Mid-continent warming will be greater than over the oceans, and there will be greater warming at higher latitudes. Some polar and glacial ice will melt, and the oceans will warm; both effects will contribute to higher sea levels. The hydrologic cycle will change and intensify, leading to changes in water supply as well as flood and drought patterns.

American Geophysical Union, Position Statement, December 2003.

Human-induced climate change is only an issue if it is large enough and rapid enough to create real problems for natural ecosystems and for human societies. In this and the following chapter we will look at the magnitude and rate of climate change, including sea-level rise and changes in extreme events, that are likely to result from human-induced emissions of greenhouse gases, and at what the effects might be on nature and society.

Given the acknowledged uncertainties, the Intergovernmental Panel on Climate Change (IPCC) tried in successive reports to state what it was confident about, and what was more or less likely or possible, but still rather uncertain. The quote from the American Geophysical Union – the non-government association of American geophysical scientists – does the same in a very summary form. The IPCC, in its report in 2001 extended this process to a treatment of possible sudden or irreversible changes in the climate system which might be catastrophic, but about which we know relatively little regarding likelihood, timing, magnitude and impacts.

Complete surprises are possible. A prime example is the sudden appearance of the 'ozone hole', which first occurred without warning over Antarctica during the 1970s in the Southern Hemisphere's spring. The ozone hole now appears far more rapidly and is far more long lasting than anyone anticipated in the early 1970s. At the time, scientists like me were worrying about possible gradual destruction of ozone in the upper atmosphere; we were taken by surprise when it happened in a few years over Antarctica, far from the sources of the chemicals thought to be threatening the ozone layer. 'Repairing' the ozone hole is likely to take the best part of a century, despite strong international agreements on doing so (see Chapter 9 for a more detailed discussion of the ozone problem). And it could have been far worse. As Paul Crutzen stated, on receipt of the Nobel Prize for his work on ozone:

> ... if the chemical industry had developed organobromine compounds [which contain bromine] instead of the CFCs [which contain chlorine] ... then without any preparedness, we would have been faced with a catastrophic ozone hole everywhere and in all seasons during the 1970s .... Noting that nobody had given any thought to the atmospheric consequences of the release of Cl or Br [chlorine or bromine] before 1974, I can only conclude that mankind has been extremely lucky.

Projected climate changes

The magnitude of eventual climate change depends to a first approximation on the accumulated emissions. On the basis of the *Special Report on Emissions Scenarios* (SRES) discussed in Chapter 3, the projected accumulated emissions by 2100, expressed in units of thousands of millions of tonnes of carbon equivalent (GtC), range from a low of 770 GtC to approximately 2540 GtC. This range compares with the earlier IPCC IS92 projections ranging from 770 to 2140 GtC, so the upper end of the range is now greater than before. Corresponding projected carbon dioxide concentrations by 2100 range from 540 to 970 parts per million (ppm).

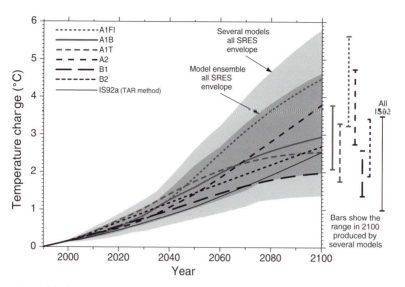

Figure 15: Global average temperature projections. Global average temperature projections for six illustrative SRES scenarios. The darker shading represents the envelope of the full set of 35 SRES scenarios used as input to the climate models, using the then accepted average climate sensitivity of 2.8°C. The lighter shading is the envelope based on a range of climate sensitivities in the range 1.7 to 4.2°C. The bars show, for each of the six illustrative SRES scenarios, the range of model results in 2100. For comparison, the IPCC IS92 range of warmings in 2100 is also shown. (Adapted with permission from the IPCC 2001 WGI report, Figure 22 (a) of Technical Summary; and from *Climatic Change* 53(4): 393–411, 2002, with kind permission of Springer Science and Business Media.)

This chapter describes projected changes in climate based on both these SRES scenarios (which are not driven by climate policies) and on some 'stabilisation scenarios' that assume policies leading to a levelling off of carbon dioxide concentrations at various values. The stabilisation scenarios are based on those provided by Wigley, Richel and Edmonds in 1996, and are referred to as the WRE scenarios after the names of the authors. The IS92 full range is added for comparison, and includes emissions scenarios drawn up in 1992 and used in the IPCC *Second Assessment Report* in 1995. Likely climate changes include surface warming, changes to rain and snowfall, increased evaporation, changes to the magnitude and frequency of extreme events such as droughts and floods, rises in sea level, and the possibilities of abrupt changes and large-scale changes of the climate system such as ocean currents or the melting of ice sheets.

Surface warming

The IPCC's 2001 report projects global average surface temperature increases ranging from 1.4 to 5.8°C by 2100 (see **Figure 15**), compared to the earlier IPCC IS92 range of 1.5 to 3.5°C. This latest projected rate of warming is roughly two to 10 times that observed during the twentieth century, which was about 0.6°C. The rate is much faster than the average warming at the end of the last glaciation. The greater warming at the high end of the range, compared to that in the IS92 range is due to both greater carbon dioxide emissions in the high emissions scenarios and less sulfur emissions.

About half the range of uncertainty in projected warming is due to the choice of scenarios, which in reality can be influenced by policy developments, and half to the uncertainty for a given scenario, which is due to scientific uncertainties. The latter essentially concerns the sensitivity of climate to a given increase in carbon dioxide concentrations. This scientific uncertainty is a high priority for further research.

The estimated transient and equilibrium warmings in the IPCC 2001 report are summarised in **Table 3**. 'Transient' warmings are reached at a certain date, while the climate system is still undergoing change. 'Equilibrium' warmings are those reached at a time when the climate system has stopped changing and settled down into a new, stable state.

The equilibrium warming scenarios are more relevant to policy, since they describe outcomes based on various prescribed emissions reduction programs, such as may be introduced to reduce the magnitude of future climate change. Concern about climate change has already (in 2005) led to policies that have reduced emissions slightly relative to the larger emissions in the SRES 'no-policy' scenario range. Comparison of outcomes under the various equilibrium warming scenarios gives some idea of the effect on climate of various emissions reduction programs.

Note, both in **Figure 15** and **Table 3,** that there is a large uncertainty range for each scenario and stabilisation level, due mainly to the uncertainty in the sensitivity of climate to specified increases in greenhouse gases. Estimates in **Figure 15** and **Table 3** are based on the IPCC 2001 range of climate sensitivity of 1.5 to 4.5°C. However, best current estimates of this range of uncertainty have changed recently, due to new probabilistic estimates of the climate sensitivity (by David Stainforth of Oxford University and others in *Nature*, 27 January, 2005) ranging from 1.9 to 11.5°C (see Chapter 8 re mitigation targets). This would extend the range of possible warmings upwards, but the new results have yet to be fully considered.

Note also that the central estimates of the warming by 2100 in Table 3 for each of the stabilisation scenarios is clearly in the bottom half of the range of warmings for the full SRES range of scenarios. Thus even following a development pathway aimed at stabilising carbon dioxide at 1000 ppm would substantially reduce impacts in 2100 relative to the impacts of the higher SRES emissions scenarios.

Table 3: Projected warmings for various scenarios of increasing greenhouse gases. Estimates of increases in global mean surface temperature (°C) for the IS92 scenario range, the full range of SRES scenario projections, and the 'WRE' stabilisation scenarios, all relative to 1990. The IS92 and SRES scenarios do not extend beyond 2100. The WRE scenarios were developed by Wigley, Richel and Edmonds in 1996, and lead to stabilisation of carbon dioxide concentrations (ppm) at levels indicated

CO_2 scenario	Warming at 2100	Warming at 2350	Equilibrium warming
IS92 revised full range	1.0–3.6	n/a	n/a
SRES B1	1.4–2.6	n/a	n/a
SRES B2	1.9–3.5	n/a	n/a
SRES A1T	1.8–3.3	n/a	n/a
SRES A1B	2.1–3.8	n/a	n/a
SRES A2	2.8–4.8	n/a	n/a
SRES A1FI	3.2–5.8	n/a	n/a
WRE 450	1.2–2.3	1.4–3.0	1.5–3.9
WRE 550	1.6–2.9	1.9–4.0	1.9–5.2
WRE 650	1.8–3.2	2.2–4.7	2.3–6.3
WRE 750	1.9–3.4	2.6–5.4	2.7–7.1
WRE 1000	2.0–3.5	3.2–6.6	3.5–8.7

It is significant that there is relatively little difference in transient warmings in 2100 for stabilisation targets above about 650 ppm. This is due to the relatively small difference in cumulative emissions by 2100 implied by the different stabilisation pathways and the slow response of the climate system, which is still catching up to the effects of earlier emissions. In other words, the warming at 2100 is largely determined by changes already in the pipeline due to past emissions.

However, differences due to different stabilised carbon dioxide concentrations at the time of temperature stabilisation (which occurs centuries beyond 2100) are substantial. Thus we can say that stabilisation pathways for any goal up to 1000 ppm would limit impacts and risks by 2100, but the higher the stabilised carbon dioxide concentrations, the greater the impacts and risks beyond 2100.

John Mitchell and colleagues at the Hadley Centre for Climate Prediction and Research in the UK have put numbers on the effects of stabilisation using the HadCM2 climate model. They compared model simulations leading to stabilisation of atmospheric carbon dioxide at 550 ppm by the year 2150, and 750 ppm by 2250, with simulations in which carbon dioxide concentration increased by 1% per year from 1990 values. They found that the global average warming between 1990 and 2100 is reduced by 55% and 40% respectively, and that average sea-level rise by 2100 was reduced by 33% and 27% respectively from the baseline result of 60 centimetre rise. Sea level continues to rise in both stabilisation cases for centuries after stabilisation of carbon dioxide concentrations.

Other transient or stabilisation scenarios of emissions will lead to different estimates of global warming for any given time in the future. However, provided their cumulative emissions fall within the range of the scenarios shown in **Table 3**, the resulting estimated warmings will lie pretty well in the range estimated here.

Regional warmings

While average global warming is of importance, most interest is in regional impacts, for which more detailed estimates of regional warming are required. Fortunately, there is broad agreement on the patterns of warming around the globe in various climate models. Warming in continental interiors and in the high latitudes of the northern hemisphere is expected to be greatest with less expected over the oceans and windward coastlines. The least warming is expected over the Southern Ocean due to its large capacity to transport surface heat into the deep ocean, and possibly in the North Atlantic region, depending on the behaviour of the ocean circulation (see later). Warming may be greater in the eastern tropical Pacific than in the west, which may lead to a more El-Niño-like average condition.

After stabilisation of greenhouse gas concentrations in the atmosphere, warming will continue for centuries in the Southern Ocean, leading to ongoing regional climate change in the vicinity, especially in Australia and New Zealand, and possibly in southern Argentina and Chile.

Precipitation and evaporation

Global average precipitation (rain or snowfall) and evaporation are projected to increase by about 1 to 9% by 2100, depending on which scenario and climate model is used. However, projected precipitation changes vary more from region to region, with increases over northern mid- to high latitudes and Antarctica in winter. At lower latitudes there are both regional increases and decreases over land areas, with some differences between different global climate models, but there are also areas of strong agreement between the models.

In the northern winter, rainfall is projected to increase in tropical Africa, show little change in South-east Asia and decrease in Central America. An increase or little change is expected in South Asia in the northern summer, but a decrease is expected in the Mediterranean region. Winter rainfall is expected to decrease over Australia.

Rainfall changes will vary greatly on finer spatial scales due to topographic and coastal effects. These changes are best simulated using regional climate models, but agreement is sometimes poor between models. Changes in rainfall intensity and seasonality are expected, but these changes are quite uncertain in many areas. Higher temperatures will mean that more precipitation will fall as rain rather than snow, changing the seasonality of river flows in many snow-fed catchments such as those in the western United States and northern Europe.

There has been an observed strengthening and poleward movement of the atmospheric low-pressure belts around the North and South Poles during the late twentieth century. This is simulated in climate models that include the effects of enhanced greenhouse gases and stratospheric ozone depletion. This effect is expected to continue through the twenty-first century, with any lessening of the ozone depletion effect being more than made up for by strengthening of the greenhouse effect. Regional effects resulting from these changes will include increased rainfall in the higher mid-latitude westerlies, but less rainfall along the low latitude edge of the low pressure belt, such as in typical 'Mediterranean-type' climates. Storm belts will also shift, and the North Atlantic Oscillation may stay in a more positive mode, affecting climate over Europe. Wenju Cai and colleagues at CSIRO, Australia, point out that in the Southern Hemisphere the increase in north–south temperature differences due to the lag in warming in the Southern Ocean will reverse after stabilisation of greenhouse gas concentrations. This may lead to a reversal of changes associated with the shift southward of the westerlies.

Extreme events

According to the IPCC, it is likely that changes in some extreme events were observed during the twentieth century (**Table 4** below), however, there is some uncertainty due to limited data. More changes in extreme events are likely in the twenty-first century. Daily maximum and minimum temperatures, and the number of hot days are very likely to increase, with fewer cold and frosty days. In general there will be a reduced diurnal temperature range (the difference between daily maximum and minimum temperatures). The heat or discomfort index is very likely to increase in most tropical and mid-latitude areas. More intense precipitation events are very likely over many areas (causing more frequent flooding), and increased summer drying is likely over mid-latitude continental interiors, with an increased risk of drought. The intensity of tropical cyclone winds and peak rainfalls is likely to increase. Greater extremes of flood and drought are likely with the El Niño-Southern Oscillation cycle (El Niño and La Niña), which is expected to continue. These changes are summarised in **Table 4**.

Table 4: Changes in extreme events. IPCC 2001 report estimates of confidence in observed changes during the twentieth century, and projected changes in the twenty-first century, for extreme weather and climate events.

Changes in phenomenon	Confidence in observed changes (latter half of the twentieth century)	Confidence in projected changes (during the twenty-first century)
Higher maximum temperatures and more hot days over nearly all land areas	Likely	Very likely
Higher minimum temperatures, fewer cold days and frost days over nearly all land areas	Very likely	Very likely
Reduced diurnal temperature range over most land areas	Very likely	Very likely
Increase of heat index[1] over land areas	Likely, over many areas	Very likely, over most areas
More intense precipitation events[2]	Likely, over many Northern Hemisphere mid- to high latitude land areas	Very likely, over many areas
Increased summer continental drying and associated risk of drought	Likely, in a few areas	Likely, over most mid-latitude continental interiors (lack of consistent projections in other areas)
Increase in tropical cyclone peak wind intensities[3]	Not observed in the few analyses available	Likely, over some areas
Increase in tropical cyclone mean and peak precipitation intensities[3]	Insufficient data for assessment	Likely, over some areas

1   The heat index is a combination of temperature and humidity that measures effects on human comfort.
2   For other areas there are insufficient observations or conflicting modelling results.
3   Past and future changes in tropical cyclone location and frequency are uncertain.

In general, any increase in the average of a climate variable such as temperature or rainfall tends to have an exaggerated effect on less frequent extremes associated with normal climate variability, such as very cold or hot days. The increase in average reduces the frequency of occurrence of extremes on the low side and increases their frequency on the high side. Changes in variability can also occur, which may strengthen or weaken the changes in extremes.

This is supported by a review of the paleo-records of natural floods, which found the magnitude and frequency of floods are highly sensitive to even modest changes of climate equivalent to or smaller than those expected from global warming in the twenty-first century. The review suggested that times of rapid climate change have a tendency to be associated with more frequent occurrences of large and extreme floods. Consistent with this, a study of great flood events in 29 river basins around the world shows an increase in frequency since 1953. Using climate models, the study finds that the frequency of such large floods will increase further during the twenty-first century, by a factor of two to eight.

A recent high spatial resolution climate modelling study finds that an increase in intense precipitation is very likely in many parts of Europe, despite a possible reduction in summer rainfall over a large part of the continent. Thus, severe flooding may become more frequent, despite a general tendency toward drier summers. Yet another modelling study finds that the proportion of total precipitation derived from extreme and heavy events will continue to increase relative to that from light to moderate events.

Kevin Trenberth of the US National Center for Atmospheric Research and colleagues critically examined the performance of some climate models in simulating the variation of rainfall with time of day. The models tended to underestimate the intensity of rain, and overestimate its frequency on an hourly basis. They argue that under global warming conditions the most likely situation is that extreme high rainfall rates will increase, and the number of light rain days will decrease, probably more than is at present simulated by climate models. The paper argues that the main changes in rainfall to be experienced with global warming will be due to the greater available moisture in the atmosphere. This will lead to higher rainfall rates and greater intervals between rain events, possibly leading to more droughts.

However, some recent analyses of pan evaporation observations (that is, measurements of rates of evaporation from a water surface in an open pan) suggest that pan evaporation, and by inference solar radiation reaching the Earth's surface, decreased in many areas from the 1960s through to the 1980s. This may have been due to increasing aerosol pollution, particularly in the Northern Hemisphere, or to changes in cloud amounts. It has been suggested that these decreasing trends challenge climate change projections that indicate increases in potential evaporation in many areas.

Against this, pan evaporation is not the same as actual evaporation, which can show an opposite trend. Moreover, pan evaporation has increased in some areas since the 1980s, and there is some evidence that solar radiation in these areas is also increasing, most likely due to decreasing aerosols. In any case, recent climate model calculations do take account of the direct effects on evaporation of atmospheric aerosols, and some models even include the indirect effects via aerosol-induced changes to cloud properties (see Chapter 2). Despite the need for improvements, recent climate models do seem to be getting the broad picture right. The fact that total global rainfall seems to have increased, especially at high latitudes, and that high latitude ocean surface waters have become fresher, suggests that the global hydrological cycle has in fact sped up as the climate models suggest.

Large floods and widespread droughts are commonly due to one or other extreme of naturally occurring variations in circulation patterns including the North Atlantic Oscillation (NAO) and the El Niño-Southern Oscillation (ENSO). The NAO consists of fluctuating pressure differences between the Icelandic low pressure region and the Azores high pressure region in the North Atlantic. ENSO is a coupled atmosphere-ocean phenomenon across the tropical Pacific involving sea surface temperature and atmospheric pressure fluctuations. These phenomena also influence other important climatic events such as the favoured tracks of storms in the North Atlantic and the location of tropical cyclones in the Pacific. Both phenomena also have long-distance or tele-connections to weather and climate elsewhere. How global warming affects these circulation patterns is very important, as it will have strong implications for storm tracks and rainfall patterns in both hemispheres.

A progressive shift in the NAO toward its more positive phase has been observed since 1950, and has been associated with a slow warming of the tropical oceans. This is supported by an analysis of observed and modelled trends in global sea-level pressure patterns, which points to a human influence, with a poleward shift in mid- to high latitude pressure patterns. Two other studies suggest that the spatial pattern of the NAO is likely to change

Future behaviour of ENSO is of critical importance to many countries affected by ENSO-related rainfall variations and storm frequency. The relationship between ENSO and rainfall has varied with time over Australia, both in the historical record and in the longer record from coral cores in the Great Barrier Reef. However, paleo-climatic data suggest that ENSO has been a feature of global climate through past warm periods. Different global climate model simulations for a warmer world show differing results, with some showing a more El-Niño like average condition, and others showing little change. This may be partly because some climate models do not simulate ENSO behaviour well, even under present conditions. The interim conclusion must be that changes in the ENSO pattern may occur, but these are still very uncertain. ENSO extremes may also be associated with more extreme floods and droughts due to the intensification of the hydrological cycle.

The situation with projections of tropical cyclone behaviour is mixed. As the IPCC concluded in its report in 2001, it is likely that tropical cyclones will become more intense by 5–10% around 2050, with corresponding rainfall peak intensities increasing by about 25%. There could also be substantial changes in the region of formation if there are changes in ENSO, although there is no evidence for changes in total numbers globally. So far there is no evidence for a substantial increase in poleward movement of tropical cyclones, either in observations or model projections.

A category of extratropical cyclones known as explosively developing cyclones, which includes some mid-latitude east coast low pressure systems, can cause severe flooding due to heavy rainfall, storm surges and high winds. Some modelling results suggest that east coast lows might intensify with higher sea surface temperatures. A statistically significant increase in explosively developing cyclones in the Southern Hemisphere has been detected from 1979 to 1999.

Global warming could also influence another class of extreme event that was not considered by the IPCC in its 2001 report, namely earthquakes. Of course earthquakes occur irrespective of climate change. They occur when one part of the Earth's crust moves against another, and can trigger tsunamis or tidal waves if they occur under the sea.

Shifts in weight on an area of the Earth's crust, due for example to the filling of large dams, can cause small local earthquakes. Such shifts in weight have occurred in the past due to the melting of glaciers and ice sheets. The weight of glaciers and ice sheets depresses the Earth's crust under them, and their removal leads to the underlying crust slowly rising. This glacial rebound is still occurring in many areas close to the former ice sheets that covered much of Fennoscandia and North America some 20,000 years ago. There is good evidence that regional earthquake fault instability increased at the end of the last glaciation.

Further melting of mountain glaciers and remnant ice sheets due to global warming over parts of Canada, Patagonia, Alaska and of course Greenland and Antarctica could lead to further land movements, triggering localised earthquakes. There is a large element of random or chaotic behaviour in earthquake occurrence, and skill in forecasting them is very limited. Nevertheless, it is arguable that the frequency of at least small earthquakes might increase as glaciers and ice sheets melt, and also perhaps as a result of rising global sea level. Sea-level rise would increase the load on the continental shelves, even far from the melting ice. How significant this is, and the timescale on which seismic effects might occur, remains to be determined, but the consequences could be significant.

The frequency and severity of other extreme climate-related events, some not discussed by the IPCC because of their small scale and a lack of studies, are also likely to be affected by climate change. These include the occurrence of flash flooding, severe thunderstorms and hail, landslides, extreme sea-level events and wildfires. Some of these will be discussed further in Chapter 6 on impacts.

Sea-level rise

Sea-level rise is obviously important, given that a rapidly increasing number of people live in low-lying coastal areas. Projections of global sea-level rise by the IPCC in 2001 range from 9 to 88 cm by 2100 (see **Figure 16**). This is appreciably lower than the estimate of 20 to 165 cm made in 1986 by the Scientific Committee on Problems of the Environment. However, it differs little from the estimates in the IPCC report in 1996 despite the higher upper limit estimates of global warming in the 2001 report. If greenhouse gas concentrations were stabilised (even at present levels), the IPCC notes that sea level would continue to rise for hundreds of years after 2100, due to the slow but continuing warming of the deep oceans, while the polar ice sheets will continue to melt due to climate change during the next several thousand years, even if climate is stabilised.

A large part of sea-level rise in the next 100 years is determined by global warming to date, since there is a large delay in its effect on sea level. **Figure 16** shows sea-level rise projections up to 2100, including ranges of uncertainty for each emissions scenario. Up to 2100 most of the total range of uncertainty is due to uncertainty in the calculations of thermal expansion and ice melting, rather than uncertainty about which scenario will be realised. Although we do not know exactly what the rise will be, it is more or less inevitable due to past emissions. The differences due to different emissions scenarios in the twenty-first century become important beyond 2100.

The IPCC estimates that by the year 2100, the main contribution to sea-level rise will be from thermal expansion of sea water, which will add some 11 to 43 cm, accelerating through the twenty-first century, with the next largest contribution coming from the melting of mountain glaciers (1 to 23 cm). The relative contributions vary with the emissions scenario and assumed climate sensitivity. According to the IPCC 2001 report, melting from Greenland is most likely to add a little to sea-level rise (−2 to +9 cm), while Antarctica may make a negative contribution due to increased snow accumulation on the ice cap (−17 to +2 cm). The latter may occur due to warmer air over Antarctica, which would have higher moisture content, leading to heavier snowfall if air temperatures remain below freezing. This would remove water from the oceans and add it to the ice cap.

Processes not adequately represented in present models of sea-level rise may also be important. The IPCC 2001 report quotes two risk assessment studies involving panels of experts. These studies concluded that there was a 1 in 20 chance that by 2100 the West Antarctic Ice Sheet (WAIS) could make a substantial contribution to sea-level rise, 16 cm in one study and 50 cm in the other. These studies also noted a 1 in 20 chance of the WAIS contributing a sea-level fall of 18 cm or 40 cm respectively, due to increased snow accumulation. It is also possible that there would be an initial sea-level fall, due to increased snow accumulation inland, followed by a sea-level rise, due to surface melting and

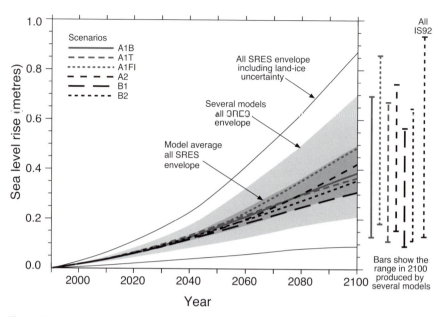

Figure 16: Projected sea-level rises. Projections of global average sea-level rise from 1990 to 2100 for the SRES scenarios. Each of the six lines in the key is the average of seven different model calculations for one of the SRES illustrative emissions scenarios. Dark shading shows the range of the average model projections for all 35 SRES scenarios. The vertical bars on the right show the range of uncertainty associated with each individual SRES illustrative scenario. (Diagram with permission from IPCC 2001 report, WGI, Figure 24 of Technical Summary.)

accelerated outflow from the outlet glaciers. Thus these experts would widen the possible range of sea-level changes, with increased risk of larger rises (which would have dire consequences for coastal populations), as well as the possibility of actual falls.

Antarctica's contribution to sea-level changes is particularly uncertain, with the possibility of surprises. Floating ice shelves, notably the Wordie and Larsen A and B shelves, broke up very rapidly during the 1990s and early 2000s following regional warming of about 2.5°C over the previous 50 years (**Figure 17**). The 1600 square kilometres of Larsen A suddenly disintegrated in 39 days during 1994–95, and the 3245 square kilometres of Larsen B in only 41 days in 2002.

The rapid regional warming around the Antarctic Peninsula was not well predicted by older global climate models. However, recent modelling by Michiel van den Broeke and colleagues suggests an explanation. They used a high-resolution (55 km spacing) regional atmospheric climate model driven by observed conditions at the boundary to compare years with a strong and a weak circumpolar vortex (upper atmospheric circulation around the pole). Results showed a change in the surface winds such that it was much warmer over the Weddell Sea and the adjacent Antarctic Peninsula when there was a stronger circumpolar vortex. The trend towards such conditions since the 1970s has been ascribed to a combination of the enhanced greenhouse effect and stratospheric ozone destruction. If this is so, the warming trend may continue, possibly affecting the much larger Filchner-Ronne and Ross Ice Shelves later this century.

The very rapid disintegration of the Wordie and Larsen Ice Shelves was unexpected. Their break-up may have been due in part to basal melting, but it is mainly due to summer meltwater (visible in the top frame of **Figure 17**) deepening crevasses, which causes major fractures in the shelves. Some of the narrow ice shelf fragments (often up to 200 metres thick) may have speeded the break-up by tipping over, releasing energy that sent shock waves through the ice shelf. These narrow shelf fragments are visible in the bottom frame of **Figure 17**.

The break-up of the ice shelves has been followed, in the case of the Larsen Ice Shelves, by an acceleration and active surging of a number of former contributory glaciers which are already making a small but significant contribution to sea-level rise. This has led to the strengthening of an earlier theory in 1978 by John Mercer of Ohio State University that ice shelves tend to hold back outlet glaciers.

The rapid disintegration of the Wordie and Larsen Ice Shelves should perhaps cause a rethink as to the stability of the West Antarctic Ice Sheet (WAIS), which, if it were to totally disintegrate, would add some six metres to global average sea level. The Ross and Filchner-Ronne Ice Shelves, which apparently stabilise the WAIS, are not immediately threatened, although Randy Showstack from *EOS* magazine reports that only a few degrees warming may be needed to threaten the Ross Ice Shelf, the largest in Antarctica. Widespread surface melting has been reported on the Ross Ice Shelf during warm summer episodes. MJM Williams of the Danish Center for Earth System Science and colleagues suggest that the Amery Ice Shelf (the third largest embayed ice shelf in Antarctica) may be threatened by a 3°C warming. Increases in basal melt rates under the ice shelves due to ocean warming and changing circulation beneath the ice shelves may be responsible.

Recent aircraft and satellite observations of the Amundsen Sea sector of West Antarctica also show that local glaciers are discharging about 250 cubic kilometres of ice each year to the ocean, almost 60% more than is accumulating in their catchment areas, and at a faster rate than in the 1990s.

There is a similar concern about more rapid disintegration of the Greenland ice sheet, which if it were to melt would cause about a seven metre rise in sea level. James Hansen of the Goddard Institute of Space Studies in New York argues that surface melt water can rapidly penetrate to the base of the outlet glaciers via moulins (near-vertical shafts worn in the glaciers by melt water),

50 km

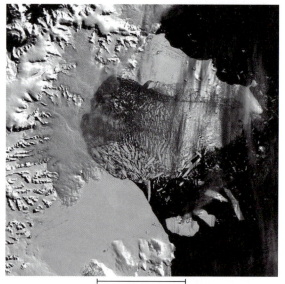

50 km

Figure 17: Satellite images of the break-up of the Larsen B ice shelf in 2002. The Larsen B ice shelf as it appeared on 31 January 2002 (top) and on 5 March 2002 (bottom). Dark areas on the ice shelf on 31 January are meltwater pools. These rapidly drained into crevices that opened up causing disintegration of the ice shelf as seen on 5 March. Note the more chunky icebergs in the lower right of the frame that are the result of normal iceberg calving from the nearby Filchner-Ronne ice shelf. Some thin cloud also appears in the bottom image. (Images provided by the US National Snow and Ice Data Center, University of Colorado and NASA's MODIS sensors.)

leading to lubrication of the glacier flow. He asserts that with global warming, not only will there be surface melt at low elevations, but also more rain rather than snow in summer at higher elevations, leading to an acceleration of this lubrication process. Moreover, as outflow accelerates, the central high elevation regions of the Greenland ice cap will be lowered, causing more rain and less snow to accumulate, reinforcing the process. Such a process, once started, may be irreversible. Hansen does not claim that such rapid disintegration will happen in a few years or even decades, but he is concerned that it will take far less than the thousands of years envisaged in the IPCC 2001 report.

The Patagonian icefields in South America have been observed to be losing volume in recent decades, with estimates based on the retreat of the largest 63 outlet glaciers increasing from a rate of 0.042 ± 0.002 mm per year in equivalent sea level, averaged from 1969 to 2000, to 0.105 ± 0.011 mm per year in the period 1995 to 2000. The latter is a rate of about 42 cubic km of ice per year, and 1 mm per decade rise in sea level. The Alaskan glaciers, which are five times larger, contribute about 3 mm per decade to global sea-level rise.

Sea-level changes will not be uniform across the world. The models show agreement on the qualitative conclusion that the range of regional variation in sea-level change over the coming century is comparable to the global average sea-level rise. This is due to different rates of regional penetration of warming into the deep oceans (and thus of thermal expansion of the water column), changes in atmospheric pressure and surface winds, and in ocean currents. However, there is little similarity in results for regional variations between models as of 2004, although nearly all models project greater than average rise in the Arctic Ocean and less than average rise in the Southern Ocean.

Further, highly localised land movements, both isostatic (the slow flexing of continental plates as the weight of ice sheets, sediments and water changes) and tectonic (earthquakes and other plate movements) will continue through the twenty-first century, causing local variations about the global average sea-level rise. It can be expected that by 2100, many regions currently experiencing relative sea-level fall will instead have a rising relative sea level as the increasing volume of the oceans due to climate change begins to dominate over local effects. Finally, extreme high water levels due to storm surges will occur with increasing frequency as a result of average sea-level rise. Their frequency may be further increased if storms become more frequent or severe as a result of climate change. For all these reasons, projections of local sea-level rise and its impacts need to be quite location-specific.

Abrupt changes, thresholds and instabilities
Complex systems do not always vary in a smooth fashion that enables easy extrapolation. This is the case for climate, where sudden changes in regime can

occur over wide areas, and are apparently associated with some shift in the circulation pattern. Abrupt changes in ecosystems have also been observed. The mathematical theory of such regime changes is still being developed.

Large-scale abrupt changes in the climate system have already been discussed in Chapter 2. Such abrupt changes also occur regionally, for example in rainfall. For example summer half-year rainfall increased over large parts of eastern Australia around 1945, largely reversing a decrease in the 1890s, while there was a sudden decrease in rainfall in the south-west of Western Australia around 1967–72, which has not reversed since. Such abrupt changes have also been found in climate model simulations. These abrupt changes may or may not be predictable, as they occur as part of natural climate variability on a time-scale of decades. They may also be brought on by gradual changes that slowly move the climate to some critical point where it flips to another regime.

The problem for climate change projections is therefore to capture the possibility and the probability of, and risk from, these abrupt changes. These changes may be either random and chaotic, or due to the existence of critical thresholds. Such thresholds may not be anticipated at all, or, even if they are anticipated, not fully understood. This problem is even more acute when we consider the possibility of large-scale changes to the climate system, which have been termed 'large-scale singular events'.

Large-scale singular events, or 'discontinuities' are an especially important category of abrupt or threshold events. The IPCC report in 2001 emphasised the potential importance of plausible abrupt or irreversible Earth system events. Although uncertain, and possibly taking a century or more to come about, such events might have such large impacts globally that their possibility becomes an important part of any risk analysis. The IPCC stated in 2001:

> Human-induced climate change has the potential to trigger large-scale changes in Earth systems that could have severe consequences at regional or global scales. The probabilities of triggering such events are poorly understood but should not be ignored, given the severity of the consequences.

Events of this type include complete or partial shutdown of the North Atlantic and Antarctic deep water formation (leading to a slowing of the 'oceanic conveyor belt' which takes heat northward in the North Atlantic), disintegration and melting of the West Antarctic and Greenland ice sheets, and major changes in the processes determining carbon dioxide concentrations in the atmosphere due to biospheric effects and methane release from seabed reservoirs. These are summarised in **Table 5**.

In 2002 the US National Research Council issued a major report entitled *Abrupt Climate Change: Inevitable Surprises* that provides a comprehensive

Table 5: Types of large-scale discontinuities. Examples of different types of large-scale discontinuities or irreversible changes in Earth systems, caused by gradual changes in the climate system. (Adapted from IPCC 2001b, Table 19–6, which contains references to relevant published papers and sections of the WGI volume.)

Type of event	Cause	Potential impacts
Non-linear response of ocean circulation	Changes in salinity and temperature could result in slow-down or regional shutdown of sinking of dense water in the North Atlantic or around Antarctica. Effects may be delayed until critical thresholds reached. (IPCC2001a, Chaps. 2, 7 and 9)	Slowing or stopping of oceanic heat transport to western Europe. Possible regional effects elsewhere, including North America, the tropics and the Southern Hemisphere. Reduced oxygen levels and carbon uptake in deep ocean.
Melting of Greenland ice sheet and disintegrating of West Antarctic Ice Sheet (WAIS)	Melting of Greenland ice over centuries due to locally warmer temperatures. WAIS disintegration could be initiated irreversibly this century, but would take centuries to be complete. (IPCC 2001a Chaps. 7 and 11)	Rapid and irreversible global sea-level rises of several metres over several centuries, threatening many coastal cities and settlements and millions of people.
Runaway carbon dynamics	Climate change could reduce the uptake of carbon by the oceans and possibly turn vegetation into a source. Thawing of Arctic tundra a source of CO_2 and methane. Gas hydrate reservoirs may also be destabilised, releasing much methane into the atmosphere. (IPCC 2001a, Chapt. 3)	Would increase rate of warming and consequent impacts of all sorts.

treatment of abrupt climate change. This has been summarised by Richard Alley and colleagues, who state that '... it is conceivable that human forcing of climate change is increasing the probability of large, abrupt events. Were such an event to recur, the economic and ecological impacts could be large and potentially serious.' They go on to say: 'Slowing the rate of human forcing of the climate system may delay or even avoid crossing the thresholds [that would lead to abrupt climate change].'

The timing and probability of occurrence of large-scale discontinuities is difficult to determine because these events are triggered by complex interactions between components of the climate system. Large or sudden impacts could lag behind the triggering mechanisms by decades or centuries. These triggers are sensitive to the magnitude and rate of climate change so that large global warmings have the potential to lead to large-scale discontinuities in the climate system.

Surface waters in the North Atlantic Ocean presently become colder and more saline as they travel north-east in the Gulf Stream. This leads to convective overturning (sinking) of the surface waters, which helps drive the currents. The slow down or complete cessation of convective overturning of the waters of the North Atlantic could arise due to several causes. These include surface warming due to the enhanced greenhouse effect, and lower salinity of surface waters due to increased rainfall at high latitudes and influxes of freshwater from rivers, melting glaciers and partial melting of the Greenland ice sheet. Already, large-scale salinity changes have been observed in the world's oceans, especially the Atlantic. Over the last 50 years, there has been an increase in surface salinity in tropical and subtropical waters and a freshening of the high latitude North and South Atlantic surface waters. This is clear evidence of strengthening of the hydrological cycle, with increased evaporation at low latitudes and increased precipitation at high latitudes. A continuation of this trend could trigger a cessation of overturning.

Also, around Antarctica the main cause of convective overturning of the surface ocean is the freezing of seawater, which leads to a rejection of salt, and thus to dense highly saline water that sinks. Global warming would lead to a reduction in sea-ice formation, and thus reduced overturning there as well.

Evidence for the plausibility and impacts of such events comes from past events recorded in the paleo-record of climate and sea level, and from computer modelling both of past and possible future events. There is also increasing observational evidence suggesting that such processes may already be underway. Besides direct impact on surface climate, reduced overturning of the oceans would reduce oceanic uptake of carbon dioxide, and thus further increase the carbon dioxide concentration in the atmosphere.

Melting of the Greenland ice sheet and/or disintegration of the WAIS, both of which could be triggered by global warming but would take centuries to complete, are potentially irreversible. These events are probably inevitable if carbon dioxide concentrations are allowed to reach two to three times pre-industrial values. The process could only be reversed if carbon dioxide were to be taken out of the atmosphere in such large quantities as to substantially reduce the carbon dioxide concentration and thus reverse global warming. Failing this, the Greenland and West Antarctic ice sheets would each contribute several metres to global mean sea level over the next thousand years or so. As discussed above in relation to sea level, the time scales for disintegration of the WAIS and the Greenland ice sheet are still under debate and there is some chance that they may occur more rapidly. Rapid melting of the Greenland ice sheet could also affect the ocean circulation.

Several mechanisms exist which could lead to an acceleration of global warming via positive feedbacks (amplification mechanisms) associated with the carbon cycle, a process known as 'runaway carbon dynamics'. One is destabilisation of the huge methane reserves stored in crystalline structures (hydrates) on the seabed of the continental shelves and slopes, and in permafrost regions on land. Estimates of the amount of carbon stored in gas (mainly methane) hydrates vary widely from more than 10,000 Gt to more recent estimates of about 1000 Gt. Even the lower estimates are comparable with other known carbon stores, and with the amount in the atmosphere. This compares with the present annual release of greenhouse gases, mainly from the burning of fossil fuels, of some 8 Gt of carbon per year. Methane is some 21 times as effective as carbon dioxide as a greenhouse gas, so even a modest leakage into the atmosphere from gas hydrates would greatly accelerate global warming.

Warming of permafrost, which is already widely observed across the Arctic region, could lead to local, but in total, massive releases of methane from gas hydrates on land. In Arctic coastal areas sea ice is receding and increased wave action is already accelerating erosion of shorelines. Melting of permafrost and loss of structural integrity of hydrate deposits will increase slope failures, landslides and avalanches and threaten human infrastructure such as buildings, roads and pipelines. The effect of the thawing of permafrost on greenhouse gas emissions in particular locations is unclear. It will likely depend on the moisture status of the organic matter after thawing. Dry organic-rich soils tend to release more carbon dioxide and less methane, whereas moist conditions favour methane-making microbes, but also peat accumulation, which stores carbon. Projected increasing rainfall in high latitudes would favour wet conditions. Some methane released from hydrates will be absorbed and broken down before it reaches the surface, both in permafrost regions on land and in ocean floor hydrate deposits. On land, since methane is much more effective as a greenhouse gas, and much of the thawed permafrost will be wet, the net effect is likely to be to increase global warming.

On the continental shelves and slopes warming of seawater at intermediate depths may melt gas hydrate deposits and cause massive slumping of sediments, not only releasing lots of methane, but also creating tidal waves or tsunamis. There is evidence that such a process has occurred in the past, notably some 7000 years ago off the coast of Norway, where the Storegga slide, which was the size of Wales, apparently produced a 20 metre tsunami that may have wiped out Neolithic communities in north-east Scotland. However, the hydrate deposits would tend to be stabilised by the increasing pressure caused by the sea-level rise. Calculations suggest that at present rates of warming the pressure effect may win, but if warming accelerates and sea-level rise lags, deposits may be destabilised. Regional differences in this balance between ocean warming and relative sea-level rise may lead to some local cases of destabilisation. This may be particularly evident on time scales of centuries as ice melts from Greenland and parts of Antarctica, causing the adjacent continental slope to rise due to loss of the weight of ice ('isostatic rebound'). Isostatic rebound after the last glaciation is still occurring in parts of Scotland, Norway and Sweden, where relative sea-level fall is occurring.

In a 2002 review, Euan Nisbet of the University of London concluded that the case is open for a major methane release in the twenty-first century, possibly from a large pool of free methane gas trapped below a hydrate deposit. He points to the possibility of large riverine floods, brought about by a more intense hydrological cycle, depositing large amounts of sediment that could destabilise hydrates through slippage in sediment deposits on continental slopes.

Other possible feedbacks on the carbon cycle include decreased efficiency of the oceanic and terrestrial biospheric sinks of carbon due to global warming. Oceanic feedbacks include increasing stability and reduced overturning of the surface layers of the oceans (leading to reduced uptake of carbon dioxide from the atmosphere), and reduced solubility of carbon dioxide in warmer waters. In addition, increasing acidity of the oceans due to higher carbon dioxide concentrations would affect many oceanic organisms in complex ways, possibly also reducing the biological uptake of carbon dioxide in the oceans.

The terrestrial biosphere, which presently acts as a sink of carbon dioxide, could become a source by 2050, and the ocean sink may also be reduced due to greater stratification of the surface layers of the ocean. Carbon dioxide sinks vary due to changes in ocean circulation associated with ENSO, carbon dioxide fertilisation of terrestrial forests, and temperature and rainfall effects on terrestrial plant growth. The main reason for the expected change of the terrestrial biosphere from a sink to a source by 2050 is increased respiration and decay of the increased biomass and soil carbon at higher temperatures. Two different climate models with interacting carbon cycles indicate that global warmings could be increased by one or more degrees by 2100 due to these interactions. Increasing fire frequencies and intensities may also cause faster increases of atmospheric carbon dioxide. Widespread forest and peat fires were observed to contribute significantly to carbon dioxide increases in 1994/95 and 1997/98 when large biomass burning took place in tropical and boreal regions.

Other, possibly lesser, but still widespread climate changes are possible. For example, the IPCC 2001 report discusses the possibilities of major changes in the behaviour of the continental monsoons, the ENSO and other patterns of climate variability.

Several recent studies have identified the importance of large-scale singular events in global estimates of risk, and in cost/benefit analyses as to the optimal timing of mitigation action to reduce the risk of such events. The possibility of such events increases the overall risk of dangerous impacts of climate change, making early action to reduce climate change more pressing.

Scenarios in a nutshell

In summary, the full range of IPCC SRES emissions scenarios would lead to a wide range of global warmings (1.4 to 5.8°C) and sea-level rise (9 to 88 cm) by 2100. About half the range in global average warming is due to the range of emissions scenarios and half to uncertainties in the science, mainly in the climate sensitivity. This leaves a lot of room for choice of emission reduction policies leading to lower emissions, and thus less climate change. Emissions policies that aim at stabilising greenhouse gas concentrations in the atmosphere anywhere below 1000 ppm of carbon dioxide equivalent would lead to smaller warmings than those resulting from the higher SRES scenarios. A target concentration of 450 ppm at stabilisation would lead to an estimated warming by 2100 in the range of 1.2 to 2.3°C, while a target of 1000 ppm would lead to 2.0 to 3.5°C. However, warmings and sea-level rise would continue long past 2100, even in the stabilisation scenarios.

Changed frequencies and intensities of extreme weather events are likely with global warming, including more hot days, fewer cold nights, greater heat stress, more droughts in mid-latitude continental areas, more intense rain events, and increased intensity and rainfall from tropical cyclones or hurricanes.

Possibilities exist for sudden rapid and long-term changes in global-scale climate-related systems, including more rapid sea-level rise due to more rapid disintegration and melting of the Greenland and West Antarctic ice sheets, major changes to the circulation of the oceans with regional climate impacts (especially in regions bordering the North Atlantic), and accelerated release of methane and carbon dioxide into the atmosphere which would accelerate global warming.

The possibility that climate sensitivity may be higher than the range adopted by the IPCC in 2001 (which was 1.5 to 4.5°C for a doubling of atmospheric carbon dioxide concentration) raises the possibility of climate changes greater than those projected in the 2001 report. New estimates by a UK team of scientists in 2005 put the climate sensitivity range at 2 to 11°C. This would mean a much greater chance of more severe climate changes and impacts.

Even the projected global warmings reported by IPCC in 2001 lead to climate-related changes that would have major impacts on human and natural systems, as we shall see in the next chapter. This means that the stakes are high, and suggests there is a need for reducing greenhouse gas emissions so we can follow low emission pathways. How this might be achieved is the subject taken up later in the book.

6

Impacts: Why be concerned?

Humanity is conducting an unintended, uncontrolled, globally pervasive experiment whose ultimate consequences could be second only to a global nuclear war. The Earth's atmosphere is being changed at an unprecedented rate by pollutants resulting from human activities, inefficient and wasteful fossil fuel use and the effects of rapid population growth in many regions. These changes represent a major threat to international security and are already having harmful consequences over many parts of the globe.

International Conference on the Changing Atmosphere:
Implications for Global Security, Toronto, June 1988.

Human induced climate change is one of the major challenges confronting the world this century. The potential for climate change is real and addressing it will require changes to the way the world produces and uses energy.

John Howard, Prime Minister of Australia, National Press Club, 15 June 2004.

The key question for policy-makers (including you the reader) is whether projected climate changes due to greenhouse gas emissions are likely to lead to unacceptable impacts on human and natural systems. The United Nations Framework Convention on Climate Change seeks to avoid 'dangerous interference to the climate system', so we should ask whether what is projected would be dangerous. If so, we must try to avoid it by adopting appropriate policies.

In 1988, despite having rather primitive climate models at their disposal, scientists at a major conference in Toronto reached the rather startling conclusion (quoted above) that human-induced climate change is a major threat to international security. Today we have much more advanced climate models and improved understanding of the effects of climate change on human and natural systems. The Intergovernmental Panel on Climate Change (IPCC) conclusions in its 2001 report largely confirm the 1988 statement by providing much more detail and a better basis. However, our understanding is still far from complete, and both climate and the systems that are affected are extremely complex. What is needed now is a clearer focus on the urgency of the problem, and what can be done about it.

Climate change impacts are complex in that they can be both direct and indirect. For example, more rain may lead directly to either greater or smaller crop yields, depending on factors such as the type of crop, the soil and the present climate. Indirect effects could include changes in supply and demand as a result of these larger or smaller yields, and thus changes in commodity prices; the profitability of farming; and the affordability of food and effects on human health. Moreover, impacts can often be made more favourable by changing strategies so as to minimise losses and maximise gains. This is called adaptation, and is the subject of Chapter 7. In the present chapter we will mainly consider direct impacts of climate change, with some allowance for the more likely adaptations and some comments on indirect effects. But it is difficult to anticipate all potential adaptations, since many will derive from research and development yet to be done and will largely be inspired by the perceived needs as climate changes.

Direct impacts, adaptation and indirect effects are largely conditioned by the nature of the relevant human society, including its institutions, how well informed people are, and how readily they can adapt. These characteristics of society will change with time through population and economic growth (or decline in some cases), new technologies and changing institutional arrangements. Another important factor, which has not been adequately studied, is the *rate* of change of climate, not just the magnitude of change. This is particularly important because rapid change requires rapid adaptation, and a subsequent need to change capital investments (for example in irrigation or flood control systems, building design, or port facilities), which will tend to be more expensive and not always possible.

Studies of specific local impacts of climate changes have been conducted by hundreds of research groups, many from organisations concerned with such matters as seasonal crop forecasts, water supply and coastal protection. These groups have found that climate change and sea-level rise of the magnitude and rates suggested would greatly affect many natural systems like forests, rivers and wildlife, as well as human activities and society.

Examples include:

- Changes in natural productivity and biodiversity, with an increased rate of extinctions.

- Decreases in cereal crop yields in most tropical and sub-tropical countries, and in temperate countries for large warmings.
- Increased water shortages in many water-scarce regions.
- Adverse economic effects in many developing countries for even small warmings, and for developed countries for larger warmings.
- Tens of millions of people on small islands and low-lying coastal areas at severe risk of flooding from sea-level rise and storm surges.
- Increased threats to human health.
- Increase in inequities between poor and richer countries.
- Increased risk of abrupt and irreversible climate changes.

These studies have been based in part on observations of past variations in climate and their effects on crop yields, river flow, flood and drought frequency and so on. Some projections of future effects have thus been based on extrapolations from past experience, while others have used mathematical models of known behaviour of systems to estimate future effects. For example, crop productivity models that simulate how plants grow and develop fruit or grain, that take into account soil moisture, temperature, soil nutrients and carbon dioxide in the air, are used to predict crop yields. These are the same models used for seasonal forecasts, but with climate change inputs. Similarly, simple causal models can predict river flows by calculating how much rain falls in a river catchment, how much evaporates, how much penetrates into the soil and how much runs off.

When such models are used to calculate the present yields or river flows we say they are used to perform 'control simulations'. We can check how good such models are by comparing the control results with observations, especially for seasonal or year-to-year variability and observed variations. The models are then run with changes in climate according to some possible future, and a new climate change simulation result is produced. The difference between this and the control is the estimated effect of the assumed climate change.

Climate change impacts – reasons for concern

Many studies of impacts for various regions, industrial sectors, times in the future, and scenarios were summarised in the IPCC report in 2001. However, it was difficult to compare and summarise these quantitatively, especially for the full *Special Report on Emissions Scenarios* (SRES) range of climate changes, since most studies were based on earlier scenarios, and nearly all were based on transient warming rather than stabilised conditions. The IPCC, however, did summarise the impacts qualitatively under five categories or '*reasons for con-*

cern', which may be considered separately. They are not all expressed in economic terms, since many impacts involve non-market factors.

The reasons for concern are:

- *Risks to unique and threatened systems*: where reliable studies over two decades or more have correlated observed temperature changes with changes in physical and biological systems, the vast majority show changes in the direction needed to maintain their normal temperature range (usually to higher elevation or polewards where that is possible). Natural systems are vulnerable to climate change, especially where migration is not possible or too slow, and increasing numbers will be irreversibly damaged as global warming increases.

- *Risks from extreme climate events:* changes in the frequency and severity of extreme events are expected, and will likely be a major cause of damages to ecosystems, crops, and society. This is demonstrated by the observed rise in damages from extreme climatic events in recent decades. Whether or not the rise in damages to date is due to changes in extremes, the increase in damages shows increasing vulnerability, which is due to population growth and other developments. Clearly damages will increase further with greater climate change.

- *Distribution of impacts*: impacts of climate change will not be distributed equally over the globe. Adverse impacts are likely to be greater and to occur earlier in low-latitude developing countries than in mid- and high-latitude developed countries. This is mainly because low-latitude countries are near or above optimum temperatures for many crops and activities already. Such countries are also less able to adapt both because more heat-tolerant species and cultivars are less available and these countries tend to have less adaptive capacity. As warming increases with time even the more developed countries will experience adverse effects, but the poorer countries will remain more seriously affected. Thus inequality between countries will be made worse.

- *Aggregate impacts:* the consensus is that the total of all the market impacts globally may be small positive or negative (1 or 2% of GDP) at small global warmings (less than 2 or 3°C), but will become increasingly negative at greater warmings. The majority of people are expected to be worse off even at small warmings. Such impacts are poorly quantified and multiple measures are necessary as many impacts cannot be expressed objectively in monetary terms.

- *Risks from future large-scale discontinuities*: While not well understood, there is a strong possibility that large-scale and possibly irreversible changes in Earth systems will result in large impacts at regional and global scales. Changes to the global-scale ocean circulation and the El Niño-Southern Oscillation (ENSO) are possible in the twenty-first century, and other changes may occur later, possibly made inevitable by climate change this century. The latter may well include long-term melting of the Greenland and West Antarctic ice sheets, leading to several metres rise in sea-level over several centuries.

Before we discuss these reasons for concern in more detail, it is worth looking at a group of phenomena that cuts across all of them – the pervasive influence of what are termed 'non-linear effects', thresholds and abrupt changes. These are effects that cannot be anticipated by simple extrapolation from recent experience. For example if we are pushing a cart up a slope, then we expect that a further push will lead to a similar movement as the last push. This is true if the slope is steady, but if we reach the top of a hill, all of a sudden the next push may lead to the cart taking off down the hill. This is a non-linear effect. We have reached a point or threshold, in this case the top of the hill, where conditions change rapidly. An even more abrupt and irreversible change would occur if our cart then reached a cliff top and went over. Climate change confronts us with many potential thresholds and possibly some rather large cliffs.

Thresholds and abrupt changes

Threshold events signal a distinct change in conditions. These may be due to direct physical limits or barriers, or to exceeding a level or benchmark nominated by society or economics. Climatic thresholds include frost, snow or monsoon onset. Biophysical thresholds represent a distinct change in conditions, such as the drying of a wetland, the cessation of flow in a river, floods, or breeding events. Behavioural thresholds are set by benchmarking a level of performance such as crop yield per hectare or net income. Operational thresholds might include sustainable herd size for grazing grasslands, design standards for buildings or drain sizes, heights of levee banks or the size of dam spillways. Movements of variables across such thresholds can have much larger consequences than similar magnitude movements that stay below the thresholds. They may take us into a region where drastic and perhaps unacceptable or dangerous change occurs in the functioning of a system.

An interesting example is set by the damage to buildings caused by wind gusts. Australian insurance figures indicate damage rises dramatically for peak wind gusts in excess of 50 knots, or 25 metres per second (**Figure 18**). This is a very important threshold, since wind damage is one of the major economic impacts of climatic extremes, which may change in frequency or intensity with

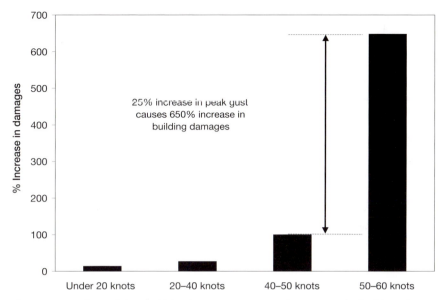

Figure 18: Wind speed threshold for damages. Insurance Group Australia building claims costs versus peak wind gust speeds show a disproportionate increase in costs when wind speeds exceed 50 knots (about 25 metres per second). A 25% increase in gust wind speed above this threshold causes a 650% increase in building damages. This is partly due to the 'snowballing' effect of flying debris. (Diagram after T. Coleman, IGA, 2002, with permission.) (1 knot ≈ 0.5 metres per second.)

global warming according to how frequently and by how much the threshold is exceeded. In the period 1995–2002, the average cost of windstorm damage in the US from hurricanes, tornados and severe thunderstorms was about US$5 billion annually.

Abrupt changes also occur in ecological systems. Studies of lakes, coral reefs, oceans, forests and arid lands have all shown that smooth change can be interrupted by sudden shifts to some contrasting state. Such sudden changes in system behaviour often arise from an element of the system reaching a limit or threshold at which instability sets in, and the system moves into a new stable state. When a system is close to such a threshold, even quite small random events or trends can force the system into a different state. In more mathematical terms, it may take the form of a switch from a negative to a positive feedback. According to Scheffer and colleagues, distance from a threshold of this sort is a measure of system resilience or ability to cope with small variations in conditions.

Abrupt changes, and exceeding thresholds, can occur in many climate change impact situations, ranging from water stress in an individual plant, through the topping of flood levee banks, to economic crises or forced migration due to rapid sea-level rise. The potential for such events lies behind many of the impacts within each category of reasons for concern identified in the IPCC 2001 report. These categories are discussed below.

Risks to unique and threatened systems

Some of these impacts have already been observed over the last several decades, for example changes in the ranges for some already threatened species of plants, animals and birds, retreat of glaciers, shorter duration of river- lake- and sea-ice and melting of permafrost. However, as we saw in Chapter 1, attribution of such observed changes to the rather minor global warming of the last century is often difficult in individual cases because of other possible causes, but made more convincing by their widespread and varied nature. The IPCC in its 2001 report did an overall analysis of observed evidence for about 100 physical processes and some 450 biological species. It found that more than 90% of the changes documented worldwide were consistent with how the physical and biological processes are known to respond to climate warming trends.

This circumstantial evidence is useful, but the real question is how projected climate changes, which are much larger than those of the twentieth century, will impact on physical and biological systems. **Table 6** lists some of the threatened and unique entities identified in the IPCC 2001 Working Group II report.

Closed lakes are particularly vulnerable to increased evaporation from higher temperatures, as are lakes with outlets that are small compared with total evaporation from their surfaces. Many of these lakes have shown large fluctuations in the past, and some (most notably the Aral Sea, Lake Chad and the Great Salt Lake) have been affected greatly by withdrawal of water from tributary rivers for irrigation. Only large increases in precipitation in their catchments, reduced withdrawals or river diversions will save them from shrinking further in a globally warming world.

Tropical glaciers in Asia, Africa and Latin America, as well as New Guinea (where they mostly disappeared during the twentieth century) are most sensitive to global warming because they tend to be marginal and suffer little year-to-year variation in temperature. Their loss will mean a loss of cold-loving species of plants and animals, as well as changes to melt-fed rivers affecting riverine species. Accelerated melting will cause floods in many upper reaches of rivers especially in spring and summer, until the glaciers have disappeared, when lack of meltwater will cause serious water shortages especially in summer and autumn. Similar effects are expected in temperate glaciers and glacier-fed rivers, which are important for irrigation and water supply in many countries including the western United States, parts of China, India, Pakistan, Europe and Latin America.

Table 6: Some of the threatened and unique entities identified in the IPCC 2001 report.

Category	Entities	Comments
Water bodies	Closed lakes, especially small ones, but including Caspian & Aral Seas, and Lakes Balkash (Kazakhstan), Chad (Africa), Titicaca (S. America) and Great Salt Lake (USA). Other lakes also affected, especially African Great Lakes	Fine balance between inflow and evaporation in closed lakes, and in some others with large areas and small outflows. Impacts on fisheries, local climate etc.
Glaciers	Tropical glaciers most sensitive, but many small glaciers will disappear	Impacts on related ecosystems, tourism and seasonal water storage
Ecosystems	Alpine ecosystems, coastal wetlands, Cape Floral Kingdom and succulent Karoo (Africa), coral reefs, mangroves, fire-prone species	Ecosystems bound by altitude, coasts or land use change most vulnerable. Increased fire risk widespread. Many coastal wetlands and mangroves cannot retreat inland due to topography or development.
Coastal settlements	North Sea coast (Europe); Gulf Coast (US); many low-lying islands and populous coasts of higher islands; Bangladesh; coastal cities of China, Indonesia, Africa, Nile delta.	Adaptations such as sea walls are expensive and create problems of sea access, drainage etc. Could displace many people.
Indigenous communities	Inuit/Arctic settlements and lifestyle. American Indian and Australian Aboriginal communities in arid or coastal areas.	Traditional hunting and food gathering threatened. Reduced water supplies, coastal flooding and erosion.

Vulnerable ecosystems are those unable to migrate due to altitude limits, coasts on the colder boundaries (for example, coastal South Africa and the south-west of Australia), or where natural ecosystems are no longer possible beyond present boundaries due to land clearing or other development. Others at risk include species that cannot migrate fast enough to keep up with climate change, or species that cannot adapt when they lose the combination of temperature and precipitation necessary for their survival. Many species that rely on each other for food or shelter will be lost as some species die out due to climate changes, leaving dependent species bereft of support. Increased summer aridity will increase fire risk and severity in many locations, leading to repeated fires that will change ecosystems.

Freshwater and mangrove coastal areas will be threatened by sea-level rise, often with little opportunity to retreat inland due to steeper topography or human imposed boundaries such as farms, roads or embankments.

Coral reefs are at particular risk. They are widespread in warm tropical waters and provide large economic benefits from tourism, fisheries and coastal protection. They are already subject to damage from non-climatic problems such as over-fishing, mining and pollution. Increasingly they are also threatened by coral bleaching and death from warmer water, slower growth rates due to increased ocean acidity from higher carbon dioxide concentrations, and in some cases by rapid sea-level rise.

Coral bleaching is a threshold phenomenon, with onset of bleaching at a critical temperature that varies from one location to another, due to different species composition and adaptation. However, adaptation is thought to be slow compared to projected rates of warming, and repeated bleaching may lead to widespread death of particular types of corals, with more affected as temperatures increase. Bleaching episodes have already occurred with increasing frequency worldwide, associated with peaks in the ENSO cycle superimposed on a slow background warming. Increased coral calcification rates at higher temperatures are likely to be outweighed by deaths due to bleaching. **Box 4** summarises issues relating to coral reefs.

One study of the economic benefits of tourism to coral reefs, which focused on the Australian Great Barrier Reef, estimated the annual benefit to the Australian economy as between US$700 million to 1.6 billion, with wider benefits to more distant countries.

Coastal settlements will also be threatened by sea-level rise, often exacerbated by subsidence due to groundwater or oil and gas withdrawal from underlying strata. Where this occurs in heavily built-up areas in rich countries protection by building sea walls is possible, but often at great financial and amenity costs. In poorer countries, or for small settlements, such defences may be uneconomic or impossible. Many millions of people will be involved in developing countries, leading to their displacement within countries and pressure for migration in some cases. Populations of low-lying countries and islands will be particularly seriously affected, losing not only their homes but in many cases traditional ways of life, ancestral connections, and even community and national identity or sovereignty.

Small indigenous communities will also be threatened, not only from sea-level rise in coastal communities, but in some cases from loss of water supplies due to increased aridity, or loss of food supplies as native species are lost due to climate change. Indigenous Arctic peoples will have to cope with loss of sea ice for hunting and fishing, changed migration routes of animals, coastal erosion due to wave action on ice-free coasts, loss of permafrost, and changes in the

---

Box 4: Threats to coral reefs

Recent reports (see notes on website) indicate that coral reefs are valuable resources that are severely threatened by global warming and other stresses. Key points are:

- Coral reefs are unique and valuable ecosystems, and provide major services to humanity including fisheries, gene pools, coastal protection and a tourism industry worth billions of dollars (US).

- Coral reefs are already declining due to over-fishing, mining and pollution.

- Outbreaks of coral bleaching have increased in frequency and magnitude over the last 30 years and are tightly linked to increasing water temperatures.

- Projected increase in temperatures will cause more frequent and intense coral bleaching unless adaptation is rapid.

- Repeated bleaching will mean some coral reefs will die, but others will change.

- Increases in atmospheric carbon dioxide concentrations will increase acidity of oceans and slow calcification rates (growth) of coral.

- Sea-level rise may invigorate growth of some shallow reef species, but drown others.

- Adaptation to global warming will be slow, incomplete and leave different devalued reefs.

- Coral reefs are global canaries warning of major changes to ecosystems.

- Management policies including protected areas, no-take zones and reduced pollution can prolong reef survival, but early and major reduction in emissions of greenhouse gases is necessary to prevent ongoing major damage to reefs.

---

abundance of traditional food sources on land and in the water. More generally, there will be risks from pests and diseases, especially vector-borne, respiratory or other infectious diseases, as traditional food supplies are threatened, lifestyles change, and water supplies for hygienic purposes are in some cases reduced.

Risks from extreme climate events

Extreme climatic events occur naturally in an unchanging but variable climate, virtually by definition. It is difficult to predict their individual occurrences more than a few days ahead, and to a first approximation their occurrence can be considered to be random. Nevertheless, we can develop statistics for their occurrence from observations of the recent past, and use these to state probabilities and risk of occurrence of a particular type and magnitude of extreme.

As discussed in Chapter 5, especially in **Table 4**, it is now widely accepted that many extreme events such as heat waves, heavy rain events, floods and droughts will increase in frequency and magnitude in many regions with global warming, while others, notably cold days and frosts, will decrease. Tropical cyclones, and likely other large storms, will increase in severity, and perhaps change in frequency and preferred locations. Other types of extremes, such as thunderstorms, hail, and high winds may also change, although present knowledge is limited. As certain circulation systems such as the ENSO and the North Atlantic Oscillation (NAO) may also change, regional climatic events associated with them, such as preferred tropical cyclone locations and mid-latitude storm tracks may change as well.

These changes, if they occur, will have widespread impacts. Most climatic impacts arise from extreme weather events or climatic variables that exceed some critical level or threshold and thus affect the performance or behaviour of some physical or biological system. Physical, biological and indeed human systems in general have evolved, or are designed, to cope with a certain range of variations in the weather, based on past variability. However, when weather variables fall outside those limits, the affected system under-performs or fails.

In human systems we implicitly or explicitly plan and design systems and infrastructure to cope with the established range of climate variability, based on past experience. To help in developing design criteria, engineers routinely estimate the average time between floods or high winds of a particular magnitude (the 'return period') at particular locations. This applies, for example, to the design capacities of spillways, drains and bridges, the heights of levee banks and the strength of buildings. Similarly planners consider return periods of floods or coastal storm surges, in zoning and locating urban developments, and in setbacks from rivers or coasts. Return period estimates are normally based on recent instrumental records, where necessary augmented by statistical or physical modelling or data from neighbouring locations. Typically drains are designed to cope with a 25-year return period flood, small bridges maybe 100-year and dams maybe a 10,000-year flood. The safety margin allowed for in design is related to the cost of a failure. However, climate change means that these statistics will change. Thus a central problem in planning for climate change, and estimating possible impacts, is how the statistics of extreme events are likely to change.

Similar problems arise in non-engineering applications such as the future effectiveness, economic performance or viability of activities or investments affected by the weather, such as farming, ski resorts, or health services.

William Easterling of Pennsylvania State University and colleagues in a review in 2000 point out that some apparently gradual biological changes are linked to responses to extreme weather and climate events. Sequences of extreme events, such as repeated floods or droughts, can compound damage and lead to irreversible change. For example, drought-affected forests are particularly prone to wildfire, and then to soil erosion arising from heavy drought-breaking rain. This in turn can cause siltation in rivers, sometimes filling deep waterholes that are refuges for aquatic life during low flow in rivers.

Stanley Changnon of the University of Illinois and co-workers argue that a large part of the observed increase in deaths and financial losses from extreme events in recent decades is due to population growth and demographic shifts into hazardous locations. This means that many societies are becoming more vulnerable to extreme events – in other words, societies often display counter-adaptive behaviour.

Small changes in average climate have a disproportionately large effect on the frequency of extreme events. This is because of the nature of frequency distributions (how frequency changes with magnitude). Extremes occur at the low frequency 'tails' of these frequency distributions. Frequencies in these tails change very rapidly as the frequency distribution moves up or down with the average. Moreover, variability can change, and this also rapidly changes the frequency of extremes. This is particularly important for high rainfall events, as global warming increases the moisture holding capacity of the atmosphere, and thus preferentially increases the likelihood of high intensity rainfall. Thus in many regions what was a 1-in-100 year flood in the twentieth century may well become a 1-in-25 year flood by late in the twenty-first century.

The impact of extremes often increases very rapidly with the magnitude of the extreme, as we have seen with wind speed in **Figure 18**. This is particularly true for flood damages, because the force of flowing water increases rapidly with velocity and depth, and damages increase very rapidly once flood depth exceeds zoning levels and thus the floods reach buildings not designed to withstand floods. Moreover, once a flood is large enough to damage a single building, debris washed downstream can act as a battering ram to damage other buildings. Wind damage has a similar 'snowballing' effect. Again, once floods breach levee banks a great increase in damages results. **Box 5** summarises a UK government report on future flooding in England and Wales.

Similar non-linear or disproportional increases in damages follow from coastal storm surges that exceed planning levels. This can occur due to average sea-level rise, and also from increases in the intensity of storms. In the case of tropical cyclones, the projected decrease in central pressure and increased wind speeds will both add to the increase in storm surge height, with additional stress from wind-driven waves and riverine flooding. The latter will be exacerbated by increased rainfall rates.

An example from calculations of the 1-in-100 year storm surge heights at Cairns, Australia, illustrates the problem. Under present conditions the 1-in-100 year flood height is 2.3 metres, but allowing for a small (10 hectopascal) decrease in average central pressure, possible by mid-century, the 1-in-100 year

---

Box 5: Future flooding in England and Wales

In 2004 the UK Government released a report on future flooding in England and Wales. It addressed the question: how might the risks of flooding and coastal erosion change in the UK over the next 100 years? Over 200 billion pounds worth of assets are at risk, along with disruptions to transport and power. The report emphasised the long lead times involved to influence future risk since:

- Large engineering works have long gestation times and long lifetimes.

- It could take decades for changes in planning policies to take effect.

- The time delay inherent in the atmosphere and oceans means that action to reduce risk from climate change must be taken now.

- Four different socio-economic scenarios were used, termed:

  - World Markets (global interdependence and high emissions);

  - Global Sustainability (global interdependence with low emissions);

  - National Enterprise (national autonomy and medium to high emissions); and

  - Local Stewardship (national/local autonomy with medium to low emissions).

- Some key findings are:

  - If flood-management and expenditures were unchanged, annual losses would increase under all scenarios by 2080, by less than 1 billion pounds under the Local Stewardship scenario to around 27 billion pounds under the World Markets scenario.

  - Besides flooding from rivers and coasts, towns and cities would be subject to localised flooding caused by sewer and drainage systems overwhelmed by local downpours. Damages could be huge but are not yet quantified.

  - The number of people at risk would more than double by 2080.

  - Drivers of future flood risk include climate change, urbanisation, environmental regulations, rural land management, increasing national wealth and social impacts. Climate change has a high impact in all scenarios, with sea-level rise increasing the risk of coastal flooding 4 to 10 times, and precipitation changes increasing risk 2 to 4 times.

  - An integrated portfolio of responses could reduce the risk of river and coastal flooding from the worst scenario of 20 billion pounds annual damage down to around 2 billion pounds (still double the present damages).

---

event becomes 2.6 metres, and with a 10 to 40 centimetre average sea-level rise becomes 2.7 to 3.0 metres. This leads to a potential area of inundation of 71 square kilometres, compared to about 32 square kilometres at present. The area presently liable to flooding is mainly wetlands, but the additional nearly 40 square kilometres would be mainly in the built up urban area, including downtown Cairns. This makes no allowance for increased storm runoff that would make matters worse.

Another problem with extreme events is that the impacts are often compounded by repeated events. Thus many systems may survive a single extreme flood or drought, but not repeated floods or droughts in quick succession. The interval between extremes may allow time for recovery, both of natural systems and of human systems. But if an economy is set back by large damages and disruption by one extreme event, for example a tropical cyclone, a second one shortly after might well overwhelm the capacity of the society to recover, causing far more economic disruption and suffering than the first. Even in rich countries, two or more successive extreme events may force losses on a farming enterprise. Farmers can be bankrupted and have to abandon their farms, unless they have disaster insurance. In poorer countries successions of disasters can set back economic development, for example in Bangladesh and Mozambique.

Disaster insurance often comes in the form of government-funded relief, but increasingly governments are designing relief schemes to only cope with 'exceptional circumstances', sometimes defined as a 1-in-20 year event. If climate change means that these events start to occur more frequently, governments will need to rethink the definition of exceptional circumstances, and ask whether restructuring the industry is better than continuing aid.

In other cases, private insurance companies provide disaster insurance. Many of these companies are already considering whether they need to increase their premiums or reduce their cover in the face of an increasing frequency of insurance claims.

The role of extremes in agriculture and natural systems is complex. Ecosystem type, and even crop productivity, is often related in studies to average climate conditions. However, often this is a proxy for the effects of extremes, since in an unchanging climate the magnitude and frequency of extremes is related to that of the averages. In fact, the causal relationship is usually with the magnitude and frequency of such extremes as frost season, aridity and extreme high temperatures at particular stages in plant growth. Many crops, for instance, do badly in waterlogged soils (very wet conditions) and also under severe water stress (very dry conditions). Moreover, crop yields are often dependent on temperatures and soil moisture at flowering or grain filling times in the growth cycle, with extremely high temperatures reducing fertility and thus grain yield.

Fire occurrence is the product of several variables, and of background conditions as well as extremes. It is a function of precipitation and temperature over a long interval of time, usually in excess of a single season, which determines both fuel density and its dryness. But fire outbreak also requires ignition (usually from lightning or human agency), high temperatures and winds, and low humidity on the day, if the fire is to spread. Proxy evidence of fire occurrences under past climates (see Chapter 2) and projected fire indices for future climate scenarios suggest that fire frequency and severity will likely increase in many regions under enhanced greenhouse conditions. Occasional fires can be beneficial in many ecosystems, thinning undergrowth and allowing regeneration. But too frequent fires can destroy seedlings and prevent regeneration, leading to the replacement of one species by another more fire-resistant one. This process can change mature forests to savannah or grassland.

Increased fire frequency and intensity will have a number of effects including, the changing of ecosystems, damage to buildings and infrastructure, loss of human lives, and threatening the survival of long-term carbon storage in the biosphere (forests and soil carbon). The latter means that increased fire may contribute to a magnification of the enhanced greenhouse effect by undoing the sequestering of carbon in plants and the soil that presently occurs in well-managed land ecosystems. If the huge boreal forests of the northern hemisphere continents and the vast peat deposits in the present tundra and some tropical areas (for example, Kalimantan in Indonesia) are burnt, fire may have a disastrous effect by accelerating climate change.

Distribution of impacts

The impact of global warming will not be distributed evenly among people, countries and regions. Some individuals, sectors, systems and regions will be less adversely affected, and might even gain in the short run. Others will suffer losses even with small levels of global warming. This pattern of gains and losses will vary with time. Increasing losses are projected as warming increases, but the incentive for early action may be less in countries that see early gains.

In the broadest of general terms, there are two main reasons for the uneven distribution of impacts. One is present climate or location, and the other is relative wealth and level of economic and technological development.

Countries such as the Philippines, Guyana and Nigeria, which are at low latitudes with high average surface temperatures are more likely to be early losers, along with low-lying countries such as Bangladesh and Kiribati, which are subject to flooding by sea-level rise. Warm tropical countries have less opportunity to gain by temperature increases because they are already warm enough at all times of the year, and are less able to import plant and animal genetic resources from other regions to replace existing plants and animals which cannot adjust to even higher temperatures. The main issues for these countries are human survival and economic development.

On the other hand, mid- and high-latitude countries such as the United States and Russia may gain in the early stages of global warming from longer growing seasons, and the opportunity to grow more heat-tolerant plants and crops. This advantage, however, may be negated by water supply problems in mid-latitudes, the spread of tropical pests and diseases, heat stress in summer, and other problems. And as warming continues, even mid-latitude countries may run out of options for heat-tolerance. High-latitude countries may also find with greater warming that gains turn to losses, due to the melting of permafrost, the death of many boreal forests, which may be burnt by wildfires along with peatlands, and increased flooding. There is also the possibility of sudden and irreversible effects causing marked regional climate changes and accelerated warming or sea-level rise. Key issues for these countries are equity and morality in the short term and guarding against harm to themselves in the long-term.

The second reason commonly advanced for an uneven distribution of impacts is the greater capacity of richer and more technologically advanced countries to adapt to climate change. This is because these countries can more readily afford the expense of investment in emergency preparedness, adaptations such as sea walls, plant breeding, and other research and development. Rich countries can also better afford to compensate losers within their own countries, with rehousing of displaced people, retraining and disaster relief.

In general, in today's climate, extreme climatic events such as floods, droughts and storm surges cause far more deaths in poor countries than in rich ones. This is because in rich countries the population is more likely to be warned of disasters, can be evacuated, fed and clothed, and has access to better health services. This ability to avoid casualties in rich countries is likely to continue as climate change hits home, although it may cost more.

Nevertheless, contrary to the emphasis on lives lost, damages in monetary terms from climatic disasters tend to be much higher, and to be increasing more rapidly, in rich countries than in poor ones. This is because there is much more financial investment in development, especially in disaster-prone coastal areas, in the rich countries, with a marked trend for populations to increase more rapidly in exposed areas. In this sense, rich countries are becoming less well adapted to climate change.

Overall, however, there is little doubt that global warming will increase the inequity between the rich developed countries and the poorer developing ones, with the poorer nations of Africa and the small island states especially vulnerable. Economic studies that have attempted to quantify the cost of climate change impacts by region have come up with estimates of percentage change in present GDP for modest warmings (1 to 2.5°C). They found around zero to a few per cent gains in Europe and North America, and losses of around four per cent in Africa. While these estimates have many shortcomings (see below), they suggest the idea. As warmings by 2100 are projected by the IPCC (2001) to be in the range of 1.4 to 5.8°C, and damages are expected to increase rapidly with greater warming, these estimates of uneven damages are a cause for concern.

> **Box 6: Impacts on food production**
>
> The impacts of climate change on food production, prices and numbers at risk of hunger depend on a number of factors. These include regional climate change, biological effects of increasing atmospheric carbon dioxide, changes in floods, droughts and other extreme events, existing agricultural systems, adaptive capacity, changes in population, economic growth and technological innovation. In a major international study, Martin Parry of the Jackson Environmental Institute, University of East Anglia and colleagues made preliminary estimates using the SRES family of scenarios of greenhouse gas emissions and socio-economic change.
>
> The study used a linked system of climate scenarios, agricultural models, and national, regional and global economic models. Adaptation was at the farm level, such as changes in planting dates, fertiliser applications and irrigation, and at the regional level via new cultivars and irrigation systems. Economic adjustments included changes in national and regional investment in agriculture, crop switching, and price responses.
>
> Results for all SRES scenarios showed small percentage gains (3 to 8%) in average crop yields in developed countries by 2080, but decreases in developing countries of -1 to -7%. This increased the inequity, measured by changes in yield, by between 7 and 10%. The authors state that 'While global production appears stable, regional differences in crop production are likely to grow stronger through time, leading to significant polarisation of effects, with substantial increases in prices and risk of hunger among the poorer nations, especially under scenarios of greater inequality (A1FI and A2).' Cereal price increases by 2080 under most scenarios were between 8 and 20%. Clearly, as the developed countries have a far smaller population than the developing countries, the majority of people will be worse off.
>
> Results are highly dependent on the benefits from increased CO_2 concentrations as measured in experiments, which are uncertain in the real world, and on effects of pests and diseases, which have not been estimated. It should be noted that these results are for climate change scenarios simulated with only one climate model, that from the Hadley Centre in the UK. Other climate models would give different results. These results are broadly consistent with the conclusions of the IPCC (2001).

Uppermost in many people's minds is the moral concern over increased inequity. This is given strong emphasis in international bodies. However, inequity between countries is clearly not of great practical concern in many rich countries, if the evidence of small and declining aid programs from some rich countries is anything to go by. There are, however, other more practical reasons why growing inequity between nations should be of concern to the rich, and which should lead to a genuine commitment to reduce inequity, rather than lip service to the ideal (see Chapter 10).

Aggregate impacts

A number of studies have attempted to estimate the overall global cost of climate change impacts. These are beset by a number of problems that have only been partly overcome. Difficulties include:

- choosing appropriate measures of impacts, since many costs such as loss of species or lives cannot be put objectively in monetary terms;

- the need to overcome knowledge gaps and uncertainties to provide a complete picture, for instance in the understanding of the effects of changes in extreme events;

- forecasting changes in exposure to climate change, which is affected by economic growth and population change,

- anticipating adaptation given its dependence on wealth and technology;

- problems in aggregating across different countries with different standards of living; and

- allowing for the passage of time in monetary costing (the so-called 'discount rate' or value of future consumption relative to today's value).

Agricultural and coastal impacts have been fairly well quantified, as has health to some extent (although it is controversial). Estimates of the cost of the loss of species and ecosystems are very uncertain. More generally, different studies get different results. This is partly due to whether they factor in the effects of extreme events and possible disasters, and how optimistically they estimate the capacity to adapt. Cross-links between water resources and agriculture, and the costs of learning and delays in adaptation, have not been well taken into account. Costs associated with exceeding critical impact thresholds, which may cause rapid increases, are usually neglected, but may dominate costs at larger warmings. Effects of rates of climate change have not been included in most studies, although it is clear that costs will be greater for rapid rates of change because adaptation will be more difficult and costly. Costs of non-market impacts such as health or species loss are subjective and perhaps best expressed in non-monetary terms.

Overall, the IPCC 2001 report states that 'our confidence in numerical results from aggregate studies remains low', and they 'may underestimate the true cost of climate change'. IPCC 2001c discusses costing methodologies but mainly in relation to costing reductions in greenhouse gas emissions.

Results to date suggest that the majority of people may be negatively affected at average global warmings of 1 to 2°C, although the net aggregate monetary impact may be slightly positive due to the dominance of rich countries in monetary terms. At higher levels of warming, estimated monetary impacts generally become negative, and studies allowing for disastrous possibilities can reach high negative outcomes, such as about 10% loss of world GDP for 6ºC warming in studies by the American economist William Nordhaus. Estimates of aggregate costs will only be realistic when more is known about the potential for future large-scale discontinuities in the climate system.

Waking the 'sleeping giants'

As discussed in Chapter 5, projected climate changes during the present century and beyond have the potential to initiate future large-scale and possibly irreversible changes in various Earth systems, resulting in impacts at continental or global scales. Fred Pearce in the *New Scientist* (12 February 2005) aptly referred to these possibilities as 'waking the sleeping giants'. They are suggested by some model simulations and by past historical and palaeo-records (see Chapter 2). Their likelihood within the next 100 years is in most cases considered to be low, although some scientists argue that more rapid changes are possible. In any case, gradual but ongoing climatic changes set in train in the next several decades may make some of these large-scale discontinuities inevitable in the following centuries as thresholds for discontinuities are reached, with possibly huge impacts on natural and human systems.

Some of these possibilities have been identified in the previous chapter (see **Table 5**). The risk of such events is at present poorly quantified, both as to their likelihood in this or later centuries and the magnitude of their impacts on natural and human systems. In view of the plausibility of very large impacts, the mechanisms and preconditions for such events should be intensively studied, both via computer modelling, and by close study of analogous past historical and paleo-events. Modelling and paleo-analysis must extend not only to the basic physical events but also to their global and regional impacts including changes in rainfall, aridity, flooding, and impacts on ecosystems and cropping potential. Studies of past episodes of rapid climate change such as the Younger Dryas event deserve special attention, with a focus not only on mechanisms but also on regional impacts. Attention should also be paid to records and modelling of more regional non-linearities and discontinuities. There is much evidence to suggest that past climatic fluctuations have not been smooth, but rather have often involved rapid changes from one circulation regime to another.

Some scientists who are familiar with these past large variations in climate, react by saying that if such changes happened before due to natural causes and life survived, what is there to worry about now? However, human populations at the time of the last deglaciation were relatively small, and people could migrate more or less freely to more suitable regions. That would be very difficult now, with more than six billion people, national borders and immigration restrictions.

Thus, despite the fact that the potential human consequences of each of these possible large-scale discontinuities have not been fully explored, it is worth looking briefly at the scope of the possible impacts.

Effects of a breakdown in the ocean circulation

Slow-down or cessation of the convective overturning in the North Atlantic (see Chapter 5) and around Antarctica would cause regional cooling, as well as connected changes elsewhere in the world. This overturning powers what has been described as the oceanic 'conveyor belt', which redistributes heat around the globe. North of 24°N the Gulf Stream presently conveys roughly a million gigawatts of energy northwards from the tropics, warming much of Europe by 5–10°C. Without deep-water formation, the Gulf Stream runs further south without releasing so much heat.

Partial or slow reductions in the North Atlantic overturning would lead to only small relative cooling in the Western European region, and this is likely also in parts of North America, as polewards heat transport is reduced. If this happens slowly, it could be outweighed by general global warming, such that temperatures in Western Europe and parts of North America would not fall below the present. However, altered temperature differences with neighbouring regions would lead to changes in storm tracks, variability and severe weather events. The impacts of such events have not yet been quantified.

A study by Michael Vellinga and Richard Wood with the UK Hadley Centre climate model suggests that weakening of the overturning in the North Atlantic may also lead to large shifts in precipitation in the tropics due to shifts in the thermal equator. Using an ecosystem model, they find that weakening of the oceanic circulation causes worldwide changes in ecosystem structure and function, including expansions of desert in the north of South America, West Africa and Australia, but reductions in desert in North America. These changes far from the North Atlantic are mainly due to precipitation changes, and have strong implications for food production. They are still quite uncertain, but point to wide implications, well beyond Western Europe.

If complete cessation of overturning were to happen this century, which is unlikely but not completely impossible, it might lead to colder temperatures in the North Atlantic region than at present, with greater warming elsewhere. A return to regionally cooler conditions in Europe and North America would have disastrous impacts on food production, health, economics and ecosystems. This could be worse than at the time of the Little Ice Age because of far larger human populations, and the greater inter-connectedness of global economies. Even if there were no direct climate change impacts elsewhere, if the economies of Europe and North America were to catch a cold, others would sneeze.

Most global climate models that have been run for such scenarios have only projected complete cessation of overturning for carbon dioxide concentrations exceeding twice pre-industrial levels, and at a point in time well beyond 2100, when the whole world would be considerably warmer than now. However, these computer simulations have not in general taken account of simultaneous forcing from decreased overturning around Antarctica, nor of accelerated melting of the Greenland ice sheet due to meltwater lubrication of outlet glaciers, as emphasised by James Hansen of NASA. Moreover, the models used have in general had insufficient detail (spatial resolution) to separately model the various small centres of action in the North Atlantic.

Modelling suggests that any such shutdown of the ocean circulation may be long-lasting relative to human lifetimes. Moreover, the paleo-climatic analogy of the Younger Dryas and similar events near the end of the last glaciation is only partial. At that time the Earth's orbital changes favoured a 'quick' recovery (which occurred after 1200 years), whereas there is no such force for recovery operating this time. We are thus not just talking about a short-term disaster from which the world might recover, but one that might last for millennia.

In a paper entitled *Abrupt Climate Change: Should We Be Worried?* Robert B. Gagosian, President and Director of the illustrious Woods Hole Oceanographic Institute in Massachusetts, USA, states that two scenarios are useful to contemplate.

Scenario 1: Conveyor slows down within next two decades. This could quickly and markedly cool the North Atlantic region, causing disruptions in global economic activity. These disruptions may be exacerbated because the climate changes occur in a direction opposite to what is commonly expected, and they occur at a pace that makes adaptation difficult.

Scenario 2: Conveyor slows down a century from now. In this case, cooling in the North Atlantic region may partially or totally offset the major effects of global warming in this region. Thus, the climate of the North Atlantic region may rapidly return to one that more resembles today's – even as other parts of the world, particularly less-developed regions, experience the unmitigated brunt of global warming. If the Conveyor subsequently turns up again, the 'deferred' warming may be delivered in a decade.

Clearly the consequences of either of Gagosian's scenarios are serious, although the first is the more alarming because of its rapid onset. The report to the US Pentagon by Peter Schwart and Doug Randall, widely reported in the media in 2004, seems to have taken the first scenario as its starting point, 'as an alternative to the scenarios of gradual climate warming that are so common'. While the resulting geo-political scenario has been widely criticised as sensationalist and even irresponsible, it seems to me that as a worst-case scenario it fulfils a purpose for the Pentagon, whose business is to plan for unlikely but not impossible scenarios. Schwart and Randall suggest that such an abrupt climate change scenario would lead to food shortages, decreased water supplies in key regions, and disruption to energy supplies, with likely downstream risks for US national security, including border management, global conflict and economic malaise. Given a major theme of this book is risk management in the face of possible climate change, such possibilities deserve some careful, albeit critical, attention.

A paper presented by Michael Schlesinger of the University of Illinois, and colleagues at a conference on 'Avoiding Dangerous Climate Change' in England in 2005, states, on the basis of their simplified climate and economic modelling, that in the absence of an emissions reduction policy, there is a 50% chance of a collapse of the North Atlantic circulation by 2205. Even with the implementation of an immediate carbon tax of US$100 per tonne of carbon, to reduce emissions, they calculate that the chance may still exceed 25%.

The effects of a slowdown or cessation of Antarctic deep-water formation have been investigated by Australian oceanographers Richard Matear and Tony Hirst. Using a simulation up to 2100, and later multi-century climate change simulations from the CSIRO climate model, they projected the impact on marine biogeochemical cycles. The key results were:

- reductions in the global oceanic uptake of carbon dioxide by about 14% by 2100;

- reductions in dissolved oxygen levels in the ocean interior over several centuries, causing expansion of an anoxic region in the mid-water of the eastern equatorial Pacific; and

- reductions in nutrient concentrations in the upper ocean, causing an expansion of regions that are nutrient limited and reducing biological production in the upper ocean, thus affecting fisheries.

Rapid sea-level rise from melting ice sheets

The ideas discussed in Chapter 5 regarding possible rapid melting of the Greenland and West Antarctic ice sheets suggest an outside chance that sea-level rise may be more rapid than suggested by the IPCC 2001 range of 9 to 88 centimetres by 2100. Even in 2001, IPCC noted an estimated 5% chance of rises greater than that. The growing evidence that surface meltwater penetration through crevices in outlet glaciers leads to lubrication and acceleration of outflow, suggests that more rapid outflow and melting is possible. Moreover, if more rapid outflow were to happen on Greenland, a lowering of the altitude of the Greenland ice sheet would lead to less snow accumulation and more lubrication of the outflow, further accelerating the process.

While the time scale for complete disintegration of Greenland and the West Antarctic ice sheets under these faster scenarios is still uncertain, the above ideas suggest that sea-level rises of the order of a metre in the twenty-first century, and several metres in the following centuries are possible. Only the broadest of estimates have been made of what impacts such large sea-level rises would have economically and on the numbers of people displaced. Martin Parry of the Jackson Environmental Institute, University of East Anglia, and others estimate that for the more modest sea-level rises expected by 2100 under the IPCC 2001 report scenarios, 50 to 100 million people may be subject to coastal flooding. Such estimates depend greatly on what assumptions are made about population growth in the coastal zone, and the affordability and effectiveness of adaptation measures such as sea walls. For the faster sea-level rise scenarios, the number affected by 2100 could be twice as large, and of course ongoing sea-level rise in the following century would at least double it again.

Apart from the huge economic costs of such coastal flooding, accommodating the huge numbers of people forced to leave the present coastal zones would be a major social and political issue. The internal disruption in many populous developing countries such as China, Indonesia, Bangladesh, Egypt and Nigeria would be enormous, with the likelihood of internal conflicts, poverty and disease. A number of low-lying island countries may be made uninhabitable, forcing migration, loss of national sovereignty and cultural identity and bringing demands for compensation. Cross-border migrations would be an issue in many regions.

Even in developed countries, the cost and loss of amenity from sea walls and other defences, and accommodating and compensating people displaced from the coastal zones and cities would cause enormous economic and social strain. Large regions that are low-lying and in some cases already subsiding will be threatened, for example eastern parts of England, the Low Countries of Western Europe, Venice and other parts of the Adriatic coast, Florida, parts of the Gulf Coast, the Chesapeake Bay region and much of the Atlantic coast in the US, and parts of coastal cities in Australia. Loss of coastal wetland habitats would be sweeping, and many coastal coral reefs such as the Great Barrier Reef in Australia would be effectively drowned, exposing coasts to full wave energy, enhanced erosion and storm surges. Many local thresholds for impacts would be exceeded, as natural barriers and sea walls would be progressively overtopped.

At what level of global warming these rapid melting and ice sheet disintegration processes will get underway is not clear, but once started they are likely to be unstoppable. Rapid sea-level rise could continue until both Greenland and the WAIS are completely melted, leaving the world with a sea-level rise of up to 12 metres lasting for millennia. This would be quite a legacy for our descendents.

Runaway carbon dynamics

As discussed in Chapter 5, runaway carbon dynamics (rapid increases in carbon dioxide concentrations in the atmosphere due to positive feedbacks) would lead to an acceleration in global warming. It includes the likely reversal of the land-based carbon sinks in the plants and soil, which today absorb carbon from the atmosphere, especially due to increasing plant growth caused by the fertilising effect of higher concentrations of carbon dioxide in the atmosphere.

Other contributors to an acceleration in global warming include more frequent forest fires, the thawing of permafrost (which allows the decay of peat stored in the Arctic tundra) and the release of methane stored in ice-like hydrate crystals on the ocean floor (see Chapter 5).

These effects add up to a more rapid increase in greenhouse gas concentration in the atmosphere, adding to the enhanced greenhouse effect, accelerating the global warming and leading to a greater and more rapid onset of all climate impacts. Exactly how rapid this process will be, and how far it will go is not yet understood, but once it gets under way it may be difficult to stop.

Stabilisation of greenhouse gas concentrations

All the five 'reasons for concern' about global warming increase in severity with the amount of warming. The big question for climate change policy is at what degree of warming does this become unacceptable, and therefore what concentration of greenhouse gases in the atmosphere should be considered the upper limit? This will determine what emissions reduction strategies must be put into place.

The IPCC did make some preliminary comments in 2001 on the effects of emissions reduction actions and stabilisation of atmospheric concentrations of greenhouse gases. These can be summarised as follows:

- The projected rate and magnitude of warming and sea-level rise can be lessened by reducing greenhouse gas emissions.

- The earlier and greater the emissions reductions, the smaller and slower the projected warming and sea-level rise would be.

- There remains a range of uncertainty in the amount of warming that would result from any particular stabilised greenhouse gas concentration. The ranges are given in **Table 3**, for stabilisation at concentrations of carbon dioxide equivalent of 450 to 1000 parts per million (ppm).

- Emission reductions that would eventually stabilise carbon dioxide concentrations at a level below 1000 ppm would limit global warming to 3.5°C or less at the year 2100 (assuming the then accepted IPCC range of climate sensitivities), but warming would continue to a possible high of 8.7°C at stabilisation, several centuries later.

- Sea level and ice sheets would continue to respond to warming for many centuries after greenhouse gases have been stabilised.

- Reducing emissions of greenhouse gases to stabilise their concentrations would delay and reduce damages caused by climate change.

- Mitigation actions to stabilise atmospheric greenhouse gases at lower concentrations would generate greater benefits in terms of less damage. This includes keeping below critical thresholds for various biophysical systems and possible major changes to the climate system.

- Comprehensive quantitative estimates of the benefits of stabilisation at various levels of greenhouse gas concentrations do not yet exist.

Other key points to note include:

- Stabilisation of concentrations of greenhouse gases will take a century or more, and stabilisation of warming, and especially of sea-level rise and ice sheet melting, will take many centuries.

- Any policy on reducing greenhouse gas emissions needs to take account of potential impacts and the benefits of avoiding them, centuries into the future. This is especially the case since potential impacts at high warmings could well be catastrophic rather than marginal, and therefore should not be discounted as is commonly done for marginal costs.

- Time lags in the climate system mean that early action to reduce emissions may reap larger benefits than delayed action to achieve the same eventual level of greenhouse gas concentrations.

- The wide range of uncertainty as to eventual warmings at stabilisation at any particular concentration of greenhouse gases means that policy should be based on the risk of exceeding a chosen threshold or level of damages, rather than on any one critical concentration.

- Recent probabilistic estimates of the climate sensitivity suggest that greater warmings may occur with given greenhouse gas concentrations, putting a premium on lower stabilisation targets.

A study published in 2002 by a consortium of UK scientists provides a concrete illustration of these general findings. The study reported on an assessment of the global scale implications of the stabilisation of atmospheric carbon dioxide at 750 ppm (by 2250), and 550 ppm (by 2150). Simulated climate changes, obtained using the Hadley Centre climate model were applied in single impact models for each of six sectors, namely natural vegetation, water resources, coastal flood risk, wetland loss, crop yield and related food security, and malaria. The study used a

Table 7: Effects of stabilisation in UK global study

Impacts	Unmitigated emissions	Stabilisation at 750 ppm (by 2250)	Stabilisation at 550 ppm (by 2150)
Delay in warming by 2050 relative to unmitigated case	–	50 years	100 years
Loss of tropical rain-forests and grasslands	2050s	2100	no loss
Change of biosphere from carbon sink to carbon source	2050s	2170s	equilibrium by 2170 (neither sink nor source)
People flooded in storm surges in 2080	94 million	35 million	18 million
Loss of coastal wetlands by 2080	12%	8%	6%
People exposed to water stress in 2080	2.8 to 3.4 billion	2.9 billion	0.7 billion
Change in population at risk of falciparum malaria in 2080	257 to 323 million	174 million	253 million
Change in population at risk of hunger in 2080	69 to 91 million	16 million	43 million

single set of population and socio-economic scenarios about the future similar to those in the old IS92a emissions scenario. Results are shown in **Table 7**.

There are important caveats in the UK study. Particular concerns include the use of: only one climate model; only single simulations of each of the stabilisation scenario climates; only one socio-economic future scenario; and considering only changes in average climate not changes in extremes. Changes in precipitation, which has large decade-to-decade variability in reality and in climate models, are particularly uncertain. This may explain peculiar results for malaria exposure and people at risk of hunger, as these are especially dependent on precipitation estimates.

The authors of the UK study concluded 'While this study shows that mitigation avoids many impacts, particularly in the longer-term (beyond the 2080s), stabilisation at 550 ppm appears to be necessary to avoid or significantly reduce most of the projected impacts in the unmitigated case.'

A further development of the UK study examined the effects of the different underlying socio-economic scenarios, which were used in generating the SRES emissions scenarios, on vulnerability and resilience to climate change. More detail is also available on estimated regional differences in effects. What emerges from these new studies is that the differences in vulnerability and adaptive capacity due to differing development pathways are in some cases more important than climate change in determining the scale and regional distribution of global and regional impacts. Thus climate change and development are intricately linked, not only in how development determines the human influence on climate change, but also in how it affects society's ability to cope with climate change. We will return to these links in Chapter 9.

Growing reasons for concern

Despite acknowledged uncertainties, it is clear from this review of the potential impacts of climate change that there are substantial reasons for concern, which increase with global warming. Risks to unique and threatened systems and from extreme climate events are expected to increase. Global aggregate impacts are expected to turn negative at around 2 to 3°C warming, while impacts will hit hardest at poorer countries, thereby increasing international inequity.

Moreover, there is growing concern that the risk of substantial and potentially catastrophic changes in the climate system, which may be unstoppable once they commence, will rise greatly for larger warmings. This may well dominate any risk assessment, and set relatively low limits for increased concentrations of greenhouse gases if such potentially dangerous changes are to be avoided. Warmings of only about 2 to 3°C may set such largely irreversible changes to the climate system in motion, and this may not become apparent until it is too late to avoid the consequences.

We may be able to adapt to small changes in climate, but in some cases this may be costly or have unwelcome side effects. We examine the capacity to adapt in Chapter 7, and the costs and benefits of reducing the rate and magnitude of climate change in Chapter 8. The message for now is that the projected climate changes are large enough and rapid enough to cause some pretty big problems which we need to take very seriously indeed.

7

Adaptation: living with climate change

One thing we must be aware of is that even if the Kyoto Protocol is implemented in full, the emission of greenhouse gases will result in our having to contend with the effects of climate change for decades to come in the form of more frequent and more intensive natural catastrophes.

Munich Reinsurance Group, *Annual Review: Natural Catastrophes 2001,* **2002.**

To a nation such as Bangladesh, adaptation is an option not by choice, but by compulsion, as insurance to its efforts in achieving sustainable development. Even with the envisaged mitigation as under the Kyoto Protocol, adaptation would be necessary because of the impending effects of the already accumulated greenhouse gases in the atmosphere.

Saleemul Huq, Chairman of the Bangladesh Centre for Advanced Studies and Mizan Khan, North South University, Dhaka, Bangladesh.

Adaptation concepts and strategies

Adaptation is an automatic or planned response to change that minimises the adverse effects and maximises any benefits. It is one of the two possible means of coping with human-induced climate change and sea-level rise. The other option is to reduce the magnitude of human-induced climate change by reducing greenhouse gas emissions. This is called mitigation and is discussed in the next chapter. Adaptation is essential to cope with the climate change and sea-level rise that we cannot avoid now and in the near future, while mitigation would limit the extent of future climate change.

Adaptation is necessary because climate change is already happening, and the long lag times in the climate system make further climate change, and especially sea-level rise, inevitable. This further climate change is already built in to the system by past greenhouse gas emissions, that is, we are already committed to it. The effect happens decades to centuries after the cause and cannot readily be stopped. Further change is also made inevitable by the long time, at least several decades, between *deciding* to reduce emissions, and the socio-economic system changing enough to *actually* reduce greenhouse gas emissions sufficiently to stop making the situation worse.

Very substantial reductions in greenhouse gas emissions will be necessary before greenhouse gas concentrations stop going up. In fact, for centuries to come atmospheric carbon dioxide concentrations will not fall much below whatever maximum levels are reached, even after major reductions in emissions. This is due to the large reservoirs of carbon dioxide in the ocean, soil and biosphere, which are in decadal time-scale equilibrium with the atmosphere. The permanent sinks are much slower to act. In short, we cannot simply turn off climate change, so we must learn to live with it. That is why adaptation is essential.

Because there are uncertainties about future amounts and effects of climate change and sea-level rise, adaptation must be a risk management strategy, which takes account of the probabilities as well as of the costs and benefits. Moreover, adaptation has limits, beyond which it is too expensive or even unacceptable in terms of the changes it requires. For example, one adaptation to increasing flooding due to sea-level rise in low-lying island countries would be to emigrate, but that may be unacceptable for the people who would have to leave their homelands, and may not be welcomed as a solution by potential host countries.

If our ability to adapt reaches its limits we have an unacceptable or damaging situation that, at least at the local level, could be considered 'dangerous'. That can only be avoided if we can reduce the level of climate change so as to stay within the limits of adaptability. In the broadest global terms, our ability to adapt is what must determine the targets we set for reducing greenhouse gas emissions, that is, mitigation policies should aim to avoid situations where we exceed the limits of adaptability. For this reason, understanding adaptability is vital, not only so that people can adapt where possible, but also to determine how urgently, and by how much we must reduce global greenhouse gas emissions.

Methods of adaptation will vary with the activity or industry, with location, and on different scales in time and space. Generally local farmers, for instance, will adapt on a year-to-year basis to drier or warmer conditions by varying planting dates, crop varieties or irrigation use. But at the district, state or national level longer term planning may be necessary to breed better-adapted crop varieties, conserve water, or develop more irrigation supplies. If the worst happens, governments may have to aid farmers, or even assist them to leave the industry if it is becoming unsupportable.

It is argued by some that the best way to ensure adaptability is to increase resilience or the capacity to cope with natural year-to-year climate variability such as flood or drought years. This is true up to a point, but as climate change increases it will lead to extremes that are outside the limits of natural variability. In such cases ordinary resilience based on past climate variability may not be enough. Moreover, increasing resilience to cope with even greater extremes will be uneconomic, or at least inefficient, unless guided by an understanding of the direction and magnitude of climate change. Increasing the capacity to cope with more tropical cyclones or hurricanes, for instance, does not make much sense if climate change is likely to lead to fewer tropical cyclones at that location. Thus, efficient adaptation strategies must be guided by an understanding of what to expect, that is, by informed foresight.

Foresight is also needed for adaptation because most adaptations cost money and thus require investment, and because they take time to put in place. For example, adaptation to more severe storms may require changes to building design or drainage systems, and these are best made in the design and construction phase of buildings or other investments, not as retrofits later when the need is urgent and the cost is greater.

A handbook on methods for climate change impacts assessment and adaptation strategies has been developed by the United Nations Environment Program which discusses the principles and strategies for adaptation. These can be summarised in eight alternative but not exclusive strategies:

1 *Bear losses*. This is the baseline response of 'doing nothing'. Bearing loss occurs when those affected have failed to act until it is too late, or have no capacity to respond in any other way (for example, in extremely poor communities) or where the costs of adaptation measures are considered to be high in relation to the risk or the expected damages. The big problem with this solution is that losses may become unbearable.

2 *Share losses*. This involves a wider community in sharing the losses. Sharing takes place in traditional societies and in the most complex, high-tech societies. In traditional societies, mechanisms include sharing losses with extended families, villages or similar small-scale communities. In societies organised on a larger-scale losses are shared through emergency relief, rehabilitation, and reconstruction paid for by government funds or public appeals, or through private insurance. However, insurance usually applies only when the risk is considered random and uncertain for the individual insured, not when it is predictable. Even with shared losses, the accumulated loss to society may eventually become unacceptable, at which point other actions must be taken.

3 *Modify the threat.* For some risks, it is possible to exercise a degree of control over the specific environmental threat. For 'natural' events such as a flood or drought, possible measures include flood control works (dams, dikes, levees) or water storages. For climate change, the major modification possible to reduce the threat is to slow the rate of climate change by reducing greenhouse gas emissions and eventually stabilising greenhouse concentrations in the atmosphere. (Note, however, that in Intergovernmental Panel on Climate Change (IPCC) terminology, measures that reduce climate change are referred to as 'mitigation' of climate change, in distinction to 'adaptation', which is reserved for an optimal response to a given climate change.)

4 *Prevent effects.* A frequently used set of adaptation measures involves steps to prevent the effects of climate change and variability. Examples for agriculture would be changes in crop management practices such as increased irrigation, additional fertiliser, and pest and disease control.

5 *Change use.* Where the threat or reality of climate change makes the continuation of an economic activity impossible or extremely risky, consideration can be given to changing the use. For example, a farmer may choose to switch to crop varieties more adapted to lower soil moisture. Similarly, agricultural land may be returned to pasture or forest, or other uses may be found such as recreation, tourism, wildlife refuges, or national parks.

6 *Change location.* A more extreme response is to change the location of economic activities. For example, major crops and farming regions could be relocated away from areas of increased aridity and heat to areas that are currently cooler and which may become more attractive for some crops in the future. This may be possible in some countries, but not in others where migration to cities or other countries may be the only alternatives.

7 *Research.* Possibilities for adaptation can also be opened up by research into new technologies and methods of adaptation, such as greater water use efficiency, cheap water desalinisation, or new crop cultivars.

8 *Educate, inform, and encourage behavioural change.* Dissemination of knowledge through education and public information campaigns can lead to adaptive behavioural change. Such activities have been little recognised and given little priority in the past, but are likely to assume increased importance as the need to involve more communities, sectors, and regions in adaptation becomes apparent. Water conservation and fire prevention campaigns and regulations are already major adaptive trends in countries such as Australia.

There are many examples of adaptation strategies and choices. Some examples are given below. **Figure 19**, adapted from a study of the threat of climate

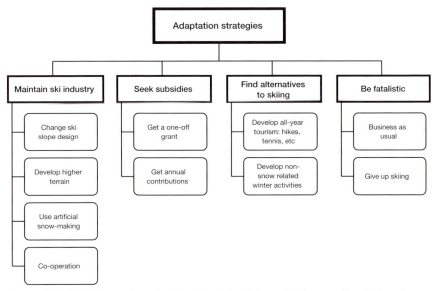

Figure 19: Adaptation options for the ski industry. Schematic showing the choice of adaptive strategies for a ski industry faced with the threat of global warming. The choice that is actually made will depend on the resort location and features, nature of competing tourist resorts, rate of warming and the views and preferences of stakeholders, including skiers, staff and resort owners. Cost and return on investments will be a major factor, and environmental considerations such as water supplies for artificial snow-making, power usage and visual impact will also be important.

change to tourism in the European Alps, illustrates many of the above points. A similar schematic diagram could be drawn up for most sectors and activities.

Costs and benefits of adaptation

Let there be no mistake about it: adaptation to climate change will cost money, time, effort and changes to how and why we do things. Adaptation will usually require planning and investment in new techniques, new infrastructure and/or new habits and lifestyles. These responses will have their advantages, or else we would not do them, but these advantages must be weighed against the costs of adaptation. Adaptation can have side benefits. It may also cause problems that lead to negative effects on other people or activities.

Examples are not hard to find. Take adaptation to sea-level rise and coastal flooding from increased storm surges. The IPCC projections for global average sea-level rise are 9 to 88 centimetres by 2100 but even if greenhouse gas emissions are stabilised, sea-level rise will continue at about the same rate for hundreds of years due to the large lag in the warming of the oceans. And we expect that the intensity of tropical cyclones will increase by about 10% for doubled carbon dioxide concentrations, likely in the latter half of the twenty-first century. So suppose you want to build a sea wall to protect a low-lying coastal city which is occasionally affected by storm surges from tropical cyclones. What height would you build it to, where would you build it, and who or what would you protect? Would you allow for protection only until 2050, or would you think it best to build it to last longer, say to provide protection until 2100? The latter would be cheaper in the long run, but more expensive now. Obviously this would cost millions of dollars, so who is to pay for it? Perhaps more importantly, will it have undesirable side effects? Well, probably. First, it would have to go along the beach, so it would stop the view of the ocean from the city streets. (You can see this now, for example in Mali, the island capital of the Maldives, and Apia, Samoa.) It might also lead to the disappearance of the beach, since as sea-level rises the beach line on a sandy beach would normally retreat inland. This would lead to destruction of the attractiveness of the beach to residents and tourists alike. In that case costly beach 'nourishment' would be needed (that is, dumping of more sand from somewhere else) to maintain the beach, and this might lead to erosion of nearby beaches beyond the ends of the wall. So there would most likely be ongoing costs, and disputes with neighbouring residents about loss of sand from their beaches.

Take another example. Climate change will likely increase the incidence of heavy rain events, interspersed with possibly more arid conditions reducing vegetation cover on land. This in turn may lead to increased soil erosion by wind and water. An obvious adaptation is planting more trees to hold the soil, reduce surface wind speeds, prevent erosion and provide shade for the animals. This could be done as extensive forestry plantations, or by more modest 'farm forestry' that is, rows or blocks of trees breaking up the wide-open landscape, but not completely replacing farming activities. Forest plantations have the added advantage of storing more carbon in the trees and soil, which would lead to financial gain in countries that engage in carbon emissions trading (where financial credit is gained for storing or reducing carbon emissions) under mitigation schemes such as those being implemented under the Kyoto Protocol.

In some situations planting more trees will also reduce dryland salinisation, which occurs in some countries due to rising water tables that bring salty groundwater near the surface, where the water evaporates and leaves the salt. However, there may be costly side effects as well, not the least of which is that trees use more water than grass so they may reduce runoff to the rivers, and thus water supply downstream.

Implementation

Adaptation can be purely reactive, autonomous or automatic in response to some perceived change in the climate. In natural systems this is the only type of adaptation, although humans can intervene to facilitate adaptation, in which case the systems become managed. For example, as climate changes natural species will die out in areas that become unsuitable, and may spread to other areas that become suitable. This is often a slow process, taking decades for seed to spread, germinate and grow into mature plants. Where there are obstacles, such as unsuitable soils or developed land, spread may be halted. Human intervention can facilitate and speed up such species migration by creating corridors, planting seeds or seedlings in new areas, or by eliminating competition from other species.

However, in the case of natural ecosystems, which consist of a mix of interdependent species of plants and animals, whole ecosystems may not be able to move due to different mixes of changed climatic conditions. Changed climates may become more suitable for some species from the existing ecosystem but not for others. For example, increasing temperature may favour some species moving in one direction, but decreasing rainfall may favour movement in another direction. In this case species will migrate in different directions, breaking up the former ecosystem, and perhaps losing some species altogether as species formerly dependent on each other become separated.

In many situations farmers already adapt to variations in seasons on a year-to-year basis, for instance by planting later in the season if it is unusually cold or dry, or applying irrigation in dry years. In particularly bad years farmers may plant smaller areas, or even not at all, thus saving on the cost of seed, labour and fuel. Such adaptations to natural variability reduce losses, but often mean that income is less than in a good year, and is only made up to a living in the long term by gains in good years. These forms of adaptation can be carried over into a situation of climate change without any conscious recognition that the climate is changing, but merely as a reaction to the current or recent past seasons.

However, where climate is changing, other longer-term adaptive strategies will be more appropriate, such as changes in crop cultivars or varieties, diversification, or even changing crops or activities altogether. To make these sorts of adaptations requires recognition of the problem, and foresight. It becomes crucial to look at alternative strategies for their cost and effectiveness, make choices, and make the necessary investments. This becomes active or planned adaptation.

Optimal adaptation strategies will only be adopted if there is a degree of foresight as to what is likely to happen and how it will affect people. Confidence is needed that the projected climate changes will occur, with understanding of possibilities and alternatives. Uncertainty can never be totally eliminated, so any strategy must contain an element of hedging one's bets, by doing something that will be beneficial even if climate change does not happen quite as expected. Diversification is such a strategy. Agreement will also be necessary that the cost/benefit ratio for action is favourable, and the necessary human, economic and technical capacity to act must exist. If these conditions are not met, adaptation will be less than optimal. The first task in seeking optimal adaptation strategies is to become better informed.

One example of successful adaptation, in the face of sudden climate change and great uncertainty, is that of the water supply authority for Perth in Western Australia (see **Box 7**). The best current explanation for the decrease in rainfall that occurred in the Perth catchments in the 1970s is that it was a combination of natural climate variability, the enhanced greenhouse effect and the effects of the depletion of ozone in the upper atmosphere. The circum-polar westerly winds have strengthened but moved further south, and the rain-bearing low-pressure systems have moved with them (see discussion in Chapter 1).

A key problem in assessing the likely success of an adaptation strategy is judging how well the process is likely to be put into practice. This requires an understanding of the problem, and a conviction that adaptation is necessary and worthwhile. As in the Western Australian rainfall case, early acceptance that there may be a long-term problem rather than a short-term fluctuation is critical if large investments are needed. This requires good scientific understanding, and is not helped by unfounded scepticism or contrarian advocacy that confuses decision-makers and delays action.

The degree and success of adaptation is a key factor in assessing likely climate change impacts. Early climate impact assessments often assumed that no adaptation occurred, thus exaggerating likely impacts. In the literature this is sometimes referred to as the 'dumb farmer' assumption. In some later impacts assessments the contrary assumption was made, that of perfect adaptation, or the 'prescient farmer' assumption. Obviously, the most likely situation lies somewhere in between, and will depend on effective provision of reliable information to the farmer, planner, industry or government agency. Well-targeted research, to address all relevant questions for the decision-maker in the local situation, is essential. Series of consultations or representation of interested parties on research and implementation panels is advisable, so that adaptation options are understood, relevant and supported by all parties.

Key points regarding early adaptation include the following:

- Adaptation can increase the robustness of infrastructure and capital investments to climatic stresses such as floods, storm surges, extreme temperatures and high winds.

- Immediate benefits can often be gained by stopping present maladaptive policies and practices (such as building on flood plains or too close to sandy beaches).

- Climate change cannot be totally avoided and may occur more rapidly than anticipated.

Box 7: Adaptation of water supply in WA

The south-west of Western Australia has already experienced the effects of climate change: in the 1970s a decrease in rainfall of roughly 10 to 20% resulted in a 40 to 50% reduction in inflow to the city of Perth's water supply; and this has not returned to previous levels in the last three decades (see **Figure 20**). As early as 1987, projections of climate change due to the enhanced greenhouse effect suggested that rainfall in the region would decline, although not appreciably until well into the twenty-first century.

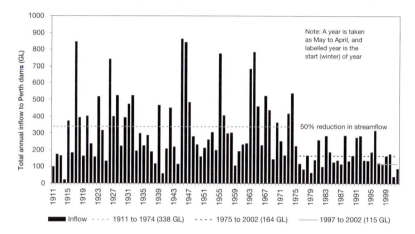

Note: A year is taken as May to April, and labelled year is the start (winter) of year

50% reduction in streamflow

Inflow · · · · 1911 to 1974 (338 GL) · · · · 1975 to 2002 (164 GL) ——— 1997 to 2002 (115 GL)

Figure 20: Annual streamflow into the water supply dams for Perth (Western Australia). Averages before and after the rainfall decrease of about 10–20% (depending on location) that occurred in 1974–75 are shown, and the even lower average from 1997 to 2002. The decrease in water supply was about 50%. (Figure courtesy of the Water Corporation, WA).

Following the recommendations of a review paper by Brian Sadler (now Chair of the Indian Ocean Climate Initiative) and others in 1987, the Water Authority of Western Australia adopted a strategy that effectively assumed that the rainfall and yield would continue its decline. In an initial adjustment, the water system yield was written down by some 13%. This led to earlier development of work on alternative future water sources and promotion of water conservation. Research was encouraged into the causes of the rainfall decline and decisions were to be reviewed periodically based on experience and advances in climate science.

As Brian Sadler stated in 2003 '[The 1987] decision by water managers was controversial at the time and remained so for many years. However, against what has transpired, a decline of some 50% in streamflow by 2002, not 2040, the decision was far from extreme.' It is a good example of what Sadler calls 'informed adaptation', which is subject to adjustment as new information comes to light.

Consistent with this approach, the Indian Ocean Climate Initiative (see: http://www.ioci.org.au/) was set up by the Western Australia

> **Box 7: Adaptation of water supply in WA (Continued)**
>
> government in 1998 to investigate the reasons for the decline, methods of seasonal forecasting in the region, and the possible future implications of the enhanced greenhouse effect. More recently, the Western Australia government has adopted a greenhouse strategy to both mitigate and adapt to climate change and, in response to a further decline in water supply, work was initiated in 2004 on a water desalinisation plant.

- Early adaptation is more effective and less costly than last minute, emergency measures and retrofitting.

- Climate change can bring opportunities as well as threats, so adaptation may be profitable.

- Planning for ongoing adjustments and reduced economic lifetimes for investments is prudent as climate changes.

- Resilience of natural systems can be enhanced by reducing other non-climatic stresses and barriers to adaptation (for example pollution of coral reefs, creating eco-corridors).

- Adaptation can be facilitated by improving societal awareness and preparedness, for example through education and setting up early warning systems and evacuation plans.

Effects of different rates of climatic change

Rapid climatic change allows less time to adapt than slow change of the same eventual magnitude, and may incur larger costs in terms of investment in new farming practices, rezoning and new design standards for engineered structures such as buildings, bridges, drains, dams and levees. Moreover, natural ecosystems have not only limited absolute ranges of adaptability, but also limited rates of adaptation. And human beings will find it psychologically and politically easier to respond appropriately to climatic change if it is slow and well established statistically, than if it is rapid but less clearly a part of some long-term change. For example, a short drying trend may be interpreted as a decadal-scale drought, for which normal drought assistance is appropriate, rather than part of a long-term trend requiring structural adjustments.

Nevertheless, few impact assessments have quantified the effects of rates of change as compared to the magnitude of change. Most have assumed that adaptation is to some new steady condition, or else occurs instantaneously. Time lags and transitional costs have seldom been considered. This is one major reason why the IPCC 2001 report, in its consideration of the five reasons for concern, used an essentially qualitative approach: there is simply not a sufficient body of evidence to assess the effects of different rates of change. What the IPCC report had to consider was whether rates of change within the projected range of 1.4 to 5.8°C per century, based on the *Special Report on Emissions Scenarios* (SRES), would substantially vary its conclusions. Clearly the more rapid rates would have greater effects, but the IPCC 2001 report considered that even the lowest estimated rate of change during this century would have serious effects increasing with time.

Rates of change of climate after stabilisation of greenhouse gas concentrations will in general be much slower, and may therefore be less difficult to adapt to (apart from the higher base temperature by then), although such a slowing is not expected to occur for sea-level rise for centuries to come.

Studies concerning the effects of rates of change on natural and human systems are essential to understand what faces us in the twenty-first century and beyond, especially if rapid changes occur beyond some threshold warming. Questions arising include: How quickly can societies adapt and change, and at what social and financial costs? What is necessary to motivate behavioural change, and how can this motivation be increased? How dependent is it on reducing uncertainties and on learning from recent experience? To what extent will people respond to theoretical projections rather than past experience? How can humans facilitate desirable adaptive change in erstwhile natural systems? So far, we cannot answer these questions.

Equity issues in adaptation

Adaptation raises serious questions about equity between countries and even within countries. This is mainly because adaptation is necessary for people or systems that are adversely affected by climate change, but not necessarily for the people or systems that have historically caused the problem. This is a major source of contention between some rich developed countries, whose historical emissions are the main cause of climate change up to now, and the poorer developing countries that will experience some major impacts in the twenty-first century. This issue is developed further in Chapter 10.

Equity is already an issue in some Pacific Island countries that are moving roads and buildings further inland to avoid damaging storm surges, which they attribute to sea-level rise and climate change. They say they are not responsible for climate change, but the rich countries are, so the rich countries should be paying the costs of adaptation. Indeed, the government of Tuvalu in 2001 asked Australia to consider taking migrants from their very low-lying atolls, where people are already feeling threatened by sea-level rise. So far Australia has refused to give such an undertaking, instead asking for more proof that climate change is responsible.

Rich developed countries in general have more capacity to adapt. This is because they can afford the expense of new systems to counter adverse impacts, they can replace old systems and infrastructure made unworkable by climate change, and they can compensate losers through disaster relief, internal migration, employment programs, retraining and so forth.

An anecdote from my experience at meetings of the IPCC may clarify the point. At one IPCC meeting the scientific authors were listening to the concerns with their draft report from government representatives. A delegate from Saudi Arabia questioned the statement that global warming would cause heat stress in dairy cattle, reducing milk production. He argued, with undoubted sincerity, that this is no problem since dairy cattle can be kept cool in air-conditioned sheds. Again, when mention was made of potential water shortages from increasing aridity in some countries, he argued that desalinisation plants could easily solve this problem. In both cases, this was true in his experience in Saudi Arabia, but such adaptations are too expensive for most countries in the developing world. Both points were retained in the report.

It is only when all countries are as rich as Saudi Arabia that such expensive and energy-intensive adaptations would be possible for all, and at the cost of a huge increase in energy demand and probably more greenhouse gas emissions.

The IPCC has identified a number of barriers to adaptation in many developing countries and some of the poorer members of the former Soviet Union (referred to as 'countries in transition'):

- Uncertain prices, lack of capital and credit.
- Weak institutional structures and institutional instability.
- Rigidity in land-use practices, and social conflicts.
- Poor access to modern technology.
- Lack of information and trained people.

Ironically, development in many poor countries has tended to reduce resilience to climate change. There has been an erosion of ancient principles of mutual support in local communities, and in some cases replacement of complex, multi-species mixed farms with more vulnerable monocultures. Population growth, deforestation and increasing use of marginal land also adds to vulnerability. There are also examples where replacement of traditional structures by modern ones has increased vulnerability. For example, traditional houses in Samoa were elliptical in shape with thatched roofs. These have been replaced by rectangular structures roofed with imported sheet iron. While thatched roofs were liable to blow away in tropical cyclones, they were easily replaced. Moreover, flying roofing iron is highly lethal and destructive of neighbouring structures. In addition, traditional house frames were stronger.

Poor developing countries tend to be located at low latitudes, where crops and natural ecosystems are already near the highest temperatures on Earth. There is therefore little prospect of importing, or even breeding, crops that can tolerate even higher temperatures, because the genetic material does not exist and would be difficult to engineer. Many of these countries are also subject to tropical cyclone and flood damage to a greater extent than temperate countries.

Benito Muller of the Oxford Institute for Energy Studies has summarised the problem clearly. (Note that he uses the common diplomatic language where 'North' refers to developed countries and 'South' to developing countries, which is inappropriate for countries such as China, Australia and New Zealand.)

> *A surprisingly clear North–South Divide exists in the views on what is the paramount climate change equity problem. In the Northern hemisphere, where the relevant discussion is spearheaded by non-government stakeholders (academic, NGO), it is regarded to be the issue of allocating emission mitigation targets; in the South, the concern – backed by many governments – is above all about the discrepancy between the responsibility for, and the sharing of climate impact burdens.*
>
> *… One of the root causes of this divide is a fundamental difference in the perception of climate change itself. In the industrialised North there is a widely held 'ecological view' of the problem. Climate change is perceived as a problem of polluting the environment, of degrading the eco-system. As such, its essence is seen to be that of a wrongful act against 'Nature.' Accordingly, environmental effectiveness – the capacity to 'make good' the human-inflicted harm on Nature – becomes a key criterion in assessments of climate change measures. The chief victim from this perspective is Nature, mankind's role is primarily that of culprit. And while climate impacts on human welfare are regarded as potentially life-style-threatening, they are taken to be self-inflicted and hence largely 'deserved.' Environmental integrity ('to do justice to Nature'), is the overriding moral objective. Issues of distributive justice are only of concern insofar as they could become obstacles in the pursuit of this paramount objective.*
>
> *The reality in the South is quite different: climate change has primarily come to be seen as a human welfare problem – not least because of the assessment work carried out by the Intergovernmental Panel on Climate Change (IPCC). The harm is against humans, it is largely other-inflicted, and it is not life-style, but life-threatening. In*

*short, the chief victim of climate change is not 'Nature', but people
and the paramount inequity is one between human victims and human
culprits. Climate change is a development problem, no doubt! But for
the developing world it is not a problem of sustainable development –
in the technical sense of 'learning to live within one's environmental
means' it is a problem of unsustainable development, in the non-
technical sense of failing to survive.*

This is not to say that developing countries are not concerned about limiting
greenhouse gas emissions, which they agree is necessary. It is merely to point
out that their first priority is the welfare of their people in the face of increasing
climatic disasters and the need for ongoing economic development. What these
poorer countries ask for, in return for limiting their greenhouse gas emissions, is
help in disaster management and relief, development aid, assistance with adaptation to climate change and access to new less carbon-intensive technology. At
the Earth summit in 1992, the developed countries committed themselves to
devoting 0.7% of GDP to international aid, as first proposed by the United
Nations back in 1970. However, up to 2004 only a handful of western European
countries have achieved this goal. The industrialised world currently gives about
0.22% of GDP, with the United States and Australia (who have not signed the
Kyoto Protocol) giving far less, especially when military aid is excluded.

Enhancing adaptive capacity

Ability to adapt depends on the state of development. Under-development limits
adaptive capacity because of a lack of resources to hedge against extreme but
expected events. Thus enhancing adaptive capacity requires similar actions as
promotion of sustainable development, including:

- Improved access to resources.
- Reduction of poverty.
- Reducing inequities in wealth and resources between groups.
- Improved information and education.
- Improved infrastructure (roads, railways, power supplies, etc.).
- Assurance that responses are comprehensive and inclusive of the people,
  not just technical.
- Active involvement of all parties to ensure that actions are related to
  local needs and resources.
- Improved institutional capacity and efficiency.

Adaptive capacity needs to be a major consideration in development, both in the lesser-developed countries and also in the developed countries, which are still subject to growth and change. This applies particularly to poor and remote communities within developed countries, such as indigenous peoples, and others particularly exposed to the impacts of climate change. All investments in growth and development need to take account of possible climate change and sea-level rise impacts and factor in ways to optimise the situation. Special attention needs to be paid to counter-adaptive trends such as population growth and building in flood plains, on low-lying coastal areas, on marginal lands, and on steep hillsides or regions potentially exposed to tropical cyclones.

Most capital investments in buildings and infrastructure have return periods or lifetimes of decades or more. Therefore they must be designed and located to take account of future changes in climate. If not, they will need to be written off and replaced before their design life is complete, with great economic cost.

There are many hundreds of specific potential adaptation actions for particular sectors and communities. **Table 8** summarises some of these in general

Table 8: Generalised examples of impacts and adaptations by sector

Sector	Potential impact	Potential adaptation	Comments
Hydrology and water resources	Increased floods and droughts Water deficit in some areas Saltwater intrusion in some island and coastal aquifers	Flood plain zoning, review levees and dam safety Management, pricing, conservation, recycling Desalinisation plant	Major dams and irrigation developments are possible, but ongoing climate changes may create problems
Land based ecosystems	Biodiversity loss in bounded areas including mountains Increased fire risk Weed invasion Salinisation	Landscape management, eco-corridors Fire protection Weed control Management	Increased management of 'natural' ecosystems, with some loss of natural state
Aquatic ecosystems	Salinisation of coastal aquifers and wetlands Low river flows Eutrophication	Barriers to saltwater intrusion (where possible) Changed water allocations Increase environmental flows, reduce nutrients	Impacts will compound problems from increased population and water demand
Coastal ecosystems	Coral bleaching More toxic algal blooms	Reduce other stresses, seed coral? Reduce nutrient inflows	Population growth and pollution are other vital factors

Table 8: Generalised examples of impacts and adaptations by sector (Continued)

Sector	Potential impact	Potential adaptation	Comments
Agriculture, grazing and forestry	Increased drought and fire risk Effects on global markets Spread of pests and diseases Increased soil erosion Initial benefit from increased CO_2 later offset by climate change	Management and policy changes, fire prevention, seasonal forecasts Market planning, niche crops, carbon trading Exclusion spraying Land management Plant breeding, changed farm practices, change crop or industry	Sustainability in question
Horticulture	Reduced winter chill for fruiting, pests and diseases	Change management, relocate, chemical sprays	Opportunities for tropical fruits
Fisheries	Changes recruitment, nutrient supplies	Research, monitoring, management	Not well understood
Settlements and industry	Increased extreme event hazards	Zoning, design standards, disaster planning	Coastal settlements worst hit
Electricity industry	Need increased peak capacity for air conditioning	Building design, shade, solar powered air conditioning	Efficiency also affected, trend to renewables
Tourism	Increased heat index Loss of some attractions for example, snow resorts, coral reefs, coastal wetlands	Cool tropical resorts, expand cooler resorts Alternative industries or relocate people	Losses and gains
Insurance	Increased exposure to natural hazards	Revised building codes, rate incentives, zoning, reduced cover	This is happening now
Human health	Expansion of range of vector-borne diseases	Quarantine, eradication, control, window screens, medication, repellents	Wealthy countries can cope, others may suffer

terms, and there is a comprehensive guide published by the United Nations Development Programme in 2005.

We have seen above that there are good reasons for adaptation to climate change, and many possibilities for improving adaptive capacity. There are some who argue that human inventiveness means that we can adapt to almost any climate change, and therefore do not need to reduce emissions. However, others argue that we can reduce greenhouse gas emissions very rapidly if only we have the will, and so do not need to adapt.

The fact is that both strategies are needed, and both require a good measure of technological innovation and resourcefulness. Indeed, it is interesting to reflect on the role of technology, and the common tendency to look for 'either/or' solutions to problems. The problem of coping with climate change is so complex, especially as it interacts with other environmental and socio-economic problems, that no single solution is sufficient. In particular, both adaptation and mitigation have essential roles to play.

8

Mitigation: limiting climate change

*There is no substitute for energy: the whole edifice of modern life is
built upon it. Although energy can be bought and sold like any other
commodity, it is not 'just another commodity', but the precondition of
all commodities, a basic factor equally with air, water and earth.*

E F Schumacher, *Energy International,* **September 1964.**

*... if energy is used in a way that saves money, the rate of burning
fossil fuels will not increase but decrease. This is because identical,
and even greatly increased, energy services can still be provided using
less total energy – but using it more productively – and also by
replacing most or all of the remaining fossil fuel supplies with
renewable sources.*

Amory Lovins and others, *Least-Cost Energy: Solving the CO$_2$ Problem,* **1981.**

Why mitigation is necessary

The projected climate changes in the twenty-first century are so large that, even
at the low end of the range of possibilities, impacts will require costly adaptations, and in some cases our capacity to adapt will not be enough to avoid serious damage to individuals and society. It will therefore be necessary to reduce
climate change by reducing nett greenhouse gas emissions to the atmosphere. In
the language used by the Intergovernmental Panel on Climate Change (IPCC)
and the United Nations Framework Convention on Climate Change (UNFCCC),
this is called 'mitigation'. The big questions are how much should emissions be
reduced, how can this be done, and what will it cost?

The interplay of adaptation and mitigation as policy responses to increasing
global warming is illustrated schematically in **Figure 21**. The black curves are
the upper and lower bounds of the potential warming up until 2100, according to

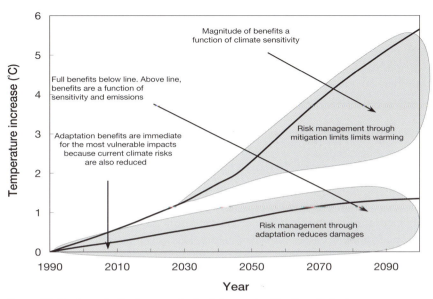

Figure 21: Regions of effectiveness of adaptation and mitigation strategies as responses to projected climate change in the twenty-first century.

the IPCC Third Assessment in 2001, using the *Special Report on Emission Scenarios* (SRES) highest and lowest plausible scenarios, respectively.

The figure indicates, in the lower shaded area, that adaptation is effective where climate change is small enough for adaptation strategies to significantly reduce damages and take advantage of any opportunities posed by global warming, without unacceptable monetary or other costs. Adaptation can produce immediate gains over inaction, particularly because it can improve societal responses to climatic extremes occurring now. It is also necessary to cope with global warming that is already inevitable due to past emissions, and which will become inevitable due to future emissions until they are reduced to levels leading to stabilisation of climate.

Mitigation, in contrast to adaptation, needs time to take effect due to the lags in the climate system and the time necessary to reduce emissions sufficiently to stabilise climate. The Figure shows how mitigation (upper shaded area) acts to reduce the upper bounds of projected warming, and thus to avoid the most extreme and damaging possibilities. Mitigation action taken now will have its most significant effects decades into the future, but is necessary to limit climate change to that which can be adapted to.

If we take as our working definition of 'dangerous climate change' a change that exceeds the limits of acceptable adaptation strategies, and thus incurs unacceptable costs and damages, what we see in the diagram is that this will occur if the two regions of effectiveness of climate response strategies (the shaded areas) do not overlap. That is to say, a dangerous situation will arise if mitigation is too small or too slow to avoid global warming exceeding that for which adaptation strategies can work. If the two areas of policy response overlap we will be OK, but if they do not, we are in trouble.

How much mitigation is needed?

The percentage reduction needed in greenhouse gas emissions to avoid dangerous changes to the Earth's climate is large, around 60–80% by 2100, but uncertain. Stabilising the Earth's climate requires total emissions at some time in the future to be less than or equal to the total removal of greenhouse gases from the combined atmosphere–shallow oceans–land–soil biota system. Removal can occur by natural processes or it can be artificially accelerated. This is illustrated schematically in **Figure 22**.

Here the broad upward arrow represents emissions from the burning of fossil fuels while the solid downward arrow denotes the natural long-term removal of carbon from the combined carbon reservoirs of the atmosphere–shallow ocean–land–soil biota, which are in equilibrium over a matter of a year or so (indicated by the double-headed arrows). To stabilise greenhouse gas concentrations in the atmosphere the alternatives are either to reduce emissions by limiting the consumption of fossil fuels by such measures as energy efficiency or substitution of renewable energy, or to remove and sequester the carbon dioxide from the use of fossil fuels in additional biomass and soil storage (increased 'carbon sinks'), in geological formations or into the deep ocean (dotted arrows). The last might be accomplished in one of two ways, either directly by pumping carbon dioxide into the deep ocean, or via increased biological activity stimulated artificially in the shallow ocean. Increasing carbon sinks effectively tilts the balance between the atmosphere and land/soil biota (the centre vertical 'CO_2 exchange' arrow). The feasibility, risks and costs of these methods of sequestration are being debated (see below).

The precise reduction in emissions needed depends on what is the upper limit to concentrations of greenhouse gases that will avoid dangerous climate change, taking account of possible abrupt and irreversible changes in the climate system as well as gradual climate change. It also depends on how rapidly we need to achieve stabilisation to avoid excessive sea-level rise over centuries to come, and to avoid rates of warming that might lead to abrupt changes. The longer emission reductions are delayed the faster they will need to be reduced later to reach the same stabilised atmospheric concentration of greenhouse gases.

However, there are two major uncertainties in deciding what concentration of greenhouse gases is a suitable target to aim for. The first is uncertainty regard-

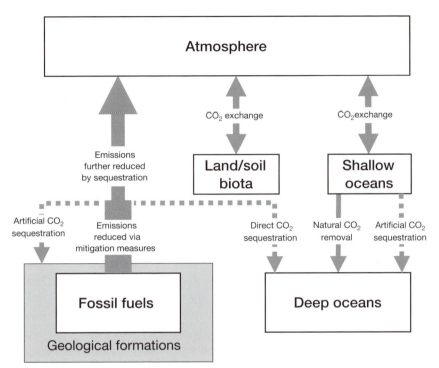

Figure 22: Broad types of mitigation options. In this schematic, mitigation options include: reducing fossil fuel emissions (upwards arrow) through energy conservation and efficiency and use of renewable energy; artificial sequestration of carbon into geological structures (left dotted arrow), or into the deep oceans (right dotted arrow) via fertilisation of plankton; and direct sequestration by pumping of carbon dioxide into the deep ocean (centre dotted arrow).

ing how sensitive the global climate is to various increases in greenhouse gases. According to the IPCC in 2001, this uncertainty is large – a doubling of atmospheric carbon dioxide could cause an eventual increase in global average temperature ranging anywhere from 1.5 to 4.5°C. However an estimate in 2004 by UK scientists James Murphy and others puts the 95% confidence range as 2.4 to 5.4°C, that is, there is only a 1 in 20 chance of being above or below this range. A follow-up study by David Stainforth of Oxford University and others found a range from 1.9 to 11.5°C, with a 4.2% chance of being greater than 8°C. Thus there now appears to be only a small chance of a climate sensitivity as low as 1.5°C, and a considerable chance that it may be well above 4.5°C. This makes it far more likely that temperatures will reach dangerous levels, and will require lower limits of stabilised greenhouse gas concentrations to avoid such risks.

The second major uncertainty in deciding on a target concentration of greenhouse gases is in determining what is a 'dangerous' level of global warming. As we have seen in Chapter 6, there are many different impacts of global warming on different sectors of society, and in different regions of the globe. Thus what may be 'dangerous' in one locality or to one entity (industry, group, activity or species) may not be dangerous somewhere else or to another entity.

In a global sense any decision as to what is a dangerous level will require consideration of a range of effects at any particular concentration, and competing interests and claims for relief or justice. Since different groups or countries will experience different impacts of climate change, defining a dangerous level of climate change becomes a value-laden moral and political process, not a scientific one. Economic assessments are not enough since climate change will have value-laden impacts not readily expressed in monetary terms, such as species extinctions or loss of cultural property and values (for example, loss of homelands and independence in the case of some low-lying island nations).

Despite these difficulties, there seems to be wide agreement, at least among the non-governmental environmental organisations, and some governments, especially those in the European Union, that global average warmings of around 2 or 3°C may be considered 'dangerous' in the terms of the UNFCCC. Such a level of warming is likely to lead to mass coral bleaching and the death of many coral reefs, and to the flooding of many low-lying islands and coasts.

Even if it becomes a firm political consensus, the problem with using such a level of warming to determine targets is that it still does not relate uniquely to a particular concentration of greenhouse gases because of the large uncertainty about climate sensitivity to greenhouse gases. Instead, any particular level of greenhouse gas concentration will lead to a range of possible global warmings, with a most probable warming but also a probability of warmings that are higher or lower than this central estimate. Indeed, we have already seen this to be the case in Chapter 5, where **Table 3** gives estimated ranges of warmings for each of a number of different scenarios of increases in greenhouse gases.

Referring to **Table 3**, we see that if dangerous climate change is thought to occur for warmings of 2 to 3°C, then each of the 'WRE stabilisation scenarios' leads to a range of warmings at 2100 that overlaps to some extent with the dangerous range; when equilibrium warmings are reached some hundreds of years later the overlap is more serious. Thus, stabilising equivalent carbon dioxide concentrations at 1000 ppm (as in the WRE 1000 scenario) leads to estimated warmings of 2.0 to 3.5°C by 2100 and, by the time climate has stabilised, to warmings of 3.5 to 8.7°C. So 1000 parts per million (ppm) is a concentration that is very likely to cause dangerous impacts. If the above judgement about what is globally dangerous is correct, 1000 ppm is too high. Note also that the ranges of warmings in **Table 3** are based on the IPCC assumed range of climate sensitivities, of 1.5 to 4.5°C for a doubling of carbon dioxide.

According to **Table 3**, stabilising according to the WRE 450 scenario, that is, at a concentration of 450 ppm, leads to a warming of only some 1.5 to 2.3°C by

2100, which barely overlaps with what is considered dangerous. However, by the time of a stabilised climate several centuries later, warming will have reached 1.5 to 3.9°C and completely overlaps with what is thought to be dangerous. This suggests that aiming to initially stabilise equivalent carbon dioxide concentration at 450 ppm leads to only a small risk of dangerous impacts by 2100, but leaving the concentration at 450 ppm for centuries thereafter would lead to dangerous consequences for future generations. Fortunately, it might be possible in the centuries after 2100 to further reduce the greenhouse gas concentrations by artificial sequestration of carbon dioxide so as to avoid at least some of the later dangerous consequences.

It would seem then that *if* it is possible to achieve an initial stabilisation of equivalent greenhouse gas concentration at 450 ppm, and reduce this further after 2100, we may well avoid dangerous global climate impacts, but it is not certain. There are three important provisos to add here:

1 Stabilised greenhouse gas concentrations can be reached by various pathways. These may result in slightly different impacts in the centuries before climate stabilises, and in different mitigation costs, but we will not go into that level of detail here.

2 As discussed in Chapters 5 and 6, we do not yet fully understand the likelihood or impacts of sudden or abrupt changes to the climate system (such as cessation of the North Atlantic deepwater formation). We do not know at what level or rate of warming such potentially catastrophic events may occur. If these were to occur for warmings of only 2–3°C then dangerous consequences are possible even for a target equivalent carbon dioxide concentration of only 450 ppm. (An equivalent carbon dioxide concentration is one that treats all six major greenhouse gases [see Chapter 1] as if they were the equivalent amount of carbon dioxide that would cause the same warming.) Some scientists working on these possibilities believe that a 2–3°C warming might indeed cause catastrophic climate changes.

3 The uncertainty ranges are not well known. Thus the new estimates of climate sensitivity for a doubling of carbon dioxide equivalent of 2.4 to 5.4°C suggested by Murphy and colleagues in August 2004, and of 2 to 11°C suggested by Stainforth and others in 2005, instead of the IPCC range of 1.5 to 4.5°C imply a greater likelihood of warmings exceeding 2–3°C by 2100 for a 450 ppm stabilisation concentration. That is to say, the warmings may be greater for the same greenhouse gas stabilisation level. This suggests that we should aim for as low an equilibrium concentration as possible if we want to be on the safe side.

Leaving these important caveats aside, the emission reductions necessary to stabilise equivalent greenhouse gas concentrations at various levels have been

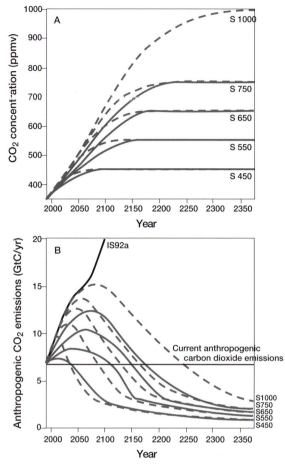

Figure 23: Projected carbon dioxide emissions leading to stabilised concentrations. Part A shows the IPCC 1995 and WRE scenarios leading to stabilised concentrations of carbon dioxide as indicated. Part B shows carbon dioxide emissions that would lead to these stabilisation scenarios. The old IS92a emissions scenario (sometimes known as 'Business-as-Usual') is shown for comparison in B. In each case two different pathways to stabilisation are shown: those used by the IPCC in its 1995 report (dashed lines labelled S) and the WRE profiles from Wigley, Richels and Edmonds in 1996 (full lines). (From the IPCC 2001 report, WGIII Figure 8.12, used with permission.)

calculated for two different pathways to stabilisation as shown in **Figure 23**. Part (A) shows the two alternative concentration profiles for stabilisation of carbon dioxide concentrations at levels of 450, 550, 650, 750 and 1000 ppm by volume. Parts (B) shows the corresponding emissions trajectories needed to achieve these concentrations.

In all cases, global emissions have to be reduced to well below the present levels (currently about 8 Gt of carbon per year) by 2300. To achieve the lower and safer stabilisation levels, global emissions need to peak before 2050 and then reduce to a fraction of the present emissions by 2150. An equilibrium concentration of 450 ppm requires a reduction to below present emissions by 2050.

The WRE scenario pathways to stabilisation indicate that to stabilise carbon dioxide concentrations at 1000 ppm (some time after 2300), total global emissions of carbon dioxide would need to reach a maximum of about 14 to 17 Gt of carbon per year around the mid- to late twenty-first century, with rapid reductions thereafter to about 4 to 6 Gt carbon per year by 2300 (and then be still declining). However, as we have seen, this concentration leads to probably quite dangerous climate change and is therefore unacceptable.

To stabilise at 450 ppm (reached in the WRE scenario by about 2250) requires much greater reductions in emissions. Following the WRE pathway, it allows a small increase from 1990 levels to a peak of about 7 to 13 Gt of carbon per year in about 2010–20, followed by a steep decrease to less than 4 Gt by 2100, and an eventual decline to less than 2 or 3 Gt per year.

However, climate-carbon cycle interactions, which amplify the rate of increase in carbon dioxide in the atmosphere, may further reduce the peak emissions allowable. These were not included in the calculations in **Figure 23**. Two recent simulations using interacting climate and carbon cycle models suggest that global warming will lead to a decline or reversal in the natural carbon storage in the biosphere. Thus critical concentrations of carbon dioxide in the atmosphere may be reached earlier, and more rapid reductions of emissions will be needed to counter this effect.

Figure 24 shows schematically how mitigation targets might be set. The figure indicates where scientific information is needed, and where value-judgements and politics take over. Mitigation targets result from a scientific understanding of the climate, natural and human systems, with value-judgements as to what thresholds of change are to be avoided, and socio-political negotiation as to processes to achieve emissions reductions. The uncertainty regarding the target for greenhouse gas concentrations and related emission reduction targets must lead to the setting of pro tem targets which should be subject to periodic reassessment as uncertainties are reduced due to better science, observed changes and progress on mitigation. The success of legislative and market mechanisms in achieving emissions reductions must also be assessed.

The important question is not what the exact target should be, but how such a large emission reduction might best be accomplished in the decades ahead. Such a demanding technological target is not unprecedented. Previous tall technological targets that were achieved through strong national commitments include the US/UK Manhattan Project to produce nuclear weapons during World War II and the US race for a landing on the moon in the 1960s. However, reaching the present greenhouse emissions reduction target requires much more

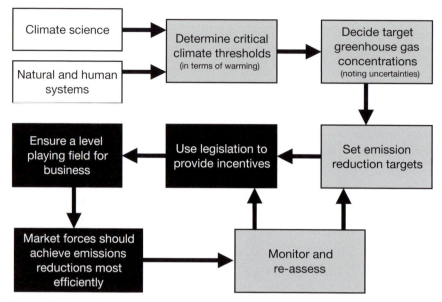

Figure 24: How mitigation targets might be set. In this schematic, white boxes indicate where scientific input is dominant, grey boxes indicate where both scientific input and value-judgements are needed, and black boxes where socio-economic and political processes take over.

societal participation. It is a matter of motivation, incentives and technological innovation. Its feasibility will be resolved by action. The importance of the UNFCCC and the Kyoto Protocol (the present target of which is much less ambitious) is not so much the targets set, but the setting of a framework and tone within governments, businesses and society that drives urgent action for mitigation. Setting a long-term target, even if subject to periodic revision, provides a degree of certainty in planning and expectations that facilitates action and commitment. It establishes a mindset necessary for success.

Where we are now

Mitigation, or emissions reductions, must start from where we are now. For this, some facts are necessary. In the year 2000 (the latest I could find with reliable numbers for all countries), global greenhouse gas emissions, measured as the equivalent amount of carbon dioxide, were 59% from fossil fuel carbon dioxide, 18% from carbon dioxide from land-use change (deforestation minus regrowth forests), 14% from methane, 8% from nitrous oxide, and 1% from several other highly active greenhouse gases.

Methane (CH_4) comes from biomass decomposition, coal mining, natural gas and oil system leakages, livestock, wastewater treatment, cultivation of rice, burning of savannah and some from burning of fossil fuels. Nitrous oxide (N_2O) comes from agricultural soils (especially where too much nitrogen fertiliser has been applied), industrial processes, automobiles and other fossil fuel burning, human sewage and animal manure. Other highly active greenhouse gases are mostly substitutes for ozone-depleting substances, and various industrial processes including semi-conductor manufacture, production of aluminium and magnesium and electrical equipment.

While carbon dioxide from fossil fuels dominates total emissions of greenhouse gases, emissions from land-use change are important, particularly in some developing countries with large rates of forest clearing. Generally, developed countries currently contribute very little directly to carbon dioxide emissions from land-use change (although they buy rainforest timber), but some 35% of emissions from developing countries is from land-use change, and more than 60% in the least developed countries. This largely reflects much higher proportions of the economy related to agriculture and forestry. Emissions from land-use change have figured in international negotiations because some countries believe they can reduce these emissions, or develop sinks (that is, remove carbon dioxide from the atmosphere) by reforestation and better retention of carbon in soils through minimum tillage and other measures. However, there is substantial uncertainty in estimating sources and sinks of carbon dioxide from land-use change, and also about definitions and permanence of carbon storage in forests and soils. Hence most of the following statistics do not include land-use change effects.

Table 9 summarises some useful information for the year 2000 on total emissions of greenhouse gases (GHG) for each of the 25 major emitting countries, the emissions per person, and carbon intensity (carbon emissions per unit economic output), as well as percentage changes in carbon intensity and GDP for the decade 1990–2000. These statistics demonstrate a wide variety of national situations, and help to explain various perceived national interests and negotiation stances on mitigation policies.

It is apparent from the table that a relatively small number of countries contribute most of the greenhouse gas emissions. These countries in general have either large populations or high gross domestic product (GDP), or both. These are the two main drivers of high emissions, although carbon intensity is also important. Carbon intensity varies greatly between countries, depending on economic structure, the mix of fuels used, and energy efficiency. There is a downward trend in carbon intensity in many developed and developing countries, however, in most of the 25 major emitting countries GDP is rising more rapidly. Furthermore, the statistics for changes are for the decade 1990–2000, during which there was an economic decline in the former Soviet Union countries, with the closure of many carbon-intensive industries. This economic decline is

Table 9: Emissions data for major greenhouse emitting countries.

Emissions data are shown for the 25 top greenhouse gas emitting countries. Data includes CO_2 from fossil fuels and cement, and five non-CO_2 greenhouse gases (collectively, GHG), but not emissions from land-use (LU) change. Statistics are also given for the 25 present me·mber countries of the European Union as a single unit, as well as the major member countries separately, and for developed and developing countries as groups. Data are based on that aggregated by the World Resources Institute and published by the Pew Center on Global Climate Change in December 2004. CO_2 intensity is in units of CO_2 emissions per unit Gross Domestic Product (GDP), expressed in units of Purchasing Power Parity (PPP) ·or comparability. The abbreviation tCe is tonnes carbon equivalent, and is the carbon equivalent of the six GHGs emissions as if they were all CO_2.

Country	Total GHG emissions in 2000 (except LU change)		GHG emissions per person in 2000		Carbon intensity tCe/$M GDP (PPP)	Carbon intensity change 1990–2000 (%)	GDP-PPP change 1990–2000 (%)
	% of world	rank	tCe	rank			
Argentina	0.9	24	2.1	17	86	-16	56
Australia	1.4	17	6.8	1	193	-11	42
Brazil	2.5	8	1.3	21	73	18	30
Canada	2.1	9	6.3	3	172	-8	32
China	14.8	2	1.1	22	201	-47	162
European Union 25	14.0	3	2.8	11	107	-21	22
France	1.5	15	2.3	16	72	-20	20
Germany	2.9	7	3.2	6	111	-28	18
India	5.5	5	0.5	25	99	-4	70
Indonesia	1.5	16	0.7	23	127	30	51
Iran	1.3	18	1.9	18	223	6	50
Italy	1.6	11	2.5	15	87	-8	17

Table 9: Emissions data for major greenhouse emitting countries. (Continued)

Country	Total GHG emissions in 2000 (except LU change)		GHG emissions per person in 2000		Carbon intensity tCe/$M GDP (PPP)	Carbon intensity change 1990–2000 (%)	GDP-PPP change 1990–2000 (%)
	% of world	rank	tCe	rank			
Japan	4.0	6	2.9	10	104	-2	15
Mexico	1.5	14	1.4	20	125	-11	41
Pakistan	0.8	25	0.6	24	112	11	47
Poland	1.1	21	2.7	12	230	-41	43
Russia	5.7	4	3.6	5	427	3	-34
Saudi Arabia	1.0	23	4.3	4	260	41	25
South Africa	1.2	19	2.6	13	200	-2	19
South Korea	1.6	12	3.1	8	185	2	82
Spain	1.1	20	2.6	14	104	4	30
Turkey	1.1	22	1.5	19	149	5	42
Ukraine	1.6	13	2.9	9	483	28	-57
United Kingdom	2.0	10	3.1	7	110	-23	26
United States	20.6	1	6.6	2	162	-14	38
Developed countries	52		3.9		147	-20	24
Developing countries	48		0.9		147	-11	59
World			1.5		147	-13	30

unlikely to continue. China shows a large fall in carbon intensity accompanying an even larger rise in GDP, but this rapid decline in carbon intensity may not continue, as it was at least in part due to the closure of inefficient industries during a period of economic reform, and the accuracy of the figures has also been questioned. The relatively low carbon intensity in France is due largely to its high percentage of nuclear power generation. Note the large range in per capita emissions, from 0.5 tons per person in India to in excess of 6 tons per person in Australia and the United States.

Statistics on cumulative emissions from 1850 to 2000 show that the developed countries dominate, with 29.8% of emissions originating from the US and 27.2% in total from the EU member countries. Russia is next with 8.3%, while China contributed 7.3% and India 2.0%. Brazil, Indonesia and Pakistan each contributed less than 1% (0.8%, 0.4% and 0.2% respectively). This helps to account for the developing countries' argument that the primary responsibility for early emissions reductions lies with the developed countries.

We will discuss the politics of setting mitigation targets further, as it relates to the UNFCCC, in Chapters 10 and 11, and to possible future mitigation measures in the final chapter.

How difficult is mitigation?

Reducing emissions of greenhouse gases is characterised by some economists, business people and politicians, as severely limiting economic growth, and likely to lead to reductions in future standards of living. They allege that it is opposed to progress, to the interests of the poor, and is overall too costly. As EF Schumacher put it in 1964, 'there is no substitute for energy' and energy is 'the precondition of all commodities'. They point out that greenhouse gas emissions have been closely tied to fossil fuel energy use for a century or more.

An alternative view is that of Sir David King, the UK Chief Science Adviser, in an article in *Science* magazine in 2004. He states '... it's a myth that reducing carbon emissions necessarily makes us poorer. Taking action to tackle climate change can create economic opportunities and higher living standards.'

King cites the British experience, where between 1990 and 2000 the economy grew by some 30%, and employment by 4.8%, yet greenhouse gas emissions intensity (GHG emissions per unit GDP) fell markedly. He also noted that over the same period the Chinese economy grew very rapidly, yet their emissions intensity also fell. Developing countries in particular have the opportunity, as they grow new industries, to use the most energy- and carbon-efficient technologies, and thus avoid the mistakes made by the developed countries.

Whether or not emissions reduction is a burden or an opportunity depends in part on a societal state of mind. In an old economy with high-carbon emission based industries, much economic and emotional capital is tied up in industries and infrastructure (such as factories, roads and power stations) that rely on burning fossil fuels and which are expensive to replace. A new low carbon-emissions society relying on energy-efficient and renewable energy technologies will be structured to make the most of the new technologies, with trained workers, the necessary infrastructure, and a positive market value placed on the new technologies and skills. The problem is the transition from one to the other. The forward-looking low-carbon emissions technologies and skills will have a growing market edge as these become the wave of the future. Hence the new motto of British Petroleum of 'Beyond Petroleum' and the Royal Dutch Shell focus on solar power, hydrogen as a carrier of energy, and other renewable technologies. Those countries, businesses and individuals who anticipate coming changes are more likely to grow and profit from opportunities in the new economy.

Many economists and businesses have argued that there is no such thing as a 'free lunch' in relation to mitigation: if businesses could save money by being more energy efficient they would have done so already. However, emissions savings are possible at no cost, as has been shown many times by businesses that have accepted the challenge to look at what savings could be made. In businesses where energy costs have traditionally been only a small fraction of capital or labour costs, many have simply not bothered to look for savings in the 10% or so of their expenses that are related to energy. However, when they do take up the challenge they find that substantial savings can be made, thus increasing their overall profits. These are called 'no regrets' emissions reductions and are far more pervasive than was once thought.

Amory Lovins at the Rocky Mountain Institute in the US and colleagues have published several studies suggesting that people can transform industrial production so as to use less natural resources to produce higher standards of living in ways that are profitable. They give many examples, and more can be found at www.natcap.org. They point out that during the second oil crisis in the United States, most new US energy-using devices such as cars, buildings and domestic appliances, doubled in energy efficiency. In the period 1973–1986 there was a 35% increase in the economy with roughly zero growth in energy use.

Lovins and colleagues maintain that energy efficiency can be improved by raising energy prices as in the oil crisis, *or* by paying attention to the issue. They argue that creating an informed, effective, and efficient market in energy-saving devices and practices can be more powerful than a bare price signal. Saving energy is profitable and benefits the national economy.

The whole question of mitigation options, methods and costs is discussed at great length in the IPCC *Third Assessment Report* (IPCC 2001c). Economic studies give widely different estimates of the costs of reducing emissions. Differences between estimates depend on assumptions about economic growth, the costs and availability of existing and new technologies, the availability of resources, the extent of 'no regrets' options and the choice of policy instruments or ways of achieving reductions.

Conclusions regarding the costs of emissions reductions also depend on:

- the timing and rate of emissions reductions,
- economic assumptions regarding discounting the future,
- the mix of economic measures such as trading in emissions permits (the buying and selling of emissions allowances) and the removal of institutional barriers to new technologies, and
- transfer of technologies to developing countries.

Emissions reductions will be less expensive if any associated tax revenues, or revenues from the sale of emissions permits, are used to reduce existing taxes which add to the costs of economic production, such as payroll taxes or taxes on capital. Cost estimates for emissions reduction are lowest when there is full trading globally in emissions permits, since then emissions reductions can be made where it is cheapest both geographically and by industrial sector. Trading also minimises inequities and hedges against uncertainties regarding costs and targets, which may change with time. Where reductions take place is then less dependent on who pays for the reductions.

Emissions reductions can have both co-benefits and ancillary costs. Co-benefits occur, for example, with reductions in the burning of coal in power stations, as this reduces greenhouse gas emissions and also emissions of other pollutants that have detrimental health effects and cause acid rain. This saves on health and other costs, and could lead to a 'no-regrets' situation. Similarly, present estimated health costs of pollution from fossil-fuelled road transport are large (around A$3 billion annually in Australia alone). This could be greatly reduced with present petrol-electric hybrid technology, and completely eliminated by a future change to hydrogen-fuelled vehicles. Another example is that of carbon dioxide removal from the atmosphere by growing trees, which has the co-benefits of providing wind-breaks, reducing erosion, and eventually providing timber. However, ancillary costs might occur also, for example, growing forests increase water use, and thus reduce runoff and downstream water supplies.

The IPCC reported that in 2050 the global average reduction in GDP resulting from emissions reductions would typically be in the range of 1 to 3% for a target concentration of 450 ppm, less than 1% for a target of 550 ppm, and near zero for targets of 750 ppm or greater. These estimates from the IPCC are shown in **Figure 25**. Costs would tend to be at the lower end of these ranges if there is full global emissions trading, since this favours lower cost mitigation options.

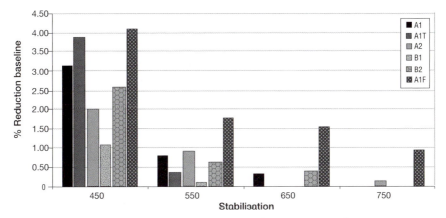

Figure 25: IPCC estimates of global average GDP reduction in 2050. The estimates are for stabilisation targets ranging from 450 ppm (left hand group) to 750 ppm (right hand group) for the six IPCC SRES reference emissions scenarios. In these scenarios there are no policies aimed at emissions reductions. Scenarios that stabilise at or below the target concentrations show zero costs. (Source: IPCC 2001c, Figure 8.18, published with permission.)

Note that these costs are estimated relative to the SRES range of emissions scenarios, which were considered by the IPCC to not be driven by climate change policy considerations (see **Box 3**). Thus for each stabilisation target, cost estimates vary according to which SRES scenario is taken as the reference. If we take the high emissions A1F scenario as the reference, for example, costs of stabilisation are relatively large, whereas if we take a low emissions scenario such as B1 as the reference, costs are relatively small. The SRES authors did not assign probabilities to the SRES scenarios, but common sense suggests that neither the extreme high nor extreme low emissions scenarios are as likely as some scenario nearer the middle of the range.

James Hansen from the Goddard Institute for Space Studies argues that initially it may be easier and less costly to reduce emissions of greenhouse gases other than carbon dioxide, for example methane and nitrous oxide, and also carbon black. This would lessen the urgency of reducing carbon dioxide emissions in order to stabilise equivalent carbon dioxide concentrations in the 450 to 550 ppm range; however, substantial reductions in carbon dioxide emissions would still be necessary.

Interestingly, some opponents of early mitigation measures have tended to contest the reality of the A1F high emissions scenario but give more credence to the B1 low emissions scenarios. They argue that this justifies less policy intervention to reduce emissions. It would indeed be nice if this were true, but in reality it seems unlikely that the B1 scenarios would be followed without some motivation from climate change concerns. My position is that the B1 type future is indeed possible, at relatively little cost, but only by deliberate choice and policy decisions by both governments and private enterprise.

The costs of emissions reductions need to be weighed against the potential costs of climate change impacts if emissions are not reduced. Costs of impacts that would be avoided by reducing emissions are discussed in Chapter 6. Such avoided costs increase with the amount of global warming, and thus with time and rate of emissions. In general, costs of emissions reductions are more immediate, and the avoided costs of impacts are greatest later. Thus, how near-term costs are compared with long-term costs is important in any cost-benefits analysis. This is usually done using what is called a 'discount rate'. Normally, for short-term cost-benefit analysis, immediate costs are discounted to take account of a preference to have goods now rather than later, or of what benefit could be gained from money spent now on mitigation if it were instead invested in something else. Discount rates are usually roughly equal to interest rates or rates of inflation, but can vary from one activity to another.

The trouble with using conventional discount rates for comparing emission reduction costs with later avoided costs of climate change is that over periods of decades or centuries, avoided costs of millions of dollars would be discounted by factors of tens to hundreds. A number of economists have argued that this is inappropriate, in part because avoided costs cannot just be expressed in monetary terms (for example, there may be species or heritage losses), but more importantly because future climate change costs could be disastrous and irreversible. These economists argue that future discount rates are very uncertain, and could be zero or even negative in the case of negative economic growth due to socio-economic disasters including climate change itself. Not only are future discount rates uncertain, but so too are future climate change impacts. This means that simple cost-benefit analysis is inappropriate to the issue of what is an appropriate rate of emissions reductions. Given large uncertainties, policies should rather be risk-averse, that is, they should aim to reduce the risk of potentially dangerous climate change impacts as rapidly as is economically viable.

Importantly, the estimated costs of emissions reductions should be compared with the rates of economic growth. Given expected growth rates of several per cent per annum in GDP, a total decrease in GDP of anything from zero up to a few per cent by 2050, due to emissions reductions, is in reality only a delay in reaching the same much higher GDP figure (two or more times the present GDP) by a year at the most. The loss of zero to a few per cent would be made up for by the next year's growth in GDP.

It is also pertinent to note that the IPCC 2001 report states that technological progress relevant to greenhouse gas emissions reductions has been faster than anticipated in 1995. For example there has been:

- rapid deployment of wind turbines
- rapid elimination of industrial by-product gases
- efficient hybrid gasoline/electric car engines
- advancement of fuel cell technology
- demonstration of underground storage or sequestration of carbon dioxide.

While few of these technologies are as yet making large reductions in greenhouse gas emissions, their potential is large.

The looming peak in oil production

The coming peak in global oil production is a potentially important issue that may well influence the ease with which mitigation policies can be carried out, their costs, and indeed their urgency. When this peak will occur has been controversial since 1956 when M. King Hubbert predicted that US oil production would peak in the early 1970s and then begin to decline (which it did). Nevertheless repeated global oil shortages in recent decades have caused sharp, if temporary, rises in the market price for oil, with downstream impacts on national and global economies. Security of oil supply (irrespective of price) has also emerged as a major concern in many oil-consuming countries.

Greater awareness of the imminence of a peak in global oil production by governments and industry could lead to several alternative and perhaps complementary responses:

1   Higher priority in foreign policy to security of oil supplies, leading to oil-driven power politics, and a greater commitment to securing oil supplies at home through oil exploration and the opening up of presently closed areas such as designated wilderness areas.

2   Research, development and investment in alternative fossil fuel sources of oil or other transport fuels, such as shale oil and tar sands, sea-bed methane, and gasification of coal.

3   Emphasis on research and development of carbon capture and sequestration, or nuclear power to enable large increases in coal-based electricity and hydrogen for fuel cells.

4   Strong support for renewable energy source such as solar, wind and biomass.

5   Demand limitation through energy efficiency and less energy-demanding lifestyles. (This raises equity issues in regard to the developing countries that aspire to higher standards of living.)

The first alternative comes at a political, economic and environmental price, but is already evident to a degree in the foreign and domestic policies of a number of major countries. The second and third alternatives have their advocates in countries such as the US, Australia, China and Japan, but will likely lead to more expensive fuel, with higher carbon dioxide emissions unless carbon dioxide capture and sequestration is made mandatory in all new fossil-fuel energy enterprises. The fourth is a solution favoured by most environmentalists, and may in fact become more economically competitive due to increased fuel prices resulting from the other alternatives. The fifth is arguably the most cost-effective, but faces an acceptability hurdle related to personal perceptions of welfare and a good life.

The faster the oil peak looms on the horizon the more urgent these responses become. From the climate change mitigation point of view this makes it critical that the focus should be on the third, fourth and fifth alternatives, which ensure that greenhouse gas emissions do not rise even faster. Some combination of these last three approaches would seem most likely to succeed in coping with the climate change issue, but traditional 'business-as-usual' attitudes would tend to favour the first two. Alternatives 1 and 2 are in line with the SRES A1FI scenarios, while alternatives 3, 4 and 5 are more consistent with the storyline behind the SRES B1 or low-emissions scenario. Clearly, achieving a low-emissions scenario is only likely to happen through conscious choice by governments and industry.

Mitigation options

Mitigation, or greenhouse gas emissions reductions, can be achieved in several general ways: through increased energy efficiency, fuel substitution, use of non-fossil-carbon fuels (including nuclear power and renewables), carbon sequestration (or removal from the climate system), and infrastructure and lifestyle changes. The challenge, if we are going to reduce the risk of dangerous climate change, is, as we have seen, how best to achieve a future like that described in the SRES B1 scenario (see **Box 3**) which relies less on high materials use and more on clean and resource-efficient technologies.

Increased energy efficiency

Historically, carbon dioxide emissions were closely related to the gross domestic product (GDP) of individual countries during the early part of the twentieth century, but at the time of the oil crisis in 1973, when the real price of oil rose sharply, emissions fell away relative to GDP, which continued to rise. This was especially so in the United States, and was due to a sudden increase in energy efficiency (energy use per unit GDP), including more fuel-efficient automobiles, turning down the thermostats in buildings, and other emergency measures. In the United States, energy efficiency, measured in terms of carbon dioxide emissions per unit GDP, and indeed total emissions, continued to fall until about 1983, after which emissions started to increase again, but more slowly than GDP.

Japan also showed a fall off in the rate of increase in emissions of carbon dioxide relative to continued rapid growth in GDP, beginning about 1978. China has shown an even more dramatic increase in energy efficiency, with rapid economic growth but much slower growth in emissions, although the accuracy of the statistics has been questioned. Russia and other former Soviet Bloc countries have shown decreases in both GDP and in emissions, although that is changing as their economies improve.

These experiences show that, given enough incentive, reductions in emissions per unit GDP can be achieved, and that lessons learnt from these experiences can continue to influence future emissions.

The building sector contributes about 30% of global energy-related emissions of carbon dioxide. Growth in emissions has been about 2% per annum, largely due to increased dwelling sizes and numbers, increase in the commercial sector, and increased use of appliances, particularly heating in winter and cooling in summer. Key areas for improvement include better building design to reduce the need for artificial heating and cooling by insulation, coatings on windows to reduce heat loss and reflect summer solar radiation, shading in summer, and passive solar heating in winter. Demonstration energy-efficient buildings show that large savings in running costs can be achieved at little or no additional capital expense. Even large office blocks can in many climates become almost independent of external energy supplies. The headquarters building of the World Meteorological Organization, in Geneva, is one such building. Another such building in Cairns, Australia, uses 40% less energy than similar office buildings in the same region, with an annual saving of some A$26,000 per year in power bills.

Combined heat and power systems for large buildings and compact neighbourhoods result in large gains in efficiency. Isolated power stations achieve about 30% efficiency, but if their waste heat is used they can achieve efficiencies nearer 85%. This may be best achieved through the use of natural gas powered fuel cells, with versions becoming commercially available which can supply individual houses or buildings, generating electricity, and at the same time providing hot water and central heating.

Energy-efficient lighting is now achievable through a range of technical innovations including energy-saving light bulbs, fibre optics and movement and light sensors to turn off lighting in empty or naturally lit rooms. Developing and choosing more energy efficient individual appliances is another major potential saving, as is getting into the habit of setting heating in winter to lower temperatures (along with putting on a sweater), and cooling in summer to higher settings (and dispensing with jackets and ties).

Simple and acceptable lifestyle changes or habits can save both energy and money. It is estimated for example, that in a typical office building, cooling the interior to 25°C rather than 18°C, when the outside temperature is 32°C, would make energy savings of 25 to 50%, depending on the amount of waste heat generated inside the building. All that is needed is more appropriate clothing. Similar considerations apply to air-conditioning in automobiles. Adherence to inappropriate sartorial fashion can be a great waster of energy, as well as a source of discomfort.

Globally, about 20% of carbon dioxide emissions come from the transport sector. These emissions are growing at about 2.5% per annum. There are large potential improvements in fuel efficiency in road transport, with hybrid gasoline-electric vehicles already on the market, with great gains from regenerative braking and gasoline engines running at their most efficient speeds, and fuel cell powered vehicles reaching feasibility. Toyota is already selling its second generation Prius car in many countries, and Honda is marketing its Civic Hybrid, both with fuel consumption about or under 5 litre per 100 kilometre. Lightweight materials such as light metal alloys and ceramics are also likely to reduce fuel needs. However, more economical vehicles may encourage greater usage, so that improved public transport, car pooling and reduced travel needs through better urban design and work arrangements are also needed.

Robert Jackson and William Schlesinger of Duke University estimate that for the United States a total reduction of 10% in carbon emissions could be achieved by a complete conversion to hybrid car technology, which would double fuel efficiency from about 10 km/l to over 20 km/l. Hybrid car technology is already taking off. With appropriate incentives, including higher oil prices, it could be a major contributor to greenhouse gas emissions reductions within the next decade.

Fuel substitution

This is generally regarded as the substitution of one readily available fuel for another, as distinct from development of new alternative fuels or energy sources. As long as fossil fuels continue to dominate energy production, switching from coal to oil or gas can reduce greenhouse gas emissions. If energy efficiencies remain unchanged, shifting from coal to oil leads to a reduction in carbon emissions of about 26%, oil to gas about 23.5% and from coal to gas about 43%. Leakage of methane in the case of coal and gas, however, slightly increases the gap between coal and oil, but reduces the gap between oil and gas.

The opportunity and likelihood of making substantial reductions in carbon emissions by such substitution varies from country to country, with some major developing countries, notably China and India, being richly endowed with coal but poorly endowed with oil and gas. They can only make large substitutions by increasing imports, which they can ill afford. Nevertheless, China is switching to natural gas, largely because of regional pollution problems, with the development of international pipelines and gas terminals. Richer countries, such as the United States, Japan, Australia and western European countries can afford fuel substitution, and in some cases have their own gas supplies. However, some 70% of gas reserves are in the former Soviet Union and the Middle East. This raises energy security problems for potential importing countries.

In countries in Africa and South America, substitution of gas will also be hampered by lack of pipelines, requiring large investments in infrastructure.

Exploitation of coal-bed methane has the double advantage that it reduces leakage of methane from coal mines as well as being less carbon intensive as a fuel. This is a potentially substantial source of methane in some countries. For example in the coal-rich Australian State of Queensland, coal-bed methane now accounts for 25% of the high-growth Queensland gas market. However, some gas sources contain a large fraction of carbon dioxide, sulfur and other pollutants that would require large amounts of energy to remove, thus increasing the effective carbon intensity of these sources.

Unconventional oil reserves such as shale oil are generally more carbon-intensive to exploit than conventional sources, and may also become less competitive with other energy sources as costs for the latter are reduced.

In some countries, the phasing out of nuclear power is leading to an increased reliance on fossil fuels, and in Brazil constraints on its former reliance on hydro-power, as its economy expands, is increasing reliance on fossil energy.

Over several decades, limited availability of established reserves of natural gas and costs may limit switching to gas supplies for power generation, although large reserves of methane exist as methane hydrates. Methane hydrates are cage-like molecular lattices of ice, inside which molecules of methane are trapped. They exist in permafrost regions, and beneath the ocean floor at depths exceeding 500 metres, where high pressures occur. While both forms are susceptible to catastrophic release due to climate change and sea-level rise (see Chapter 5), they constitute a huge source of methane, which could be used, if they can be accessed, to substitute for coal and oil. According to the US Department of Energy in 2004, the worldwide potential of methane hydrates approaches 400 million trillion cubic feet, compared to the 5000 trillion cubic feet of the world's currently proven reserves of natural gas. Moreover, they exist in many different localities around the world. A Japan–US–Canada consortium is currently exploring the possible exploitation of methane hydrates for gas supplies.

However, if a target greenhouse gas concentration as low as 450 ppm is desired, substitution of natural gas or methane for coal and oil would, by itself, still not enable such a target to be reached.

Nuclear power

Nuclear power globally accounts for about 7% of total energy supplies, although this varies greatly between countries. France gets the vast majority of its electricity from nuclear power, but many other countries have none. Some countries are phasing out nuclear power stations on environmental grounds. Growth has stalled in recent decades because of public concern heightened by the Chernobyl accident in 1986. Moreover, lower fossil-fuel prices and high costs of licensing and safety precautions have made nuclear power uncompetitive. This is especially so in countries where power stations are run by the private sector, which expects high returns on capital investment. Many existing nuclear power stations are reaching their design lifetimes and are to be phased out in coming decades.

With the expansion of the European Community in 2004, there are now 156 nuclear reactors operating in the EU, producing over 30% of its electricity. However, most are old, with an average age in 2004 of 22 years. The Euratom treaty commits the EU to a 'powerful nuclear industry', but a number of EU countries are unhappy with this objective, and safety concerns are leading to demands for phasing out of some older reactors, especially in Lithuania and Slovakia.

The Director General of the International Atomic Energy Agency (IAEA) in June 2004 stated that nuclear power is not in competition with renewable energy sources, but has the advantage of supplying reliable base-load electricity needed to replace fossil fuel plants. He also pointed to its potential to supply hydrogen for fuel cells used in transport.

The future of nuclear power depends on it meeting several concurrent criteria:

- transparently safer operations and security from terrorist attack,
- increased safeguards against nuclear weapons proliferation,
- convincing solutions to long-term radioactive waste disposal, and
- competitive economic costs.

Each of these points remains, at best, controversial at present, with heightened fears of terrorism adding to the safety and proliferation concerns.

A consortium of ten nations, the Generation IV International Forum, is pooling its research expertise to choose designs for a new generation of fail-safe nuclear reactors. These would operate at higher temperatures, allowing more efficient electricity generation and the possibility of generating hydrogen from the thermochemical splitting of water. The latter could be used to fuel transport. However, to generate enough hydrogen to replace gasoline in the US would require hundreds of new nuclear power plants. Moreover, the need for new coolants and more corrosion-proof materials will be huge challenges. New demonstration reactors are unlikely to be delivered before the 2020s. A recent study by the Massachusetts Institute of Technology (MIT) looked at the potential for the power generated by nuclear reactors to triple by 2050, which would avoid nearly two billion tonnes of carbon emissions. However, the MIT report suggested this would not be economically competitive with fossil fuels, while the cost of renewable energy could fall dramatically over this time.

Another consideration is the energy pay-back time for nuclear reactors. The large materials investment in the building of a nuclear power station, such as in concrete and steel, requires large energy input. This leads to what are called 'embedded emissions'. Thus the pay-back time before there is a net reduction in carbon dioxide emissions, may be several decades for each reactor, and longer if hundreds of reactors are to be built over the next fifty years.

These considerations suggest that nuclear reactors are unlikely to play a major role in replacing fossil fuels and reducing total emissions by 2050, even in countries such as France, China or Japan that may put energy independence before cost. However, nuclear fusion could also be an option in the latter part of the twenty-first century, with far less radioactive waste, if feasibility can be demonstrated in the next few decades. The Bush Administration in the US has placed considerable emphasis on cooperative international research programs to develop safe nuclear power and nuclear fusion, but these will not lead to significant reductions in greenhouse gas emissions over the next several decades.

Hydropower

Globally, hydropower provides some 2.3% of energy supplies, although in some countries such as New Zealand, Norway and Brazil the proportion is much higher. While there is considerable potential for increases, for example in China and India, there are increasing concerns about the environmental and social impacts of large dams on fisheries, displacement of populations, riverine ecosystems, and other issues. Another significant obstacle is the distance between potential users and the potential sites for hydropower generation, leading in some cases to large costs and losses of power in transmission.

Another important consideration is the changing water balance due to climate change itself. Global warming will increase the rate of evaporation and globally averaged precipitation (rain and snowfall), but this will be uneven in space and time, with changes in seasonality of rainfall, loss of storage in snowpack and glaciers, increased aridity in many subtropical regions, more frequent droughts and intense rain events. These impacts will complicate planning for hydropower dams, their operational requirements and security of supply, as plans will have to take into account changes in flood control and water supply measures needed for irrigation and other industrial and human uses.

Solar energy

Solar energy has huge potential, with the lowest estimates of supply, taking account of such factors as land availability, being some four times current global energy consumption. However, present costs of electricity from photoelectric solar cells, or 'photovoltaics', are not competitive with fossil fuels, except in areas not served by electricity distribution systems. Nevertheless, in late 2002 the total power that existing solar installations could generate worldwide was more than 1300 MW, following growth of about 30% per annum over the previous five years. Approximately 1.5 billion people are at present without access to electricity in developing countries and these provide a huge potential market for locally produced solar electricity as cheaper photovoltaic systems become available. According to a recent study, high growth rates are likely to continue for photovoltaics, wind power and fuel cells. The *Clean Edge* report estimates a 10-fold growth over the next decade, that is, a sustained growth of some 26% per year. Costs of photovoltaics are being rapidly reduced by improved technologies.

Photovoltaics can be incorporated in window coatings in buildings, and could help to make many office buildings energy self-sufficient in lighting, heating and cooling. These and photovoltaic devices in individual houses are already incorporated into electricity grids in many locations so that any electricity generated surplus to requirements is fed into the grid.

Concentrating solar-thermal power plants have lower costs. These focus solar energy at high temperatures onto boilers or other generators of electricity that can be fed into power grids. Nine plants in the Mohave Desert near Los Angeles, USA, have been supplying more than 350 MWe of power since 1989.

Solar hot water systems are already in use in many private dwellings around the world, especially in locations where sunshine is plentiful. Here, as with photovoltaics, a key problem is the relatively high initial capital cost for individual households, which takes some years to recover through decreased charges for use of fossil fuel energy. Schemes to finance this initial cost and write it off over time can facilitate such investments.

A novel solar tower is planned for a site near Mildura, Australia, with a capacity of 200 MWe. It relies on what is in effect a giant circular glasshouse of diameter 5 km, which warms air that rises through a 1 km high chimney at its centre. As the air is drawn into the tower it passes through air turbines that generate electricity. It also heats thermal storages (rocks or water tanks), enabling it to continue operation during the night. A 50 kW pilot system operated for seven years in Spain in the 1980s.

Photosynthesis is the most successful natural solar converting system on Earth, enabling crop production for food, fibre and energy. Artificial photosynthesis would make it possible to use sunlight to produce large quantities of hydrogen from water, cleanly and cheaply. Research currently under way in several laboratories may eventually lead to artificial photosynthesis, hopefully competitive with other energy sources.

A central problem with solar energy is the need for storage to counter its intermittent nature over the daily and annual cycles and with cloud cover. As storage becomes cheaper, solar energy will become more attractive. Cheaper and more efficient batteries are the conventional solution, but generation of hydrogen for use in fuel cells (see below) may be more promising, and only a decade or so away. A major advantage of solar energy in a warmer world is that it will be at its maximum just when it is needed to provide power for summer air conditioning, in what will increasingly become a peak load situation.

Wind power

Wind power is the fastest growing renewable energy source, with rapid growth both in numbers and installed capacity of 'wind farms', and in their energy efficiency with lowered cost. International Energy Agency estimates for 2020 project 1200 GW (1 GW is one thousand million Watt) of installed capacity, compared to 32 GW at the end of 2002. The former would provide almost 3000 TWh (1TW is a million million Watt) per annum of electricity. Global economic potential is estimated at between 20,000 and 40,000 TWh per annum. Denmark already generates 18% of its electricity from wind power, and has a rapidly growing export market in wind turbines. Germany has 12 GW of installed wind power capacity, and is planning for 25% of its electricity to come from wind power by 2030. A report by the governments of Eire and Northern Ireland indicates that some 3300 MW of wind power can be fed into the Irish electricity grid from wind generation by 2010, saving E250 million on fossil fuels each year.

Wind farms occupy less land than any other energy conversion system, with roads and tower bases less than 2% of a typical farm, and continued cropping and grazing possible on the rest of the land.

The main problems with wind power are public resistance to wind farms on-shore and high costs for them offshore. Objections have centred on claims of unsightliness, noise and danger to birds, and there have been some clumsy public relations and installations. Noise is a rapidly vanishing problem with better, almost silent designs. Unsightliness is partly due to some unfortunate locations in special areas, but mainly in the eyes of some beholders, who seem to tolerate ugly power stations, smoke plumes, pollution and high-voltage transmission lines, which are features of industrialised societies. Clive Hamilton, an Australian environmental economist, argues that environmentalists need to take account of the greater good:

> *When some people look at a wind farm they see a symbol of*
> *industrialism despoiling a beautiful headland. Others see majestic*
> *and elegant machines that power our cities with zero pollution,*

proving with every rotation that humans can live in the world without destroying it. The latter vision must prevail.

Martin Pasqualetti, an American expert on wind power, suggests that potential sites for wind power should be ranked not only by wind speeds but also by compatibility with local communities. He suggests two general strategies: work to change public opinion in favour of wind power, or install the turbines out of view, preferably on lonely farms which need rental income.

Studies in Australia suggest that the danger to birds has been grossly exaggerated. Rotation speeds of modern wind turbines are slow enough for birds to avoid the windmill blades. Nevertheless, careful siting in relation to nesting areas and flight paths, especially in relation to rare and endangered species, and with respect to scenic areas, is advisable, if only to minimise objections from the public. US studies indicate that far more birds are killed by glass windows, house cats, cars and trucks, transmission lines, agriculture and hunting.

Sites for wind farms depend critically on annual average wind speeds, with power generated varying as the cube of the wind speed, so that an 'excellent' site with an average annual wind speed of 8 m/s generates over 40% more power than a 'good' site with 7 m/s. If costs can be lowered to make 'good' sites economically viable, many more sites become available, enabling a greater choice of sites that have minimal visual impact.

As with solar energy, the intermittent nature of wind power requires either storage devices or integration into a widespread grid that would enable power generation to be averaged out over large areas experiencing different wind regimes. Backup for occasions of low output across the whole grid can be from hydropower or relatively cheap gas turbines that need to be operated only rarely. Wind forecasting can be used to schedule backup generators. Such backup is needed with coal-fired power stations anyway, in case of break down, so the problem is not new. One potentially viable alternative use of intermittent power would be to generate hydrogen as a fuel.

Biomass energy

Historically, biomass, that is the accumulation of organic material from plants and animals, has been a major energy source, especially in less developed areas, where it is used for fuel for stoves and heating, usually in the form of wood or cattle dung. With population growth, and for reasons of health, local and indoor air pollution, land degradation and exhaustion of supplies, use of traditional biomass burning is now often being phased out in favour of fossil-fuel generated electricity from urban and rural grids. Development of cleaner and more efficient stoves is helping at the local village level, but the real future for biomass energy is at the larger regional scale.

Sustainable biomass energy effectively reduces greenhouse gas emissions because, even if renewable biomass is burned and the resulting carbon dioxide is released into the atmosphere, the fuel results from plants that take a similar amount of carbon dioxide out of the atmosphere. Biomass burning effectively harvests solar energy and recycles the carbon.

If carbon dioxide from biomass burning were to be removed and more permanently sequestered underground or elsewhere, it would result in actual reductions in atmospheric concentrations of carbon dioxide. This may prove necessary in the future to reduce greenhouse gas concentrations to a safe level, below the maximum concentrations reached in the next century or so, thereby slowing or stopping sea-level rise from thermal expansion of the oceans, or the melting of ice sheets.

Greenhouse gas emissions can be reduced in three ways using biomass:

- solid and gaseous biofuels can be substituted for fossil fuels in generating heat and electricity,
- gaseous or liquid biofuels can substitute for oil in transportation, and
- biomass, in the form of timber or compressed fibrous sheeting, can replace much more greenhouse intensive construction materials (that is materials formed using lots of fossil fuel energy) such as concrete, steel or aluminium.

The first use is dependent on access to large quantities of biomass, either agricultural or forestry waste or purpose-grown material. In some cases this can be combined with incineration of urban garbage, but in either case a key consideration is the elimination of potentially hazardous or unhealthy pollution. The other main problem is the need to transport the fuel from dispersed sources to the power plant. This both costs money and uses energy for transport. So the economics dictates an optimal size for an exclusively biomass power station, although co-firing biomass in an existing coal-fired power station is possible.

Biomass can be gasified by heating it with steam and air, or via bioreactor cells and anaerobic digesters. Liquid fuels, methanol, ethanol and bio-oil, can be produced from biomass, the last by pyrolysis. These can all be used to generate stationary energy and in transport vehicles. Methanol burns more cleanly and efficiently than petroleum in internal combustion engines. It can also be used in fuel cells to generate electricity, including those in electric vehicles. This may become the mainstay of a future hydrogen economy (see below).

Brazil pioneered the use of ethanol, from sugar-cane waste, for automobiles in the 1970s. The industry has grown strongly in recent years in the United States, Europe, Africa and Asia, with total consumption of about 38 billion litres in 2002. However, this is still only about 1% of global transport fuel usage. In Brazil, gasoline supplies contain up to 25% ethanol, while India and China are both aiming at 10% blends. Ethanol is seen as the preferred substitute for the octane enhancer methyl-tertiary-butyl-ether (MTBE), and as a means of increasing the viability of many agricultural enterprises otherwise in need of subsidies. It also reduces reliance on imported oil. Tax breaks and other subsidies are being used to enhance use of ethanol. In 2001, the European Union established a goal of 20% biofuels by 2020

Senator Richard Lugar and James Woolsey, a former Director of the Central Intelligence Agency in the US, have advocated the large-scale use of biomass ethanol in the United States not only to reduce greenhouse gas emissions, but also to reduce American reliance on Middle Eastern oil, which they suggest causes 'dangerous foreign policy compromises'.

The economics of biomass energy can be assisted by its generation and consumption in isolated communities where transmission costs would be high, and by any credits for its contribution to reducing climate change, and in some cases reducing groundwater salinity. Large areas of degraded land, particularly from over-grazing, could be stabilised by biomass plantations. Multi-purpose facilities such as plants producing activated carbon, vegetable oils and electricity are also possible. Many species of deep-rooted trees can be coppiced for fuel, that is, the above ground growth is harvested for fuel while the roots survive and grow new shoots. This can reduce waterlogging in wet areas, reduce dryland salinity, provide shelter for stock, reduce wind and water erosion and increase biodiversity and aesthetic values. A device has recently been demonstrated which produces electricity from human waste sewage, which could mean that sewage treatment will pay for itself.

Constraints on the use of biomass include the necessary balance between the production of food, fodder and energy, especially in a world with growing population and demand. Land availability is thus an issue, especially if further land clearing is to be avoided because of its effect on biodiversity. In dry areas the additional water use may also be an issue, especially in a warming climate that will place a premium on water supplies. Increased potential for wildfires, discussed in Chapter 6, may also be a problem, especially for large-scale biomass plantations. Maintaining biodiversity and an ability to resist widespread attack by diseases and pests may argue against large monoculture plantations. Diverse on-farm plantations, which provide shelter for crops and animals and protect watercourses, may be preferable. Sustainability may also require a return of trace nutrients to the soil, either from the residue from biomass consumption or from fertilisers.

Substitution of biomass products for energy-intensive material such as steel and aluminium may be achieved by the use of products such as laminated wood and agricultural waste. At present the trend is rather the opposite, with greater use of steel and aluminium due to diminishing resources from old growth forests and the huge demand for wood pulp for making paper. Reduced usage of paper, perhaps through electronic communications, and increased recycling of paper, would contribute greatly to freeing up wood products for other uses, which would reduce carbon dioxide emissions.

Tidal, wave and geothermal energy

Richard Carew in his *Survey of Cornwall* in 1602 wrote:

> *Amongst other commodities afforded by the sea, the inhabitants make use of divers his creekes for grist mills, by thwarting a banke from side to side, in which a floodgate is placed, with two leaves; these the flowing tide openeth, and, after full sea, the waight of the ebb closeth fast, which no other force can doe: and so the imprisoned water payeth the ransome of driving an under sheete [undershot] wheel for his enlargement.*

The tide mill at Looe, Cornwall, was built between 1614 and 1621, possibly at the suggestion of Carew, and was still in practical use in the early twentieth century, when it was replaced by electricity.

As is the case today, such tide power installations required a large tidal range, but today much larger inlets or estuaries need to be dammed. A 240 MW tidal power station has been operating at La Rance in France since 1967. However, such installations can greatly affect the tidal ecosystems and there are not many suitable sites, and these are often far from consumers. Other sites under consideration are on the Severn estuary in the UK, in the West Kimberley region of Western Australia, Long Island Sound in the US and the Bay of Fundy in Canada. In some cases co-benefits include road links and flood control, but capital costs are very large. Turbines can be designed to generate power on both the ebb and flow of the tides. Another refinement is a 'double basin' type where incoming tides top up a high basin and outgoing tides drain a low basin. With a channel connecting the two, there can be a constant flow of water from the high to low basins. It is also possible to use a tidal-powered pump to lift water to a high basin, allowing for constant power to be generated from the latter irrespective of the tidal cycle.

Lessening the ecosystem effects is possible using turbines installed on the sea floor to capture power from the currents rather like windmills do on land. Although the speed of tidal or other ocean currents is generally less than that of the wind, the much higher density of water means that ocean currents can provide the same power with smaller turbines than the wind. A 300 kW experimental tidal current turbine is being installed off the coast of Devon in the UK, and others are operating experimentally at Hammerfest in Norway and in Shetland's Yell Sound.

Harnessing wave power is possible using oscillating air columns, or buoys to drive turbines, but is generally expensive and subject to damage by extreme wave conditions. Largest wave energy is generally in the deep ocean, which would require expensive transmission of power generated to shore.

Geothermal power can also be harnessed. This derives from hot dry rocks at depth below the Earth's surface, and requires engineering processes such as drilling and hydraulic fracturing of rock so that water can be circulated through it. These are techniques used by the oil and gas industry, and have been applied in plants in New Zealand, California and Iceland. While the potential is large, and generation can provide reliable base load electricity, capital costs are high. In suitable situations such as Iceland, geothermally heated water can be used for district heating, but there may be concerns about contamination of the water.

The hydrogen economy

Hydrogen is not an energy source but an energy carrier like electricity. It can be generated by the use of fossil fuel, by renewable energy or by using nuclear power. It is of enormous interest because when it is burned to provide energy in a turbine, or used to produce electricity in a fuel cell, its only waste product is water. It is thus a clean fuel at its point of use, which is good if it means that mobile sources of carbon dioxide, such as internal combustion engines in cars and trucks can be eliminated. The crunch, though, is how hydrogen can be generated without the emission of carbon dioxide. If it is produced from fossil fuels it is not free from greenhouse gas emissions, or from local pollution at its point of production.

To achieve a reduction in greenhouse gas emissions, hydrogen must be generated without the release of carbon dioxide to the atmosphere. This means it must be generated by renewable energy, nuclear power, or from fossil fuels in a process in which the carbon dioxide is removed from the emissions and disposed of other than in the atmosphere. The process of removal and long-term storage or 'sequestration' is discussed below. The most likely means of production of hydrogen are the reforming of natural gas, or the hydrolysis of water using electricity.

Hydrogen gas has a very low amount of energy per unit volume. Therefore, in order to store and transport hydrogen, it has to be compressed or otherwise contained at high density. This uses the equivalent of some 10% of its intrinsic energy. Pipelines exist in Europe and the US to transport hydrogen, but these use higher pressure than natural gas pipelines, which adds cost. However, at least in a transition phase to using mainly hydrogen, it can be mixed with natural gas and transported in natural gas pipelines. Also, the existence of natural gas pipelines means that easements already exist along which hydrogen pipelines could be built, so reducing costs. Alternatively, high-pressure linings could be inserted in natural gas pipelines.

Much effort is going into research on technologies to generate hydrogen and to use it as a fuel in automobiles. US President Bush has requested a US$1.2 billion budget for a Hydrogen Fuel Initiative and the 'FreedomCAR Partnership' to foster an industry decision by 2015 to commercialise hydrogen-powered fuel cell vehicles. The main focus is on generating hydrogen from natural gas and coal, to 'provide the transition to a hydrogen economy' with carbon sequestration to avoid 'adding to concerns over the build-up of carbon gases in the atmosphere'. A principal aim is to reduce the US's dependence on foreign oil.

It has been argued, however, by Demirdoven and Deutch of the Massachusetts Institute of Technology that hybrid petrol- or natural gas-electric vehicles are as energy efficient as hydrogen-fuelled fuel cell cars, and are available now. If the hydrogen comes from fossil fuels without carbon capture and sequestration, then there is no carbon dioxide emissions advantage. They argue that more effort should go into improving, and developing the market for hybrid vehicles, perhaps with tax credits, with hydrogen-fuelled fuel cells later. This is supported by a 2003 American Physical Society report, and a book by Joseph Romm *Hype About Hydrogen*. Romm, who is Executive Director of the Center for Energy and Climate Solutions, drives a hybrid and says 'If your concern is global warming, hydrogen cars are not what you'll be doing for the next 30 years.'

In Europe, the European Union and nine European cities have joined together to carry out a practical trial of hydrogen fuel cell buses in the Clean Urban Transport For Europe project (CUTE). The cities of Amsterdam (Netherlands), Barcelona and Madrid (Spain), Hamburg and Stuttgart (Germany), London (UK), Porto (Portugal) and Stockholm (Sweden) are each trialling three Mercedes-Benz Citaro fuel cell buses, with hydrogen production in each city via electrolysis of water or natural gas reformers, and high pressure refuelling stations. The first CUTE bus started operation in Madrid in 2003. If these technologies are made competitive they will reduce European dependence on imported oil, clean the air in the cities, and, depending on the source of the hydrogen, substantially reduce greenhouse gas emissions.

Shell Hydrogen, with various partners, is working on projects in Iceland, Washington DC and California (USA), and Tokyo (Japan) as well as the CUTE project. The Icelandic government has announced its intention to transform Iceland into the world's first hydrogen-based economy by 2050, and is trialling hydrogen-powered buses made by DaimlerChrysler. Another hydrogen-fuel cell bus experiment is underway in Perth, Western Australia, in collaboration with CUTE and BP, who are supplying the hydrogen.

Hydrogen may be produced in future from biomass, including a small device that converts liquid ethanol into hydrogen, which is then used in a fuel cell. This device may be suitable for safe portable power supplies, including drives for automobiles. The use of micro-algae or solar furnaces to split water into hydrogen and oxygen is being developed at the French laboratories CNRS. Several car manufacturers, including General Motors, BMW and Daimler-Chrysler are working on hydrogen-powered fuel cell car technology. A review by Seth Dunn in *Renewable Energy World*, July–August 2001, lists many other initiatives on the way to a hydrogen economy.

There are some potential concerns about the widespread use of hydrogen. One is safety, hydrogen being an odourless gas that burns with an invisible flame, although it must be in a higher concentration with air (more than 13%) than methane before it can cause an explosion. Another is the leakage of hydrogen into the atmosphere. If it gets into the upper atmosphere it could react with hydroxyl (OH) radicals to form water vapour, adversely affecting the climate and the ozone layer, while even in the lower atmosphere its reaction with hydroxyl radicals may allow methane to last longer, thus adding to the greenhouse effect. The result will depend on how large the leakage of hydrogen is, and on natural sinks for hydrogen in the soil. The sinks are not well known, and estimates of possible leakage vary from 10 to 20% down to about 0.1%. Knowledge of these problems may lead to ways of avoiding them.

In summary, the increased use of hydrogen as an energy carrier could lead to a substantial reduction in greenhouse gas emissions through:

- sequestration of carbon or carbon dioxide in large centralised plants generating hydrogen from fossil fuels,
- efficiency improvements from using hydrogen in fuel cells, and even burning hydrogen in internal combustion engines,
- generation of hydrogen using renewable energy sources and its subsequent use in transport.

Estimates of potential progress in moving to a hydrogen economy by mid-century vary wildly, but it is possible it may account for 25–40% of fuel use by 2050. However, a recent review in *Science* entitled 'The Hydrogen Backlash' states 'By focusing research on technologies that aren't likely to have a measurable impact until the second half of the century, the current hydrogen push fails to address the growing threat from greenhouse gas emissions from fossil fuels.'

This reflects the views of some notable critics of the focus on a hydrogen economy, such as Ulf Bossel, a prominent consultant on fuel cell technology. They base their concern mainly on the physical nature of hydrogen as the lightest gas, which requires the use of significant amounts of energy for its packaging, storage, delivery and transfer as an energy carrier. They compare this unfavourably with the use of electricity or methane as carriers of energy. For example, they cite volumetric heating values for hydrogen at one atmosphere pressure and 25°C of about 11 kJ/litre, compared to methane at about 35 kJ/litre.

This means that hydrogen must be highly compressed, liquefied or stored in hydrates, or transported in high-pressure pipelines. All of which consumes energy. They therefore oppose a 'pure-hydrogen-only-economy', preferring either electricity as a carrier of energy, or else a hydrocarbon such as methane. Where hydrogen is generated by renewable energy, they favour its use at source, either for local heating or to generate electricity. They state:

> ... hydrogen generated by electrolysis may be the best link between –
> mostly physical – energy from renewable sources and chemical
> energy. It is also the ideal fuel for modern clean energy conversion
> devices like fuel cells and can be used in modified IC [internal
> combustion] engines. But hydrogen is far from ideal for carrying
> energy between primary sources to distant or mobile end users.

Bossel and colleagues prefer a 'synthetic liquid hydrocarbon economy' based on biomass distillation or fermentation. However, this may be limited by the restricted availability of biomass fuel, given other constraints on land use such as food production. Provided hydrogen is generated from renewable sources, such as solar powered electrolysis, and is also used for powering its compression at source, loss of overall energy efficiency may be acceptable to avoid carbon dioxide emissions.

Carbon capture and sequestration

While increased energy efficiency and more non-fossil fuel energy both have the potential to decrease carbon dioxide emissions significantly over the next several decades, these alone may not be enough to avoid likely damaging climate change. An additional means to reduce emissions is to capture carbon dioxide at large point sources such as coal-, oil- or gas-fired power stations, and keep it out of the atmosphere. This is called carbon capture and sequestration. The goal is to produce energy from fossil fuels free of carbon dioxide emissions, at an affordable cost.

Even more exciting is the possibility of carbon capture and sequestration from biomass fuels. This would not merely result in zero emissions, but would actually remove carbon dioxide from the atmosphere. This will be necessary to return atmospheric concentrations of carbon dioxide to values less than the maximum at stabilisation, as represented in **Figure 23** above. As we have seen, the risk of dangerous interference in the climate system remains appreciable even at stabilisation levels of 450 ppm, especially if the global climate sensitivity is not at the low end of the IPCC estimated range (as the latest results suggest). Efforts will therefore be needed to bring the carbon dioxide concentration down after stabilisation in as short a time as possible.

The value and need for carbon removal and sequestration was not prominent in the IPCC 2001c summary conclusions, although it did say 'After 2010, emissions from fossil and/or biomass-fuelled power plants could be reduced substantially through pre- or post-combustion carbon removal and storage.' There are numerous other references to this subject in the text of the report. For example, on p.159 it states 'Climate stabilization requires the introduction of natural gas and biomass energy in the first half of the twenty-first century, and either nuclear energy or carbon removal and storage in the latter half of the century as the cost effective pathways.' It goes on to say that carbon removal and storage has a special role to play in otherwise high emissions scenarios such as the SRES A1FI and A1B scenarios. In other words, if you want to continue to use fossil fuels in a big way, carbon removal and storage is essential.

In general, carbon sequestration possibilities include underground or geological storage, injection into the deep ocean, biological sequestration in the oceans spurred on by iron fertilisation, and biological sequestration on land. Options for underground or geological disposal include:

- use of carbon dioxide in enhanced oil recovery,
- use of carbon dioxide in enhanced coal-bed methane recovery,
- depleted oil and gas reservoirs,
- deep un-minable coal beds,
- large cavities or voids, and
- deep saline water-saturated reservoirs.

Removal of carbon dioxide from post-combustion fumes uses either a membrane that allows only the carbon dioxide to pass through it, or amine solvents to scrub flue gases. In the latter case, the amine is then heated to release the pure carbon dioxide and is then re-used. However, low concentrations of carbon dioxide in the power station flue gases means that large volumes have to be treated, requiring large equipment and large amounts of energy to generate the solvent, all of which is expensive. Pre-combustion capture avoids some of these problems, but requires the use of hydrogen as the carrier of energy. Steam reforming of natural gas produces carbon dioxide and hydrogen. The carbon dioxide is then separated from the hydrogen. Hydrogen can also be produced from oil, coal or biomass and the carbon dioxide removed similarly. Only in the case of biomass does this result in a net removal of carbon dioxide from the air.

Global storage capacities in geological formations are estimated by the IPCC to range from 1500 to 14,000 Gt of carbon. This compares with present global emissions of about 8 Gt of carbon and IPCC SRES projections of total emissions by 2100 in the range 770 to 2540 Gt of carbon (see Chapter 5). So storage capacity is not likely to be a limit on carbon sequestration provided the storages have long-term security from leakage, and it is economical to use them.

Cost estimates vary with techniques and distance from source to storage area. They range, according to the International Energy Agency (IEA) in 2002, from US$25 per tonne of carbon to US$60. This cost may be reduced with improved technology, and can be substantially reduced where the carbon dioxide is used to enhance oil or coal bed methane recovery. In fact, IEA estimates that there could be a net benefit in some cases. Such a scheme is already in operation in the Sleipner offshore drilling platform run by Statoil in the North Sea.

Experimental carbon geo-sequestration projects are under way in several other countries including the United States, Australia, Canada and Japan. In most cases they are joint government and fossil fuel company projects subsidised by government funding. Key questions to be answered are:

- Can geo-sequestration handle the large volumes of gas from point sources such as power stations?
- Can this be achieved at a reasonable economic cost?
- Is it proven to be safe, secure and permanent?
- What percentage of carbon dioxide will not be captured?

Clearly governments and the fossil fuel industries are hopeful on all these points, as they are investing many millions of dollars into research and development. However, some environmental groups and advocates of renewable energy argue that the cost of carbon capture and geosequestration will likely make the cost of fossil fuel energy greater than that of many renewables, and that in the meantime funding is being diverted from research and development of renewables. These groups also argue that safe sites for geosequestration are limited and that geosequestration is unproven. They see it as at best a temporary solution until renewables can take up the slack.

The problem of leakage of sequestered carbon dioxide back into the atmosphere is particularly serious, as simple arithmetic easily demonstrates. If carbon sequestration were to be the principal means of reducing emissions into the atmosphere this century, it would need to take up the majority of the SRES projected emissions of 770 to 2540 Gt of carbon by 2100. Let us take 1500 Gt of carbon as a moderate estimate. Now consider that only 1% of the sequestered carbon dioxide leaks back into the atmosphere each year. This amounts to a leakage at year 2100 of some 15 Gt of carbon, or about twice the present global annual emissions. However, to stabilise carbon dioxide concentrations in the atmosphere at more or less safe levels, we have already seen that we must reduce net emissions to nearer 2 Gt of carbon per year. This requires nearer 0.1% as the maximum rate of leakage. This is a tall order. It suggests that geosequestration should not be seen as a long-term solution, since the total sequestered, assuming increasing use of fossil fuels, rapidly grows to a very large amount, requiring extremely low leakage rates. Moreover, this leakage rate from what is sequestered may be dwarfed by the amount of carbon dioxide not captured and sequestered, if reliance on fossil fuels continues without a full 100% carbon capture and sequestration.

Injection of carbon dioxide into the deep ocean in liquid form has been proposed. In principle, a large fraction of the carbon in known and recoverable reserves of fossil fuels could be stored in the oceans and calcareous ocean sediments. It would be pumped to a depth of 1000 metres or so, and there it would dissolve into the water. If sites were well chosen, this water would normally stay at depth for 1000 years or so, but it would change the chemistry of the deep ocean, including a slight reduction in pH, or increase in acidity. This could harm local sea life. Most deep-sea organisms are highly sensitive to small changes in water acidity, even as small as 0.2 to 0.5 units of pH.

As carbon dioxide is likely to be classed as an industrial waste under the terms of the London Convention on the prevention of pollution from ships, injection of carbon dioxide would also be unlawful in international waters. Moreover, verification of any emission reduction under the UNFCCC would depend on satisfying concerns about permanence, with respect to leakage and security.

Another controversial technique is to fertilise the ocean surface with iron, since low iron concentrations are known to limit biological productivity in many parts of the ocean. Several experiments have tested this in a limited way, and some commercial groups are interested in fertilisation of the ocean to increase fisheries production. Adding iron in iron-poor regions of the oceans has caused algal blooms detectable from satellites, and this may indeed remove some carbon dioxide from the atmosphere. However, such algal blooms may cause undesirable changes in the ocean by reducing oxygen levels in the water, encouraging bacteria that may produce other greenhouse gases such as methane and nitrous oxide, possibly causing toxicity and altering the food chain.

These ocean 'dumping' techniques are likely to be opposed by the public, according to a survey conducted by the Tyndall Centre for Climate Change Research in the UK, on the grounds of possible biological impacts and doubts about the permanence of any carbon storage.

Land-based carbon sinks

Biological sequestration on land includes better management of existing forests to safeguard and increase carbon stored in trees and soil, farm-scale or large-scale tree plantations, and farm management practices such as minimum tillage, which increase carbon stored in the soil. The IPCC 2001c report estimated that biological sequestration on land could sequester up to 100 Gt of carbon in total by 2050, which is equivalent to about 10% to 20% of projected fossil fuel emissions of carbon in that interval. Beyond 2050 the capacity to store more carbon will decrease as forests reach maturity and decay starts to match growth. This decline may well be accentuated as global warming increases, and even turns forests and soils into sources of atmospheric carbon rather than sinks due to increased decay, forest die-back, selective changes in species competition and the danger of increased wild fires. Fire protection, cessation of land clearing, and continuation of minimum tillage practices are essential to maintaining a biological carbon store. If plantations are to act effectively as permanent carbon stores, any harvesting of mature timber or other biomass generated must be used to replace fossil fuel emissions through biomass energy, to substitute for energy-intensive materials such as steel or aluminium, or for long-lasting timber such as in furniture or buildings. Verification of actual amounts of carbon permanently stored would be difficult and contentious.

Biomass growth, and thus carbon storage, will rise with increasing atmospheric carbon dioxide due to fertilisation effects, but may be positively or adversely affected by climate changes, with adverse effects tending to dominate for large warmings or decreases in soil moisture. Increased carbon stored in managed land ecosystems can only partly offset fossil fuel usage, and must be considered as a partial delaying mechanism until other mitigation measures take over. Moreover, consideration must be given to destruction of soil carbon content by any large-scale clearing for plantations, especially if accompanied by burning of trash, as is often done.

Other considerations regarding large forest plantations are their effect on the albedo or reflectivity of the Earth's surface to solar radiation. Forests in general absorb more sunlight than bare soil or grassland. Additional forests will therefore lead to additional warming, either locally or downwind due to the transport of latent heat from the increased evapotranspiration by the trees. This radiation absorption effect may go some way to cancelling out the effect of plantations in removing carbon dioxide from the atmosphere. In addition, plantations tend to use more water than bare soil or grasslands, which will reduce runoff and thus water supplies. Especially in regions where water supply problems may be aggravated by climate change, this may be critical for dependent local communities.

Plantations also tend to displace existing farming activities and people dependent on them. This is already the cause for opposition to plantations in some rural areas of Australia, and in some developing countries where large numbers of people may lose their livelihoods. Trees, however, may reduce dryland salinity, decrease soil erosion and in some cases increase local income. All in all, plantation forestry needs to be considered on a case-by-case basis, taking into account a complex web of factors.

The UK Royal Society in a special report in 2001 summed up the role of land carbon sinks in mitigating global climate change in its final statement:

... our current knowledge indicates that the potential to enhance the land carbon sink through changes in land management practices is finite in size and duration. The amount of carbon that can be sequestered in these sinks is small in comparison to the ever-increasing global emissions of greenhouse gases. Projects designed to enhance carbon sinks must therefore not be allowed to divert financial and political resources away from the restructuring of energy generation and use (e.g. increased use of renewable energy), technological innovation (e.g. increased fuel efficiency, sequestration at source) and technology transfer to less developed countries. It is these that must provide the ultimate solution to the problem of reducing the concentration of greenhouse gases in the atmosphere.

Changes in infrastructure and behaviour

Evolutionary or adaptive structural changes to society are implicit in most forms of mitigation. How to reverse the increasing reliance on private automobile transport for commuting, shopping and other activities in modern cities is one example. Clearly a more compact city, or one designed so as to minimise the necessity for travel would help. It is also possible to provide better public transport services, which obviate the necessity to use private transport.

Such measures would encourage walking and bicycle use instead of cars for short trips, and car-pooling or public transport for longer trips. Measures include provision of bicycle lanes or separate bicycle paths, walking paths and pedestrian malls, more pedestrian friendly urban design, and suburban parking areas and computerised linkup schemes for car-pooling and buses on demand, or parking facilities at suburban transport hubs.

There are many examples where such strategies have worked, such as in Toronto, Canada, and Perth, Western Australia. In Perth, a deliberate strategy to encourage use of public transport included full electrification of three existing rail lines in 1991, and the opening of a new northern suburbs line in 1993. Rail patronage in Perth has risen from about 8000 daily in 1991 to nearly 30,000 in 1997. This contrasts with Adelaide, South Australia, a similar sized city where rail patronage has remained almost unchanged since 1991.

Another example is the issue of cars fuelled by less polluting means than petroleum. In the case of fuel cells fuelled by hydrogen, car manufacturers are unlikely to build fuel cell cars unless they can be assured that the vehicles can be refuelled at a network of stations, because customers require that convenience. Fuel providers, meanwhile, would be unlikely to provide hydrogen at their stations unless they were assured of a market for the hydrogen. Several solutions are apparent. One would be for car manufacturers to build cars that can generate hydrogen for their fuel cells on board from a hydrocarbon fuel. Another would be for a planned program with incentives or subsidies to make hydrogen-fuelled fuel cells cheaper and more attractive, coupled with incentives for refuelling stations to carry hydrogen. Here, choices about the structure of the market place may decide which fuel becomes the fuel of choice. A similar situation with the introduction of unleaded petrol and suitable car engines was managed successfully in many countries.

Much of the inefficiency in supplying electric power is in the wasted heat generated at the power stations, and losses in the transmissions lines. Both these inefficiencies can be greatly reduced if decentralised power generation can be encouraged, where heat can be used for industrial or domestic heating and there are no transmission losses. This would be helped by government incentives and more appropriate public or private planning, for example encouraging the generation of electricity and heat in buildings from natural gas fuelled fuel cells.

Technological innovation: attitude is vital

Technological change has been rapid and accelerating over the last century or so. The invention and refinement of the automobile, and later the aeroplane, radically changed society, urban structures, trade and warfare in the twentieth century. Communication technology has also increased rapidly, especially in the last few decades as computers and the world wide web have made the flow of information almost instantaneous for those with the wealth to afford it. Computer technology has leapt ahead so rapidly that many older but well-educated citizens have been left behind, while science has been able to achieve miracles in the area of computer modelling which now guide scientific developments and even manufacturing.

Nevertheless, people have an ambivalent attitude to technology. This is reflected in their policy preferences in relation to climate change. Many people (often associated with business) believe that, given climate change will happen, society has the ability to adapt, but that reducing carbon emissions would be too costly. This attitude displays technological optimism in the area of adaptation but pessimism regarding technology for mitigation. In effect, these people put the onus to innovate on those who will be affected by climate change (by saying it is easy), rather than on those whose activities may cause it (by saying it is too hard).

Other people, usually of an environmentalist bent, believe that carbon emissions can be reduced dramatically within a few years, but that adaptation will be unacceptably costly or impossible. These people have optimism about technology to reduce emissions (which in simplistic terms is not their responsibility), but pessimism about adaptation (which they would need to do).

This dichotomy is of course too simplistic. Most people stand somewhere between these extreme views. If we are to solve the problem of human-induced climate change we need to both adapt and mitigate. Therefore, we need to innovate in both areas, and have the optimism or faith to go ahead and try, then learn

by doing. If technological change was increasingly rapid in the twentieth century, why cannot it be even more rapid in the twenty-first, when we see the
urgent need, and the direction in which we need to innovate? If, indeed, dangerous interference in the climate system is rapidly approaching, why can't we initiate urgent programs to innovate our way out of the problem, both by
adaptation and mitigation? Private corporations and individuals set goals and
programs for development and change every day, and in the area of defence governments do it all the time on the basis of perceived but uncertain threats, at
great expense, and by setting very demanding research and development goals.

Technological optimism is perhaps well expressed by Wilson Tuckey, a conservative Australian politician. In a 2003 speech linking the hydrogen economy
to a proposed tidal power project in Western Australia, he stated:

> So why are we panicking today? The basic technology exists at every
> level, refinement and financing is the challenge. …. We have got to
> develop our options. It does not matter that there will be other options
> for low emission energy production or hydrogen creation. But if we
> are going to maintain our standard of living … then we have got to
> have 'Greenhouse with Grunt'.

A further exhortation to view climate change policy as an opportunity comes
from the book *Natural Capitalism,* by Paul Hawken and others in 1999:

> … in the next half century, the climate problem could become as faded
> a memory as the energy crises of the seventies are now, because
> climate change is not an inevitable result of normal economic activity
> but an artefact of carrying out that activity in irrationally inefficient
> ways …
>
> If we vault the barrier, use energy in a way that saves money, and
> put enterprise where it belongs, in the vanguard of sound solutions,
> climate change will become a problem we can't afford, don't need,
> and can avoid with huge financial savings to society.

If some of us are indeed panicking today it is because too many governments, industries and entrepreneurs have not yet fully taken up the challenge of
technological innovation to deal with climate change. Technological optimists
say it can be done. We must find the will to produce solutions through ingenuity
and innovation. Attitude is vital.

The road to effective mitigation

It is sometimes said that if the enhanced greenhouse problem is real, someone
will find a way to make money out of a solution, and so the market will take care
of it. That is partly true. However, there are barriers or obstacles that can slow or

prevent the spread of technologies and practices that could potentially reduce greenhouse gas emissions.

The most obvious are so-called market failures, such as subsidies for fossil fuel industries, lack of competition and inadequate information about alternatives. Others include initial capital costs, even though these costs may be exceeded by savings in a matter of a few years to a decade or so. An interesting example is rented housing, where the tenant pays the energy bills, but the landlord pays the upfront costs for energy-consuming equipment such as lighting, heaters and air-conditioners. This provides no incentive for the landlord to pay more for energy efficient equipment. Overcoming such barriers, for example by changing tax structures, giving innovative industries an initial tax break or subsidy, or extending capital loans at cheap rates, would lead to net savings over time and an economically viable alternative to some greenhouse gas intensive industries and technologies.

A second class of barrier is due to people's preferences and other social and cultural barriers to the spread of new technologies. Examples include preferences for private transport over public because of perceived convenience and safety, or for architectural styles that are not appropriate to energy-efficient living in a particular climate. These barriers can be overcome once they are recognised and addressed, for example by improving the timing, routing, staffing, security and reliability of public transport, or by information or guidelines on the savings to be made by energy-efficient housing design, such as having wide eaves or verandas on the sunny side of houses, adequate insulation, and so on. Subsidies and other incentives may also help. These can be removed once better practices have been widely adopted and become the norm. The idea that people's preferences are somehow fixed is nonsense, as any serious consideration of changing fashions in clothes or popular music will show. People react to many things that may change their preferences and habits, including new information, new technology, advertising campaigns, cheap introductory offers, examples and peer pressure.

This class of barriers includes the provision of the necessary large-scale infrastructures necessary for the adoption of some technologies, for instance generation and distribution networks for hydrogen or other alternative fuels, user-friendly public transport, or energy-efficient urban planning and regulation. These can be achieved through local, regional or national government planning, preferably in collaboration with private industry, driven by consideration of long-term issues of sustainability and public good.

A third class of barrier is economic, for those technologies which would reduce greenhouse gas emissions, but which are presently too expensive for consumers. These economic barriers can be overcome by including in the price of competing technologies the environmental and social costs of pollution, thus making plain the benefits of switching to cleaner technologies. This can be achieved by imposing surcharges or taxes on polluting technologies, or by providing equivalent subsidies for non-polluting ones. If the most cost-effective non-polluting technologies are to be employed, such price penalties or incentives should be based on accurate estimates of the environmental and social costs and benefits. Such measures should be constructed so as to avoid bias towards one non-polluting technology over another that might be more efficient. This includes the concept of embedded energy emissions, discussed earlier.

Stabilising greenhouse gas concentrations is part of the objective of achieving sustainable development, since, without a stable climate sustainable development is impossible (see Chapter 9). In reviewing a book on energy and the challenge of sustainability, Walt Patterson from the Royal Institute of International Affairs in the UK said:

> *The authors ... realise that overcoming the economic, social, and political obstacles to sustainable development will take time. The long life cycles of some investments resist efforts to accelerate changes. Even after environmentally friendly technologies are developed, they must become affordable and available in the quantities and at the locations necessary for them to be effective. Inertia in human behaviour and consumer choices will have to be overcome. Today's purchasers are reluctant to pay for benefits that will not be delivered until some uncertain time in the future. The transition to an energy framework that will support sustainable development will require widespread public support along with informed political leadership and policy-making.*

Overall, the market tends to react to short-term signals, measured in days to years, whereas the enhanced greenhouse problem acts on a longer time scale of decades to centuries. Also, the market normally takes into account only what has a market price, so issues like long-term sustainability, species extinctions, and even community health, are often neglected. For the market to work in relation to long-term problems, especially on issues that are not usually measured in dollars, mechanisms need to be built into the market to help it account for non-market values and to bring in the longer-term perspective. That is a role for governments and far-sighted businesses. Investments in initially unprofitable low-carbon technologies may well pay off in the long run as market niches, and eventually, economies of scale are created.

Some governments have placed greatest emphasis on voluntary action by industry to reduce greenhouse gas emissions. This is achieved through education, technical advice, and in some cases subsidies. However, such programs lack a sense of urgency, and usually only succeed where emissions reductions can be achieved on a 'no regrets' basis within the existing price and taxation structures. They tend to focus on drawing industry attention to the energy savings that can be made in that small percentage of industry budgets devoted to energy costs, which has often been neglected by industry. However, many of the institutional obstacles mentioned above apply to voluntary and relatively unco-ordinated actions.

Industry needs a level playing field where those who are far-sighted and innovative are not penalised by the market. This certainly requires elimination of large subsidies presently paid to many fossil fuel or energy-intensive industries, such as:

- tax incentives for oil and gas exploration;
- energy subsidies for some energy-intensive industries such as aluminium manufacturers;
- regulatory systems favouring established industries;
- huge tax-derived expenditures on road networks favouring private energy-intensive transport over more efficient public transport;
- tax subsidies or flat rates for taxes on 'gas-guzzling' heavy vehicles often used for recreation;
- and preferential tariffs.

Carbon taxes are often advocated as the best method to discourage the use of carbon intensive fuels. Just as often they are argued against. The argument against is that they add too much to industrial costs and thus slow the economy, create unemployment and reduce the surplus needed to devote to environmental benefits. There is some truth in both arguments.

However, carbon taxes should be part of an array of measures to foster a switch to a low-carbon economy. Such measures should include at least initial subsidies for non-carbon energy sources and the fostering of measures to create economies of scale for low-carbon alternatives. By itself, any tax that increases the overall tax burden on industry and investment is likely to have a negative effect on the economy through raising costs and prices. However, if the revenue from that tax is used to reduce other taxes, or fed back into the economy in the form of subsidies and incentives for low-carbon energy or improved energy efficiency, there may be an overall benefit to the economy. Such a package of measures can increase employment, increase efficiency, and reduce reliance on imported fuel.

Special attention should be paid to measures designed to encourage innovation in low-carbon emitting technology. These could include subsidies on research and development, low interest loans for initial capital investments by both suppliers and consumers, and public education. Other measures might include, where appropriate, regulated energy efficiency standards such as fuel economy in vehicles, and minimum proportions of renewable energy on electrical grids. Regulatory measures may be needed to require electricity suppliers to buy back excess electricity generated by home solar energy units, or to expedite siting for solar energy collectors and wind generators.

Local and district combined electricity and heat generation should be favoured over centralised power stations where heat is wasted.

Building and planning regulations should be modified to encourage energy efficiency through insulation, proper siting with respect to the Sun, eaves and verandas on the sunny sides of houses, double glazing, solar hot water and other renewable energy devices. Urban planning is essential to provide denser population near to public transport facilities and to minimise daily travel requirements. Facilities for home offices and electronic commuting, such as planning permits and cabling, should be made.

The list of such measures will grow as new technologies are developed. Their urgency and stringency will need to be varied according to their effectiveness, acceptability and ongoing risk assessments of the reality of climate change and projections of its likely impacts.

Economic concerns require that the most economically efficient low-carbon technologies are developed, consistent with other environmental and social objectives. This requires care not to pick winners between alternative low-carbon technologies without good reason. It is better to use measures that maintain competition while fostering innovation. Thus tax concessions and subsidies should be based less on specific technologies and more on performance in terms of energy efficiency, low-carbon intensity, and ancillary social benefits. Various forms of carbon emissions trading, both within and between countries, may well provide incentives to reduce carbon emissions at least cost.

Carbon trading (sometimes called 'cap-and-trade') consists of issuing permits to emit certain amounts of greenhouse gases (or specifically carbon dioxide), which are then bought and sold. The amount of emissions permitted under each permit can be reduced with time, in order to meet more stringent overall reduction targets as required to mitigate climate change.

In rapidly developing countries the need for new infrastructure can be seized upon as an opportunity to invest in low-carbon emissions technology, thus leapfrogging over the more energy- and carbon-intensive technologies hitherto developed in the industrialised countries. Less emphasis on freeways and more on improving mass transit is essential in the mega-cities of the developing world. This will have many co-benefits in terms of minimising urban air pollution, and avoiding social costs such as road deaths. Similarly, emphasis on decentralised renewable energy supplies rather than centralised power grids is an opportunity rather than a burden. Access by developing countries to the latest low-carbon and energy-efficient technologies is vital, and should be a big part of any effort by the developed countries to minimise inequity and foster sustainable development.

In the more developed countries, old carbon-intensive technologies will need to be phased out as quickly as possible, with a need to write off old infrastructure and invest in the new. Again, this is likely to have co-benefits in terms of increased efficiency, regional employment, reduced urban pollution, and a greater sense of community. New investments in old carbon-intensive technologies and industries should be actively discouraged.

Deep reductions in emissions of carbon dioxide are necessary to stabilise climate. Under most scenarios, according to the IPCC 2001 report, this will require the increasing introduction of natural gas and biomass energy in the first half of this century, and, for high energy use scenarios, either nuclear power or carbon removal and storage in the latter half of this century, as cost effective pathways.

However, as we have seen in our review above of mitigation options, none of these solutions by themselves will solve the problem. Certainly, continued large-scale use of coal and oil can only be considered in the short term, and then only with rapid application of carbon removal and sequestration. But the stringent requirement of extremely low leakage of sequestered carbon back into the atmosphere, once amounts of sequestered carbon grow to hundreds of Gt of carbon, means that this cannot be seen as a long-term solution. Similarly, terrestrial biomass sequestration is only a short-term solution, useful only as a delaying mechanism, since the terrestrial biosphere is likely to change from a sink to a source within a matter of decades.

Efficient use of natural gas through fuel cells may well increase energy efficiency and reduce carbon emissions substantially, but not totally eliminate carbon emissions. Continued growth in populations, economies and energy use will eventually require the almost complete phasing out of natural gas as well as coal and oil. Indeed, the continued growth of populations and per capita energy use, but not necessarily of a more clever low-carbon economy, must eventually be questioned if emissions of greenhouse gases are to be stabilised. Rapid development of renewable energy sources such as solar, wind, biomass and tidal power, and perhaps nuclear power, along with a decline in growth of energy use through increasing energy efficiency and decreasing demand, are thus the only really long-term solutions. Each of these technologies, and maybe others not yet thought of, has its problems, but all will need to be pursued in the future, with a growing sense of urgency.

9

Climate change in context

Local, regional, and global environmental issues are inextricably linked and affect sustainable development. Therefore, there are synergistic opportunities to develop more effective response options to these environmental issues that enhance benefits, reduce costs, and more sustainably meet human needs.

IPCC *Third Assessment Report, Synthesis Report,* **2001, p.29.**

In the short term, population growth will be the main pressure on scarce water resources. In the long run, climate change may exacerbate the problems, causing irreversible impacts, especially in arid and semi-arid zones.

James Evans, Acting Director, World Bank Environment Department, 2004.

A common reaction to climatic change research by scientists in other disciplines, and by many decision-makers, is that there are other global change issues (such as land use change, water supply or economic development) deserving of greater priority both for research funding and for policy concern and action. Up to a point this is undoubtedly true. The climate change issue should be put in context and given its due weight and not more. However, climate change is a truly global phenomenon, and over periods of several decades it will have appreciable impacts on many sectors and on the policy reactions required for these other problems. Climate change is one of a suite of problems and issues, and its true effects and appropriate policies cannot be understood without reference to the joint effect of other problems and stresses. There are multiple causes, multiple effects, possible synergies and other interactions between problems.

Donald Kennedy, Editor of *Science* magazine in the US, put it this way:

... we have a great many pressing problems in the world. There's a population problem associated with economic development and pressure on resources. There is a continuing global security crisis augmented by the rise of terrorism. There is the chronically inequitable distribution in resources between the rich nations of the North and the poorer nations of the South. And, finally, there is the steadily growing body of evidence that we're about to undertake a major reorganization of the global climate regime.

The proposition is simple. It is that the last issue is of great concern to us because it directly relates to the future of our children and grandchildren, but it's also important because it relates in an indirect way and a very powerful way to every single one of the other problems I've just listed.

In its 2001 report, the Intergovernmental Panel on Climate Change (IPCC) made a first attempt to put climate change in the context of other cross-cutting issues such as sustainable development, equity, decision-making processes and uncertainty. Nevertheless, the result falls well short of complete success. In part this is inevitable in the light of IPCC's primary task of reporting on climate change issues, not on every other world problem. While some critics have argued that the IPCC did not deal adequately with, for example, land use change effects on climate, the IPCC itself produced a special report on *Land Use, Land-Use Change, and Forestry*. Similarly, international reports by the United Nations Environment Program and the World Meteorological Organization deal with the problem of ozone depletion.

What is still needed, though, are more studies that attempt to include all the various causes and effects, and their interaction, on systems of interest. Such studies are termed 'integrated assessments'. This is already well underway with a number of global integrated models, referenced in the IPCC report, however, these are often simplistic in their characterisations of many complex processes. This is understandable, given limited computing and other resources, but more comprehensive impact assessments are needed.

Several of the interactions between issues merit separate discussion and are explored below. A simple schematic diagram, shown in **Figure 26** might help to visualise the connections.

Surface air pollution and climate change

There are a number of connections and feedbacks between surface air pollution and climate change.

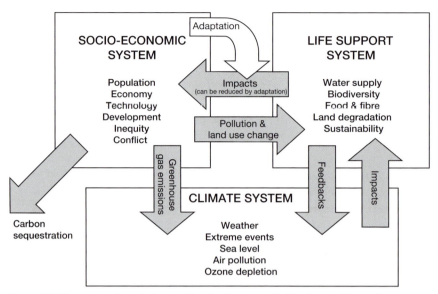

Figure 26: The connections between climate change and other issues. The socio-economic system and the life support system (for humans, animals and plants) interact independently of climate change. However, the climate system is affected by the socio-economic system and in turn affects the life support system. Feedbacks from the life support system also affect climate, while the socio-economic system has a limited capacity to adapt to changes in the life support system brought about by climate change.

First, near-surface ozone air pollution and the emissions that drive it are important contributors to global climate change. Pollutants such as nitrogen oxides, carbon monoxide and volatile organic compounds lead to ozone pollution in urban environments and to a global increase in ozone concentrations in the lower atmosphere. Ozone in the lower atmosphere is the third largest human-induced contributor to global warming, after carbon dioxide and methane.

Second, the precursors of surface ozone pollution mainly come from the combustion of fossil fuels, so reducing fossil fuel emissions has co-benefits by limiting both global warming and urban air pollution.

Third, global warming tends to make urban air pollution and surface ozone concentrations worse by affecting the chemistry of the atmosphere.

Fourth, another major air pollutant in the lower atmosphere is sulfate particles and the resulting acid rain, formed from sulfur emissions from the burning of fossil fuels. Sulfate particles cause some local cooling by reflecting sunlight back into space and are largely responsible for so-called 'global dimming' as discussed in Chapter 2.

Finally, acid rain has widespread adverse effects on land-based and aquatic ecosystems, human health and on many building materials. It adds to the adverse effects of climate change on agriculture and food supplies. So, once more, reducing the combustion of sulfur-rich fossil fuels can have desirable effects on two environmental problems, global warming and acid rain.

Stratospheric ozone depletion

There are also a number of links between climate change and stratospheric ozone depletion. Several of the chemicals causing ozone depletion in the stratosphere, notably the chlorofluorocarbons (CFCs), are important greenhouse gases and have been largely phased out of production because of their effects on ozone. However, other halocarbons that are less damaging to the ozone layer, namely hydrofluorocarbons, have been used as substitutes for the CFCs, but these are also greenhouse gases.

Another connection is that destruction of ozone in the stratosphere, or upper atmosphere, leads to less absorption of ultraviolet radiation from the Sun, so more ultraviolet radiation reaches the surface. This causes an increase in skin cancers and eye cataracts. It also adds synergistically to stresses on some food crops, and on coral reefs, which are adversely affected by both increased ultraviolet radiation and by climate change.

Ozone destruction in the stratosphere also leads to less absorption of solar energy in the upper atmosphere and therefore a cooling of the stratosphere. This impacts on the atmospheric circulation by increasing the equator to pole temperature difference, because most ozone destruction occurs at high latitudes. This increases the transport polewards of westerly angular momentum in the atmosphere, due to the rotation of the earth, leading to stronger westerly winds that form the westerly low-pressure vortices around the Arctic and Antarctic regions. Like giant whirlpools, these strengthened vortices contract towards the poles. This in turn means that weather systems in the lower atmosphere move further polewards, with serious consequences for rainfall and storm patterns at the Earth's surface. These changes may also contribute to more rapid warming and melting of polar ice, at least along the Antarctic Peninsula. Because the CFCs have a long lifetime in the atmosphere, the effect of ozone destruction, while now limited by cessation of production of CFCs, will continue for decades to come, so influencing climate well into the mid-twenty-first century. This is a prime example of the importance of time lags in the atmospheric system.

Ozone destruction, and the way it is being dealt with under the Vienna Convention for the Protection of the Ozone Layer and the Montreal Protocol, sets an important precedent for dealing with the enhanced greenhouse effect. The time lag between remedial action under the Montreal Protocol and its effect, some 50 years or more, is also an object lesson that early action is needed on the greenhouse problem if we are to avoid dangerous impacts later this century.

Biodiversity, agriculture and forestry

Changes in land-based and marine plant and animal systems occur for many reasons, including land-use change, pollution, climate change and increasing atmospheric concentrations of carbon dioxide.

In turn, changes in these biological systems affect climate by changing the exchange of greenhouse gases including carbon dioxide, methane and oxides of nitrogen between the land and ocean surfaces and the atmosphere. Land surface cover by vegetation also has an important effect on the reflection and absorption of sunlight at the Earth's surface, and thus on temperatures and evaporation. This should be taken into account in climate models, by including a variable biosphere that responds to climate change. Such combined models have now been run and show that an interactive biosphere can speed up the increase in greenhouse gases in the atmosphere.

Natural climate variability, from year to year and decade to decade demonstrates that the biosphere is sensitive to climate, and thus to climate change. But the effects of other stresses such as erosion, fire, sea-level rise, salinisation and air pollution are also evident. These can amplify the effects of climate change, or at least add to stresses on humans reliant on the biosphere for food, fibre and shelter. Climate change effects on crop production are of course of vital importance, while changing patterns of crop growth and irrigation affect surface reflectivity, temperature and evaporation, and thus have an effect on climate, at least at a regional level.

Other stresses on the biosphere, such as land-clearing, air pollution and overexploitation also increase the vulnerability of the biosphere to climate change and sea-level rise. Coral reefs are a notable example, with pollution and overfishing having deleterious effects on their survival. They may be pushed to the edge of extinction, at least locally, by climate change. Similarly, loss and fragmentation of habitat due to land clearing renders many species and ecosystems more vulnerable to climate change by restricting opportunities to adapt by migration. Conversely, climate change renders species and ecosystems more vulnerable to land use change. Moreover, climate change can enhance the risk from the spread of pests and diseases and the risk from monocultures, which can suffer widespread damage from a single pest or disease.

Land degradation and desertification

Projected levels of climate change would worsen the land degradation and desertification that has occurred over the last several centuries as the human population has expanded, water resources have been harnessed and diverted, monocultures established and forests cleared.

Extreme climatic events historically are the main cause of land degradation, amplified by unwise land clearing in marginal areas where soil needs vegetation cover to remain fertile and to prevent erosion. Increased frequency and severity of droughts and floods, and increased fire frequency and intensity, will increase wind and water erosion of soil and loss of soil fertility in many regions.

As populations grow and demand for food increases, more marginal land is likely to be exploited, increasing the synergetic interplay between climate change and loss of land cover, erosion and reduced soil fertility. Floods, land-slides and related natural disasters will cause increased damage, loss of life and poverty. The pressing need to substitute biomass for fossil fuels will also place further pressure on land resources, with possible unfortunate consequences for sustainability, food production and human equity, although reforestation and biomass plantations may in some cases help protect or restore degraded land.

Any increase in fire and soil erosion will further decrease forest and soil carbon storage, adding to the rapidity of climate change and tending to defeat attempts at mitigation through sequestration of carbon on land. This is already a major issue in Kalimantan, Indonesia, where large areas of peat swamps were drained for agriculture, leading to large surface and underground fires during drought conditions, creating smoke haze and large greenhouse gas emissions.

Freshwater

As stated by the IPCC in its 2001 report, all three classes of freshwater problems – too little, too much, and too dirty – may be made worse by climate change. Freshwater is essential for food supplies, sanitation and human health. It is also critical for natural ecosystems and for many industrial processes.

When water withdrawals are greater than about 20% of the total renewable resources, water is often a limiting factor in development, while withdrawals of over 40% mean serious water stress. In many arid regions this is being overcome by withdrawals from underground reservoirs, which were laid down over thousands of years, leading to lower water tables and diminishing resources. Others rely for irrigation and hydro-power on meltwater from glaciers, which increase temporarily with global warming, until the glaciers are gone, when drastic reductions in river flow follow. Such unsustainable situations apply in wealthy countries like the United States, as well as in developing countries like Pakistan, Peru and Nepal. In 1950, groundwater accounted for 23% of total irrigation water in the United States, while in 2000 it accounted for 42%. Seasonal snow-fed supplies are also under threat in the US due to higher temperatures.

One global study in 2000 reported that rising demand would greatly out-weigh greenhouse warming in defining the state of global water systems by

2025. However, the international *Dialogue on Water and Climate*, in 2004 concluded:

> *Our results suggest that water is going to be more plentiful in those regions of the world that are already 'water-rich'. However, water stresses will increase significantly in those regions and seasons that are already relatively dry. This could pose a very challenging problem for water resource management around the world. For soil moisture, our results indicate reductions during much of the year in many semi-arid regions of the world, such as the south-western regions of North America, the north-eastern region of China, the Mediterranean coast of Europe, and the grasslands of Australia and Africa.*

In the year 1990, about a third of the world's population lived in countries using more than 20% of their water resources. By the year 2025 it is estimated that some 60% of the then larger global population will be living in such water-stressed countries, simply due to population growth.

Climate change will add to these problems. The *Dialogue on Water and Climate* also states:

> *The hydrological cycle is speeding up. That means more frequent and extreme storms, floods and droughts in many parts of the world. ... The problems of climate variability are with us now. Every year, floods kill many thousands of people, make millions homeless and destroy the lives and hopes of millions more. ... annual losses from hydro-meteorological disasters increased tenfold between the 1950s and the 1990s ... including a rise from US$75 billion in the 1980s to more than $300 billion in the 1990s; successive droughts in Kenya in 1997–8 and 1999/2000 are estimated to have cost the country more than 40% of its GDP ... and Mozambique suffered a 23% reduction in its GDP after the 1999 floods ... It is the poor in the developing world who suffer most. Their fragile livelihoods and precarious homes are the first to go when disaster strikes, while poverty constrains their capacity to protect themselves in advance or to recover afterwards. Repeated disasters set back national economic progress and threaten the achievement of Millennium Development Goals.*

Strains on urban water systems are likely to increase due to global climate change. Typical strains are likely to include:

- increased water demand in hotter, drier seasons when water supply is at a minimum;
- floods exceeding the design capacity of protection works;

- more extreme rainfall events exceeding sewage design capacities, leading to overflows;
- less dilution of wastewater discharges into rivers with less dry-season flow;
- increased eutrophication and reduced water quality due to high nutrient loadings, low water flows and high temperatures;
- conflicts in the management of dams to simultaneously protect against greater floods, limit eutrophication, generate electricity and store water for dry seasons.

Other areas of concern include restoration of environmental flows to preserve riverine ecosystems and maintain freshwater fisheries, and the potential effects on runoff of reforestation (for various purposes, such as control of soil erosion and salinisation, and for carbon sequestration). A comparative study in Australia indicates that in one inland catchment, reforestation of 10% of the upper catchment would reduce runoff into the water storages by as much as the climate change by 2030. The combined effect would be far worse than either effect alone.

Major technological fixes or adaptations being considered include water diversions between river systems in China, India and elsewhere. However, these are very costly and controversial, involving ecological problems and displacement of large numbers of people. Other costly solutions include desalinisation plants (recently projected for Perth in Western Australia), which need large energy supplies. Alternative adaptations include demand management through water conservation and pricing and recycling of water. Reducing the extent and rapidity of climate change through mitigation actions appears necessary, as discussed in Chapter 8.

Population growth

Ever since Thomas Malthus' *Essay on the Principle of Population* in 1798, global population growth has loomed as a major environmental issue. The Malthusian argument is that population growth would outstrip the capacity of the Earth to support the population. Applied to the greenhouse effect, this relates to the Earth's capacity to accept additional greenhouse gas emissions without harm. In 1965, E Boserup offered the contrasting view that high population densities favour technological innovation that enables the environment to support more people. Applied to the greenhouse effect this suggests that technological innovation may avoid harm by either increasing our capacity to adapt, or by providing less carbon-intensive means of supplying energy services.

Empirical evidence from data from 1975 to 1996, analysed by Anquing Shi of the World Bank, indicates that greenhouse gas emissions increased more rapidly than population in developing countries, but less rapidly than population in developed countries.

Greenhouse gas emissions are a product of population, energy use per person, and carbon intensity of energy production. Population is thus a key driver of greenhouse gas emissions. However, as indicated in **Table 9**, emissions per person are more than 10 times as large in the United States and Australia than in the least developed countries such as India and most of Africa. Sustainable development in these developing countries clearly must include declining rates of population growth in order to safeguard many aspects of sustainability, including a stable climate. However, the real question is how this is to be done, given traditional attitudes, the development context in these countries, and questions of equity and human rights.

As we saw in Chapter 3, global population is expected by many experts to peak during this century. Population is already declining in most developed countries. This is thought to be a result of increased income, growing family security, and the education of women, which provide both the incentive and the means to limit population growth. This is often referred to as the 'demographic transition' that comes with development. Population in the United States and Australia is still increasing, but in both cases this is largely due to immigration, much of it from poorer countries.

This suggests that until developing countries reach development levels at which a demographic transition begins, both their populations and emissions are likely to continue to increase rapidly unless there is a rapid transition to low-carbon technologies, or disease and malnutrition take their toll. Moreover, as yet, most of the richer countries still have increases in emissions per person, starting from a much higher base rate: even with zero population growth developed countries need to greatly decrease their emissions.

The population issue boils down to one of sustainable development, with population growth declining when conditions are ripe for a demographic transition. Towards this end, a global population policy has in fact been devised through the United Nations International Conference on Population and Development in Cairo in 1994.

As suggested by Brian O'Neill and colleagues in their book *Population and Climate Change* (Cambridge University Press, 2001), population and climate policy need to be linked. They point out, however, that due to population age structure, family planning will take a generation or more to take effect, and thus will not substantially reduce emissions in the short term. Thus population measures, however necessary they may be in the long run, should not detract from the need for urgent reductions in emissions per person, especially where this is already high. Fostering energy conservation and low-carbon technology therefore remain critical.

Synergies and trade-offs

The numerous connections between climate change and other issues inevitably means that there are ways in which action on any one issue may have an effect on another. In considering comprehensive greenhouse gas emission reduction measures, there will thus be co-benefits and synergies, but also possible trade-offs where action on climate change may aggravate some other issue.

Environmental benefits from reducing greenhouse gas emissions include reduction of environmental problems such as urban air pollution and acid rain; and protection of forests, soils, watersheds and biodiversity. Socio-economic benefits would include reduced subsidies and taxes that presently distort the economy; greater energy efficiency; reduced road congestion and traffic accidents; decentralisation of energy supply and employment; and induced technological change and diffusion, with spin-offs into sustainable development and increased international equity.

Some mitigation measures may have both positive and negative impacts on other problems, depending in part on how mitigation is implemented.

Thus, reducing the carbon-intensity of energy supplies, with desirable effects on air pollution and acid rain, can be achieved through increasing the share of lower carbon emitting fuels, more energy efficient fossil fuel technologies, and renewable energy technologies. However, increased use of biomass as a substitute for fossil fuels could have positive or negative impacts on soils, salinisation, biodiversity and water availability. This will depend on how it is managed, what land-use patterns it displaces, and whether, for example, it increases water demand, displaces food production, or destroys wildlife habitat. Similarly, carbon sequestration by plantation forestry can enhance carbon sinks and protect soils and biodiversity, but depending on how it is managed, could reduce biodiversity and water supplies.

Some policies aimed at reducing other environmental problems may have major benefits for climate change reduction. This applies particularly to policies aimed at reducing urban air pollution, and at encouraging the use of public transport for economic and urban planning reasons. However, restricting sulfur emissions because of their impacts on human health and vegetation is already reducing sulfate particle concentrations in the atmosphere in some regions, which otherwise would help to reduce global warming. Moreover, some pollution control measures reduce the energy efficiency of power plants, thus increasing carbon dioxide emissions for the same amount of useable power.

Increasing energy efficiency has many benefits, including reduced pollution, reduced need for investment in power stations and electricity grids, improved export competitiveness, and reduced reliance on imported fossil fuels. Increased reliance on renewable energy, which generally comes from dispersed sources, increases decentralisation, and thus reduces urban sprawl.

Reducing vulnerability to climate change generally has many benefits in better managing climate variability, protecting threatened ecosystems from other stresses, reducing land degradation, and better managing freshwater resources. The converse is also true – better management for climate variability and extremes, and of threatened ecosystems and water resources provides better adaptability to climate change.

Integration, sustainable development and equity

The above synergies, co-benefits and conflicts point to the need to integrate climate change policy decisions into the framework of decision-making on other issues. Climate change policy needs to be included in routine consideration of other social and environmental issues. Only then will the full benefits of consistent and well thought out policies become achievable. Thus, for example, any decision-making procedure related to such issues as building design; urban planning; water supply; capital investments in agriculture, buildings, energy, transport or other infrastructure, should consider impact on and resilience to climate change in any checklist of considerations. This is not a trivial matter, but in the long run it may save a lot of later changes and expenses. Retrofitting is in general less efficient than forward planning.

Climate change policy also needs to be linked to broader social and political issues such as equity. Equity, within countries, between countries, and between generations, is a major concern that must be considered.

- Without equity within countries and between countries, policies to address climate change will not be widely supported by those who feel disadvantaged by such policies. This requires acceptance of responsibility on a user-pays principle, compensation or assistance to those harmed by climate change or policies to prevent it, and fairness in applying policies.

- Without wide acceptance of climate change mitigation and adaptation policies, those implemented will not be the most efficient. In particular, unless both developed and developing countries can agree that fair policies have been proposed they are unlikely to fully participate in achieving the necessary reductions in greenhouse gas emissions.

- Growing inequity related to climate change will exacerbate existing political tensions, instability and conflict, and may well create new tensions.

Equity issues will be considered further in the next chapter.

Integration of climate change policies into policies for sustainable development is the most likely way to ensure that the lesser- and more-developed countries can work together on this problem.

It is important to note that, besides the United Nations Framework Convention on Climate Change (UNFCCC) (New York, 1992) and the related Kyoto Protocol (Kyoto, 1997), many existing international agreements originally conceived for other concerns are relevant to the climate change issue. These include:

- The Antarctic Treaty (Washington, 1959)

- Convention on Wetlands of International Importance Especially as Waterfowl Habitat (the 'Ramsar Convention') (Ramsar, 1971)

- International Convention for the Prevention of Pollution from Ships (London, 1973)

- Convention on International Trade on Endangered Species of Wild Fauna and Flora (Washington, 1973)

- Convention on the Prevention of Marine Pollution from Land-based Sources (Paris, 1974)

- Convention on the Conservation of Migratory Species of Wild Animals (Bonn, 1979)

- UN/ECE Convention on Long-Range Transboundary Air Pollution (Geneva, 1979)

- United Nations Convention on the Law of the Sea (Montego Bay, 1982)

- Vienna Convention for the Protection of the Ozone Layer (Vienna, 1985), and the related Montreal Protocol (Montreal, 1987)

- Basel Convention on the Control of Transboundary Movements of Hazardous Wastes and Their Disposal (Basel, 1989)

- UN/ECE Convention on the Protection and Use of Transboundary Watercourses and International Lakes (Helsinki, 1992)

- Convention on Biological Diversity (Rio de Janeiro, 1992)

- UN Convention to Combat Desertification (Paris, 1994)

- Stockholm Convention on Persistent Organic Pollutants (Stockholm, 2001)

- United Nations Forum on Forests (New York, 2001).

Other agreements that arguably are relevant are the 1951 United Nations Convention and the 1967 Protocol Relating to the Status of Refugees, because climate change and sea-level rise may lead to the displacement of populations within and across national borders. Although these agreements do not include economic or environmental causes in their definition of refugees, it has been argued that the definition should be extended to do so.

The Global Agreement on Tariffs and Trade (GATT) and the World Trade Organisation (WTO), and associated agreements, should also be considered. These may affect the application of any subsidies and the enforcement of any trade restrictions or penalties under the UNFCCC, which are designed to encourage or ensure international compliance with mitigation and other measures. The issue here is whether environmental values and sustainability should rate more highly than principles of free trade applied to environmentally damaging goods or services.

As we have seen in this chapter, climate change should not be viewed in isolation. It is inevitably connected to many other issues in terms of multiple or common causation, effects which interact with other issues, and potential solutions which need to be examined for their co-benefits and tradeoffs. Impact assessments, and adaptation and mitigation strategies must consider these interactions; otherwise they run the danger of unexpected side effects and conflicts that may render them unacceptable or ineffective.

10

The politics of greenhouse

*Everyone has the right to a standard of living adequate for the health
and well-being of himself and his family, including food, clothing,
housing and medical care.*

*Everyone is entitled to a social and international order in which the
rights and freedoms set forth in this Declaration can be fully realized.*

Universal Declaration of Human Rights, Articles 25 and 28.

*The Parties should protect the climate system for the benefit of present
and future generations of humankind, on the basis of equity and in
accordance with their common but differentiated responsibilities and
respective capacities.*

**From Article 3, United Nations Framework Convention on Climate Change
(UNFCCC)**

Whole volumes have been written on the politics of the enhanced greenhouse
effect. Learned journals devoted to policy related issues publish dozens of
articles each year. In this chapter I will confine myself to a brief general discussion of key issues that divide decision-makers and which require agreement in
order to ensure the most effective international action is taken. Previous
chapters have dealt with a number of these issues, but a summary, placed in the
context of the decision-making process, is useful.

Is the science credible?

As noted in Chapters 4 and 5, there are many uncertainties in relation to climate
change. Nevertheless, the overwhelming body of evidence from relevant scientists is that there is a high probability that human induced global warming, with
associated changes in other climatic conditions, is happening. Moreover, the

evidence is that warming will continue, at an accelerating pace, through the twenty-first century and beyond, unless urgent measures are taken to slow and eventually reverse the increase in greenhouse gases in the atmosphere.

These conclusions are hotly contested by a relatively small number of contrarians, discussed in Chapter 4, who for various reasons accuse so-called 'establishment scientists' of bias and poor science. Genuine sceptics exist and are welcomed, as they keep scientists on their toes and ensure that what is accepted is well based and relevant to the real world. However, contrarians often present misleading arguments, and frequently seize upon any discussion of uncertainty as an excuse for dismissing the whole topic. Too often they repeat old arguments that have already been thoroughly discredited.

Where relevant, common arguments by the contrarians have been dealt with above. The truth is that in the reports by the Intergovernmental Panel on Climate Change (IPCC) we have the most thoroughly peer-reviewed and carefully written series of reports summarising the science of a major issue that have ever been published. Each report has gone through two sets of peer reviews by scientists. Moreover, the scientific authors have considered, but not necessarily accepted, comments from representatives of governments holding many different views and interests, including China, Russia, Saudi Arabia, the United Kingdom and the United States. Such diversity does not allow for a single party line. Indeed, a guiding principle of IPCC has been to present policy-relevant but not policy-prescriptive assessments.

Examples of the discussion at plenary sessions of the IPCC, where government representatives are present, illustrate the detailed level of debate. In Chapter 7 on adaptation, I gave the example of claimed methods of adaptation to heat stress in dairy cattle, and to water shortages, where scientists rejected unwarranted generalisation from the special Saudi Arabian experience.

Another example concerns a draft that mentioned that many cereal crops would switch from gains to losses in productivity as global average warming increases beyond 2–3°C. Such an effect is shown in numerous crop simulations for different locations and scenarios of climate change, but with a range of numerical results. The effect is due to the changing balance between the beneficial effects of increasing carbon dioxide concentrations on crop growth and the effects of warming and rainfall changes. The latter turn negative due to increases in water stress and crop intolerance at too high temperatures. The argument from Russia was that regional warmings greater than 3°C would still be beneficial there, while some tropical countries argued that losses would start at less than 1°C. Some scientists suggested a compromise of replacing '2–3°C' by 'a few °C', since there are uncertainties and the number was not meant to be precise. However, China and other non-English speaking countries commented that a translation of 'a few' into their languages might convey a meaning of up to more than 3°C, while other countries wanted to stick to 2–3°C. In the end the scientists agreed on 'a few', and asked that any translators pay special attention to the English meaning. It being a scientific report, what the scientists agreed was accepted. The whole process took upwards of half an hour, on a fairly minor point, but the process was painstaking and true to the science. That is typical of IPCC deliberations.

What about the uncertainty?

The role of uncertainty is of course central to the question of climate change. As discussed at length in Chapter 4, two main sources of uncertainty about the future nature and effects of climate change exist: one scientific, and the other due to future human and societal behaviour. Both are important and well recognised. Thus, any projection of the future will be uncertain and depend in part on human behaviour. There is nothing new in that. Every politician, business person and decision-maker lives with uncertainty every day, and has to make policy, investment and planning decisions despite uncertainty. It is done by assessing the risks of alternative courses of action and seeking to minimise risk and maximise gain. That is how it should be with climate change. We must get away from the idea that we should dismiss concerns or possibilities that lack certainty. Ordinary people make a risk assessment every day when they look at the weather forecast and decide whether or not to take a coat or an umbrella.

What is fairly new in the climate change issue is to recognise that the risks include much more than the relatively well understood ones due to gradual warming and slow changes in average rainfall. Possible changes in the frequency and intensity of extreme events like floods, droughts and severe storms also need to be taken into account, as well as the possibility of large-scale or sudden, and possibly irreversible changes to the climate system. This last category is particularly worrying because such events are very uncertain as to timing, likelihood and impacts. The likelihood of sudden large-scale changes in climate may be small, and they may not occur for decades or centuries. However, the possible magnitude of their effects may be so large that they cannot be considered as damaging only at the margins of society – they may cripple society as we know it. The risk posed by such possible disasters must be reduced, even at significant cost.

As mentioned previously, the common analogy used to justify some sort of investment in action to avoid climate change damages is taking out an insurance policy. It is not too bad an analogy, but it misses one important point. In the case of insurance we are spreading the risk to an insurance company that can compensate us if the worst comes to the worst. But in the case of global-scale climate change there is no outside insurer to pay compensation. If it happens, we lose. The point must be not how we can rebuild after the disaster happens, but how to ensure that it never happens.

Another aspect of uncertainty is the role being played by natural climate change. We know that small and large climate changes, some of them sudden, have occurred before. They could occur again. Some argue that this means that we can survive climate change, and there is nothing we can do about it anyway. Both points are essentially wrong. First, no previous large climate change occurred when there were over 6000 million people living on earth – we are in new territory here, and many of us would not survive. Second, past large-scale climate changes, especially abrupt ones, occurred when some natural change in external forcing was driving gradual climate change, and the climate system hit a threshold which triggered rapid change. Right now, humans are providing a driving force that is producing gradual, if rather rapid, climate change. This is making it far more likely that the climate system will hit a threshold where abrupt change occurs. Third, the more seriously we take the possibilities of human-induced abrupt climate change the more we will learn about how to predict, avoid or cope with both human-induced and natural abrupt climate change.

Uncertainty is being used as a delaying tactic by those with a short-term interest in prolonging the use of fossil fuels. This is similar to the classic tactics adopted by the tobacco industry, and asbestos manufacturers, which delayed action and cost many lives. Despite the contrarians, the weight of evidence that global warming is happening, and is in large part caused by human action, is now overwhelming, even if the details are still uncertain. Decisions must still be taken, on the basis of minimising risk in accordance with prudent foresight.

Uncertainty places us on a fast learning curve. We must learn how to minimise the risks posed now, given the uncertainties, and how to reduce the uncertainties as fast as possible, so that we can better understand what must be done to avoid or adapt to climate change. This is not something we can put off while we get richer or while we deal instead with some other problems. Accumulating greenhouse gases and large time lags between cause and effect require that we address the climate change problem now.

How realistic are the scenarios?

This is an important question. Some economists have argued that for technical reasons the high emissions scenarios used by the IPCC 2001 report, such as the *Special Report on Emissions Scenarios* (SRES) A1F or A2 scenarios (see **Box 3** and **Figure 15**) are wrong, or at least highly unlikely. Thus they argue that the high end of the range of estimates of global warming by 2100 shown in **Figure 15** is too high and unnecessarily scary. It gives total global emissions at 2100 of about 30 Gt of carbon per annum compared to the present figure of about 8 Gt. (The dubious validity of this argument is discussed more fully in Chapter 3).

However, irrespective of the technical arguments of the sceptics on this point, simple arithmetic suggests that if 8 billion people in 2100 were each to emit nearly as much per head as the average US or Australian citizen does today (say 5 tonnes per annum), then global emissions would be about 40 Gt in 2100. This makes the A1F and A2 scenario estimates look pretty moderate as an upper estimate for a fossil-fuel intensive global society.

Some contrarians also argue that the low SRES emission B1 scenario gives such low emissions (about 5 Gt or less by 2100) that no urgent emissions reduction actions, which they think would be damaging to the global economy, are needed. This is the thinking of those who believe that the so-called 'free market' will solve every problem, and in this case will automatically take the low emissions development path. This ignores the fact that the free market tends to operate on a short time scale while climate change operates on a longer time scale, with large lags built in. By the time the free market responds to an already-occurred impact it may be too late to prevent a far worse impact later on.

The IPCC 2001 report acknowledges, however, that the SRES scenarios are hypothetical futures, not predictions, and attaches no particular probability to them, just saying that they are 'plausible'. The SRES scenarios were in fact predicated on the idea that no policy actions determined by concern about climate change were included. This is why the contrarians have homed in on the low emissions scenarios, to argue that no policy actions are necessary.

The real point about the SRES scenarios is that they were never intended as predictions, but as a reasonable range over which to look at the sensitivity of climate change impacts to emissions. Any use of the IPCC results as unconditional predictions is wrong, although they do highlight possibilities, some of which we might well wish to avoid. (It must be conceded that many climate scientists and even the IPCC, let alone journalists and others, have been careless in the use of language when discussing scenarios, projections, and predictions. It is a matter of semantics and nuances, but the fact remains that the SRES scenarios are not, and were never intended to be, predictions, but rather projections based on story lines for plausible futures (see Chapter 3 for a discussion of these distinctions).

We may well ask, however, if the very low emissions in the B1 scenario are likely without policy action to limit climate change. We might well hope so. However, the IPCC description of the B1 scenario is of a future economy 'with rapid change in economic structures toward a service and information economy, with reductions in material intensity and the introduction of clean and resource-efficient technologies' and 'with emphasis ... on global solutions to economic, social and environmental sustainability, including improved equity ...'. Is this really all that likely unless there are strong policies to ensure it happens? I doubt it, but that is what the advocates of business as usual would have us believe.

Choosing global and local emissions targets

The need for emissions reduction targets and their rough dimensions were discussed in Chapter 8, driven largely by the impacts as described in Chapter 6 and the uncertainties, which require that we take a risk reduction approach. As recognised in the UNFCCC, emissions reduction targets should be driven by estimates of the concentration of greenhouse gases in the atmosphere that would lead to dangerous impacts. As discussed earlier, what is dangerous is a value-laden subject, due to non-monetary values related to, for example, extinctions and loss of heritage, and uneven impacts on different countries and sectors of society. Moreover, we have to take account of possible large-scale or abrupt changes to the climate system, and the wide range of uncertainty in the climate's sensitivity, which determines the relationship between greenhouse gas concentrations and global warming.

The choice of a low warming target, and its achievement, is crucial to eventual outcomes. As Donald Brown of the Pennsylvania Consortium for Interdisciplinary Environmental Policy put it, in a paper on the ethical dimensions of climate policy:

> *Because this target will determine which people, plants, and animals will survive rising temperatures, increased disease, rising oceans, more intense storms, and increased floods and droughts, the greenhouse gas atmospheric target level issue raises profound ethical questions.*

As we consider the policy implications of projected climate impacts, we should note that the various stabilisation scenarios, which are examined in the 2001 IPCC report, are far more policy-relevant than the SRES scenarios. Summary results in terms of global warmings at 2100, 2350 and at equilibrium, are shown in **Table 3**. When applied to regional impact assessments, comparisons of projected impacts for different levels of stabilisation demonstrate dramatically the value of achieving low greenhouse gas concentrations at stabilisation.

Figure 27 shows such an intercomparison for the full SRES range and for stabilisation at 450 and 550 ppm. The full range of uncertainties due to different possible climate sensitivities, and in the SRES case due to different plausible emissions scenarios, is shown. (Additional uncertainty may be appropriate to account for regional downscaling from the global climate models.)

It is apparent from these results, derived by CSIRO in Australia for the Government of New South Wales (NSW), that widespread reductions of the

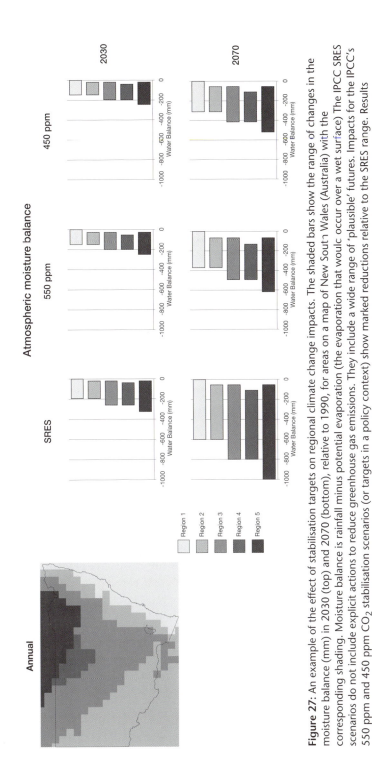

Figure 27: An example of the effect of stabilisation targets on regional climate change impacts. The shaded bars show the range of changes in the moisture balance (mm) in 2030 (top) and 2070 (bottom), for areas on a map of New South Wales (Australia) with the corresponding shading. Moisture balance is rainfall minus potential evaporation (the evaporation that would occur over a wet surface) The IPCC SRES scenarios do not include explicit actions to reduce greenhouse gas emissions. They include a wide range of 'plausible' futures. Impacts for the IPCC's 550 ppm and 450 ppm CO_2 stabilisation scenarios (or targets in a policy context) show marked reductions relative to the SRES range. Results courtesy of CSIRO and the NSW government.

moisture balance, that is, drier conditions, are more likely than not in NSW under any of the scenarios. Severe drying appears likely without a greenhouse gas reductions policy, particularly in the north-central regions of the state. However, following the 550 ppm stabilisation scenario results in much less drying, and for 450 ppm stabilisation the effect is even less. It also shows that the benefits of emissions reductions, relative to the no-policy SRES scenarios, become greater with time. In this example, the range of reductions in moisture balance is halved in 2070 in the 450 ppm stabilisation scenario, relative to the no-policy range of scenarios. The relative reduction in impact would be even greater at later dates.

This is a policy-relevant result, as it demonstrates the advantages of a low stabilisation target. If some unacceptable level of drying can be determined from its potential impact on the state, this can lead to the adoption of a regionally appropriate target for emissions reductions to avoid such drying. This in turn may lead to the adoption by the Australian government of a target for reductions in emissions to be advocated internationally in order to serve Australia's national interest. Ideally, similar assessments should be made in other countries and for other potential impacts, some of which may be far more serious than regional drying in Australia. It would be highly policy-relevant, and it is to be hoped that such results will emerge from the next IPCC report.

Given the uncertainties, I suggested in Chapter 8 that equilibrium greenhouse concentrations equivalent to 450 to 550 ppm might lead to a globally acceptably low level of risk of overall dangerous impacts, although the uncertainty about climate sensitivity suggested that we should aim for concentrations as low as possible to be on the safe side.

Reference to **Figure 23** suggests that such a target in the range of 450 to 550 ppm requires a global reduction in emissions of about 40% by 2050, and maybe 60–80% by 2100. This figure is of course subjective. It is determined by a choice of an acceptable level of risk. This choice is not a matter for science, but of opinion as to what is an acceptable level of risk, given regional and sectoral variations in impacts, and ultimately this is determined by politics.

But next consider that the developed countries historically have emitted the most greenhouse gases, and still do, and have a great capacity to conserve energy and develop less carbon-intensive technologies. Developing countries, however, historically emitted little, are rapidly developing and need to increase their energy use, and most likely their emissions, in order to alleviate poverty. This brings in the equity issue, discussed further below, but let us make some small allowance for equity considerations here. International equity suggests that a round figure for developed countries might be in the ballpark of a 60% reduction in emissions by 2050, while developing countries should also try as hard as possible to limit their emissions even as they achieve stronger economies in the next few decades. Perhaps they should aim at rapidly reducing their emissions per unit GDP. This would allow for growth, but be a start towards an

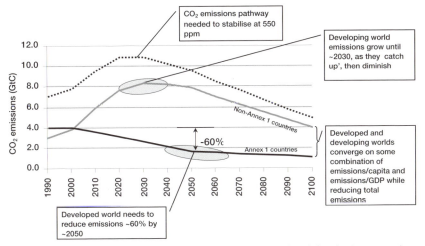

Figure 28: A projection of emission pathways for developed and developing countries. The top curve shows a global CO_2 emissions pathway that would achieve a stabilised concentration of 550 ppm. The lower two curves show how this might be split up between developed and developing countries, allowing developing countries further growth in emissions until about 2030, while developed countries start to decrease their emissions starting about now. How this split is made is one of the most serious areas of disagreement between some of the richest countries (the United States and Australia) and the poorer developing countries. (Diagram courtesy of Dr Greg Bourne, WWF Australia.)

ultimate convergence of living standards and emissions per person between rich and poor. Help with the latest technology from the rich countries might accelerate this process. **Figure 28** shows the idea. Even with this allowance for equity, people in developed countries would still be emitting more greenhouse gases per person in 2050 than those in developing nations.

It should be clear from this that two key policy issues are which target concentration provides an acceptable level of risk, and how the necessary emissions reductions should be split between the developed and developing countries. These are highly contentious issues. The above suggestion that the global target must be less than 550 ppm (indeed, less than 450 ppm if the latest estimates of climate sensitivity are correct) is subject to revision as we learn more about the costs, achievability of the target, and the risks from climate change. Clearly, the choice of how to split the task of reaching this target concentration between developed and developing countries is another highly political one, with considerations of justice and achievability paramount. My hope, indeed the hope for the world, is that large reductions in emissions may be easier than most of us think.

How urgently do we need to act?

One other key policy question, hotly contested politically, remains: how urgent is it to start reducing emissions? **Figure 23** supplies part of the answer. That is, early emissions reductions (the full lines) lower the peak of the emissions curves, and produce earlier reductions in greenhouse gas concentrations, and thus smaller global warmings before reaching equilibrium. This reduces the risk from high rates of global warming. Moreover, early emissions reductions allow a slower rate of emissions reductions later, which may well have less severe effects on global economies and be more technologically feasible. Against this, those who prefer to gamble on the problem being exaggerated, possibly because early emissions reductions might cost them money, will push for delays in emissions reductions. My view is that the risk is large and therefore emissions reductions are urgent, and should proceed as fast as technically and economically feasible. Any delay cuts off options for stabilisation at low concentrations, and raises the price for future generations.

How much will reducing emissions cost?

This question is often answered by considering only the cost of mitigation measures in isolation. In fact these costs must be weighed against the potential costs of damages due to climate change. Estimates of the latter have a strong ethical values-laden component that is often overlooked, namely non-market or uncertain costs such as damages to human health and the environment, disproportionate effects on the world's poor, the potential for catastrophic damages or surprises, possible irreversible changes, and the increased danger resulting from delayed emissions reductions.

As discussed in Chapter 8, the IPCC 2001 report estimated the cost of emission reductions necessary to achieve a target stabilisation concentration of 450 ppm at 1 to 3% of the global average GDP by 2050. The estimated costs depend on what is taken as the reference scenario, that is, the scenario with no reductions in greenhouse gas emissions due to concern about climate change (such as in the SRES scenarios). For high emissions scenarios in the SRES range (see **Box 3**, and **Figure 15**), for example the A1T and A1FI, costs are at the high end. For low SRES emissions scenarios, such as the B1, the cost is nearer the 1% estimate. Thus it is evident that different development pathways, pursued for reasons other than greenhouse policy, strongly influence the costs of emissions reductions. However, the likelihood of the world following either the extreme high or extreme low emissions scenarios in the absence of greenhouse policies seems to me to be small.

It bears repeating also, that if economic growth continues at rates of several per cent per year, GDP doubles in only a few decades. In that case, a 1% lower GDP by 2050 due to emissions reductions only delays the achievement of the same GDP by a few months. Arguably, this is a small price to pay for greater safety in the face of climate change.

Another consideration is that research and development in carbon-efficient and low-carbon energy technologies, and their implementation in the market place are open-ended and almost impossible to predict, beyond what is already in the pipeline. As we saw in Chapter 8, huge potential sources of renewable energy are available, as well as possibilities for carbon-removal and storage or sequestration. Cost study estimates so far have tended to confine themselves to existing technology, or modest innovations, with little allowance for dramatic reductions in cost likely to follow from human ingenuity and inventiveness.

Moreover, the present trend in some developed countries towards personal fulfilment through ever larger and more energy-demanding automobiles, dwellings and lifestyles, may be reversible through education, infrastructure planning and tax or other incentives. Examples of such behavioural changes include the rapid spread of recycling of waste in many developed countries, successful campaigns to reduce sunbathing because of ozone depletion and skin cancer, the wearing of seatbelts in cars and helmets on bicycles, decreases in smoking, and greater use of public transport where it is convenient and safe (as in many European cities and Perth in Australia). Profligate energy-wasting lifestyles are certainly not sustainable and impose many penalties on society such as pollution, urban sprawl and ever-larger road systems, traffic congestion and accidents.

One interesting lifestyle suggestion that strikingly illustrates simultaneous benefits to the environment and other societal issues is that overweight people in developed countries, who are an increasing health problem, might be persuaded to walk or use bicycles instead of driving cars for short journeys. Such a change would lead to a healthier population, reduce medical expenses and at the same time save fossil fuel emissions. Paul and Millicent Higgins of Stanford and Michigan Universities estimate that if the 39 million obese and 90 million overweight men and women in the US walked or biked instead of using cars for short journeys they would not only become healthier but might save up to 10% of US carbon dioxide emissions as at 1990 levels.

Resource-intensive trends such as those followed historically in developed countries cannot be reproduced in the more populous countries of Asia, Africa and Latin America without unacceptable social costs. Increasing energy demand from China is already affecting the global oil price and adding to concerns about fossil energy supplies and the security of supply for developed countries. The geo-politics of oil may yet play a large part in motivating the developed countries to reduce reliance on fossil fuel. The co-benefits of reduced fossil-energy use may well become increasingly obvious.

Many opportunities are opened up by climate change mitigation, not only in specific low-carbon technologies, but also in the finance industry. This is perhaps epitomised in the paper *Climate Change and Finance: New Business Opportunities*, from the major international bank UBS, which points to a 'new market potential for a climate value investment product related to the implementation of the Kyoto Protocol mechanisms'.

It is also true that fossil fuel industries are at present heavily subsidised in many developed and developing countries. Economists Kym Anderson and Warwick McKibbin in 1997 calculated that reducing coal subsidies and trade barriers would lower emissions of carbon dioxide in OECD (developed) countries by 13% and global emissions by 5%. They also found that if low domestic prices for coal in major developing countries were raised to the level in international markets, their carbon dioxide emissions would be reduced by 4%. These market reforms are already under way in some European countries and in China, and are increasing economic efficiency rather than economic costs.

The European Environment Agency estimates that subsidies on coal, oil and gas in the then 15 European Union member countries totalled about 22 billion Euros in 2001. Riedy and Diesendorf estimated Australian subsidies for fossil fuels at A$6.5 billion in 2003. Subsidies are presumably there for supposed socially desirable ends. What needs to be asked now is what are the relevant socially desirable ends, given the climate damages we are risking from continued greenhouse gas emissions.

As pointed out in the recent book *Society, Behaviour and Climate Change Mitigation*, edited by E Jochem and colleagues, policy analysis is not a matter of a price comparison between different options, but of a choice between different interests, cultures and values. As one reviewer wrote:

> *Costs and benefits, as well as rights are all social constructs. What makes reduction of greenhouse gases, a cost? The same thing that made freeing slaves or giving women the vote, a cost? How would we feel if the same greenhouse mitigation activity was labelled an investment?*

It is what we value that counts, not what it costs in dollars and cents.

Meeting targets most efficiently

Two main issues are at stake regarding reducing greenhouse gas emissions to reduce the risk from climate change. One is whether changes to reduce fossil fuel emissions can be done without slowing economic growth or lowering economic standards. Some economists, some others with vested interests in fossil fuel industries, and technological pessimists say it can only be done at great cost and with a lowering of living standards. Others are more optimistic, believing that targeted research and development, together with economic incentives, can lead quickly to prosperous low-carbon-emissions futures.

The other argument is whether emissions reductions are best achieved by a 'top-down' setting of mandatory emissions reduction targets, or best left to the so-called 'free market' on the basis that if there is a real problem, someone will find a way of making money out of solving it. A middle position, which I favour, is that this is an artificial dichotomy, since there is no such thing as a perfect free market, and the one we have is driven largely by short-term considerations of profit. The market is therefore best at deciding how to proceed most economically once long-term goals are set. Thus we need a combination of top-down goals and bottom-up market economics.

The goal should be to minimise the risk of dangerous climate change, rather than setting immutable but debatable numerical targets. Interim targets need to be set, as discussed above, but these should be regularly revised in the light of experience and new knowledge. A number of general principles seem to apply to efficiency in meeting such a broad policy aim as the reduction of greenhouse gas emissions, especially when no one technical measure seems likely to provide all the emissions savings needed. Such principles are listed in **Box 8**.

Several measures may be employed to foster these goals. They include the issuing of 'cap and trade' greenhouse gas emissions permits at provincial, national or global levels. Under this system, permits to emit greenhouse gases are issued according to some formula related to present emissions, and the amount that can be emitted is periodically reduced to meet progressively more stringent emission reduction targets, as needed. Permit holders can buy or sell their permits (termed 'carbon trading'), which logically means that those who can most easily and most economically reduce their emissions will do so and sell the excess permits to those who find it more difficult. This ensures that reductions in emissions are achieved at the least cost. Cap and trade permits were pioneered in the United States in relation to sulfur emissions, with great success, and came into operation for carbon dioxide in the EU in 2005, as well as being planned for a number of US and Australian states at present (see below).

The cap and trade system serves to encourage non-carbon emitting energy producers such as wind and solar power generators by making their products more competitive with the carbon-emitting producers. This is because carbon-emitters have to keep buying more permits to emit as the amount allowed under their existing permits shrinks with time, thus raising their prices. Moreover, as the market share of non-carbon emitting energy suppliers increases, their costs will decrease due to economies of scale and improved technology and infrastructure, and they will become more competitive.

An alternative measure often proposed is a carbon tax that is introduced gradually but increases with time so as to eventually recover from energy users the full costs of energy production from whatever source, taking account of the environmental and health costs inflicted on the community. Such taxes are based on a 'user-pays' principle where users of polluting fuels pay for the costs inflicted on society by their use. For economic efficiency, these taxes must be

---

Box 8: Efficient reduction of greenhouse gas emissions

Some principles applicable to efficient reduction of greenhouse gas emissions are:

- Be open to a wide range of contributions to a solution, including both short-term (next two decades) and longer-term (next 20 to 100+ years) measures.

- Avoid favouring one technology over another without good reasons.

- Set broad standards and goals, thereby ensuring a stable and level playing field for public and private enterprise, encouraging long-term planning and investment.

- Provide incentives for research, development and market penetration that taper off with time and market share so as to ensure competitive and economical solutions.

- Ensure that any carrots (incentives) and sticks (penalties), such as subsidies or carbon taxes, apply equitably.

- Redistribute any tax revenue so as to stimulate rather than harm the economy, for example using revenue to reduce employment taxes.

- Facilitate the early retirement of energy- and carbon-intensive infrastructure through incentives, rapid depreciation allowances and facilitation of replacement infrastructure.

- Provide retraining and incentives for those otherwise adversely affected.

- Facilitate the transfer of energy- and carbon-efficient technology to developing countries through technological aid programs.

---

varied from source to source according to the true external costs of their energy production. Based on the present cost of generation of electricity, wind and hydro-power (which are already competitive with coal and natural gas) would be more competitive if the external costs of generation from coal and natural gas were taken into account. With improved technologies, solar cells or newer solar technologies may well become competitive also.

The principal argument against carbon taxes is that they will increase the price of energy, thus adversely affecting the economy. However, reducing taxes on production costs other than energy (for example payroll tax), and cheaper renewable energy as economies of scale and new technologies reduce costs, may negate this argument. Renewable energy is in general more labour intensive. This would also increase employment and thus reduce social service costs and increase income tax revenue.

Increased support for research and development for renewable energy and related infrastructure is being applied successfully in the EU. This includes mandatory targets for achieving market shares, to bring these technologies into the market with economies of scale. Fossil fuel industries could also retain legitimacy by research and development of carbon sequestration methods, although this would raise their costs, creating more of an opening for renewables.

The process by which, decade by decade, the changing price structures for fossil fuel versus renewables might lead to a rapid increase in the market share of renewable energy is shown schematically in **Figure 29** with a corresponding reduction in greenhouse gas emissions.

In the first decade national or regional carbon taxes or carbon emission permits would marginally increase the price of fossil fuels, while renewable energy sources would be demonstrated and begin to penetrate the market. This is already happening in some countries, notably in the EU and in some states of the United States such as California. By the next decade market penetration by renewables would have grown, with decreasing costs, and fossil fuel emissions would be reduced either by decreased use, or carbon sequestration (which would gain credits under any carbon tax or permit system). In the third decade proven renewable technologies would begin to increase rapidly both in developed and developing countries. Decentralised renewables would often be preferred in developing countries due to lower infrastructure costs and more available sunshine in low latitude and arid countries.

The key to achieving such a technological scenario is a general realisation that it is essential to reduce risks from climate change. Energy businesses need to face up to the threat from competitors, customers, regulators and legislatures. Success in this new milieu will come from forward thinking, entrepreneurial activity, innovation, technological breakthroughs and start-ups. Progressive CEOs and entrepreneurs will win through at the expense of those who remain rooted in the past. The new industrial revolution is inevitable, but unpredictable in detail. It will happen as people embrace it.

International equity: what is fair?

Historically, developed countries have emitted the most greenhouse gases since the industrial revolution and become rich in the process. Advocates from less-developed countries argue that equity therefore requires that less-developed countries should be able to continue to use fossil fuels to develop, or else be compensated and assisted by richer countries if they are to reduce their reliance on fossil fuels. However, a simple extrapolation of recent growth rates in emissions in major developing countries such as India and China indicates that their emissions will start to dominate global emissions within the next several decades. Thus, if we are to limit climate change through global emissions reductions, the cooperation of developing countries is essential.

Any successful international effort to limit climate change and to cope with its impacts requires that both developed and developing countries play a significant

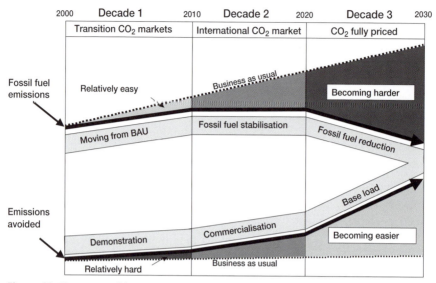

Figure 29: How renewables energy might increase their share of the total energy market. The upper black curve shows notional changes in fossil fuel emissions. The lower one shows the reduction in total emissions due to low-carbon energy. BAU is 'Business As Usual'. (Schematic courtesy of Dr. Greg Bourne, WWF Australia.)

role. Success will not be forthcoming if the key concerns of all major greenhouse gas emitting nations, including the United States, China and India are not adequately taken into account in the future development of the climate change regime under the UNFCCC. The support of lesser emitting nations, who will be adversely affected by climate change, is also essential. International equity is thus not only a matter of ethics and fairness, but also an essential means to persuading all relevant countries to adopt a joint action plan.

As Tom Athanasiou and Paul Baer put it in their book *Dead Heat: Global Justice and Global Warming*:

> *A climate treaty that indefinitely restricts a Chinese (or Indian) to lower emissions than an American (or European) will not be accepted as fair and, finally, will not be accepted at all. Climate equity, far from being a 'preference', is essential to ecological sustainability.*

Some developed country advocates argue that limiting global carbon emissions would slow economic growth in both developed and lesser-developed countries and that this would harm all countries. This argument is essentially a result of technological pessimism about economical emissions reductions. However, it merely postpones the problem and makes it more acute in the future, as more drastic reductions will be needed later on to stabilise the climate. If emission reductions are needed urgently now to reduce the risk from present and future climate change, postponing action is indeed dangerous. If time lags between cause and effect are important, it is urgent to act now.

Moreover, impacts of climate change will not be equitable. As the IPCC 2001 report authors concluded:

> *There is high confidence that developing countries will be more vulnerable to climate change than developed countries, and there is medium confidence that climate change would exacerbate income inequalities between and within countries.* (IPCC 2001b report, p.916)

This means that progress on managing climate change risk requires that human impacts on climate, and historical responsibility for them, must be acknowledged and taken into account in the multilateral negotiations under the UNFCCC. Notwithstanding the necessity to negotiate extensions to the emissions reduction regime established under the Kyoto Protocol (see below) beyond the first commitment period (which expires in 2012), the issue of sharing climate impact burdens must be fully acknowledged, since many climate change and sea-level rise impacts have now become inevitable. How to do this is unclear, as it includes weighty questions such as what to do about 25 million Bangladeshis likely to be rendered homeless this century by sea-level rise.

Benito Muller of Oxford University argues that a first step in this direction might be a call for a legally binding, mandatory Disaster Response Instrument under the UNFCCC. Other possible responses include an insurance fund, financed by the industrialised countries, to pay costs of climate change impacts, as was proposed by the Alliance of Small Island States, or a general increase in international aid for sustainable development. These measures would assist developing countries to cope with inevitable climate change, and predispose and enable them to work towards reducing greenhouse gas emissions.

As stated by John Ashton of LEAD International (UK) and Xueman Wang in a valuable essay on equity and climate, 'equity', whether based in philosophy, morality or human nature, is an ideal that shapes our view of what is right or just. It is predicated on the notion of the common good, and at times may call on some to sacrifice for the sake of others. 'Interest', on the other hand, is what is best for the individual or nation. Interest, and especially national interest, may include equity as a consideration, but not necessarily the dominant one. Ashton and Wang note that the UNFCCC and the Kyoto Protocol both convey a palpable sense that the negotiators bent over backwards to find a package of outcomes that all could consider fair.

Ashton and Wang identify five aspects of equity:

- *Responsibility*: when our interests are harmed, the question of who is to blame usually arises. This gives rise to the 'polluter pays' principle.

- *Equal entitlements*: all human beings have equal rights or entitlements, notably to liberty, security, impartial justice and opportunity. This is embodied in the United Nations Charter and in many national constitutions and laws. Such rights may include rights to land, water, food, housing and cultural identity, all of which may be threatened by climate change and sea-level rise.

- *Capacity*: the idea is that the most able should contribute most to the provision of a public good. This is the basis of progressive taxation and of philanthropy by the rich.

- *Basic needs*: this is the idea that the strong and well-endowed should help the weak and the poor in meeting their most basic needs, and is the basis of a 'safety net' in many countries for the poor and disadvantaged.

- *Comparable effort*: this compares the efforts of different parties to any overall effort, to ensure that they are 'fair' given the different circumstances of the parties. What people do about those in need may differ according to circumstances, but it should be fair.

Based on such considerations, Eileen Claussen and Lisa McNeilly of the Pew Center on Climate Change suggest a set of principles for climate change negotiations, shown in **Box 9**. Many of these, and related principles such as the Precautionary Principle, are already included in the text of the UNFCCC and the Kyoto Protocol, but their consequences do not yet seem to have been adequately taken on board by all the countries which are parties to the UNFCCC.

Box 9: Principles for climate negotiations

Eileen Claussen and Lisa McNeilly of the Pew Center on Global Climate Change suggest the following guiding principles for climate negotiations:

- All nations should be able to maintain or improve standards of living under a global climate change mitigation regime. Consequently, climate change mitigation should focus on alternative low-carbon development paths that don't reduce economic growth.

- More broadly, the outcome of UNFCCC negotiations should not undermine or hinder progress toward the goal of sustainable development.

- The countries most responsible for greenhouse gas concentrations in the atmosphere should be leaders in the effort to reduce emissions.

- All nations should work to the best of their abilities – or with help from other countries – to reduce emissions either absolutely or relative to business-as-usual trajectories.

- The world should take advantage of emission reduction opportunities where they exist.

The United States and Australia, although parties to the UNFCCC, have objected to the provisions of the Kyoto Protocol, which attempts to define how the aims of the Convention might be implemented in the short-term (until 2012). Indeed the US has withdrawn from the 'Kyoto process', on the grounds that the mandated emissions reductions for developed countries would retard economic growth, and that in the first round of reductions in emissions no commitment is required of the lesser-developed countries. The latter is characterised as 'unfair' by many US Congress members and some Australian politicians. Australia has said that it will not agree to the Kyoto Protocol until the US, as the world's largest emitter of greenhouse gases does so, and supports the US objections.

The charge of unfairness by the US and Australia is based on the idea that mandated emissions targets in developed countries but not in developing countries would lead to emissions intensive industries being transferred to developing countries. They suggest this would lead to loss of jobs in developed countries, and no real decrease in global emissions. However, a suitably framed system of emissions credits would largely obviate this problem, as would a revision of developing country obligations beyond 2012, the end of the first commitment period under the Kyoto Protocol. Many ideas are being put forward, from both developed and developing countries, regarding how this might be done.

The arguments regarding unfairness of the Kyoto provisions tend to ignore many of the above considerations regarding equity, and confuse a short-term view of national self-interest with the question of equity. These arguments also ignore the fact that, for a variety of reasons, many developing countries, notably China, Brazil and India, have voluntarily reduced their emissions well below business-as-usual through various measures. These include removal of energy subsidies, fostering of renewable energy, and in the case of China substitution of natural gas for coal.

The American ethicist Thomas W Pogge of Columbia University argues that there are three basic reasons why increased inequity should concern us:

1 A duty to help people in distress.

2 A duty to oppose and reject systems and institutions which lead to or perpetuate poverty and from which we benefit.

3 Prudential considerations that others being poor may make us worse off (in the long run, for example, through loss of trade, instability, cross-border migration pressures, radical movements, and even terrorism).

These reasons suggest a need for concern about inequity and poverty in general. Regrettably however, they have not been persuasive enough to make rich countries substantially eliminate inequity and poverty so far. Indeed, the percentage of rich nations' GDP being devoted to non-military aid has in recent decades significantly decreased. Nevertheless, it is worth looking closer at these reasons for concern in the narrower perspective of climate change.

The *first* reason is a positive duty to help people in distress. It is taught by all the world's great religions, but is usually followed only by some people in some cases: we quickly become overwhelmed by the needs of others and tend to close our eyes and ears except to those nearest to us. It is easy to recognise when people are in distress, but also easy in many cases to rationalise not helping them.

Too often we find ways of blaming the poor for their poverty instead of seeking constructive ways to help. Moreover, reporting by the media of people in distress is highly selective, so that we are often unaware of the real extent of poverty and inequity. Not to put too fine a point on it, one rich person who dies in a traffic accident is often more newsworthy than a hundred poor people who die of starvation in Africa. Moreover, people in far off places, or from different religious or ethnic groups are often of less concern. That is why the Parable of the Good Samaritan is so powerful in Christian thought.

The *second* duty is a more stringent negative one: not to uphold injustice, and not to contribute to or profit by the unjust impoverishment of others. Here the moral duty is plain, but recognising when we are indeed upholding unjust systems, and profiting by them, is more difficult and may be contentious.

Pogge develops a detailed set of criteria for determining when such unjust systems and institutions exist, including a shared institutional order that is shaped by the better-off and imposed on the worse-off, the possibility of an institutional alternative which would reduce the inequity, and the absence of other explanations for the inequity.

Applying these ideas to the question of climate change impacts, it is plain that continued and indeed increasing emissions of greenhouse gases are leading to increasing inequity, and that the developed nations are the main emitters historically, and on a per capita basis for the foreseeable future. This is historically the result of institutional arrangements that have allowed unrestricted emissions, with no strong incentive to reduce our reliance on carbon-intensive industry and development. Clearly, with the advent of the UNFCCC and the Kyoto Protocol there is an alternative institutional arrangement which seeks initially to limit emissions, and which foreshadows attempts to greatly reduce them. This would lead to a reduction in climate change and thus in the additional inequity increasing emissions would otherwise cause.

On this analysis, the second reason clearly applies: developed countries actively contribute to a system that increases inequity, and they have historically profited by it through the provision of cheap energy and higher living standards. Again, the real problem for most people in rich countries is to realise the extent of their complicity in increasing inequity. This is a matter for analysis and education.

This concern for justice does motivate many people in developed countries, notably the churches and others of religious faith. Groups such as the *Evangelical Environmental Network* and *What Would Jesus Drive* campaign (which campaigns against the growing use of 'gas-guzzling' recreational vehicles) base their position squarely on a Biblical understanding of justice, concern for the poor and stewardship of God's creation. Indeed, Senators Joseph Lieberman and John McCain called their bill, placed before the US Senate to create a national carbon emissions cap-and-trade regime, the *Climate Stewardship Act*. Senator Lieberman states:

> *The word stewardship in the title of the act was not chosen*
> *coincidentally, [but rather] because John McCain and I believe we*
> *have a stewardship responsibility over the earth and the people on it,*
> *who are, after all, God's creations.*

Lieberman characterises the *Climate Stewardship Act,* which gained 43 votes out of 100 in the US Senate, as 'a faith-based initiative'.

The *third* reason for concern about growing inequity is a more selfish one, justifying moral action (according to the first two reasons above), 'only' because reducing the hunger and poverty of others may increase our wellbeing or security. Nevertheless, in a world where profits and security are higher priorities for many in positions of power than altruistic moral conduct, prudential arguments may in the end be the more powerful for many decision-makers. Moreover, they need not exclude the moral arguments, but merely reinforce them.

So what are the prudential reasons for seeking to avoid an increase in inequity due to climate change? Some possible reasons are shown in **Box 10**. These are listed with little explanation and argument, although references to relevant literature are provided in the notes on the web (see p. 296). These are each complex issues, and it is not possible to argue them fully here, but I skim lightly over them below.

Development has already been historically slowed in countries exposed to climatic disasters, such as Bangladesh (floods and typhoons), Mozambique (floods), several Pacific islands (tropical cyclones), and Honduras, Haiti and other Caribbean countries (hurricanes and floods). As this increases with climate change, more aid will be needed and more forced migration will occur for environmental and economic reasons.

Outbreaks of SARS and other diseases (for example malaria and dengue fever), transmitted internationally by air transport, illustrate the threat from these and other possibly climatically-induced disease outbreaks. The uncontrolled transmission of diseases may well increase with increased climate change and sea-level rise induced cross-border migration, especially if it is unofficial or illegal, that is, not part of a regulated immigration or refugee program.

The problem of economically- and environmentally-forced migrations, both internal and across borders, is increasing. A paper presented at the International Association for the Study of Forced Migration in 2003 states:

Box 10: Prudential reasons for minimising inequity

Growing international inequity due to climate change might:

- Slow development in poor countries.
- Reduce trade between the developed and developing countries.
- Create more problems for aid programs.
- Add to trans-border health problems.
- Lead to millions of displaced people, either internally within countries, or across borders as environmental 'refugees'.
- Increase migration pressures on the borders of the rich countries.
- Foster political instability and radicalism in developing countries.
- Stimulate anger, hatred and hopelessness leading to potential terrorists, both among the poor and indeed among the idealistic or radical rich.

Addressing humanitarian crises involving mass migration is integral to maintaining international security and sustainable development. This is particularly the case post-September 11, when it has become apparent that such countries as Afghanistan that experience prolonged humanitarian emergencies can too easily become breeding grounds for terrorism.

The paper points out that such forced migrants do not as yet share the same status in international law as refugees from political or other persecution, and urges a widening of the definition of 'refugees'. Many of these environmental refugees are unlikely to be able to return home.

In a study on the environment and sustainable development, the International Council for Science states

It could be forecasted with very high level of probability that the total number of environmental refugees will increase both in relative and absolute quantity. ... Appearance of large numbers of environmental refugees could be one of the biggest problems for government in the 21st century.

Of the world's 19 megacities, 16 are situated on coastlines, and many will be vulnerable to sea-level rise, as will many other people living on low-lying islands and coastlines. A one-metre rise in sea level would displace tens of millions of people in Bangladesh, Vietnam and elsewhere. Who will accept responsibility for them? Considering the possibilities, Molly Conisbee and Andrew Simms of the New Economics Foundation (UK) write:

The spectre of wholesale relocation of populations raises fundamental questions about citizenship and nationality. Once land has been lost,

*will residual nationality be able to persist, or does there need to be a
new category of 'world citizen'? Could such a status be created in
acknowledgement of the fact that climate change is a collective
problem and requires a collective solution?*

These are not going to be easy questions to address, but they will increasingly be consequences of climate change.

There will always be radical groups and individuals bent on extremism and anti-democratic behaviour, often wedded to some extreme ideology. However, poverty and a sense of inequity, injustice and hopelessness opens up grievances in the broader population and creates fertile ground for recruitment to radical groups. This occurs not only among the poor, but also among the richer and better educated elite, who for idealistic reasons identify with the poor and the oppressed. We have seen this in many places including Northern Ireland, Palestine and throughout the Islamic world and in the UK in 2005. It may not lead to logical behaviour, is often accompanied by extremism and is often counter-productive, but it is fostered by perceived injustice and inequity.

It is not stretching things too much to see that such instability and extremism may be exacerbated by an increase in poverty and inequities associated with climate change and climatic disasters, especially if they can plausibly be blamed (at least in part) on the rich. This is hardly in the interests of the rich, although many in rich countries do not seem to see the connection.

A lot has been written about 'environmental security'. This means different things to different people. To some it is ensuring that each country secures its environment by military means if necessary, for example to protect water supplies or prevent mass movements across borders. To others it means demonstrating the inadequacy of a purely military approach to security in the face of environmental threats that cross borders, such as acid rain, oil spills or climate change. Environmental issues, and particularly climate have little respect for borders, although some countries will be more seriously affected than others. In an increasingly globalised economic system, climate changes that adversely affect sections of the human race are likely to adversely affect the rest of us eventually, so we all have a stake in environmental security. The UNFCCC concept of 'dangerous' levels of climate change encapsulates the idea. Just because we may be rich does not mean we are immune from the effects of climate change.

The importance of equity within countries

Equity within countries is also an issue, as it is with many environmental and development issues. Different sectors and regions within countries will be differently affected by both climate change effects and emissions reduction measures.

Climate change will affect the most vulnerable, who are usually the poor and isolated, often living in low-lying flood-prone areas or on hillsides vulnerable to erosion and landslides. Others live in communities where water is scarce and medical services inadequate. In developed countries this often includes indigenous communities and people in polluted urban slums. Communities dependent on particular affected sectors such as farming or tourism may also be adversely affected by increased aridity, changing markets or loss of tourist attractions such as coral reefs or beaches. Adaptation in these cases will include compensation, relief and special help in the form of improved health and emergency services, relocation and retraining.

Alice Fothergill of the University of Vermont (US) and Lori Peek have documented this phenomenon in the United States where the poor are more vulnerable to natural disasters due to such factors as place and type of residence, building construction and social exclusion. A recent report for the Congressional Black Caucus Foundation in the US concluded that:

- African Americans are already disproportionately burdened by the health effects of climate change. This includes deaths during heat waves and from worsened air pollution.

- Economic hardship and unemployment associated with climate change will fall more heavily on African Americans.

- African Americans are less responsible for climate change than other Americans.

- Policies to reduce climate change can generate large health and economic benefits for African Americans.

Emissions reduction programs will impact unevenly on sectors and communities, with those dependent on fossil fuels adversely affected and in need of retraining, relocation or other assistance. This should be made easier by the growth in employment in renewable energy sectors, although in some cases the same people may not be easily transferred from one job to another. In general, renewable energy is more labour intensive, so more jobs may be forthcoming, as well as less unemployment relief expenditure and more income taxes. Correctly managed, the move to less carbon-intensive industries should be an opportunity to lesson inequities within countries.

Proper provision for people adversely affected by greenhouse gas emission reduction programs will be vital, not only as a matter of equity, but also in order to obtain community support for necessary changes. Indeed, the most influential opposition to mandatory greenhouse gas emissions programs, including the Kyoto Protocol, comes from people directly dependent on the fossil fuel extraction and energy-intensive industries, and who therefore see themselves disadvantaged by such programs.

Provision must be made for orderly and non-threatening transitions from fossil fuels to renewables, with reinvestment of capital with accelerated investment cycles, and preferential redeployment of displaced labour. Carbon removal and sequestration programs in the fossil fuel industries may well play a major role in this transition, although, for reasons discussed earlier, it is unlikely to be economic or sustainable in the long run. Foresight and planning by fossil fuel companies for alternative technology investments and employment can play a big role in reducing the potential inequities of emission control measures. This has been shown already by several large corporations including BP and Shell, which have both established renewable energy businesses.

Equity between generations

Climate change will alter and possibly restrict the choices and opportunities of generations to come, especially if sudden, large-scale and irreversible changes to the climate system are triggered, such as those discussed in Chapter 6. Future generations will not be responsible for the climatic situation bequeathed by us, but they will be entitled to access to energy and also to an acceptable environment and livelihood. If we continue to emit large quantities of greenhouse gases, the effects of which may take many decades to work their way through the climate system, future generations will be obliged to emit far less if they are to keep the climate within safe limits.

We cannot know how easy it will be for future generations to cope with a climate that we have changed, nor what sort of extreme or rapid changes they may experience. Nor can we know how easily they will be able to make do with much reduced use of fossil fuels, which they may have to face if they are to stabilise climate after we fail to act. Under these circumstances we have an obligation to adhere to the Precautionary Principle (see Chapter 4). The onus is on the present generation to make decisions regarding emissions of greenhouse gases that will not pose a significant risk of serious adverse consequences to future generations.

It is almost axiomatic that the faster we bring climate change under control, the less likely it is that we will damage the interests of future generations through climate change itself. However, many economists argue that expenditure now on reducing greenhouse gas emissions reduces the opportunity to invest in other developments that could benefit future generations. As discussed earlier, this is usually allowed for by applying a discount rate, or rate of devaluation of future costs as against present costs. This rate is usually close to that of inflation, interest rates or rate of return on investments.

However, future costs from the impacts of climate change may not be merely marginal. They could be disastrous, leading to deflation and the collapse of economies. In that case normal discounting would not be sensible, the applicable rate is uncertain and could be zero or even negative. Uncertainty about future climate change impacts, with a risk of large adverse effects, makes early action to minimise climate change more desirable as a form of insurance or precaution. Moreover, uncertainty about the real costs of emissions reduction, given possible technological advances that might rapidly reduce costs, makes early action to stimulate appropriate new technology through research, development and market penetration more advisable.

The role of governments and NGOs

Modern democracies consist of representative governments usually elected for terms of three to six years. However, global economic forces and the behaviour of markets often limit their freedom of action. Such market forces are often driven by short-term considerations, but in the case of major corporations longer time perspectives may apply. Governments also operate in a political climate where the voices and support or opposition from business groups, trade unions and community organisations play a vital role. Short-term thinking drives some of these organisations as well, but many have a longer time perspective and greater continuity than particular government administrations.

Issues such as climate change are highly complex, with imperfect information, highly technical and scientific connections, issues of human behaviour and values, and large uncertainties. In the case of climate change this is further complicated by large time lags between actions regarding greenhouse gas emissions, and their eventual consequences, which may be large but delayed by decades to centuries.

The electoral cycle for democratic governments is very short compared to the timescale on which climate change usually takes place. Moreover, politicians and the media too often focus on the short-term in terms of income, profits, taxes and jobs rather than on planning or investing for the following decades and generations. A key question is how longer-term thinking about cause and effect can be built in to the decision-making process, both of governments and of businesses. In part this must come from an informed and highly educated electorate. Institutions that have a longer time perspective than the next election are vital, because they can bring a greater level of foresight to government and the political process.

Examples include business companies and corporations, trade unions, trade and business associations, educational and research institutions, religious groups, environmental advocates, social justice advocates, professional bodies and many other associations, many with their own form of total or partial democracy. Collectively these groups are termed non-governmental organisations (NGOs). They, and their hopefully peaceful manner of operating, are often referred to as 'civil society'.

It is a legitimate and indeed necessary role of civil society to influence both governments and voters, especially regarding longer-term issues. In democracies, such influence is subject to the will of all citizens at government elections. Ideally, the role of governments vis-à-vis civil society is to take note of the concerns, and where necessary to mediate among often competing elements of society, before acting for the common good. In particular, governments have a role to encourage cooperation and competition across a level playing field, with a long-term perspective, in the long-term interests of the whole society.

Governments have a duty, therefore, to set standards, goals, and rules of behaviour on an equitable basis. Governments can facilitate the attainment of goals, although in most cases actually achieving change is up to individuals and groups, including businesses, consumers, investors and innovators. Policies and laws are only effective if civil society in the main wants them to work: otherwise they are empty rhetoric or worse. Governments can in general offer a mixture of carrots and sticks. The contrast between how this is being done in relation to climate change policy, in the UK and the EU on the one hand, and the US and Australia on the other, is discussed in Chapter 11. The pros and cons depend very much on their likely success in limiting climate change, and the effects of emissions reductions on the economy, both in the short and longer terms. Crucial to any judgement is to take account of the urgency of the measures and how successful they might be in avoiding damages and reducing risks from climate change both in the near future and for future generations.

What role should business take?

Businesses are in existence to invest money and labour in producing and selling things, so producing income for themselves and their shareholders. Climate change will affect them directly via impacts on their activities, including raw material and production costs, insurance, prices and competitive position. They will also be affected by how greenhouse gas emission reduction measures may influence their costs and activities, and ultimately their competitive position. Whether or not business people believe that human induced climate change is happening, they will be affected by how their competitors, governments and society perceive the problem.

As with previous technological revolutions, such as the introduction of the steam engine, electricity, plastics, electronics and computers, industries will have to adapt to the push for a low-carbon emitting economy. Particular businesses will either change and adapt, or deny the need for change and eventually go under. Innovators and early movers will be at an advantage, as will businesses that live in a regulatory environment that facilitates change and fosters innovation.

In a paper on the strategic implications of climate change policy for business, Andrew Hoffman, of the Boston University School of Management, states:

> *Many companies today are taking proactive steps on climate change by reducing or even sequestering their greenhouse gas emissions. But one cannot, as many now do, generalize from these examples the proposition that all companies can benefit from greenhouse gas reductions. Climate change controls represent a market shift; the formation of new markets in pollution, pollution credits, money and emission abatement technology. And in any such transition, there will be winners and losers, those that embrace the shift and those that resist it. The difference between these two postures lies in strategic factors such as capital asset management, market competencies, global competitiveness and managing institutional change.*

Similar sentiments are expressed in a cover story on global warming in *Business Weekly* (16 August 2004) that begins 'Consensus is growing among scientists, governments, and business that they must act fast to combat climate change. This has already sparked efforts to limit CO_2 emissions. Many companies are now preparing for a carbon-constrained world.' The article concludes 'Companies have begun to respond, but there is a long way to go, and only two choices: Get serious about global warming – or be prepared for the consequences.'

Business needs to act now to limit greenhouse gas emissions and prepare for changes already happening. They can play a significant role in providing solutions that are both profitable and socially desirable. This is already being demonstrated by many businesses, including some based in the fossil fuels sector, although others are holding out against change, based on a short-term view of their stockholders' interests. Robert Bradley of the Institute for Energy Research in Houston, Texas, expresses such a view when he argues for a narrow strategy that does not go beyond short-term 'no regrets' actions. This seems to be based in a sceptical view of the reality of climate change, and ignores the possibility of opening up new opportunities for growth.

The experience of BP is salutary. Back in 1997 they decided to set a target of a 10% reduction in their in-house greenhouse gas emissions, and achieved this nine years ahead of schedule. This was done through a compulsory internal emissions trading scheme, which led to the identification of lots of business value. After three years they had generated an extra US$650 million of shareholder value. This is only from their internal operations, which generate about 100 million tons of carbon dioxide each year. The emissions from their products are about 15 times as much. They publicly favour a global emissions reduction target aimed at keeping global warming below about 2°C. They estimate that this will require a new carbon-free primary energy industry equal in size to the present fossil-fuel based industry by 2050, and are setting about creating such an industry under the motto 'Beyond Petroleum'.

Many governments are implementing domestic legislation and policies that are creating direct requirements to reduce greenhouse gas emissions and imposing liabilities on various sectors. This is happening at national levels in both developed and developing countries, and regionally in the European Union. Even in Australia and the US, despite the opposition of the respective federal governments to the Kyoto Protocol, there is considerable movement at the state and local levels, including fuel efficiency measures, design criteria, and incipient carbon emissions permit trading.

As Martijn Wilder of the international law firm Baker & McKenzie put it in a recent paper:

> For corporations, and in particular multi-nationals, the emergence of a diversity of climate related laws, in both developed and developing countries, means that a clear understanding is required as to the nature of legal liabilities that now exist or are likely to exist in the future and how best to position themselves. Companies should be fully aware of the extent to which market based mechanisms within these regimes present opportunities to create carbon assets and offset liabilities or at the very least aware as to how to preserve ownership of such opportunities. ... and to be able to understand the carbon ramifications of key investment decisions and acquisitions.
>
> It is also critical for corporations to be aware of the way in which global capital – especially within the investment and insurance industries – is reassessing investments for carbon risk, and the growing reluctance of shareholders to tolerate corporate non-performance on greenhouse matters. When coupled with the recent commencement of climate litigation, companies and their directors need to be fully aware of the ramifications of such matters ...

Wilder goes on in his paper to detail various legal actions being pursued in the US and Australia by environmental groups and local governments, some acting on behalf of individuals. One action against a proposed coal-fired power station at Redbank in New South Wales was lost, but the state minister rejected an application for a second power plant due to high greenhouse gas emissions. This adds credibility to possible further legal actions in NSW against high emitters of greenhouse gases.

The Pacific nation of Tuvalu has previously threatened to bring a lawsuit against the US, the UK and Australia in the International Court of Justice for their alleged failure to limit greenhouse gas emissions that could eventually render Tuvalu uninhabitable due to sea-level rise. In the US several legal actions are in process against the US EPA variously for failing to further limit emissions from motor vehicles, failure to regulate carbon dioxide emissions under the *US Clean Air Act*, and failure to update emission standards for power plants. These actions have been brought by several environmental organisations and the States of Connecticut, Maine and Massachusetts.

In July 2004 eight US states and New York City sued five large electric power companies that between them operate 170 power plants that are responsible for some 10% of the national total carbon dioxide emissions. The case, under federal common law of public nuisance, calls for cuts of 3% a year in carbon dioxide emissions to 'curb air and water pollutants emanating from other states'. The Connecticut attorney general cited the states' successful suits against tobacco companies as evidence that such efforts can succeed.

Wilder quotes an article in the *Financial Times* in 2003 in which it was said:

> *First it was tobacco and asbestos. Then it was the turn of the food sector. Now litigators have a new target in their sights: those responsible for climate change.*

The main barrier to success in these litigations, according to Wilder, is in establishing causation – that is showing the link between the action of the emitting party and the damage suffered by the plaintiff or damage to the environment. This is difficult to prove at present, but as with the case against the tobacco industry, as science progresses the link may become clearer. Attribution of an individual climate disaster to global warming may not be 100% certain, but if the change in probability of such disasters due to global warming can be established, then a percentage of the damages might be attributed to climate change.

The insurance industry has been one of the first to face up to the consequences of climate change. A report by the Association of British Insurers in 2004 states:

> *Climate change is no longer a marginal issue. We live with its effects every day. And we should prepare ourselves for its full impact in the years ahead. It is time to begin planning for climate change in the mainstream of business life.*

The Association went on to say that insurers are uniquely placed to contribute to the climate change debate because they understand risk and their customers. Insurance needs to manage its own risks and to engage with government and others who affect that risk.

In 2002 the United Nations Environment Program Finance Initiatives presented a report that highlighted the need for financial institutions and professionals to:

- become more familiar with the threats and opportunities posed by climate change issues;
- incorporate climate change considerations into all business processes, and
- work directly with policy-makers on effective strategies for mitigation and adaptation.

The mining industry has also recognised that it needs to take climate change seriously. The Australian Minerals and Energy Foundation in a report in 2002 stated that:

> Climate change is a major concern in relation to the minerals sector and sustainable development. It is, potentially, one of the greatest of all threats to the environment, to biodiversity and ultimately to our quality of life.
> … [It] clearly raises important issues for the minerals industry's operations; relations with the broader community; and willingness to internalise important sustainable development principles, including the precautionary principle.

Innovest Strategic Value Advisors, on behalf of 97 institutional investors with more than US$10,000 million worth of assets under management, wrote in 2003 to 500 of the world's largest companies, asking about their greenhouse gas emissions. In their report they point out the consequences of increased natural disasters amounting to US$70 billion in 2003 on key sectors and commodity markets, such that climate risk must now be considered. They also point out that carbon finance is now a reality, with the European Union's Emissions Trading Scheme in force as of January 2005, and that the future 'cost of carbon' is already of concern. They note that FT500 companies are major participants in the global clean technology sector. Innovest reports that these trends have not been ignored, with more companies quantifying their carbon emissions, more 'carbon-neutral' products and companies being created, and more active climate risk management. It states that the concepts of corporate leadership, transparency and brand value underpin approaches to climate change. Innovest has developed a 'Climate Leadership Index' to gauge company performance.

In addition to the EU Emissions Trading Scheme, the Chicago Climate Exchange already exists. This is a self-regulating exchange that administers a multi-national and multi-sector marketplace for reducing and trading greenhouse gas emissions. It is a 'voluntary, legally binding commitment by a cross-section of

North American corporations, municipalities and other institutions to establish a rules-based market for reducing greenhouse gases'. It was started with 28 large companies including Ford, DuPont and BP America, and the cities of Chicago and Mexico City. It is partly driven by the expectation of some future, government-imposed emissions-reduction program in America.

The Pew Center on Global Climate Change has set up the Business Environmental Leadership Council, a group of leading companies worldwide that are responding to the challenges posed by climate change. Its website lists more than 40 major companies and the targets they have set themselves to limit greenhouse gas emissions. The companies subscribe to the following belief statement:

1   We accept the views of most scientists that enough is known about the science and environmental impacts of climate change for us to take actions to address its consequences.

2   Businesses can and should take concrete steps now in the US and abroad to assess opportunities for emission reductions, establish and meet emission reduction objectives, and invest in new, more efficient products, practices and technologies.

3   The Kyoto agreement represents a first step in the international process, but more must be done both to implement the market-based mechanisms adopted in principle in Kyoto and to more fully involve the rest of the world in the solution.

4   We can make significant progress in addressing climate change and sustaining economic growth in the United States by adopting reasonable policies, programs and transition strategies.

More details of the climate change efforts of businesses in the United States can be found in the Pew Center publication *Climate Change Activities in the United States: 2004 Update*. This report identifies numerous opportunities to reduce greenhouse gas emissions cost-effectively while achieving multiple benefits. It states that to take advantage of these opportunities and to achieve the right mix of solutions, federal policies are needed with certain ends and flexible means. It urges the US to harness market forces to spur innovation and to motivate companies and jurisdictions to identify and implement solutions that can be tailored to specific circumstances.

The positive side of the business perspective on climate change is opportunity through new and growing markets for low-carbon technology. Janet Sawin of the Worldwatch Institute points out that already in 2003 an estimated US$20 billion was spent on renewable energy development, equivalent to about one-sixth of the total world investment in power generation equipment. This includes some of the largest energy corporations such as BP, Royal Dutch/Shell and General Electric. In the decade 1993–2003 the annual increase in installed power generation capacity was about 30% for wind power, 22% for solar cells, but only 2.2% for natural gas, 1.3% for oil, 1.0% for coal and 0.6% for nuclear power. Most of this growth in renewable energy occurred in a few countries with favourable national or provincial/state policies, namely Denmark, Germany, Japan, Spain, India and the United States. Countries which have set increased minimum levels for renewable energy in the electricity grid have seen large increases in investment in renewable energy, with increases in employment and taxes. Costs per unit energy for renewables have trended down steeply in the last decade. This trend is likely to continue with new technologies and larger scale production. There is therefore a great opportunity for innovative businesses.

The role of state and local governments

In countries such as the US and Australia, where strong federal action on climate change is lacking, some state and local governments are leading the way on emissions reduction programs. Through their authority over many areas affecting the environment, such as land-use planning, transportation, building standards, regulation of natural gas and electricity supply, air pollution standards and enforcement, and economic development, these regional and local authorities are able to exert pressure to minimise greenhouse gas emissions, encourage energy efficiency, and to foster renewable energy developments.

Many states and cities are adopting polices that are reducing greenhouse gas emissions without threatening local economies, while achieving other benefits such as cleaner air and reduced traffic congestion. Some measures that are controversial at the federal level have been accepted at the state and local level, while others, including encouragement of wind power installations, are being debated and proven viable.

Twenty-eight US states and Puerto Rico have or are developing strategies or action plans to reduce greenhouse gas emissions, some with numerical targets. Some are requiring power plants to either reduce emissions or offset them with payments to funds that invest in carbon sequestration, for example in forest plantations. In Australia the refusal of the State of New South Wales to permit the construction of a new coal-fired power station, mentioned above, is a case in point.

In August 2001 a conference of governors of the US New England States and Eastern Canadian premiers approved a comprehensive Climate Change Action Plan to reduce regional greenhouse gas emissions. Progress is being made on a regional carbon dioxide cap-and-trade program for power plants, involving Maine, New Hampshire, Vermont, Massachusetts, Rhode Island,

Connecticut, Delaware, New Jersey, and New York, and possibly Maryland and Pennsylvania.

Most US states now require greenhouse gas inventories, especially for large emitters, and many states are encouraging carbon sequestration via minimum-tillage agriculture or tree planting. Energy conservation strategies are in place in many states, and more than 20 US states have various forms of public benefits funds to channel revenue from electricity customers into energy conservation or renewable energy projects. Thirteen states have established renewable energy mandates, which require a minimum proportion of electricity to come from renewable sources. Even George W. Bush's home State of Texas has set a minimum target of an additional 2000 MW of renewable electricity generation capacity by 2009, mainly from wind power and land-fill gas, with some hydropower. The California Air Resources Board is to adopt new more stringent emission standards for light-duty vehicles in 2005, which under the *US Clean Air Act* could be adopted by other states. New York is likely to follow, adding considerably to pressure on car manufacturers to comply.

In Australia, despite the refusal of the federal government to ratify the Kyoto Protocol, the states have adopted greenhouse strategies, partly influenced by state-funded scientific advice. All six Australian states, plus the Northern Territory and the Australian Capital Territory, have set up an Inter-Jurisdictional Emissions Trading Working Group, chaired by New South Wales. New South Wales has a mandatory Greenhouse Gas Abatement Scheme, started on 1 January 2002, with a target of a 3% per annum reduction in per capita emissions each year until 2007, where it remains static until 2012. The states are encouraging renewable energy projects including wind power, tidal power in Western Australia, and geothermal and solar power. Victoria has fast-tracked approvals for wind farms, despite some local opposition, and encouraged wind power manufacturers to set up in the state, leading to new jobs.

Globally, local governments have also become actively involved, in part through the organisation International Council for Local Environmental Initiatives (ICLEI). ICLEI has over 450 member towns, cities and municipal associations and undertakes international campaigns, programs and regional projects on sustainable development, including the climate change issue. Its program 'Cities for Climate Protection' (CCP) has, as of mid-2004, more than 600 towns and cities participating, including 250 in North America, 118 in Europe, 172 in Australia, 40 in Asia, 18 in Latin America and eight in Africa. The program requires councils to make inventories of greenhouse gas emissions, estimate growth, establish reduction goals, draw up local action plans and monitor their progress. In Australia, CCP programs, with the support of the Federal government's Australian Greenhouse Office (which generally fosters only voluntary programs), cover more than three-quarters of the total population, with average greenhouse gas reduction targets of 20%.

A 'Local Governments' Renewables Declaration' adopted in Bonn, 31 May 2004, by 50 mayors from many countries urges a wide-ranging shift towards renewable energy in cities. The communities see their role especially in urban and environmental planning. This includes mandating or providing incentives for renewable energy sources and efficiencies, and investing in infrastructure and facilitating cooperation and financing strategies.

Carolyn Kouskey of Harvard University and Stephen Schneider of Stanford interviewed officials or staff from 23 municipalities in the US that had enacted climate policies. They found that most policies were based on what was considered to be 'good business' or rational policy choices, driven by cost savings and co-benefits rather than public pressure. They found that in many cases at least initial reductions in emissions can be made at cost savings.

So what are the politics of greenhouse?

This chapter has only skimmed the surface of the politics of greenhouse. It is a huge subject with a huge literature. Further information is available on the website. This is a brief summary.

The first key issue is whether we have something urgent to do about climate change, and if so, what. The answer hinges on how credible the science is, and what it means in terms of risk to us, and to our children and grandchildren. Despite all that the contrarians have thrown at it, the science is credible. There is a serious risk, which grows with every tonne of carbon dioxide we add to the atmosphere. The lag between cause and effect is long, so we must act on the basis of foresight rather than proven, has-been, observable fact. We are faced with a problem of risk management.

Next, we have looked at what is required, and found that it is a big ask. This raises questions about the potential cost and how to share that cost between the rich countries and the poor, and between the present and future generations. The message is that we need to reduce global emissions of greenhouse gases by around 60–80% by 2100, and the sooner the better if we want to avoid some big risks. Whether this is possible has been debated, but there is a lot of evidence that if we try we may well be able to do it, even at rather little cost. Estimates of what it will cost depends in part on subjective value judgements and guesses about the future – there cannot be completely objective cost estimates in dollars and cents.

The really key political question is how to do it. How do we ensure that it happens? Is it a matter for the free market, which will do it automatically if the problem is real, and make money out of it? Or does it need some far-sighted top-down direction and detailed targets to achieve such a goal? My tentative answer is that the free market has a big role, but left to its own devices it tends to take a short-term view, when we are talking about a long-term problem. What we need are all elements of the civil society, including business people as well as environmentalists and others, pulling together towards shared goals. That is best accomplished through a genuine partnership between government and non-government agencies. Goals must be set together, and a level playing field established for innovation and competition to achieve emission reductions and the transition to a low-carbon economy with as little cost, and as much gain, as possible. For the sake of justice, and to ensure cooperation, we will need to help those who will be badly affected, either by climate change impacts that we cannot avoid, or by the impacts of emissions reductions. Creating the fairest and most effective possible means to achieve these goals is not going to be easy, but we have to do it.

The final question, then, which has been the biggest stumbling block so far in international negotiations, is what is a fair distribution of effort between the rich developed countries and the poorer developing ones. Historically, most of the problem has been due to emissions from the developed countries, generated while they got rich by burning fossil fuels and cutting down forests. The problem is that the poorer countries now want to catch up, but if they do so by imitating what the developed countries did, that is by burning lots of cheap coal and oil, we will all be in deeper trouble later this century and next. So we need both developed and developing countries to act, the first to reduce their emissions, and the second to limit their increase in emissions. It is a matter of fairness, and of effectiveness. Unless we reach an equitable arrangement that gets both the rich and the poor pulling together we are all in trouble. How to do that is the nub of the problem.

In the next chapter we will look briefly at the history of attempts to deal with the problem to date, and at various national interests that may affect what countries do next. We will also look briefly at what people are thinking about as possible ways forward.

11

International concern and national interests

Whether we wish it or not we are involved in the world's problems, and all the winds of heaven blow through our land.

Walter Lippmann, *A Preface to Politics*, 1913.

The Earth's atmosphere is being changed at an unprecedented rate by pollutants resulting from human activities, inefficient and wasteful fossil fuel use and the effects of rapid population growth in many regions. These changes represent a major threat to international security and are already having harmful consequences over many parts of the globe.

Statement from the International Conference on the Changing Atmosphere: Implications for Global Security, Toronto, June 1988.

A brief history

In 1827, the French mathematician-physicist Jean Baptiste Fourier was the first to suggest that the atmosphere keeps heat from escaping from the Earth, resulting in the Earth being warmer than if there were no atmosphere. John Tyndall then demonstrated in Britain in 1859 that methane and carbon dioxide control the Earth's surface air temperature by absorbing infrared or heat radiation. This led the Swedish chemist Svante Arrhenius to suggest in 1896 that increasing atmospheric carbon dioxide could cause the planet to warm, amplified by increased atmospheric moisture in a warmer world. Arrhenius issued the first warning that human activities since the Industrial Revolution could lead to changes in the Earth's climate. With remarkable foresight, he estimated that a doubling of the concentration of carbon dioxide in the atmosphere could lead to the Earth's surface warming by around 4 to 6°C, which is only about twice the range estimated by the Intergovernmental Panel on Climate Change (IPCC) in 2001of 1.5 to 4.5°C (and even closer to more recent estimates of climate sensitivity). G.S. Callendar in 1938 likewise warned of global warming from increasing carbon dioxide, and suggested that it may already be happening.

Charles Keeling of the Scripps Institution of Oceanography in San Diego, was instrumental in establishing the first carbon dioxide monitoring stations, at the South Pole and Mauna Loa in Hawaii. In 1957 he wrote:

> *Human beings are now carrying out a large scale geophysical*
> *experiment of a kind that could not have happened in the past nor be*
> *reproduced in the future. Within a few centuries we are returning to*
> *the atmosphere and oceans the concentrated organic carbon stored in*
> *sedimentary rocks over hundreds of millions of years.*

By the early 1970s, however, it was not warming but rather a global cooling trend of about 0.5°C observed in the 1950s and 1960s that was arousing concern, with some scientists fearing that it might be the beginning of a long lasting cooling or even of a new glaciation. A number of possible explanations were raised, particularly the cooling effect of increasing particulate matter (atmospheric aerosols) in the atmosphere. Moreover, it was feared that this effect might be amplified into a greater cooling by increased snow cover.

Nevertheless, Wally Broecker of Columbia University commented in 1975 that:

> *... a strong case can be made that the present cooling will, within a*
> *decade or so, give way to pronounced warming induced by carbon*
> *dioxide. Once this happens, the exponential rise in the atmospheric*
> *carbon dioxide content will tend to become a significant factor and by*
> *early next century will have driven the mean planetary temperature*
> *beyond the limits experienced during the last 1000 years.*

Doubting the reality of an ongoing global cooling, the World Meteorological Organization (WMO) in a special report in 1976 stressed the importance of shorter-term climate changes, which might be due to natural or man-made causes, which they said now required urgent attention and further study. Similar conclusions were reached by other scientific groups such as the Australian Academy of Science in 1976.

By 1979, however, the WMO's First World Climate Conference in Geneva in 1979, stated that an increased amount of carbon dioxide in the atmosphere can contribute to a gradual warming of the lower atmosphere and that the world should try to 'foresee and prevent potential man-made changes in climate that might be adverse to the well-being of humanity'.

By the 1980s it was clear that the cooling trend had ended, and many of the scientists who had been concerned about a cooling demonstrated their openness to new information by changing their minds. Continuing increases in green-house gas concentrations, and a realisation that the effective lifetime of CO_2 in the atmosphere was much longer than that of particulates, making for a greater cumulative warming effect, meant that by the early 1980s there was a growing scientific interest in assessing the likelihood and magnitude of global warming.

Indeed, a conference of scientists at Villach in Austria in October 1985, which was sponsored by the non-governmental International Council of Scientific Unions along with the WMO and the United Nations Environment Program (UNEP) agreed to a statement that raised the first collective scientific warning: '... it is now believed that in the first half of the next century a rise in global mean temperature could occur which is greater than any in human history.'

Also in 1986, the Scientific Committee on Problems of the Environment (SCOPE), a committee of the International Council of Scientific Unions, issued a major report entitled *The Greenhouse Effect, Climate Change and Ecosystems*, which reinforced the concern about global warming. The SCOPE report concluded that if the observed rate of increase of carbon dioxide continued, it would reach double pre-industrial values towards the end of the twenty-first century, and this would lead to global average warming in the range 1.5–5.5°C, with associated global average sea-level rise in the range 20–165 cm. The report went on to discuss possible impacts on agriculture, forests and ecosystems.

By 1988 this concern had turned into a demand for action to reduce carbon dioxide emissions, adopted by over 300 scientists at a United Nations sponsored 'Conference on the Changing Atmosphere' in Toronto in 1988. This called for an initial reduction in carbon dioxide emissions of 20% by 2005, stating that

Humanity is conducting an unintended, uncontrolled, globally pervasive experiment whose ultimate consequences could be second only to a global nuclear war.

In response to these concerns, the WMO and the UNEP set up the IPCC in 1988. The initial brief of the IPCC was to report to the Second World Climate Conference in November 1990, and the United Nations General Assembly, on 'the scientific information that is related to the various components of the climate change issue ...' and 'formulating realistic response strategies for the management of the climate change issue.'

It was envisaged by some that this might lead to international negotiations directed towards an agreement to eventually limit greenhouse gas emissions and to adapt to unavoidable climate changes. IPCC established three Working Groups, one to assess available scientific information on climate change, a second to assess the environmental and socio-economic impacts, and the third to formulate response strategies.

To date, the IPCC has issued three major Assessment Reports, in 1990, 1996 and 2001, and a special report entitled *The Regional Impacts of Climate Change*, in 1998. There have been a number of other IPCC reports, including the *Special Report on Emission Scenarios* (SRES) in 2000, which produced a wide range of 'plausible scenarios' for future greenhouse gas emissions up to the year 2100.

Under United Nations auspices, country representatives met in February 1991 to draw up a global Framework Convention on Climate Change (UNFCCC), to be signed at the Rio Earth Summit of 1992. This was a 'framework' convention, meaning that it set out broad principles and objectives, but left a lot of details to be negotiated subsequently. It aims at stabilising greenhouse gas concentrations in order to avoid 'dangerous anthropogenic interference with the climate system'. The UNFCCC came into force on 21 March 1994, and as of 24 May 2005 has received instruments of ratification from 189 member countries that are 'parties' to the convention.

Principles set out in the UNFCCC include:

- The need to limit climate change on a basis of equity, in accordance with each country's common but differentiated responsibilities and respective capacities. Accordingly, the developed countries were expected to take the lead.

- The need to recognise the specific needs and special circumstances of developing countries, especially the most vulnerable (such as low-lying island states and major fossil fuel exporters).

- The need for precautionary measures in the absence of full scientific certainty, qualified by the need to be cost-effective and comprehensive, by taking account of all sources and sinks, adaptation, and all economic sectors.

- The right to sustainable development, and the need to avoid unjustified discrimination or a disguised restriction on international trade.

How these principles can be worked out in practice is not easy, and involves a strong mixture of equity, overall purpose and national interests.

The first meeting of the Conference of Parties (COP-1) (the countries who signed the UNFCCC) in 1995 established a sub-group to negotiate an agreement, called the 'Berlin Mandate', aimed at strengthening efforts to combat climate change. Following intense negotiations up to and including the COP-3 meeting in Kyoto, Japan, in 1997, delegates agreed to what is now known as the Kyoto Protocol.

The Kyoto Protocol

The Kyoto Protocol commits developed nations and countries in transition (former Soviet bloc countries) to achieve quantified reductions in greenhouse gas emissions. Representatives of these countries, termed Annex I Parties, agreed to reduce their combined emissions of six designated greenhouse gases to at least 5% below levels in 1990, between 2008 and 2012, with specific targets varying from country to country.

In 1997 the Parties to the Protocol arrived at assigned amounts, which are the total allowed emissions for a country over the first commitment period 2008–12. Three mechanisms to assist Annex I countries to meet their targets at the least cost were also agreed:

1   Joint Implementation (JI). JI refers to the generation and transfer of emission reductions by investment in a project in one Annex I country by another, thereby generating credit for the investing Party.

2   An Emissions Trading Scheme. Emissions trading allows for the buying or selling of emission allowances between Annex I countries. It is expected that domestic and international trading schemes will be set up to facilitate this, as is happening in the EU in 2005.

3   A Clean Development Mechanism (CDM). The CDM is similar to JI, but generates credits for investing Annex I Parties from project investments in non-Annex I Parties.

Further negotiations in Buenos Aires in 1998 and The Hague in 2000 led to a reconvening of the Parties to the Convention in Bonn in July 2001. However, in March 2001 prior to the meeting in Bonn, the United States withdrew from the process, stating that it considered the Kyoto Protocol to be 'fatally flawed', because it would damage the US economy and because it exempted key developing countries from emissions reduction targets. The United States withdrawal from the Kyoto negotiating process heightened political interest, and probably facilitated agreement reached in Bonn.

The remaining Parties in Bonn accepted a package of agreements, and referred drafts of others on mechanisms, compliance and land use, land-use change and forestry to a further meeting in Marrakesh, Morocco in October–November 2001. Agreement was reached at Marrakesh on most points, although Australia, Canada, Japan, New Zealand and Russia had reservations on some points. In New Delhi in late 2002 further agreements were reached, including the 'Delhi Declaration on Climate Change and Sustainable Development'. This reaffirms development and poverty eradication as overriding principles in developing countries, and again recognises member countries' common but differentiated responsibilities and national development priorities and circumstances in implementing the commitments under the UNFCCC.

For the Protocol to come into force it had to be ratified by at least 55 countries, and also by enough Annex I countries to account for at least 55% of global carbon dioxide emissions in 1990. As of mid-2004, 122 countries had ratified the Protocol, but only 32 were Annex I countries and these accounted for only 44.2% of the global carbon dioxide emissions. Initially Russia was ambivalent about ratification, with deep divisions apparent among Russia's politicians and scientists, but it ratified the Protocol in November 2004 and so it came into force in early 2005. It should be noted, however, that only Parties who have ratified the Protocol (150 countries as of 27 May 2005, accounting for 61.6% of global emissions) are bound by it, hence there is ongoing controversy regarding countries that have not yet signed. The attitudes and interests of particular countries will be discussed later in this chapter.

The many rules and complications related to carbon sinks, accounting, verification, JI, CDM, funding mechanisms, and compliance procedures make the rules and procedures of the Kyoto Protocol hard to fully comprehend. I will not go into details here. Several books and many learned papers and reports address these issues and can be located via the bibliography and the notes on the web (see p. 296). I will give one example here to illustrate the complications that related to land-based sinks.

Land-based carbon sinks, that is, sequestering of carbon in plants and the soil (see Chapter 8), were not originally envisaged as part of the Kyoto Protocol for reducing greenhouse gas emissions – initially reductions were to be achieved simply by limiting the use of fossil fuels. However, some major emitters, including the US, pushed for their inclusion and this was made part of the Protocol in 1997, before the US withdrawal. What began as a simple low-cost alternative to reducing fossil fuel usage turned out to be controversial, with many complications in the detail of how the amounts are to be counted. Melvin Cannell of the UK Centre for Ecology and Hydrology has summarised some of these complications:

- *Definition of a forest.* Is it based on land-use or land-cover? Definitions and numerical criteria make a large difference to the areas that can be counted.

- *Unintended and unfair outcomes.* This relates to sequences of deforestation and reforestation in different commitment periods.

- *Sinks to be additional.* The proposed baseline of 1990 levels is poorly determined.

- *Sinks must be the direct result of human-induced actions.* This excludes natural processes or activities prior to 1990 such as recovery from earlier land-clearing, or fertilisation due to increasing carbon dioxide concentration.

- *Measurement and verification.* Sinks include biomass, soil carbon and litter, all of which are difficult to measure with accuracy across large areas.

- *Permanence and reversibility.* All land sinks are potentially reversible, but temporary storage may be valuable in delaying impacts of climate change.
- *Leakage.* Actions to increase carbon storage in one place may create pressure to reduce it somewhere else, for instance by changing the market value of forest products.
- *Equity.* Many countries party to the UNFCCC wanted the developed countries to reduce their use of fossil fuels first, and not be able to offset this by increasing carbon storage. This was solved by placing limits on what could be claimed.
- *Collateral damages or benefits.* These include environmental impacts of changing land use, and socio-economic impacts such as on commodity prices, recreation and tourism, employment and wealth or poverty.

The mandated reductions in emissions by developed countries under the first commitment period of the Kyoto Protocol (2008–12) would slow the growth in total world emissions, compared to 'business as usual'. However, unless strengthened beyond 2012, the Kyoto targets would not completely stop growth in world emissions, let alone reduce them, and greenhouse gas concentrations would continue to increase.

In 2002, the US Bush Administration proposed an alternative to setting a target of reducing total carbon emissions, namely, targeting a reduction in emissions *intensity*, that is, less emissions per unit growth in GDP. However, reducing emissions intensity would only reduce total emissions if the reduction in emissions intensity were enough to more than cancel out the effect of the growth in GDP. For example, if GDP were to double, halving emissions intensity would just leave total emissions unchanged. President Bush's stated target for the US is an 18 per cent *reduction* in US emissions intensity between 2002 and 2012. However, the US has an expected growth in GDP of about 30 per cent over the same period, so that total US emissions would in fact *increase* by about 12 per cent, and end up some 30% above 1990 levels.

Thus both the first stage Kyoto Protocol measures and those proposed by the United States in 2002 postpone any absolute reduction in world emissions until after 2012.

This lack of immediate reductions in global emissions needs to be compared with the target reductions discussed in Chapters 8 and 10, which suggest the need for a 60–80% total reduction by 2100, relative to 1990 levels. The question of urgency hinges on the understanding of the role of inertia and time lags, which means that delayed action will lead to greater long-term damages and the need for more drastic action later. It also hinges on how we value the right of future generations to inherit a world with more rather than less choices, and on how optimistic we are that future generations will be able to find technological fixes for possibly catastrophic problems we have left them.

The work of the IPCC, with its wide range of plausible scenarios, and its assessment of mitigation pathways, strongly asserts that a future world of low concentrations of greenhouse gases in the atmosphere is feasible. What is needed to achieve this is a development pathway that values sustainability and low-carbon technology over high-carbon technology, and that this is implemented with a real sense of urgency and deliberation. Development with foresight is needed. The UNFCCC has provided an international framework within which cooperation towards these ends is possible. The challenge is to convince all countries that it is in their national interest to be part of this move towards a sustainable future, and to have the agreed targets and measures greatly strengthened.

National interests and climate change

Perceived national interests are central to the politics of climate change, and the ability of the global community to avoid dangerous levels of climate change. What should determine the bottom line of governments regarding their negotiating positions and national implementation programs? This will collectively determine the rate and extent of future climate change. Narrow self-interest is what may go down best in domestic politics, although this is tempered in most countries by some ethical standards, held by at least some of the population, relating to fairness or equity. Equity (see Chapter 10) will also play a role in determining what can be agreed internationally, and for this reason must temper narrow national interest. Negotiating positions must therefore combine some mixture of national self-interest and international equity.

The questions of perceived versus real national interests, and of short-term versus long-term interests are of critical importance. These are both in part a matter of knowledge and education, but also of the time-horizons governing political discourse. Are people more concerned about short-term economic self-interest or about sustainability and the wellbeing of future generations? Here we home in, for various countries and regions, on those national interests that should convince decision-makers that limiting climate change is both necessary and urgent.

In considering individual country situations and national interests it may be useful to refer back to **Table 9** in Chapter 8, where the absolute and per capita emissions of the 25 largest emitting nations are listed, along with their carbon intensities and changes in carbon intensity and GDP over the decade 1990–2000. Clearly no one country absolutely dominates global emissions, and many must collaborate if global emissions are to be reduced substantially, including eventually both developed and developing countries.

The discussion here is more pointed than was possible in the various IPCC reports. The IPCC reports were limited in what they could say by the need for diplomacy, for avoiding 'policy-prescriptive' language, and by the requirement for unanimous adoption of the policy-makers summaries by member states at the IPCC Assemblies. Nevertheless, the uncertainties must still be acknowledged, especially when thinking about potential downstream effects of climate change, for instance on food security, population displacement and other socio-political issues. These may be sensitive and contentious issues. The points raised are not meant to be definitive, but rather provide my personal perspective and should be seen as discussion starters.

Readers interested in similar analyses for other countries would do well to study the regional impacts chapters of the IPCC 2001b report, which is accessible on the web at www.ipcc.ch, and the mitigation volume (IPCC 2001c), which discusses development and equity in the context of possible mitigation actions.

African nations

Africa is a huge and varied continent spanning the tropics, subtropics and warm temperate zones from 37°N to 35°S. Common elements across many countries include rapid population growth, low per capita income, and a relatively low capacity to adapt to climate change due to poverty and existing climate, which is often hot and arid. This is exacerbated by a long history of regional floods, droughts and famines, chronic armed conflict in several regions over the last 30 years, and in many cases governments and other institutions that are under-funded, inefficient, or otherwise not able to deal well with emergencies and long-term planning. Generalisations are risky and should not be taken as universal in application, but are made here in order to illustrate common problems across the continent that demand a policy response.

The IPCC in 2001 concluded that Africa is highly vulnerable to the various manifestations of climate change. Six areas of concern were emphasised:

- *Water resources*. Africa has the lowest rate of conversion of rainfall to runoff of any continent, averaging only 15%. Although the equatorial region and coastal areas of eastern and southern Africa are humid, the rest of the continent is dry subhumid to arid. Global warming is overwhelmingly projected to lead to reductions in soil moisture in subhumid zones and to a reduction in runoff and thus in water supplies. There has been an observed decrease in runoff in major African river basins of about 17% in the last decade. Reservoir storage shows strong sensitivity to variations in runoff and periods of drought. Lake storages and major dams have reached critically low levels in many areas, threatening irrigation and industrial activity. Climate model simulations project an increase in the frequency of such low storage episodes. Moreover, population growth will make this situation worse. World Bank estimates put the number of countries in Africa suffering water stress or scarcity (defined as less than 1000 cubic metres per year per person) in 1990 at eight, increasing to 18 by 2025 due to population growth alone. The number of Africans living in water-scarce regions would grow from about 300 million in 2000 to 600 million in 2025. The combination of demographic trends and climate change is likely therefore to cause increased human suffering and economically significant constraints in some parts of Africa.

- *Food security.* There is a widespread consensus that climate change, through increased extremes of high temperature and aridity, will worsen food security in Africa. The continent already experiences frequent major deficits in food production in many regions, and likely decreases in soil moisture will add to this burden. Thus serious impacts will occur due to higher prices for food on the world markets projected to result from climate change. As a result of water stress, inland fisheries will become more vulnerable because of episodic drought and habitat destruction. Ocean warming will also modify ocean currents and upwelling, with possible impacts on coastal fisheries.

- *Natural resources and biodiversity.* While population and development pressures will continue to be the major cause of changes in vegetative cover in Africa, climate change is projected to become an increasingly important factor by mid-century. Resultant changes in ecosystems will affect the distribution and productivity of plant and animal species, water supply, fuel wood, and other services. Losses of biodiversity are likely to be accelerated by climate change, particularly in limited regions where there are large concentrations of native species such as the Cape Floral Kingdom in South Africa, the mountains stretching from Ethiopia to South Africa, and Madagascar. In each of these areas migration of species is limited by coastal boundaries or altitude limits.

- *Human health.* Human health is very likely to be adversely affected in Africa. Temperature rises will extend the potential habitats for insect carriers of diseases (disease vectors) such as malaria, while droughts and floods will result both in increased frequency of epidemics and intestinal illnesses due to unsanitary conditions. More frequent outbreaks of Rift Valley Fever could result from increased rainfall in tropical east Africa, while warmer coastal waters could aggravate cholera epidemics. Many of these potential health threats could be overcome by adequate sanitation and health services, but unlike more developed countries, such services are lacking in many parts of Africa.

- *Coastal zones.* More than a quarter of Africa's population lives within 100 kilometres of a sea coast. Coastal zones are vulnerable to sea-level rise, particularly infrastructure such as roads, bridges and buildings. Nicholls and colleagues, in a global study of impacts for the UK government, estimated that the average number of people globally affected by coastal flooding in 2080 could increase from 1 million in 1990 to a worst case of 70 million, with many of these in Africa. Banjul, the capital of The Gambia, could disappear in 50–60 years due to coastal erosion and sea-level rise. Some fertile delta regions important for food production, such as the Nile Delta, could disappear or become saline.

- *Desertification.* Although the relative importance of causal factors such as climatic variations, versus human activities such as land-clearing and overgrazing, are uncertain, each has played a role in increasing desertification in parts of Africa, notably the Sahel. Potential increases in the frequency and intensity of drought across subhumid Africa are likely to increase desertification, and to act against any attempts to reclaim land lost to past desertification. Declines in soil fertility, and agricultural, livestock, and forest production have economic and social consequences contributing to poverty and instability in the region.

All these concerns, on top of other stresses such as AIDS and internal conflicts, add up to Africa being the region likely to be worst affected by enhanced climate change. This will add to the existing inequality between African nations and the richer developed countries. This cannot be good for Africa, nor for the developed nations, as it may limit world trade, increase political instability and tensions, and add to the problems of forced migration and necessary economic and emergency aid programs. It is clearly in the interest of African countries to see an urgent start on reducing total global greenhouse gas emissions, and it is important for the richer countries to see that this happens also, if only to avoid further growth in inequity between nations.

At present African countries in general have the lowest standards of living and the lowest per capita emissions of greenhouse gases. African countries therefore need assistance in coping with the impacts of climate change and variability, and need development to raise standards of living and to make the populations more resilient to stresses including climate change. Both objectives might best be achieved through the large-scale dissemination of renewable energy technologies to the poor. These nations will therefore be pressing for aid in achieving sustainable development, including low-carbon energy sources, but are unlikely to agree to any arrangement that restricts their economic growth.

Equity considerations suggest that Africans have a strong moral claim to assistance and to the right to increase their very low per capita emissions. Hopefully it will not be necessary for them to increase their greenhouse gas emissions to anything like the per capita amounts in the developed countries, but this can only happen through massive transfer of new low-carbon technologies. Lack of electricity grids and other centralised energy infrastructure means that wide dispersal of small-scale renewable energy generation systems (such as those based on solar and biomass energy) may be economically attractive in most of Africa. While many African countries have ratified the Kyoto Protocol, they have not so far committed to emissions reductions in the first commitment period, 2008–12, since none are Annex I countries.

Australia and New Zealand

Australia is a high per capita emitter of greenhouse gases. But when it comes to the potential impacts of climate change, Australia is almost certainly the most vulnerable developed country. All developed countries, by virtue of their wealth, and technological and institutional capacities can be expected to have great advantages relative to lesser-developed countries in terms of capacity to adapt to climate change. But, as we have seen in Chapter 7, the ability to adapt is also affected by the severity of climate change-induced stresses experienced, and to bio-physical limits to adaptation.

In Australia several factors increase the severity of exposure to climate change relative to other developed countries, and limit the capacity to adapt. These include:

- *Vulnerability to warming.* Mainland Australia is in the lowest latitude band of any developed country. This exposes Australian plants and animals, and especially agricultural and forest cropping, to optimum or above-optimum temperatures for large parts of the year. Studies of potential crop production suggest that for key crops such as wheat, warming will tend to increase yields only for the first two or three degrees Celsius, but only if local rainfall and soil moisture do not decrease. For greater warmings, yields will drop. Moreover, warming in inland parts of the country will not be moderated by the oceans and is likely to be greater than 2–3°C by the mid-twenty-first century and as much as 5–10°C by 2100 unless large reductions in greenhouse gas emissions begin soon. It is unlikely that plant breeding could provide suitable cultivars for summer temperatures, which could be well in excess of 45°C in some regions.

- *Regional reductions in rainfall.* Rainfall decreases are likely across much of southern and south-eastern Australia, which is the most populated region, with greatest agricultural production. This would seriously exacerbate the impact of warming by reducing soil moisture and runoff. Annual rainfall increases in the central and north-west are likely, but in a region that is only sparsely populated.

- *Already stressed water resources.* Water resources are already suffering from increasing stresses, and are likely to be greatly reduced, especially in southern and inland regions. Existing problems include dryland and riverine salinisation, eutrophication and toxic algal blooms, lack of environmental flows, and competition for limited supplies. Projected climate changes would lead to reductions in runoff and water supply in the Murray-Darling Basin with central estimates of around 20% reduction as early as 2030. Despite potential increases in water use efficiency and recycling, this decline in water supply would greatly inhibit irrigation of both low and high value crops, and adversely affect other water uses such as that for industry and town water supplies, especially during drought years. The major cities of Perth, Melbourne, Sydney and Canberra have already been seriously affected by water shortages due to persistent droughts, consistent with the enhanced greenhouse effect, over the last decade, and Perth is already installing a water desalination plant.

- *Vulnerable native plants and animals.* Many native Australian species of plants and animals, some already threatened by exotic predators and loss of habitat, have low tolerances to changes in climatic averages (although they are often well-adapted to short term climatic variability). This includes especially Alpine species, species in the biologically-rich south-west of Western Australian (which cannot migrate south due to the coast), and Australia's very extensive coral reefs, where corals are already showing increasing damage due to more frequent and severe bleaching events. Death of corals would have a great adverse effect on the tourism industry, and on fisheries.

- *Counter-adaptive trends.* Exposure to tropical cyclones and storm surges on the northern, western and eastern coasts of Australia is rapidly increasing due to population and investment growth in these areas, far greater than the national average. Projected increases in maximum intensities of tropical cyclones, their possible penetration further south, and mean sea-level rise, would greatly increase the magnitude and frequency of storm surges.

- *More severe droughts.* Possible changes in the behaviour of the El Niño-Southern Oscillation system (ENSO) towards a more El Niño-like average condition could greatly increase the frequency of major droughts in eastern Australia, and change the frequency of tropical cyclones, with increases in the west, but possible decreases in the east.

New Zealand is less vulnerable than Australia due to its location at higher latitudes and a climate more moderated by the oceans, which will slow warming over land. New Zealand also has ample water resources, although these differ greatly by region, with potential scarcity in the east. This could be exacerbated by a more El Niño-like mean oceanic state, and by a strengthening of the mid-latitude westerlies, which would increase rainfall on the already wet west coast, but reduce rainfall in the east. New Zealand is sensitive to an increase in storm intensities and extreme rainfalls, due to its steep terrain and frequent landslides.

Australia and New Zealand will both be particularly vulnerable to increasing pressure to take immigrants from threatened low-lying island states in the South Pacific, where emigration will be one of the few means of adaptation. As rich neighbours, Australia and New Zealand will need to accept some responsibility for aid to neighbouring countries that are threatened by sea-level rise. Indeed both Australia and New Zealand have some special responsibility, as members of the former British Commonwealth of Nations, for its developing country members, some 27 of which are also members of the Alliance of Small Island States. In his 1999 address to the UN General Assembly, the then Commonwealth Secretary-General spoke of the vital need 'to avert environmental threats like climate change and sea-level rise' and called for the Kyoto Protocol to enter into force as soon as possible, a call repeated at the Commonwealth Heads of Government Meeting in Durban later that year.

New Zealand has constitutional and other arrangements in place to accept environmental and economically motivated migrants from some nations in the South Pacific. However, Australia has so far strongly resisted any special consideration of such migration, and has taken a particularly hard line on so-called 'illegal' arrivals, which potentially would include environmental 'refugees' (see chapter 10 regarding equity issues). Increasing migrant pressures due to rising sea level and other effects in the South Pacific will therefore pose a major foreign policy dilemma for Australia, both inside and outside the Commonwealth of Nations, especially if migrants from the South Pacific increasingly use New Zealand residency as a means of entry to Australia.

Sea-level rise may also increase the pressure for migration to Australia, and to a lesser extent New Zealand, from low-lying parts of South-east Asia, including especially Bangladesh and low-lying coastal regions of Thailand, Indonesia, Indo-China, and even China. As the impacts of sea-level rise on these low-lying coastal regions increases, the threat of many tens of thousands of environmental refugees in the Australian–New Zealand region (and in other parts of the world) may become a reality. Issues of human rights and equity will be thrown into stark relief.

For all the above reasons, it is arguable that Australia has a particularly strong set of reasons for seeing effective global mitigation of climate change, as a matter of national interest. New Zealand will also have good reasons, not the least being its close economic and political relationship with Australia, and the large number of New Zealanders who have traditionally resided in Australia. Australia and New Zealand must recognise that effective mitigation of climate change will not come from a mere slowing down in the growth rate of emissions, or a decrease in the emissions per unit economic growth (as the US proposes): it can only come from real reductions in total emissions. Australia and New Zealand need to develop policies to turn this challenge into an opportunity, rather than an escalating crisis.

New Zealand has ratified the Kyoto Protocol, and hopes to meet its emissions target of no change relative to 1990, largely through forest sequestration. Australia, although a signatory to the UNFCCC, has joined the United States in refusing to ratify the Protocol. Nevertheless, the Australian Government claims to be meeting its Kyoto emissions target (which is an *increase* of 8% over 1990 levels) through voluntary energy conservation and other measures. In fact this is occurring largely through reductions in land clearing, which peaked in around 1990. The Australian Government's stated reasons for not ratifying the Protocol are listed in **Box 11**, along with some counter arguments. Many of these reasons and counter arguments apply to the US as well.

Australia has a particularly large potential for renewable energy in the form of solar power, wind power, and large amplitude tides. Over coming decades, growth in these energy resource industries (plus energy conservation) could provide ample power, a large potential for export of technology and hydrogen for fuel cells, and increased employment.

A 2004 Australian Government white paper announced several initiatives to foster renewable energy sources, and strong support for research and development in carbon capture and sequestration and cleaner coal usage. However, it refused to increase the existing Australian Mandatory Renewable Energy Target beyond the current 2% of electricity generation required to come from renewables, despite strong pleas from the renewables industry to increase it. The Government also removed fuel excise charges on diesel fuels, making them more competitive with renewables.

Contrary to the Federal Government's position, a report to the New South Wales, Victorian and South Australian State governments concluded that ratification of the Kyoto Protocol for the first commitment period would be advantageous for Australia, provided there were no open commitments for later periods. Another report, by the Australian Climate Group, consisting of a number of industry, science and environment experts, recommends that in view of Australian vulnerability to climate change, Australia should set a national emissions reduction target of 60% by 2050. The Federal Government's Chief Scientist has

Box 11: Australia and the Kyoto Protocol

The Australian Government has given a number of reasons for not signing the Kyoto Protocol. (The Bush Administration in the US has used many of the same arguments.) This summary is based on *Climate Change Policy in Australia: Isolating the Great Southern Land*, by Clive Hamilton, September 2004. See: www.tai.org.au.

Reason 1 Developing countries are 'exempted' from the Protocol and this is unfair.
Counter arguments
- The UNFCCC and the Kyoto Protocol state that all countries must limit their emissions, but rich countries should lead.

- While rich countries are mainly responsible, poor countries will suffer most. The polluter pays principle should apply.

- It will be at least 50 years before developing countries match the cumulative greenhouse gas emissions of the rich countries over the last 200 years.

- Individual Australians are responsible for between ten and twenty times the greenhouse gas emissions of individuals in many developing countries.

Reason 2 Australia is a net exporter of energy, unlike most developed countries.
Counter arguments
- Under the protocol, direct energy exports such as coal or natural gas are not counted against the exporting country's quota, but rather against countries who use that energy.

- Staying out of Kyoto cannot stop other countries reducing their energy imports. Joining Kyoto will stimulate investment in low-carbon energy industries.

- Canada, Norway, the UK and Russia are all net energy exporters but have signed.

Reason 3 Australia's fossil fuel dependence makes it harder to cut emissions.
Counter arguments
- Traditionally fossil fuels in Australia have been so cheap and abundant that energy efficiency has not been a priority. Australia has a greater opportunity to reduce emissions because many low-cost opportunities remain.

- Transport costs incurred in Australia are overwhelmingly for short-distance travel. Improved public transport and fuel efficiency would be more economic.

Reason 4 Kyoto is not in Australia's economic interests.
Counter arguments
- Costs from the Kyoto Protocol will be higher for countries that stay outside than for those who join. Those inside benefit from carbon trading and other mechanisms.

Box 11: Australia and the Kyoto Protocol (Continued)

- Economic interests do not necessarily coincide with national interests.

Reason 5 Ratifying Kyoto will result in large job losses.
Counter arguments
- Australian models show estimated job losses arise more from compliance by other countries (who have already signed) than from compliance by Australia.
- Estimates of losses generally assume a carbon tax policy that does not include job stimulation through reducing other taxes.
- Estimated losses do not take account of job growth in renewable energy and energy-efficiency industries.

Reason 6 Business will move off-shore and this will cause more CO_2 emissions and other pollution.
Counter arguments
- Energy-intensive industries enjoy cheap energy, stability and skilled labour in Australia. Future CO_2 emission and other pollution reduction obligations are likely in developing countries anyway.
- Key companies operating in Australia, such as Alcoa and Rio Tinto, have supported the Kyoto Protocol through the Pew Center on Climate Change's Business Environmental Leadership Council.
- Clean energy companies in Australia may move offshore if Australia does not ratify. (This is already happening to some degree.)
- Old energy-intensive industries in Australia are not as clean as more modern ones in developing countries.

Reason 7 Australia can take part in international emissions trading anyway.
Counter arguments
- Under the EU Emissions Trading Scheme and the Kyoto Protocol, participation by non-Kyoto countries is denied unless such countries have mandatory caps on emissions. Non-Kyoto countries cannot participate in the Clean Development Mechanism and Joint Implementation schemes.

Reason 8 Cuts required under the Kyoto Protocol are too small to make much difference to climate change.
Counter arguments
- Only true if emissions are allowed to increase after 2012.
- The first round targets under the Kyoto Protocol are only a first step.
- Australia (and the US) worked to ensure these targets were minimal, yet they now complain they are not strict enough!
- There is nothing to stop Australia (or the US) from voluntarily making larger emissions reductions.

Reason 9 Australia will meet its Kyoto target anyway, so it does not need to sign the Protocol.
Counter arguments
- If Australia will meet the target, why not sign and gain the benefits of participation? This would be the most economical way to meet the target.

> ### Box 11: Australia and the Kyoto Protocol (Continued)
>
> - Australian energy and transport emissions continue to grow rapidly. Only a one-off reduction in land clearing may allow the target to be met.
> - US emissions will be way above its negotiated target at Kyoto, with Australia supporting US policy.
>
> **Reason 10** Australia contributes only about 1.4% to global emissions so whether it signs does not matter.
>
> **Counter arguments**
> - This is unjust: each country should pull its weight.
> - Should a millionaire pay no income tax because their fraction of the national income is small?
> - Participation by Australia (and the US) would support the only systematic attempt to tackle the problem globally. The Kyoto Protocol is the only game in town (although there are other bilateral research and development agreements which could be expanded).

also called for a reduction of Australian emissions by 50% by 2050 and 80% by 2100. These long-term targets are in line with EU and UK thinking, and go way beyond the Kyoto Protocol.

One reason Australia claims to be deserving of special treatment is due to its large economic reliance on exports of direct energy commodities such as coal and natural gas as well as goods with large amounts of embodied energy (that is, goods requiring large amounts of energy to manufacture), especially aluminium and steel. This being so, Australia would benefit greatly, and perhaps equitably, from the addition of a provision to make embodied energy in manufactured exports such as aluminium and steel a charge against the emissions quota of the consuming rather than the exporting country.

China

China ranks second among nations in total greenhouse gas emissions, mainly from the burning of fossil fuels, but also as a result of methane from rice production. However, China's population is four times that of the highest emitter, the United States, and its priorities are raising living standards and promoting sustainable development

China has a long record of climatically related national disasters, including flood, drought, typhoons and famine. Major flood disasters occurred in 1852 (100,000 dead), 1887 (900,000 dead), 1931 (140,000 dead), 1954 (40,000 dead), and 1998 (3650 dead). Droughts, with associated famines, have been equally disastrous, while typhoons have frequently led to storm surge and riverine flooding in coastal regions. While major efforts have been made to control flooding and to store water for irrigation, increased population and encroachment on flood plains, as well as land clearing in catchment areas, have meant that the potential for disaster has not necessarily decreased.

For example, in the early 1950s comprehensive flood control measures were taken in the Yangtze River valley. These included construction of dikes along the river to prevent overflowing, and the creation of flood diversion areas (polders) that could be inundated during floods to reduce the discharge in the river and lessen downstream flooding. The largest of these polders (Jingjiang), built in 1952, had an area of 920 km^2, and could store 6 billion cubic metres of water. During the great flood of 1954 this prevented the number of casualties from being much greater. However, some 50 years later, almost a million people have settled in this flood basin, and it can no longer be used for floodwater diversion. Thus cities and towns downstream, such as Wuhan (population around 5 million), are now more exposed than they were in 1954.

However, due to limited resources, assessments of the impact of climate change in China have so far focused mainly on changes in average temperature and rainfall rather than on changes in the frequency and intensity of extreme events. This has led to a somewhat optimistic view of China's vulnerability to climate change. Possibly a clearer understanding of China's vulnerability would help China to adopt forward commitments, which in turn would encourage the United States to make a commitment. Therefore, a critical assessment is required of risks to China from climate change, including especially extreme events. These risks include:

- Likely increases in flood magnitudes and frequencies. Most global climate model simulations in the IPCC 2001 report show modest increases in average rainfall over most of China in summer, while a study by UK hydrologist Nigel Arnell shows increases in runoff especially in central and south-eastern China. Increases in rainfall intensity, and possibly in variability, are likely to lead to more frequent large floods, as found for China and elsewhere by US investigators Milly and colleagues in 2002.

- A tendency for more winter and spring runoff and less summer runoff in snow-fed rivers, increasing the need to operate dams more for flood control rather than maximising storage for summer irrigation.

- Possible increases in drought intensity, frequency and duration, due especially to increased year-to year variability and greater evaporation rates. Already, there has been a tendency for reduced flow and sediment discharge by the Yellow River in northern China. This may lead to increased erosion in the Gulf of Bohai and reduced water for irrigation.

- Probable increases in typhoon intensity and possibly in frequency and penetration to higher latitudes due to higher sea surface temperatures in the China Sea.

- Rising sea level adding to flooding of coastal regions, especially during storm surges or in association with river floods. This will reduce coastal wetland ecosystems as coasts retreat to areas protected by sea walls, thus reducing fish spawning grounds, and causing salt intrusion in river estuaries. It will also threaten the homes and livelihood of large numbers of people, especially in the heavily populated south-eastern region, including several large cities.

- Effects of any change in ENSO, which would affect rainfall variability and frequency of typhoons in China.

- Increased flushing of nutrients and chemicals into rivers and lakes (due to more intense runoff events). With higher temperatures this would lead to more eutrophication and algal blooms in water supplies.

China has made great strides in energy efficiency, renewable energy and reforestation, mainly for other reasons such as reducing local air pollution, economic efficiency, and controlling soil losses. Chinese official figures suggest a resulting decline in China's energy intensity (energy per unit GDP) of a remarkable 60% between 1977 and 1997. However, this may be exaggerated, with other estimates suggesting a decline of 10% during the 1990s. Two-thirds of China's energy use comes from coal, but the current five-year plan (2001–05) aims to improve the energy infrastructure, reducing coal use in favour of natural gas and modern renewables. The latter include wind, biogas and solar and photovoltaic sources, instead of the less environmentally desirable traditional burning of crop wastes, wood and dung. A rapid increase in private automobiles is a problem from the emissions viewpoint, and some policy-makers are advocating greater reliance on modern mass transit systems and smart growth policies.

Discussion on appropriate domestic and international energy policies for China is ongoing and vigorous. This includes a new generation of nuclear reactors, fostering renewables, coal gasification with carbon removal and sequestration, and eventually hydrogen generation for transport. Princeton University's Eric Larson and colleagues modelled China's energy technology choices. They concluded that by using coal gasification, co-generation, liquid and gaseous energy carriers, carbon sequestration, expanded renewables and end-use efficiency, China could still develop over the next 50 years with secure energy supplies and improved environmental quality. This would include modest near-term reductions in greenhouse gas emissions, at a cost less than 'business as usual'. Robert Williams from Princeton University also discusses how China could achieve zero emissions from coal.

China is looking to international assistance in leapfrogging over carbon intensive technology. This opens up a huge market for low-carbon technologies.

It is strongly in China's national interest to see an effective international regime to reduce greenhouse gas emissions as soon as possible, which will require limits to emissions both in developed and developing countries. China's interests would thus be well served by negotiating on the basis that progressively increasing commitments will be made by China and other developing countries once they are made by developed countries. Despite, and indeed because of potential economic rivalry between the two economic giants, China and the United States need to reach an agreement on how to bring an effective global emission reduction regime into being which allows for development in China and other developing countries, but avoids intolerable levels of climate change. Advocating a global target for reductions in energy intensity, sufficiently stringent that global emissions actually go down, may be a way forward.

European Union

The EU already has a strong commitment to an effective mitigation regime, although the degree to which this is being achieved is under debate. The reasons for the European commitment are outlined below. They demonstrate the rationality of the EU position and the need for the EU to meet its commitments and to eventually bring both the US and the developing countries into the picture.

- *Increasing aridity in the Mediterranean region.* This is one of the clearest areas of agreement between different global climate models regarding rainfall changes, with projected reductions in summer rainfall as well as higher potential evaporation. In an area already experiencing water shortages, this could bite hard in the next few decades, especially affecting agriculture and increasing the frequency and severity of wildfires. This and other regional differences will tend to accentuate the difference between the more prosperous northern parts of Europe and the less prosperous south.

- *More severe heat waves.* Higher average temperatures and possibly increased variability are likely to lead to increased frequency and severity of heat waves, causing thousands of additional deaths (see **Figure 5**). Air conditioning would reduce death rates, but would be expensive, increase energy demand – and hence emissions – and not reduce discomfort outdoors.

- *Increased flash flood risks right across the EU.* This follows from increased rainfall intensities projected by climate models, in a region where flash flooding is already a recurring problem due to close settlement, steep topography and fast runoff.

- *Increased major flood risk in northern Europe.* This follows from the broad agreement of global climate models that total rainfall in northern Europe will increase, especially in the winter half year. In many catchments warming will decrease snow accumulation, pushing peak runoff more into winter. Severe and widespread flooding has become common in northern and central Europe in the last two decades. In combination with rising sea levels, flooding will be exacerbated in coastal lowlands, particularly where storm surges slow drainage.

- *Possible changes in storminess, including extreme winds and hail.* Many modelling studies suggest that mid-latitude storms may increase in intensity due to more intense convection, and possible changes in storm tracks. Severe wind storms in western and northern Europe in recent years have caused extensive damage to forests and buildings. This tendency may increase.

- *Thawing of permafrost.* This will cause problems with buildings and infrastructure in far northern Europe, and in the Alps. In the Alps this could increase the danger of major landslides affecting mountain slopes and valleys, which will affect buildings and infrastructure such as cable cars, ski lifts, roads, railways, mountain villages and towns.

- *Loss of coastal wetlands due to sea-level rise.* This is of most concern in southern Europe, as local relative sea level will not be as severely affected in the north due to the continuing slow rebound (rising) of the land following the end of the last glaciation.

- *Pressures for population movement.* Pressure will come from both within Europe and from less-developed countries, from areas more adversely affected by climate change. This will increase pressure on both migration policies and external aid programs. Growing aridity in North Africa and the Middle East may be of particular concern.

- *Threats to peace and security.* There may be increased instability in less developed countries as they suffer adverse impacts and regional disputes over water in Europe, the Middle East and Central Asia.

- *Weakening or cessation of the North Atlantic thermo-haline circulation (THC).* The THC presently keeps Western Europe relatively warm (see Chapter 6). Regional cooling along the Atlantic and North Sea coasts by up to 6 to 8°C could occur if the THC breaks down during this century. The likelihood and impacts of such an event are poorly understood.

Several countries in the EU already have strong renewable energy sectors, notably wind power in Denmark, or the potential to develop such industries (solar energy in Spain, tidal power in the UK). These represent growth industries. Policies leading to early action, including research, development, and market building, could lead to a global technological advantage for exports.

The European Union has a comprehensive policy on climate change following its ratification of the Kyoto Protocol in 2002, and has agreed to reduce EU emissions of greenhouse gases to 8% less than 1990 levels by 2008 to 2012. The implementation of policies and measures to reduce emissions is taking place mainly at national levels, with some joint EU actions. New members of the EU, mainly from economies in transition, have commitments to reduce emissions, but some former Eastern Bloc countries are already below 1990 levels due to economic setbacks following the break-up of the former Soviet Union.

The United Kingdom has a strong policy, with a goal of a 60% reduction of carbon dioxide emissions by 2050, and an interim target of a 20% reduction by 2020. This is to be achieved by a reduction in the amount of energy consumed, plus a substantial increase in the use of renewable energy. Since 1970, the UK economy has doubled, while overall energy consumed increased by only about 15%. Besides emission trading, measures will include energy efficiency commitments, revision of building regulations, improved efficiency in transport and lower carbon fuels. A 2004 report by the House of Lords Science and Technology Committee commends the objectives but warns that their achievement is uncertain without stronger government action, especially regarding the transport sector.

Some critics claim that the EU is unlikely to meet its targets, and has to date looked good only because of the shift from coal to gas in the UK in the 1990s, the reform of the East German economy on reunification, and the relatively strong reliance on nuclear power. Nevertheless big strides are taking place in renewables and many other measures are being taken. Production of six key greenhouse gases dropped slightly in 2002 following two years of increases. Total emissions from the then 15 EU countries was about 3% below 1990 levels, compared to the Kyoto Protocol of an 8% reduction by 2008–12.

In 2003 the EU established a scheme for greenhouse emissions trading, which became operational on 1 January 2005. This is expected to accelerate reductions in emissions in EU countries.

India, Pakistan and Bangladesh

This section will focus mostly on India, which is the country with the second largest population in the world, the fourth largest economy, and a per capita income about half that of China. The neighbouring countries of Pakistan and Bangladesh share some of the same problems and climatic influences.

Global warming is expected to have profound effects on India, Pakistan and Bangladesh, although there are large uncertainties about the relative effects on the summer monsoon rains of global warming with or without taking account of aerosol (atmospheric particle) effects. Key potential impacts include:

- higher temperatures increasing potential evaporation and duration of heat waves;
- enhanced variability in summer monsoon rainfall;
- significant decline in winter rainfall leading to severe water scarcity during early summer months;
- more intense droughts over larger areas adversely affecting crop production, especially wheat and rice;
- more intense floods, especially in the flood plains of the eastern Himalayan rivers, their major tributaries and the delta regions;
- coastal flooding and salinity intrusion from sea-level rise in combination with the amplification of storm surges from more intense tropical cyclones in the Bay of Bengal;
- rapid melting of Himalayan glaciers, leading initially to greater river flows and hence sedimentation, and subsequent reduced flow, especially in the dry summer months;
- serious health impacts due to heat-related stress and vector-borne diseases.

These climatic changes would likely lead to more severe food shortages, increased loss of life and infrastructure from coastal inundation and riverine flooding, loss of life from heat stress and vector-borne diseases, and potential displacement of tens of millions of residents of low-lying coastal areas, especially in Bangladesh, causing problems of internal and cross-border migration. The IPCC 2001 report classifies south Asia as highly vulnerable to climate change in terms of food and fibre, biodiversity, water resources, coastal ecosystems and settlements, and moderately vulnerable as regards health.

Rapid industrialisation, urbanisation and population growth have already greatly increased water demand. Groundwater resources are already under severe stress and expansion is limited. In response, the Indian government has initiated plans to link rivers across India, supplying water from the present water-surplus rivers of the north and east to the drier central, western and southern river basins. This huge project is highly controversial, with concern from Bangladesh about its share of the waters, and the possibility that climate change might decrease the water supply in the north making such a scheme less viable.

India has one of the lowest per capita rates of greenhouse gas emissions, about one-twentieth that of the US, has a high population growth rate (1.5% per year), and in the 1990s its economy grew at about 6% per year. Its energy use grew roughly 7% per year over the same period, and its carbon intensity (emissions per unit GDP) began to decline after 1995. India is heavily dependent on coal and traditional non-commercial biomass use. However, economic reforms and enforcement of clean air laws, combined with renewable energy incentives and developments has led to recent decreases in energy-related carbon emissions. Nearly 60% of the Indian population lacks access to electricity.

India has ratified the Kyoto Protocol, and while its priority is sustainable development, it is committed to a 'climate-friendly' approach. India's vehicle stock has been greatly modified in recent years, with public vehicles in Delhi converted to natural gas, and European-level emission standards applied to passenger vehicles in several major cities. India has a goal of 10% of new power generating capacity from renewables by 2010, new combustion technologies in power plants, and utilisation of coal-bed methane is promoted.

Nevertheless, 'business as usual' projections suggest that Indian GDP could be nearly five times the present by 2030, with a tripling of energy use and more than a doubling of carbon emissions. Additional emission reductions would require concerted measures aided by international carbon trading, the CDM and access to new technologies.

Latin America

Latin America covers a huge range of environments, with diverse climates, ecosystems, human population distributions, living standards, and cultural traditions. Population growth and land-use changes are already exerting major pressures on the environment, so that climate change and sea-level rise are just adding to the stresses. Some considerations related to climate change include:

- *Warming patterns*. Indications are that Central and South America generally will warm at about the global average rate, although probably faster in inland South America.

- *Rainfall patterns*. Sub-regional detail is limited. However, indications are that Central America will tend to have less rainfall, with patterns in South America varying greatly from location to location, with major drying indicated in some model projections. Rainfall changes in parts of South America may be dominated by changes in the ENSO pattern, which has great influence. A southward movement of the mid-latitude westerlies and the high-pressure belt is now considered likely due to both the enhanced greenhouse effect and stratospheric ozone depletion, affecting rainfall in southern Argentina and Chile.

- *El Niño*. Under enhanced greenhouse warming, El Niño-like conditions may become more frequent and intense. This would lead to drier conditions in Mexico, the Amazon region and Central America. Higher temperatures would exacerbate such droughts by increasing rates of evaporation of existing soil moisture.

- *The Amazon region*. Some, but not all, global climate models show a reduction in rainfall in the Amazon basin. Deforestation, currently occurring due to land clearing, leads to reduced evapotranspiration (atmospheric moisture input from trees), which provides about half of the moisture in the region recycled as rainfall. Forest fragmentation and drying leads to greatly increased danger of widespread fires. This would be greatly exacerbated by more El Niño-associated droughts. The danger is that death of forests due to land clearing and fire may lead to an irreversible decline in regional rainfall, to large increases in carbon dioxide input to the atmosphere, and amplification of the greenhouse effect.

- *Agriculture*. Under climate change conditions, subsistence farming would be severely threatened in some parts of Latin America, such as north-east Brazil and Mexico. Increased temperatures may also reduce yields in other parts of Latin America, even allowing for the physiological benefits of increased carbon dioxide concentrations.

- *Health*. Higher temperatures will make urban air pollution worse in major cities. More intense rainfalls from storms generally and tropical cyclones (hurricanes) in Central America will increase the risk of flash flooding and landslides endangering lives and property. Vector-borne diseases are also likely to increase especially in poorer populations where medical services are limited.

- *Glaciers*. Those in the high Andes and the ice sheets in southern South America are already retreating, and will retreat much more. This will lead to changes in the total and annual cycle of river flow in some rivers, threatening some urban water supplies (notably in Peru), irrigation and loss of tourism.

- *Tropical cyclones*. These are expected to become more intense. They have major impacts on the Caribbean and Central American States, causing great economic and human losses, for instance Hurricane Mitch in 1998 caused losses of about 40% and 70% of the GDP in Nicaragua and Honduras, respectively.

Overall, climate change may bring some benefits to some regions of Latin America, but increasing environmental deterioration, changes in water supply and agricultural lands may make any gains negligible. Adaptability of Latin American socio-economic systems to extreme climate events is very low and vulnerability is high, especially for the many urban and rural poor.

With the exception of Venezuela and Mexico, Latin America is poorly supplied with fossil fuels, and energy imports are a large drain on the economies of the region. Brazil has been in the forefront of developing renewable energy sources, notably hydro-power for electricity (90% of total power generation in 1999) and ethanol for transport. Brazil has also been very active in climate policy negotiations, with proposals to provide for equitable participation of developing countries. However, rapid economic growth and an electric power shortage has led to a growth over the last couple of decades in coal, oil and gas based thermoelectric power generation, which can be built faster and closer to centres of high power demand. This trend is expected to continue.

Despite this recent trend to increased use of fossil fuels, Brazilian experience in initially subsidising the use of ethanol from sugarcane is instructive. Not only have costs gone down and ethanol become economically competitive with petroleum, but ethanol production has supplied far more employment per unit energy than coal, oil or hydropower. The federal government of Brazil has recently mandated a minimum share of new renewable sources in electricity generation in Brazil, and proposed similar global targets and time frames internationally. It is essential that Brazil, as one of the largest developing countries, be engaged in the post-Kyoto global mitigation regime.

The Russian Federation

The Russian Federation covers a vast territory from the Baltic Sea in the west to the Bering Sea in the east, and from south of 45°N to the high Arctic beyond 70°N. Much of northern Russia is tundra overlaying permafrost, with vast boreal forests further south, and arid areas in Central Asia. Obviously, people who are heavily snow-bound in winter with sub-zero temperatures would welcome a little more warmth. However, it is a complex business, since vegetation, ecosystems and human society have adapted to the climate over hundreds and thousands of years. Some key issues include:

- The melting of Arctic sea ice would facilitate shipping over a longer season, although melting of permafrost may restrict access to inland sites. The exposure of coasts to storm and wave action would increase erosion along the Arctic shores, made worse by sea-level rise.

- Indigenous communities dependent on hunting of reindeer, polar bear, walrus and some species of seal, for example in Chukotka in the far east, will be threatened.

- Many human settlements and developments, including buildings, roads, rail, airfields and oil and gas pipelines have been built on permanently frozen ground. As is the case in Alaska, costs from damage to these structures as foundations shift, could be large. The southern limit of

permafrost is projected to move northward by several hundred
kilometres by 2100.

- Winter heating costs could be reduced, but cooling may become
  increasingly necessary in summer.

- Some crops in more temperate regions would have longer growing
  seasons and could increase their yield at least for warmings of up to
  about 5°C, especially where accompanied by increased winter snow and
  summer rain, as is likely in many mid- to high-latitude regions. However,
  warming in inland regions is expected to be more than twice the global
  average, so it could well be 5 to 10°C warmer by 2100. Continental
  interiors may also experience summer drought, exacerbated by the high
  temperatures, leading to heat and water stress on crops. In regions where
  rainfall increases, waterlogging of crops may become a problem.

- Warming, and melting of snow cover would increase the range and
  length of season for insect pests, allowing more generations over a
  growing season, affecting crop yields and human health.

- Boreal forests would be exposed to higher temperatures, and
  increasingly frequent and severe summer droughts. Coupled with
  increased exposure to insect pests, this would lead to dieback and
  increased danger of wild fires. Eventually boreal forests may extend
  further north, but losses at their southern boundaries are likely to occur
  sooner and to be greater. According to the Canadian Forest Service such
  effects are already occurring in Canada.

- The episodic impacts of increasingly severe floods, droughts, severe
  storms and insect infestations may prove to be a major concern.

Whatever the balance between the gains and losses listed above, which
will become worse with increased warming beyond a few degrees, other considerations will impact on the Russian national interest. These include likely
deleterious effects on Russia's southern neighbours, most of which are in the
drier continental interior that will become much warmer and may not have
increases in rainfall. Growing poverty, food shortages and other factors may
lead to increasing unrest and instability, requiring Russian aid or leading to
adverse impacts from insurgencies and environmental refugees.

These and other considerations recently led to heated discussion within the
Russian Federation as to whether it should ratify the Kyoto Protocol. Russia ratified the Protocol in November 2005, despite the opposition of some influential
advisers. Argument hinged in part on what economic benefits might accrue to
Russia in the short term from possible sale of surplus greenhouse gas emission
rights, and from Joint Implementation projects. While these were initially
thought to be large due to the collapse of the Russian economy after the break-

up of the USSR, recent signs of economic recovery suggest that Russia may have less surplus emissions for sale.

The politics of Russia's relationship to the Kyoto Protocol were reviewed by Jacqueline Karas of the Royal Institute of International Affairs in March 2004. Among the Russian scientists and economists opposed to ratification of the Protocol were Professor Yuri Israel, who has long maintained that Russia will benefit from moderate global warming, and Andrei Illarionov, President Putin's economic advisor. Russia's role as a major exporter of oil and gas may have been critical to the decision to ratify the Protocol. This may have been influenced by the prospect of carbon removal and sequestration becoming a major mitigation strategy. Anna Korppoo of Imperial College, London, believes that improving Russian energy efficiency would have been unlikely without investment made possible by the Protocol, which is likely to lead to Joint Implementation projects in Russia, particularly by members of the EU.

Small Island States

Small Island States include a mixture of islands in many different locations and having different physical characteristics. These include:

- *Atolls*. These are rings of coral reefs enclosing a lagoon. Around the rim of the reef are small islands, usually with average heights above sea level of only a few metres. Obviously, these will be severely affected by sea-level rise, storm surges and wave action. Atoll nations include Kiribati (population 78,000), the Maldives (population 269,000), the Marshall Islands (population 60,000), Tokelau (population 2000) and Tuvalu (population 9000).

- *Islands with higher elevations*. These islands are usually of volcanic origin and often have low-lying fringes that contain much of the arable and populated land. Depending on their size and distribution of land, some islands such as the main islands of Fiji, Tonga and Samoa, may be severely affected by sea-level rise, although they will not become completely uninhabitable.

- *Island States*. These consist of a mixture of atolls and higher elevation islands. They will suffer various degrees of stress, especially associated with loss of resources and forced internal migration or emigration. Examples include Tonga (population 110,000), and Fiji (population 800,000).

- *Low-latitude islands*. Most Small Island States lie in tropical or subtropical waters such as the Pacific and Indian Oceans and the Caribbean Sea. Those within about six degrees of latitude of the Equator are not directly subject to tropical cyclone (typhoon or hurricane) impacts (although they may still experience storm surges from weather disturbances at a distance). Those further from the Equator may suffer direct hits from such storms.

- *Mid-latitude Small Island States*. Examples are Cyprus and Malta. These are less low-lying and less exposed to storm surge events.

There are also many other small low-lying islands, often populated, which have many of the same potential problems from sea-level rise and climate change, but which are part of metropolitan countries or are in political association with them. These include American Samoa, Guam, and the Federated States of Micronesia (all associated with the US), many low-lying islands in the Philippines and Indonesia, and the islands of the Torres Strait in Australia. We will focus here on those islands that form independent states, and thus have national interests as such, although we note that the interests of the associated metropolitan states should include those of their associated islands.

Small Island States are not major contributors to the total emission of greenhouse gases, although they may be severely affected by consequent sea-level rise and climate change. In most cases they also have very limited resources and standards of living, and thus are less able to adapt to climate change than other states, unless they receive foreign aid to do so.

Major impacts affecting national interests include:

- Mean sea-level rise, which will increase the salinity of groundwater, especially on atolls where groundwater is often the only source of freshwater for human consumption and agriculture.

- Extreme sea level, storm surges and high wave energy events, which will increasingly lead to wave overtopping and flooding of atolls and low-lying coastal fringes, threatening lives, infrastructure and property. Probable increases in the average and peak intensity of tropical cyclones (typhoons or hurricanes), and possibly of mid-latitude storms also, will exacerbate these problems. **Figure 30** vividly illustrates the existing highly vulnerable state of many inhabited low-lying coral atolls.

- Damage to coral reefs from more frequent and intense coral bleaching and wave damage, leading to loss of wave protection, loss of fisheries, and loss of attraction for the tourist industry.

- Many atolls, and some atoll states, could become uninhabitable during the twenty-first century or beyond with consequent loss of nationhood and cultural heritage. In order of vulnerability, Small Island States that could become uninhabitable in the next 50 years include Tokelau, the Maldives, Tuvalu, the Marshall Islands and Kiribati, with a total population at present of around 420,000.

- In higher elevation islands, increased rainfall intensity associated with storms will increase erosion and riverine flooding.

- Changes in weather patterns, ocean currents and sea levels associated with regional climatic phenomena such as ENSO, the Intertropical Convergence Zone (ITCZ) and the South Pacific Convergence Zone (SPCZ) could lead to major changes in average rainfall and cloud cover and inter-annual variability, including the frequency and intensity of floods and droughts.

- Threats to crop production due to higher temperatures and water demand, more saline groundwater, changed annual and inter-annual rainfall patterns, and storm damages.

- Increased costs of fossil fuels and freight, due to mitigation measures will put a premium on locally produced renewable energy and self-sufficiency.

Adaptation to climate change and sea-level rise is not easy for the Small Island States due to their limited resources, isolation and fundamental threats to their environmental support systems (land, fresh water, food supplies and so on). Disaster preparedness and relief is one option, but options are limited, and if sea-level rise continues, ultimately the Small Island States are faced with the prospect of emigration as the last resort. This would have deep personal and cultural consequences, and demands a willingness by other nations to accept responsibility.

These and other considerations mean that it will be in the interests of the Small Island States, and especially of the low-lying ones, to:

- Increase use of local renewable energy supplies and foster increased self-sufficiency.

- Reduce reliance on groundwater on atolls and in coastal zones.

- Develop a population policy, including consideration of large-scale emigration to metropolitan states. This will entail negotiated migration agreements where these do not yet exist (as they do for former New Zealand dependencies). This provides a potential bargaining point in relation to the greenhouse mitigation policies and aid policies of the metropolitan states.

- Foster pro-active mitigation policies in both developed and developing countries. This includes a mediating role between those developed states (namely the US and Australia) that resist commitments until the lesser-developed states accept commitments, and those lesser-developed states that are unwilling to make forward commitments until the developed states act.

Figure 30: Graphic illustration of the vulnerability of coral atolls. Top: The normal view from the Meteorological Service office across the airport runway from the main town of Funafuti Atoll, Tuvalu, in the South Pacific. Bottom: Inundation caused by the spring tides in 2002. (Photos courtesy of Kathy McInnes, CSIRO, Australia (top) and Chalapan Kaluwin, AMSAT, Fiji, (bottom)).

- Place emphasis on the global significance of the issues of equity, sovereignty and cultural assets raised by the possibility of populated atolls becoming uninhabitable.

Various UN and other treaties and agreements bear on these issues, as do the commitments to them already made in principle by many other states. For example, the Commonwealth Heads of Government declared in their Langkawi Declaration in 1989 that they were deeply concerned at the serious deterioration in the environment, noting especially that some islands and low-lying areas are threatened by the prospect of rising sea level. It is interesting to note that 27 of the 54 members of the Commonwealth are also members of the Alliance of

Small Island States. The Commonwealth is also committed in principle to 'a more equitable society', a principle that is seriously negated by continuing large per capita greenhouse gas emissions in developed countries.

In the words of an editorial in the *Business Island Monthly*, Suva, January 2004:

> *Along with other countries alarmed by what climate change and sea level rise predictions imply for them, the Pacific Islands have been asking the big ask for a decade. Except for the European Union countries, the response to the protest clamour from the world's great climate polluters has generally been to sidestep, prevaricate, dodge, sabotage, obstruct, make excuses or to display open hostility to the notion that they have a duty to clean up their acts.*

United States of America

In an announcement by President Bush on 14 February 2002, the United States reaffirmed its commitment to the UNFCCC and its central goal of stabilisation of greenhouse gas concentrations at a level that will prevent dangerous interference with the climate system. However, the US has withdrawn from the Kyoto Protocol process, and Bush's commitment is only to reduce its greenhouse gas *intensity* (that is, emissions per unit GDP) by 18% over the next 10 years. This is very close to the reduction in greenhouse gas *intensity* that the US achieved over the last 10 years, when *total* US emissions (not per unit GDP) increased by 12%. This increase in actual emissions was due to a much larger (32%) increase in GDP over the same period. Assuming continued US economic growth, the Bush commitment for the next decade amounts, in terms of actual emissions, to about a 30% increase above 1990 emissions levels by 2012, compared to the 7% reduction originally agreed to by the United States at the Kyoto conference.

As stabilisation of carbon dioxide levels will only occur after a massive decrease in global emissions (more than currently agreed in the Kyoto Protocol), the US stance demonstrates no real commitment to stabilisation of carbon dioxide concentrations in the foreseeable future. As the United States emits about a third of total global emissions, and its participation in global trading of carbon emissions is vital to a strong market in emissions, US policy is important to the future success of global initiatives to deal with climate change.

The stated reason for this lack of commitment to real emissions reductions is concern about what is felt to be a large cost to the US economy of real reductions. Leaving aside the question of whether this large cost is realistic (but see Chapter 10 for a discussion of evidence that it is probably greatly exaggerated), it is pertinent to examine what is most at risk for the United States if climate change proceeds as projected in the absence of large emission reductions.

The United States is particularly vulnerable to:

- Sea-level rise and storm surges on the Pacific, Atlantic and Gulf of Mexico coasts, including areas in the south-east such as Louisiana, Florida, North Carolina and the eastern shore of Chesapeake Bay. James Titus and Charlie Richman of the US Environment Protection Agency estimate that some 58,000 square km along the Atlantic and Gulf coasts is less than 1.5 m above sea level. These areas are highly vulnerable to the combination of sea-level rises of around 50 cm by the year 2100 (which have a probability of at least 50%), along with high tides and storm surges. Some 54% of the US population now live in the 17% of the land area that comprises the coastal zone, and the largest population growth during the next several decades is projected for coastal areas. The city of New Orleans already lies below sea level and could be drowned by a combination of river flooding, storm surge and sea-level rise.

- Decreases in winter snow pack in the Pacific North-west, the Sierras and the Rocky Mountains leading to increased river flow and flooding in winter and spring, and less water storage for summer irrigation. Dams will need to be operated for flood protection, by keeping water levels low, and will thus not maximise their storage for irrigation.

- Increasing aridity in the South-west and Great Plains regions and possibly elsewhere due to higher evaporation and the risk of appreciable decreases in rainfall. The South-west is among the most rapidly growing areas of the country. Of the simulations from nine different climate models used in the IPCC 2001 report, half project decreases in rainfall, except in the North-west and East in winter, and there is strong agreement on a decrease along the Mexican border. Thus over most of the central and southern regions of the US, there is at least a 50% chance of less rainfall, and more than a 50% chance of reduced runoff (due to higher evaporation). A more recent simulation by Niklas Christensen and colleagues from the University of Washington of changes in water resources in the Colorado Basin confirms this likelihood, as does a study by Princeton University's Syukuro Manabe and colleagues. Such changes would likely force rises in water prices and restrict urban and industrial growth in the South-west. They would also affect assessments of changes in crop yields, where increasing aridity may well counter any advantages from warmer conditions and increased concentrations of carbon dioxide. Lake Powell on the Colorado River, as at 19 July 2005, was 51.6% full.

- Increased frequency of major floods in the large river basins of the US. Researchers from the US Geological Survey and the National Oceanographic and Atmospheric Administration report that great floods in 29 large river basins worldwide have increased in frequency since 1953, and are projected to further increase in frequency during the twenty-first century by a factor of 2 to 8 times. This includes the Mississippi Basin.

- Increased risk of wild fires and damages, especially in the western US. There seems to be an increase in recent decades, and a further increase is projected.

- Effects of any changes in ENSO and the North Atlantic Oscillation (NAO). Both these global weather systems have large impacts on extreme events in the US. A more El Niño-like mean state is projected under global warming, and the behaviour of the NAO may also change. El Niño conditions are associated with more Pacific and less Atlantic hurricanes along the US coast.

- Increased health risks from weather-related disasters, heat waves, and air pollution in cities. This will impact particularly on the urban poor, and is a focus of concern by the Congressional Black Caucus. A study by Katherine Hayhoe of ATMOS Research and others using high and low emissions pathways looked at impacts in California. They found that a high emissions pathway led to major impacts on heat-related mortality, snow pack and water supplies.

- Risk of possibly severe impacts from a decrease or cessation in the North Atlantic thermo-haline circulation, especially for the north-east states. This effect is unlikely (but not impossible) during the twenty-first century, but it may be irreversibly set in train by continuing high emissions of greenhouse gases this century (see Chapter 6).

- Major increases in aridity in Central America, including Mexico, which would almost certainly lead to increasing pressure for economic migration to the United States across its long land border with Mexico, and to a need for economic aid.

The US will also need to address the following issues:

- The need for greater energy efficiency and less reliance on imported oil, for national security and economic competitiveness. This provides a major co-benefit of reducing greenhouse gas emissions.

- Its vested interest in political stability and international cooperation, which will be undermined by environmental stresses imposed by climate change, especially in many lesser-developed countries.

These considerations suggest that the US has a strong, if under-acknowledged, national interest in effective global mitigation of climate change. This is heightened by the fact that other countries, and notably the EU, are acting to foster energy efficiency, the use of renewable energy, and to reduce the carbon intensity of their economies. Subject to interpretation of agreements under the World Trade Organisation, new standards adopted in other countries may limit US exports to markets where US products do not comply, and where new and alternative technologies, stimulated by carbon trading, are gaining market share. A notable example at present is hybrid automobile technology, with non-US car makers further advanced in research, development and actual sales.

A 2004 study of world car manufacturers by the World Resources Institute in Washington and Sustainable Asset Management in Zurich finds that potential increases in manufacturing costs to meet carbon constraints (policy measures to limit greenhouse gas emissions), and possible loss of market share to manufac- turers of less carbon-intensive vehicles, poses risks for US manufacturers. Opportunities lie in the potential to develop lower-carbon technologies ahead of rivals. This would reap the benefits of technological leadership, brand differen- tiation and enhanced profits. The study, based on present corporate behaviour, rated Toyota as most favourably placed, and GM and Ford the least, with an esti- mated relative difference due to carbon constraints of 20% of earnings before interest and tax.

Apart from the Bush Administration's withdrawal from the Kyoto process, and its stated goal of a decrease in US energy intensity (but not in total emis- sions), the US has adopted a voluntary program of emissions reporting and energy conservation and a seemingly comprehensive low-carbon energy research program. The US Secretary of the Department of Energy, Spencer Abraham, in June 2004, described 'six pillars of collaborative research'. These are hydrogen, clean coal, safe nuclear power, fusion, energy efficiency and renewable energy. Underlying this policy, Secretary Abraham stated

> '... we've operated from a very simple point of view. Across the planet, countries including the United States have very substantial reserves of coal at their disposal, and ultimately this coal will be used.'

Secretary Abraham described the *Hydrogen Initiative* as the *first pillar* of the US climate strategy. This includes the *Freedom Car*, which is to be powered by hydrogen-based fuel cells. As hydrogen is only a carrier of energy, this in turn is based on generation of hydrogen, from electricity generated either from nuclear power stations or fossil fuel with carbon capture and sequestration, or perhaps from renewable energy sources. This is a multi-decadal program that will do nothing to reduce carbon emissions in the near future, although it may be valua- ble in the later decades of the twenty-first century.

The *second pillar* of the US program is the *Clean Coal Research Initiative*, dubbed *FutureGen*. This is a 'cost-shared program between government and industry to quickly demonstrate emerging technologies in coal-based power generation and to accelerate their commercialisation'. The aim is to use gasification to break coal down, allowing the capture of carbon emissions, efficient generation of electricity and production of hydrogen. Carbon sequestration is one of the highest priorities, with the formation of the *Carbon Sequestration Leadership Forum*, involving 15 countries and the European Commission. Goals are for development of technology within the next six years that gives 40% less carbon emissions, 50% reductions by 2020, and eventually 'practically zero emissions of carbon into the atmosphere'. This time-scale is of course for developing the technical capabilities, not for achieving a complete turnover of existing power stations to these technologies, which would take several, or indeed many decades if there are no mandatory targets and incentives.

The *third pillar* is new generation nuclear energy. This is to avoid undue dependence on other fuels, and because 'nuclear power simply has such great capacity to provide clean energy to the world'. Secretary Abraham states that it is imperative to address the safety and proliferation concerns of opponents of nuclear energy. Again, the US has developed a multi-national program, *Generation IV*, to develop new reactor designs which will be safer, more economical and secure, and able to produce hydrogen. The hope is to have candidate reactor designs by 2020. But again, actual large-scale deployment of such reactors would be several more decades away.

The *fourth pillar* of the US strategy is fusion, again aimed at production of hydrogen as well as electricity. This too is via an international collaborative project, ITER (ITER means 'the way'). First operational experiments will not take place until early next decade, and there is no certainty that fusion's potential can be realised.

Secretary Abraham recognised that some of these new technologies will not be realised for another 10 or 15 years and that others may take 30 to 50 years. So, he says, it is not enough to rely on new technology breakthroughs, which is why the *fifth and sixth pillars* are energy efficiency and renewable energy. These are being developed through the Federal Energy Management Program, and the Department of Energy with the aim to reduce the cost of renewables. Abraham pointed out that the US had more installed renewable energy capacity in 2001 than Germany, Denmark, Sweden, France, Italy and the UK combined. Again, some international collaborative efforts are underway, as well as a domestic *Climate Vision Program* aimed at reducing the growth of emissions by energy-intensive industry.

Clearly the US Administration favours collaborative international research and development programs with other countries, and cooperative voluntary programs at home. It has recognised the reality of the climate change problem, places great faith in new technology to provide long-term solutions, but has not yet signalled through actions that it recognises the urgency of short-term emission reductions.

However, many states, local governments, businesses and NGOs are calling for federal action to create greater certainty, a sense of urgency, a uniform playing field, and to maximise efficiency in US mitigation efforts.

The common interest in global solutions

This brief and incomplete survey of national interests suggests some common themes. One is that every nation will be directly and indirectly affected by climate change. There will be gains, especially in higher latitudes in the short-term, but also losses, which will increase with time. Among the indirect effects, which will reverberate around the world, is a potential increase in inequity, as the poor countries and poor people everywhere are most adversely affected. This will have unfortunate effects in an increasingly globalised society.

Even those countries that might expect to gain in the short-term from global warming, of which the Russian Federation is the prime example, are likely to suffer adverse effects in the longer term, especially from indirect effects such as increased instability on their borders. Full participation in global mitigation opportunities through Joint Implementation and emissions trading is also a decisive issue.

Countries such as the United States and Australia, and also China, India and Russia, rely heavily on fossil fuels for domestic consumption, economic development or exports. These countries have an interest in continuing the use of fossil fuels as long as possible. It is significant that the US and Australia are the two developed countries which have refused to sign the Kyoto Protocol, evidently because their governments feel that mandatory emission reduction strategies are against their national interests. Yet both countries have embarked on government-funded programs to develop 'clean coal' technologies including carbon removal and sequestration, and subsidise some other voluntary programs.

Even in the United States and Australia the dubious arguments against the reality of human-induced climate change are increasingly irrelevant to the policy debate, which has moved on to look at the most appropriate means to reduce emissions, and the urgency of doing so. Both governments now concede that there is a real problem from human-induced climate change. However, both have argued that continued reliance on fossil fuels is economically essential, and appeal to carbon removal and sequestration as the great hope for the future, with the United States adding safe and secure nuclear energy as the second technological saviour.

What is lacking in both these countries is a clear recognition of the urgency of the problem. This urgency is due to the large delays or lags in the climate system, which mean that action taken (or not taken) today will affect the climate and sea level decades, and indeed centuries, into the future. Unless urgent action is taken in the next decade or two to substantially reduce greenhouse gas emissions, it will be impossible to stabilise the climate at what may be considered safe levels of change. The UK target of a 60% reduction in emissions in developed countries by 2050 is entirely reasonable if we are to avoid high risks of climate change induced disasters. Every delay in reducing greenhouse gas emissions increases the risk of dangerous climate change impacts and makes necessary future action ever more drastic.

Carbon removal and sequestration, and indeed safe and secure nuclear energy may well be essential as part of a package of solutions, but neither is as yet proven safe and economically viable, nor is it possible to install these technologies fast enough to avert a high risk of dangerous climate change. Other urgent measures must be taken such as demand management, increasing energy efficiency, and rapid development and deployment of renewable energy technologies that are already available.

It is ironic that it is the poorer developing countries that may pioneer many of these developments. They have to build new energy infrastructure in the twenty-first century, and have the opportunity to do so using low-carbon technologies. They could leapfrog over the pollution and health problems brought on by the industrial revolution of the eighteenth, nineteenth and twentieth centuries. By contrast, the developed countries are mired in the past due to large investments in outdated technology. They require more innovative, forward-looking and entrepreneurial citizens who will bring the developed world into a new age of low-carbon technology.

12
Accepting the challenge

Taking small steps never feels entirely satisfactory. Nor does taking action without scientific knowledge. But certainty and perfection have never figured prominently in the story of human progress. Business, in particular, is accustomed to making decisions in conditions of considerable uncertainty, applying its experience and skills to areas of activity where much is unknown. That is why it will have a vital role in meeting the challenge of climate change – and why the contribution it is already making is so encouraging.

John Browne, Group Chief Executive of BP in *Foreign Affairs,* **July–August 2004.**

The whole history of international environmental action has been of arriving at destinations which looked impossibly distant at the moment of departure.

Tony Brenton, *The Greening of Machiavelli* **1994.**

When President John F. Kennedy called the United States to action in the space race, he uttered words that might apply even more convincingly to the cause of securing our civilisation from the risk of human-induced dangerous climate change. He said:

We choose to do these things not because they are easy, but because they are hard, because the goal will serve to organize and measure the best of our energies and skills, because the challenge is one we are willing to accept, one we are unwilling to postpone, and one which we intend to win.

Coping with the climate change issue is in many ways a greater challenge than the space race. It is more multi-faceted, more fundamental to our civilisation, and likely to be an ongoing challenge for this and future generations. It is a question of foresight, because it involves seeing into the future to see what is required of us today. It is a matter of risk management, because we cannot predict the future, but merely look at the possibilities, attach tentative probabilities conditional on human behaviour, and use that to decide policy today.

It is also a matter of faith – faith in science, faith in people to meet the challenge, and faith that human ingenuity and adaptability can cope with the challenge. Faith and hope, like despair, can be self-fulfiling prophecies. If people believe they can make a difference, they will act and, in so doing, *will* make a difference. If, however, they despair and choose to do nothing, they will be overtaken by events: they will have abdicated their choice. People either choose and act for a sustainable future, or they contribute to a growing environmental disaster. Climate change is serious and urgent stuff, but you can make a difference.

People hate doom and gloom – it turns people off. That is not what this is about. It is about new and exciting technologies, creating new markets, making new investments and taking advantage of new opportunities. It is about solving several problems at once, co-benefits and complementary strategies. It is about enjoying our relationship with nature and creating a sustainable future. It is about making life better.

It is a curious thing that many people choose to see climate change as an either/or problem. Either we must reduce emissions of greenhouse gases or we must adapt to climate change. In fact there is no choice – we have to do both. We must adapt to what cannot be avoided, but also act to reduce the magnitude of the climate changes to keep them within safe limits. There are limits to what humans can adapt to, and there are limits to how fast we can reduce greenhouse gas emissions. And we have to do both as best we can.

History tells us that humans are adaptable and ingenious in devising new technologies. Thus the twentieth century saw the birth and spread of many amazing new technologies such as the internal combustion engine, flight, telecommunications, and medicines that have eliminated ancient scourges.

It is therefore strange that some think we are so ingenious that we can adapt to anything, yet not be able to reduce greenhouse gas emissions at an affordable cost. And others argue the opposite – that we are so clever that we can almost instantly cut greenhouse gas emissions at acceptable cost, yet cannot adapt to even minor climate changes. Again, we can and must do both. We can simultaneously devise new technologies to reduce greenhouse emissions thus building a low-carbon economy over the next half-century, while at the same time adapt to the changes we have not been able to prevent.

On both the mitigation and adaptation fronts there are great opportunities ahead. If we seize these opportunities we can achieve wonders, and even do so while developing our economies and simultaneously reducing poverty and inequity.

An interesting developing country perspective is provided by Jose Goldemberg, former Minister for Science and Technology, Brazil:

Renewable energy is inexhaustible and abundant. It is clear therefore that in due time renewable energies will dominate the world's energy system, due to their inherent advantages such as mitigation of climate change, generation of employment and reduction of poverty, as well as increased energy security and supply.

After reviewing numerous real case studies, Paul Hawken, Amory Lovins and L. Hunter Lovins of the Rocky Mountain Institute in Colorado go further:

In the past fifty years, the world's annual carbon emissions have quadrupled. But in the next half century, the climate problem could become as faded a memory as the energy crises of the seventies are now, because climate change is not an inevitable result of normal economic activity but an artefact of carrying out that activity in irrationally inefficient ways. Climate protection can save us all money – even coal miners, who deserve the just transition that the nation's energy savings could finance a hundred times over.

In *Natural Capitalism*, Little Brown and Company (1999).

Besides *Natural Capitalism*, there are a number of other sources of information, including case studies, on how to reduce greenhouse gas emissions. I will mention two here, but there are others in the list of websites at the back of the book. One good site is that of The Climate Group, which is a group of companies, NGOs and local, regional and national governments 'committed to adopting a leadership agenda on climate protection and to reducing greenhouse gas emissions'. Another is the International Council for Local Environmental Initiatives (ICLEI), which has over 450 local government members, runs meetings and has specialist advisory groups.

It is worth reminding ourselves that in the range of scenarios for future emissions to 2100 in the Intergovernmental Panel on Climate Change (IPCC) *Special Report on Emissions Scenarios* (SRES) (see Chapter 3), one scenario (B1) resulted in emissions that would lead to less than 550 part per million (ppm) of carbon dioxide equivalent by 2100. This scenario was based on a hypothetical world with an emphasis on global solutions to economic, social and environmental sustainability, but with no overt climate change policies. So even the authors of the SRES report agree with the authors of *Natural Capitalism* that it is plausible, and maybe even desirable, to follow a safe emissions pathway in the twenty-first century for reasons other than climate change. Of course, SRES also had some alternative very high emissions scenarios – there is a choice of alternative futures.

The message is clear – we have a choice about the future, and the choice has serious consequences for future climate and for human societies. Risks associated with climate change should influence that choice. It is important here to remember that the IPCC deliberately did not attach probabilities to its SRES scenarios. However, if we examine the assumptions underlying the B1 scenario, we see that it requires reductions in material intensity (raw materials per unit quality of life) and the introduction of clean and resource-efficient technologies, with an emphasis on global solutions, sustainability and improved equity. How probable are these developments without some deliberate policy choices, and indeed without community/government decisions, goals and incentives? The SRES scenarios say this is possible, but not that it is likely without deliberate efforts to make it happen.

Business Weekly, in a feature on global warming on 16 August 2004, reports G. Michael Purdy, Director of the Lamont-Doherty Laboratory as saying that the reasons for the present lack of urgency in reducing greenhouse gas emissions is 'not the science and not the economics', but rather 'it is the lack of public knowledge, the lack of leadership, and the lack of political will.' All that is necessary is for us to create the will to make it happen.

The situation is urgent, with both adaptation and mitigation needed. Moreover, no potential contributions to emissions reduction should be ruled out on the basis of prejudice against particular technologies or socio-economic biases. Whether it is wind power, geo-sequestration or nuclear power, mitigation options should be examined for timeliness, safety, acceptability and economic potential, rather than ruled out on the basis of some pre-existing ideological position. Competitive infighting on an either/or basis is counter-productive.

Faced with the challenge of achieving rapid sustainable development, countries such as China, India and Brazil are starting to build new low-carbon technologies, and will gain competitive advantages from doing so. In so doing, they will reduce local air pollution problems, increase employment, and avoid excessive reliance on foreign sources of fossil fuels. They are not necessarily consistent in this, as the increasing use of private automobiles rather than bicycles and public transport testifies. Yet the challenge is being faced, and these and other developing countries have the opportunity to adopt strategies and to design and build infrastructures that will achieve sustainability, including a stable climate.

The poorer lesser-developed countries, such as much of sub-Saharan Africa and parts of Asia, are in many cases not yet on a rapid development pathway. Instead they are struggling to cope with poverty, natural and manmade disasters such as floods, drought and civil wars, unrest and instability. For them energy policy is a matter of survival, and climate change considerations rate low on their list of priorities. Yet, as IPCC has pointed out, they are likely to be worst affected by climate change, with reduced crop yields, more climatic disasters and flooding due to sea-level rise. For these countries sustainable development needs to come first in the form of disaster preparedness, aid in developing dispersed forms of renewable energy, and efforts by the rest of the world not to make matters worse through climate change.

The challenge in developed countries is in some ways greater because they have so much more already invested in inappropriate and unsustainable infra-structures. These include inefficient coal-fired power stations; hundreds of millions of polluting motor vehicles; vast road systems designed for private transport; under-utilised, run-down or even abandoned public transport systems; and highly energy-inefficient building stock. Much of this existing stock needs to be transformed and upgraded, or written off and replaced, in order to meet more sustainable standards.

Central to all these situations is how to foster rapid growth in renewable energy and energy efficiency, and how to minimise greenhouse gas emissions now. Urgent results can only be achieved through existing technologies such as greater energy efficiency (insulation, hybrid cars and so on) and proven renewable technology such as biomass ethanol, and solar and wind power. This must be backed up with new and emerging technology, including appropriate carbon removal and sequestration, and, if possible, safe and secure nuclear power. But these latter capital-expensive technologies will only achieve massive reductions in greenhouse gas emissions over the course of many decades, due to the need for research and development, large embedded energy costs and slow uptake. They are as yet largely unproven in the market place and require large long-term research, development and investment.

It is government policies that can engender a sense of urgency that might come from mandatory targets for energy efficiency, renewable energy and reductions in emissions. And it is tax incentives and other measures that would accelerate the development and commercialisation of low-carbon technology by internalising environmental costs. As we saw in Chapter 10, many state and local government initiatives in both the United States and Australia are being developed to fill the gaps in federal government programs in these two countries. However, these initiatives will have maximum effectiveness only when they are implemented federally, and indeed internationally, thereby achieving economies of scale and greater planning certainty for industry.

In some developed countries, notably the European Union countries, governments are accepting the challenge of developing low-carbon technology to meet necessary targets, although there is still debate about how realistic the measures being implemented are in achieving these goals.

Recognition and ownership of the climate change problem is urgent. It requires understanding and education, but also action by governments to set standards and create the business climate in which innovators and entrepreneurs can flourish. Markets may be efficient in achieving least-cost solutions when they recognise a problem or opportunity, but too often they are focused on the short-term and fail to recognise long-term challenges. Climate change requires urgent action in the short-term, to fulfil long-term goals. Mandatory targets and other government carrots and sticks can stimulate this sense of urgency.

Looking beyond the Kyoto Protocol

With the notable exceptions of the United States and Australia, most of the world has accepted that the Kyoto Protocol is a good starting point in getting greenhouse gas emissions under control. Together with its parent United Nations Framework Convention on Climate Change (UNFCCC), the Kyoto Protocol has set initial emissions targets for the developed countries, to be achieved by 2008–12, along with several principles and mechanisms. Central to the thinking in the Kyoto Protocol is the idea of differentiated responsibilities, with developed countries, who are the largest per capita emitters, taking the lead in the first commitment period, and the idea of sustainable development for all countries, especially the less developed ones.

Now that the Kyoto Protocol has come into force, pressure is growing from industry and economists in Australia for ratification of the Protocol and for involvement in more economically rational carbon emissions trading rather than piecemeal and voluntary measures. In the US, however, opinion seems to be pretty much that the Kyoto Protocol is a dead letter. This latter view may of course change now that the Protocol is in effect, or as the influence of the states, cities and businesses that want national standards and national and international carbon trading comes to prevail.

It is important to remember that the Kyoto Protocol emissions targets, and exclusion of developing countries from them, apply only until 2012, after which a new formula must be developed. Negotiations on such a formula are likely to include at least the major developing countries in one form or another. More explicit mechanisms are needed for aid to developing countries in the form of the transfer of low-carbon technologies to assist in economic development, and for aid in adapting to unavoidable climate change. Australia and the US are likely to be involved in any post-Kyoto negotiations and agreements, even if they take a different form to those in the Kyoto Protocol.

The key arguments that have been traditionally used to argue the need for international agreements on mitigation of climate change apply to new agreements going beyond the Kyoto Protocol. International agreements are necessary as they are more likely to create a level playing field where countries and businesses have equitable access to markets and standards and know what to expect, foster international equity and sustainable development, and discourage or penalise free-loaders. By creating truly international markets such agreements can also achieve greatest efficiency in emissions reductions, and in so doing foster a real sense of urgency.

How effective such a post-Kyoto agreement would be, and whether in fact agreement can be reached, is of course dependent on the outcome of the negotiations. Arguments over possible post-Kyoto arrangements are complex, voluminous and often highly specialised. A December 2004 document from the Pew Center on Global Climate Change lists some 40 proposals and provides a succinct summary. This is not the place to go into the proposals in any depth. However, I will mention some ideas and point, in the lists of further reading, websites and the notes on the web (see p. 296), to where you can follow them up.

Considerations in arriving at any new international agreement to reduce greenhouse gas emissions include:

* building on what has already been agreed;
* encouraging least-cost effectiveness in mitigation actions;
* promoting co-operative arrangements to cope with or adapt to unavoidable climate change via capacity building and emergency relief;
* achieving co-benefits, especially sustainable development;
* allowing for equity, relating to the agreed ideas of differentiated responsibilities and capacities;
* avoiding unwanted outcomes;
* minimising risk of failure;
* ensuring effectiveness in achieving rapid reductions in emissions;
* leaving room for adaptability as new information comes to hand regarding risks and effectiveness, and
* monitoring progress and enforcing agreements.

Whatever we may want – and the UNFCCC goal of avoiding dangerous levels of greenhouse gases seems like a reasonable objective – the strategy must be related to a realistic assessment of the success likely to be achieved. As Sir Winston Churchill once said:

However beautiful the strategy, you should occasionally look at the results.

A lot of thought has gone into what might follow the Kyoto Protocol. Niklas Hohne of ECOFYS, a European research and consulting company, outlines a number of possible approaches to a future mitigation agreement in work done for the German Federal Environmental Agency. Some key proposals include:

* *Continuing Kyoto.* This might include ad hoc negotiated emissions reduction targets increasing every ten years for developed countries, and

increasing participation of other countries as their GDP per capita rises closer to the global average.

- *Intensity targets.* This approach would define emissions targets in terms of emissions per unit GDP (carbon intensity), and was favoured by the US Bush Administration. It clearly allows for economic growth, but would not lead to reductions in actual emissions unless the decrease in carbon intensity is more rapid than economic growth. This is presently not the case in virtually all countries (see Table 9) including the US, and is, in a sense, the key problem. Expressing mitigation targets in such terms makes it difficult to define what actual reductions in emissions would be achieved, as these would depend on economic growth rates.

- *Contraction and convergence.* This proposal, originally from the Global Commons Institute in the UK, defines as the goal a target stabilised greenhouse gas concentration, assesses a global emissions pathway (variation in emissions with time) that would lead to this goal, and allocates emissions pathways to individual countries aimed at converging on the same emissions per capita at some future date such as 2050 or 2100. This would allow for some initial increase in emissions for some countries with present low emissions per capita, but greater reductions for countries with high emissions per capita.

- *Extended Global Triptych.* This approach would assign different emissions reduction criteria to different sectors (initially three, hence Triptych) such as domestic, industry, electricity, agriculture and forestry. It was one basis of the formula used in the EU to share the burden between different member countries under the Kyoto Protocol. The domestic sector would require convergence of per-capita emissions, industry would require growth in energy efficiency, electricity would require a proportion of renewables, agriculture would require stabilisation at 1990 levels, and forestry would aim at zero net emissions.

One interesting variation, which potentially accommodates large differences between countries, involves negotiating a package of multi-component commitments by each country based on national circumstances, negotiated from the bottom up, as in multilateral trade agreements. How far this proposal differs from what was attempted in the Kyoto Protocol is not clear. The author, Robert Reinstein, former chief US negotiator for the UNFCCC, argues that a commitment to a target for emissions reduction must be accompanied by an illustrative package of policies and measures that might be expected to result in the target. Conversely, he argues that commitment to a package of polices and measures should be accompanied by a projection of the emissions reduction expected to result. Such estimates are a key to seeing whether the targets or policies and measures are working. He adds that government actions alone will not be sufficient to achieve results, since most investment decisions and technology dissemination are carried out by the private sector. But governments can help to create an enabling environment to encourage such private sector participation.

Reinstein goes on to state that in negotiating a balanced package of commitments by all countries, it is important to distinguish between short-term and longer-term commitments. The former begin the process and send a political signal. Actions in response to short-term commitments begin to change the psychology and reinforce expectations of change, which influence market behaviour. Longer-term commitments to promote low-carbon technology and subsequent changes in capital stock and transformation of infrastructure are supported by short-term changes. Major reductions in greenhouse gas emissions will in general occur over the longer term as a result of both short-term and longer-term processes. Where I would go beyond Reinstein is to place greater emphasis on the urgency of the short-term commitments, since early reductions in emissions are crucial to reducing the risk of dangerous climate change.

These and many other approaches are open for discussion and have been modelled using various economic and energy sector models to see how they might work out. Critical to their acceptance and usefulness is how they fit in with each country's national interests and their overall effectiveness in achieving urgent and continuing emission reductions. Hohne concludes that substantial reductions of emissions in developed countries are necessary in all approaches, and that these reductions would be much larger for a 450 ppm concentration target than the emissions reductions required under the Kyoto Protocol. He also concludes that early involvement of developing countries is necessary, but that many approaches and variations on future actions are possible, with none being ideal. He suggests that a mixture of approaches may be a good compromise.

Addressing the key issues

In this book we have seen that, despite the uncertainties, there is a real and present danger that our continuing large-scale burning of fossil fuels is pushing the climate system into a situation where there is a risk of serious damage to us and our children. This danger increases with every year that we fail to take appropriate action, yet there are potential solutions out there, which we could apply.

Here are some key findings that should guide us:

- There is a need to achieve a *target of a stabilised concentration of about 450 to 550 ppm carbon dioxide equivalent*, or even lower if recent results suggesting a high climate sensitivity are borne out. Higher concentrations would lead to too great a risk of unacceptable consequences (Chapter 6). This takes account of large uncertainties and factors them into a risk assessment.

- To achieve this, *global emissions must peak before 2050,* and then decline rapidly. This requires sizeable reductions *starting as soon as possible.*

- Effective international action requires *agreement between developed and developing countries* on emissions reduction schedules consistent with sustainable development for all. This is in everyone's interests (Chapter 10), and probably requires eventual convergence on equal emissions per person across all countries.

- This requires that *emissions in developed countries must decrease by some 50–60% by 2050* (Chapter 8), and that increases in emissions in developing countries be kept as low as possible. This requires a rapid transfer to, or development of, low-carbon technology in developing countries.

- *Proven methods for reducing emissions should be applied urgently* in the next decade or two, because early emissions reductions are essential.

- *Research and development should be encouraged for other potential low-carbon technologies*, at least while they seem feasible and acceptable on other grounds. They will be needed in the latter part of the twenty-first century.

- *Government intervention is necessary* to remove direct and hidden subsidies for fossil fuels and inefficient carbon-intensive activities, and to provide incentives for low-carbon technologies via the polluter pays principle.

- *Market mechanisms* should be used to achieve maximum efficiency through real competition on a level playing field.

- *National and international carbon emissions trading* looks like the best overall mechanism to internalise the environmental costs of emissions. This mechanism has proven efficient and acceptable in the US through the trading of sulfur emissions and is already being implemented for greenhouse gases in the EU and elsewhere.

- *Some potential damages due to climate changes are inevitable* due to climate changes that cannot be avoided because of inertia in the economic and climate systems.

- *Adaptation measures will be necessary to minimise damages.* Adaptation will not avoid all damages and will require expenditure.

- *Mitigation and adaptation measures need to be integrated* into normal decision-making on all matters of development, planning, innovation and investment.
- *Aid will be necessary* for communities and countries with low adaptive capacities, and for those suffering damages.

This list provides many pointers to what must be done. With a level playing field, and proper incentives, many proven low-carbon energy sources and energy saving strategies can be implemented quickly. According to the experience of many businesses, entrepreneurs and innovators, this can be done at little cost, and may even be profitable. Possibilities for mitigation were discussed in Chapter 8. Pacala and Socolow of Princeton University in *Science* vol. 305, page 968 (2004), among others, provide an excellent summary list.

Improving energy efficiency and conservation by:

- Increasing fuel economy in cars, including petrol/electric hybrids.
- Reducing reliance on cars, with better public transport, bike paths and urban design.
- Using more efficient buildings with better use of insulation, shade, cogeneration plants, and automatic controls.
- Increasing power plant efficiency.

Decreasing carbon emissions from electricity and fuels by using alternatives such as:

- Substitution of natural gas for coal.
- Wind generated electricity.
- Solar photovoltaics.
- Renewable hydrogen.
- Biofuels.
- Carbon capture and sequestration from power plants.
- Carbon capture and sequestration from synthetic fuel plants.
- Nuclear power.

Increasing the effectiveness of natural sinks by:

- Improving forest management, including plantations and on-farm forestry.
- Improving management of agricultural soils.

Every one of these options is already operating at a pilot or industrial scale, and could be scaled up further over 50 years to provide real reductions in global emissions. With priority given to implementing the short-term solutions such as energy efficiency and conservation first, and to suit local and national situations, these options provide an excellent agenda for action.

What is absolutely crucial, however, is that options for reducing greenhouse gas emissions must be pursued with a real sense of urgency. Every extra tonne of carbon dioxide placed into the atmosphere increases the very real risk of dangerous climate change, and nobody will escape the direct or indirect consequences.

Individuals often feel helpless in the face of global situations such as these. However, decisions are made by individuals, sometimes alone and often acting together. It is the sum of all these decisions that will make the difference. We act as decisionmakers in business, as investors or entrepreneurs, as members of political parties or in government and non-government organisations, as voters, and most of all as consumers. As individuals and groups we can act to conserve energy and minimise our greenhouse gas emissions. We can adopt more environmentally friendly lifestyles, reward energy conscious suppliers and turn the market around. We can make a difference.

If we do not act now, we are in danger of inadvertently tripping the 'on' switch to disaster, with an inevitably long delay before it can be turned off again. What is done now that enhances climate change cannot be easily undone, so we should err on the side of caution. We need to reduce carbon emissions, and we need to do it fast. We owe that, at least, to our children.

Further information

Introduction

Some of the books listed are out of print, and perhaps most will not be readily available in local libraries. That is one reason why access to the world wide web (www) is so useful. If you do not have your own personal access to the web, you can generally get it at your local library. See the list of web addresses to get you started.

Look carefully at the year of publication. Some of these books and articles are somewhat out of date, and the projected climate changes are now rather different (in most cases more severe). Major revisions in climate change scenarios occurred about 1990, 1996 and 2001, but some more recent impacts studies have used older scenarios. However, old publications on historical climatology are more generally sound, as are the discussions of sensitivity to climate change and qualitative aspects of impacts. Policy discussions can become dated, but general principles may still be relevant in older publications.

Regarding books and journal articles, there are various ways of referring to them, for example by author or authors and year of publications, or in the case of reports from organisations sometimes by organisation and year. In the text I have mainly referred to publications of the International Panel on Climate Change by 'IPCC' and the year, but other publications may refer to them by chapter authors or volume editors.

Articles or papers in journals or magazines are usually referred to by scientists by author and year, but social scientists and lawyers sometimes use different conventions. In my detailed notes, published on the web at **www.publish. csiro.au/pid/4992.htm.** I have not given full details of such publications, such as *all* authors, full title of article, journal name, volume, pages and date – merely the minimum needed to locate the item in a library or on the web. What follows here in print is a list of some important or useful books and papers. Detailed references justifying many of my facts and arguments in the text are given on the website.

Bibliography/reading list

Anderson, S. and Sarma, M. 2002: *Protecting the Ozone Layer: The United Nations History*, Earthscan Publications, London.

Athanasiou, T. and Baer, P. 2002: *Dead Heat: Global Justice and Global Warming'*, Seven Stories Press, New York.

Australian Institute of Marine Sciences, annual: *Status of Coral Reefs of the World*, available on line at www.aims.gov.au.

Bradley, R.S. 1999: *Paleoclimatology: Reconstructing Climate of the Quaternary*, Second Edition, International Geophysics Series, Volume 68, Harcourt Academic Press, San Diego.

Bradstock, R.A., Williams, J.E. and Gill, M.A. (eds.) 2002: *Flammable Australia: Fire Regimes and Biodiversity of a Continent*, Cambridge University Press, Cambridge.

Bryson, R. and Murray, T. 1977: *Climates of Hunger*, University of Wisconsin Press.

Carpenter 1966: *Discontinuity in Greek Civilization,* Cambridge University Press.

Conisbee, M. and Simms, A. 2003: *Environmental Refugees: The Case for Recognition*, New Economics Foundation, London, see: www.neweconomics.org

Crocker, D.A. and Linden, T. (eds.) 1998: *Ethics of Consumption: the Good Life, Justice, and Global Stewardship*, Rowman and Littlefield, Lanham, MD.

Crowley, T. 1991: *Paleoclimatology*, Oxford University Press, New York.

Daly, J.L. 1989: *The Greenhouse Trap: Why the Greenhouse Effect Will Not End Life on Earth*, Bantam Books, Sydney.

Deffeyes, K.S. 2001: *Hubbert's Peak: The Impending World Oil Shortage*, Princeton University Press.

Dialogue on Water and Climate, c.2004: *Climate Changes the Water Rules*, available via www.waterandclimate.org/report.htm.

Dietz, A.J., Ruben, R. and Verhagen, A. (eds.) 2004: *The Impact of Climate Change on Drylands*, Environment and Policy, Volume 39, Kluwer Academic, London.

Fritts, H.C. 1991: *Tree Rings and Climate*, Second Edition, Academic Press, London.

Gelbspan, R. 1997: *The Heat is On: The High Stakes Battle over Earth's Threatened Climate*, Addison-Wesley, Reading, Massachusetts.

Glantz, M. (ed.) 2001: *Once Burned, Twice Shy? Lessons learned from the 1997–98 El Nino,* United Nations University Press, Tokyo.

Godrejk D. 2001: *The No Nonsense Guide to Climate Change*, New Internationalist Publications, Oxford, UK.

Greenpeace International/Stockholm Environmental Institute, 1993: *Towards a fossil fuel free energy future. The next energy transition*, SEI, Boston.

Grubb, M. with Vrolijk, C. and Brack, D. 1999: *The Kyoto Protocol: A Guide and Assessment*, Royal Institute of International Affairs and Earthscan Publications, London.

Hare and Meinshausen, 2004: *How Much Warming are We Committed to and How Much Can be Avoided?* PIK Report No.93. See www.pik-potsdam.de.

Hawken, P., Lovins, A. and Lovins, H.L. 1999: *Natural Capitalism: Creating the Next Industrial Revolution*, Little, Brown and Company, Boston.

Huntington, E. 1915: *Civilization and Climate*, Yale University Press.

International Council for Science (ICSU), 2004: *Environment and its Relation to Sustainable Development.* Report of the CSPR Assessment Panel, see www.icsu.org.

International Energy Agency/OECD, 2002: *Beyond Kyoto: Energy dynamics and Climate Stabilisation*, Paris.

IPCC, 1998: *The Regional Impacts of Climate Change: An Assessment of Vulnerability.* Watson, R.T., Zinyowera, M.C. and Moss, R.H. (eds.), Intergovernmental Panel on Climate Change Special Report. Cambridge University Press, Cambridge, UK.

IPCC, 2000: *Special Report on Emissions Scenarios.* Nakincenovic, N. and Swart, R. (eds.), Intergovernmental Panel on Climate Change Special Report. Cambridge University Press, Cambridge, UK.

IPCC, 2001a: *Climate Change 2001: The Scientific Basis.* Houghton, J. T., Ding, Y., Griggs, D.J., Noguer, M., Van der Linden, P.J. and Xiaosu, D. (eds.), Intergovernmental Panel on Climate Change. Cambridge University Press, Cambridge, UK. See www.ipcc.ch.

IPCC, 2001b: *Climate Change 2001: Impacts, Adaptation and Vulnerability.* McCarthy, J. J., Canziani, O.F., Leary, N. A., Dokken, D.J. and White, K.S. (eds.), Intergovernmental Panel on Climate Change. Cambridge University Press, Cambridge, UK. See www.ipcc.ch.

IPCC, 2001c: *Climate Change 2001: Mitigation.* Metz, B., Davidson, O., Swart, R. and Pan, J. (eds.), Intergovernmental Panel on Climate Change. Cambridge University Press, Cambridge, UK. See www.ipcc.ch.

IPCC, 2001d. *Climate Change 2001: Synthesis Report.* Watson, R.T. and the Core Writing Team (eds.), Cambridge University Press, Cambridge, UK. See www.ipcc.ch.

IPCC Special Report, 2000: *Land Use, Land-Use Change, and Forestry*, Watson and others (eds.), Intergovernmental Panel on Climate Change, Geneva.

IPCC Workshop Report, 2004: *Describing Scientific Uncertainties in Climate Change to Support Analysis of Risk and of Options.* See www.ipcc.ch.

Jochem, E., Sathaye, J.A. and Bouille, D. (eds.), 2002: *Society, Behaviour and Climate Change Mitigation*, Kluwer Academic Publishers, Hingham MA.

Jones, P.D., Ogilvie, A.E.J., Davies, T.D. and Briffa, K.D. 2001: *History and Climate: Memories of the Future?*, Kluwer Academic/Plenum, Dordrecht.

Kennett, J.P., Cannariato, K.G., Hendy, I.L. and Behl, R.J. 2003: *Methane Hydrates in Quaternary Climate Change: The Clathrate Gun Hypothesis*, American Geophysical Union, Washington DC.

Koppel, T. 1999: *Powering the Future: The Ballard Fuel Cell and the Race to Change the World*, John Wiley, Chichester.

Lamb, H.H. 1982: *Climate, History and the Modern World*, Methuen, London.

Le Roy Ladurie, E. 1971: *Times of Feast, Times of Famine*. George Allen & Unwin, London, and Doubleday, New York (1972

Lomberg, B. 2001: *The Skeptical Environmentalist: Measuring the Real State of the World*, Cambridge University Press, Cambridge and New York.

Lovins, A., Lovins, H.L., Krause, F. and Bach, W. 1981: *Least Cost Energy: Solving the CO_2 Problem,* Brick House Publishing, Andover, MA.

McGuffie, K. and Henderson-Sellers, A. 1997: *A Climate Modelling Primer*, Wiley, New York.

Michael D.M. (ed.) 2003: *Natural Gas Hydrate in Oceanic and Permafrost Environments*, Kluwer Academic Publishers, Dordrecht/Boston/London.

Michaels, P.J. and Balling, R.C., Jr. 2000: *The Satanic Gases: Clearing the Air about Global Warming*, Cato Institute, Washington DC.

Muller, B. 2002: *Equity in Climate Change: The Great Divide*, Oxford Institute for Energy Studies. See www.OxfordClimatePolicy.org

National Research Council (US), 2002: *Abrupt Climate Change: Inevitable Surprises*, see http://books.nap.edu/books/0309074347/html/1.html#pagetop

Oberthur, S. and Ott, H. 1999: *The Kyoto Protocol: International Climate Policy for the 21st Century*, Springer-Verlag, Berlin, Heidelberg and New York.

OECD, 2004: *The Benefits of Climate Change Policies*. See www.oecd.org.

Pasqualetti, M. 2002: *Wind Power in View: Energy Landscapes in a Crowded World*, Academic Press, London and New York.

Pew Center on Global Climate Change: The following (and other) publications can be accessed at www.pewclimate.org.

A Synthesis of Potential Climate Change Impacts on the U.S., 2004.

Beyond Kyoto: Advancing the International Effort Against Climate Change, 2003.

Climate Change Mitigation in Developing Countries, 2003.

Climate Data: Insights and Observations, 2004.

Coping with Climate Change: The Role of Adaptation in the United States, 2004.

Coral Reefs and Global Climate Change, Buddemeier, Kleypas and Aranson, 2004.

Designing a Climate-Friendly Energy Policy: Options for the Near Term, 2002.

International Climate Efforts Beyond 2012: a Survey of Approaches, 2004.

Observed Impacts of Global Climate Change in the U.S., 2004.

Pittock, A.B., Frakes, L.A., Jenssen, D., Peterson, J.A. and Zillman, J.W. 1978: *Climatic Change and Variability: A Southern Perspective*, Cambridge University Press, Cambridge and New York.

Pittock, A.B. 2002: What we know and don't know about climate change: reflections on the IPCC TAR. *Climatic Change* Vol.**53**, pp.393–411.

Pittock, B. (ed.) 2003: *Climate Change: An Australian Guide to the Science and Potential Impacts*, Australian Greenhouse Office, Canberra. See www.greenhouse.gov.au/science/guide/pubs/science-guide.pdf.

Potter, T. and Colman, B. (eds.) 2003: *Handbook of Weather, Climate, and Water: Dynamics, Climate, Physical Meteorology, Weather Systems, and Measurements*, John Wiley, Chichester and New York.

Retallack, S. 2005: *Setting a Long-term Climate Objective.* A paper for the International Climate Change Taskforce. See www.ippr.org.

Roberts, P. 2004: *The End of Oil*, Houghton Mifflin, Boston.

Romm, J. 2004: *Hype About Hydrogen,* Island Press, Washington DC, at www.islandpress.org/books.

Schneider, S.H., Rosencranz, A. and Niles, J.O. (eds.), 2002: *Climate Change Policy: A Survey*, Island Press, Washington, DC.

SCOPE, 1986: *The Greenhouse Effect, Climate Changes, and Ecosystems*, Bolin, B., Doos, B. R., Jaeger, J. and Warrick, R.A. (eds.), John Wiley & Sons, Chichester, London.

Sense About Science, 2004: *Peer Review and the Acceptance of New Scientific Ideas*, by a Working Party, see www.senseaboutscience.org.uk/.

Smith, J.B. and others, (eds.) 1996: *Adapting to Climate Change: An International Perspective*, Springer-Verlag, New York.

Stuart, D. 2000: *Anasazi America: Seventeen Centuries on the Road from Center Place,* University of New Mexico Press.

Trenberth, K.E. 1992: *Climate System Modelling*, Cambridge University Press, Cambridge.

UNDP, 2005: *Adaptation Policy Frameworks for Climate Change: Developing Strategies, Policies and Measures*, Lim, B. (ed.), Cambridge University Press, Cambridge, UK.

UNEP, 1998: *Handbook on Methods for Climate Change Impacts Assessment and Adaptation Strategies*, United Nations Environment Program, Nairobi.

United Nations Environment Programme, 2002: *Global Environment Outlook 3,* Earthscan Publications, available at www.unep.org/geo/geo3

US Global Change Research Program, 2000: *Climate Change Impacts on the United States: Potential Consequences of Climate Variability and Change,*

US National Assessment, Cambridge University Press. See www.gcrio.org/
NationalAssessment/foundation.html

Washington, W.M. and Parkinson, C.L. 1986: *An Introduction to Three-
Dimensional Climate Modelling*, Oxford University Press, Oxford, UK.

Weart, S. 2003: *The Discovery of Global Warming*, Harvard University Press,
Cambridge Massachusetts. See www.aip.org/history/climate.

Wigley, T.M.L., Ingram, M.J. and Farmer, G. (eds.), 1981: *Climate and History*,
Cambridge University Press, Cambridge, UK.

Williams M.A.J. and others, 1993: *Quaternary Environments*, Edward Arnold,
London, New York.

Websites

This list of websites all worked as at 7 January 2005. In general, other relevant organisations can then be found by a search on a search engine such as Google. Climate change science and policy is a rapidly developing subject. Readers are therefore urged to keep as up to date as possible by using the many websites listed. In many cases these websites add new documents and news items quite frequently. Many items can be read online or else downloaded and studied at leisure. By monitoring a range of websites with different expertise, interests or viewpoints, readers can continue to obtain a balanced view of new developments. Be aware, also, that websites can stop showing particular documents, change, or even go out of existence altogether. I cannot guarantee their continued operation, nor do I necessarily endorse their content.

I have made a simple classification of websites into a number of categories to make it easier to find relevant ones, but sometimes the categorisation is a bit arbitrary, so look in overlapping categories if you do not find what you want the first time. My apologies for all the other relevant websites not included.

Business and economics

Association of British Insurers: www.abi.org.uk. See 2004 report *A Changing
Climate for Insurers*.

Carbon Finance magazine: www.carbon-financeonline.com. Monthly, with in-
depth coverage of the global markets in greenhouse gas emissions.

Chicago Climate Exchange: http://www.chicagoclimatex.com. Trades in
greenhouse gas emissions.

The Climate Group: www.theclimategroup.org. Companies, NGOs and
governments 'committed to adopting a leadership agenda on climate
protection and to reducing greenhouse gas emissions'.

CO2e.com: www.CO2e.com. One of the major players in carbon emissions
trading. It is an example of what is already happening in business.

Hydrogen and Fuel Cell Investor: www.h2fc.com

Munich Reinsurance: www.munichre.com. A major reinsurance company with a strong interest in natural disasters and climate change impacts.

Shell Hydrogen: www.shell.com/hydrogen.

Swiss Reinsurance: www.swissre.com.

Energy technology and climate policy

African Energy Policy Research Network: www.afrepren.org. Includes many publications and a newsletter.

Climate Options for the Long term: www.wau.nl/cool. This is a Dutch project to develop options for reductions in greenhouse gas emissions.

Climate Policy journal: www.earthscan.co.uk/

Climate Strategies: www.climate-strategies.org. A clearing point for information on climate policy and solutions.

CO_2 Sequestration Website: www.co2captureandstorage.info. Run by the International Energy Agency.

Energy Policy journal: http://www.sciencedirect.com/science/journal/03014215.

Environmental Science and Policy journal: www.elsevier.com/locate/envsci.

Future International Action on Climate Change Network: www.fiacc.net.

Oxford Institute for Energy Studies: www.OxfordClimatePolicy.org. Numerous articles and reports on climate change policy.

Peak Oil: www.peakoil.org. Focus on the implications of declining oil supplies.

Wuppertal Institute for Climate, Environment and Energy: www.wupperinst.org.

Development

African Studies Centre, University of Leiden: http://asc.leidenuniv.nl/climatechange/. Studies relating to climate change issues in Africa.

Bangladesh Centre for Advanced Studies: http://bcas.net/.

Development Alternatives: www.devalt.org. Promotes sustainability in India.

Dialogue on Water and Climate report: http://www.waterandclimate.org

International Institute for Environment and Development (IIED): www.iied.org. Covers development issues, especially adaptation to climate change.

International Institute for Sustainable Development: www.iisd.can. Includes the *Earth Negotiations Bulletin* reporting international climate change negotiations.

One World: www.oneworld.net. News and resources on environment and development, with a campaign on climate change.

Stockholm Environment Institute: www.sei.se. Climate and energy program focuses on sustainable energy in developing countries.

Tiempo: A bulletin on climate and development: www.cru.uea.ac.uk/tiempo/
   Presents information on climate change relevant to developing countries.
   Useful links.
United Nations Development Programme: www.undp.org/cc/ Works with the
   Global Environment Facility (GEF) that funds climate change related work
   in developing countries.

Environmental and climate NGOs

Australia Institute, The: www.tai.org.au. A think tank 'for a just, sustainable,
   peaceful future'.
Australian Conservation Foundation: www.acfonline.org.au. A major Australian
   environment NGO.
Carbon Calculator: www.safeclimate.net./calculator. Online calculator of
   greenhouse gas emissions.
Centre for Science and Environment: www.cseindia.org. India-based
   organisation promoting environmental awareness and climate issues, with a
   magazine.
Choose Climate – Flying off to a Warmer Climate?: www.chooseclimate.org/
   flying. Calculates your greenhouse gas emissions from air travel.
Climate Action Network: www.climatenetwork.org. Coalition of more than 340
   groups campaigning on climate change in many countries.
Climate Ark: www.climateark.org. Climate change portal site, with web search
   facility, directories and latest news.
Climate Justice Programme: www.climatelaw.org. Related to Friends of the
   Earth. Aims to use environmental law to enforce reductions in greenhouse
   gas emissions.
EcoEquity: www.ecoequity.org. Explores equity issues related to climate
   change, by the authors of *Dead Heat*.
Evangelical Environmental Network: http://www.creationcare.org. Evangelical
   Christians concerned about the environment.
Environmental Defense Fund: www.environmentaldefense.org. US NGO.
Friends of the Earth: www.foe.co.uk. Environmental organisation with many
   national and international branches. Sponsors legal challenges to major
   GHG emitters.
Future International Action on Climate Change Network: www.fiacc.net.
Global Commons Institute: www.gci.org.uk. Home of the *Contraction and
   Convergence* policy, complete with an online calculator.
Greenpeace: www.greenpeace.org. A major international campaigner for
   environmental policies. Mounts 'direct actions'.
Heat is Online: www.heatisonline.org. Website from Ross Gelbspan, with latest
   news, and a special section on climate sceptics.

International Emissions Trading Association: www.ieta.org. Association of businesses set up to support the UNFCCC via emissions trading.

Kyoto Now!: www.rso.cornell.edu/kyotonow. University groups campaigning for US ratification of the Kyoto Protocol.

National Resources Defense Council: www.nrdc.org. US-based NGO with a strong focus on climate change.

Natural Capitalism: www.natcap.org. Based on the book by Paul Hawken and others, it promotes entrepreneurial ideas on business adapting to a limited world.

New Economics Foundation, London: www.neweconomics.org. Reports on climate related issues such as environmental refugees.

Oilwatch: www.oilwatch.org.ec. Network of developing country groups campaigning to stop oil exploration and production, and in support of indigenous people.

Pew Center on Global Climate Change: www.pewclimate.org. Non-partisan US NGO sponsors reports and meetings on climate change. Lots of material on web.

PlanetArk: www.planetark.org. News on environmental topics, with search facility.

RealClimate: www.realclimate.org. Fast-reaction website where some scientists reply to contrarian criticism of action to stop climate change.

Rising Tide: www.risingtide.org.uk. Groups campaigning against global warming.

Rocky Mountain Institute: http://www.rmi.org/. Fosters 'efficient and restorative use of resources to make the world secure, just, prosperous, and life-sustaining'.

Royal Institute of International Affairs (UK): www.riia.org. Reports on climate change policy issues.

Union of Concerned Scientists (USA): www.ucsusa.org. Promotes 'innovative thinking and committed citizen advocacy to build a cleaner, healthier environment and a safer world'.

World Resources Institute: www.wri.org. Good source of reliable information.

World View of Global Warming: www.worldviewofglobalwarming.org. This project of the Blue Earth Alliance, Seattle, WA, documents in words and pictures how the world is changing.

Worldwatch Institute (US): www.worldwatch.org/. US NGO with strong environmental informational and advocacy role.

Worldwide Fund for Nature (WWF). International: www.panda.org. Global NGO with a strong climate change program, and links to national websites.

Government agencies, national and international

Australian Bureau of Agricultural and Resource Economics (ABARE): www.abare.gov.au.

Australian Greenhouse Office: www.greenhouse.gov.au. The Australian federal government's agency for coordinating action on climate change.

Canada, Taking Action on Climate Change: www.climatechange.gc.ca/english/default.asp.

Carbon Sequestration Leadership Forum: www.fe.doe.gov/programs/sequestration/cslf.

European Environment Agency: www.eea.eu.int.

German Advisory Council for Global Change: www.wbgu.de.

Global Environment Outlook: www.unep.org/GEO/geo3. A state of the environment report from UNEP, released in 2002.

India, Ministry of Environment and Forests: www.envfor.nic.in.

International Atomic Energy Agency: www.iaea.org.

International Council for Local Environmental Initiatives (ICLEI): www.iclei.org. Local governments concerned about environmental issues and policies.

International Energy Agency Greenhouse Gas R&D Programme: www.ieagreen.org.uk. Publishes *Greenhouse Issues*, with material on alternative energy and greenhouse mitigation technologies including carbon removal and sequestration. See also its CO_2 Sequestration Website, at www.co2captureandstorage.info.

International Partnership for the Hydrogen Economy: www.state.gov/g/oes/rls/fs/2003/25983.htm.

Organisation for Economic Cooperation and Development: www.oecd.org. Statistics and publications relevant to climate policy.

UK Climate Change Indicators: www.nbu.ac.uk/iccuk.

UK Climate Change Programme: www.defra.gov.uk/environment/climatechange.

UK Energy Policy: www.dti.gov.uk/energy.

UK Environment Agency: www.environment-agency.gov.uk.

United Nations Development Program (UNDP): www.undp.org/cc.

United Nations Environment Program (UNEP): www.unep.net. UNEP and the World Meteorological Organization (WMO) are the parent bodies of the IPCC. Access to publications on climate change issues.

United Nations Framework Convention on Climate Change: www.unfccc.de. Access to the full text of the UNFCCC and related Protocols.

United States energy programs:

Clean coal initiative: www.fe.doe.gov/programs/powersystems/cleancoal/.

Energy Efficiency and Renewable Energy: www.eere.energy.gov.

Fusion program ITER: www.iter.org.

Generation IV Program (nuclear power): http://gen-iv.ne.doe.gov.

Hydrogen: www.fe.doe.gov/programs/fuels.

Other programs: www.climatevision.gov, www.epa.gov/climateleaders,
www.epa.gov/smartway

United States Geological survey on water use: http://water.usgs.gov/watuse.

Renewables

American Physical Society studies: http://www.aps.org/public_affairs/popa/
reports/occasional.cfm Occasional Papers on hydrogen fuel cell vehicles
and wind energy.

Bioenergy International: http://www.novator.se/bioint/aboutus.htm

California Fuel Cell Partnership: www.drivingthefuture.org

Canadian Hydrogen Society: www.h2.ca

Clean Edge: www.cleanedge.com. A research and strategy firm re clean energy.

Clean Power Now: www.cleanpowernow.org. Community group in New
England, USA, supporting wind power in Nantucket Sound, despite strong
opposition.

Curry and Kerlinger: www.currykerlinger.com. Consultants to the wind power
industry. Includes data on bird kills from many other causes.

European Hydrogen Society: www.dwv-info.de.

European Renewable Energy Centres Agency: www.eurec.be.

Hydrogen and Fuel Cell Letter: www.hfcletter.com.

Hydrogen critique by Bossel and others: http://www.efcf.com/reports.

Hydrogen Initiative (USA): http://www.fossil.energy.gov/programs/fuels.

HyWeb Gazette: www.hydrogen.org.

International Association for Hydrogen Energy: www.iahe.org.

National Hydrogen Association (US): www.ttcorp.com.

National Renewable Energy Laboratory, US: www.nrel.gov. The prime US
DOE laboratory on renewables.

Refocus, the International Renewable Energy Magazine: www.environmental-
expert.com/magazine/refocus.

Renewable Energy World magazine: http://www.jxj.com/magsandj/rew.

Renewables Canada: www.renewables.ca.

Solar Tower (Mildura, Australia): www.enviromission.com.au.

Tidal power world survey: http://www.worldenergy.org/wec-geis/publications/
reports/ser/tide/tide.asp?

Wind power birdkills: www.currykerlinger.com/birds.htm.

World Renewable Energy Network: www.wrenuk.co.uk. Non-profit
organization, affiliated with UNESCO. Holds biennial world congresses.

Science: biological, physical and social

Arctic Climate Impact Assessment (ACIA): www.acia.uaf.edu. Multinational
effort to assess potential climate change impacts on the Arctic region.

American Institute of Physics: www.aip.org/history/climate. Documents the history of the climate change issue.

Australian Greenhouse Office, Hot Topics in Climate Change Science: www. greenhouse.gov.au/science/hottopics/.

Australian Institute of Marine Sciences:www.aims.gov.au. Access to latest surveys of coral reef damage due to coral bleaching and other causes.

Association for the Study of Peak Oil and Gas: www.peakoil.net. Interested in the date and impact of the peak and decline of global production of oil and gas. Newsletter online.

Austrian Climate Portal: www.accc.at.

Benfield Hazard Research Centre: www.benfieldhrc.org.

Brookings Institute, The: www.brook.edu/. Studies on economics, the environment and policy.

Carbon Dioxide Information and Analysis Center: www.cdiac.ornl.gov. Part of the US Oak Ridge National Laboratory, and the World Data Center for Atmospheric Trace Gases.

Carbon Mitigation Initiative: www.princeton.edu/~cmi. A joint project of Princeton University, BP and the Ford Motor Company.

Center for International Climate and Environmental Research, Oslo: www.cicero.uio.no.

Climate Change Knowledge Network: www.cckn.net. Members aim to increase knowledge and capacity re climate change.

Climate History: www.aip.org/history/climate. American Institute of Physics website specialising in climate history.

Climatic Research Unit, University of East Anglia: www.cru.uea.ac.uk/.

CSIRO Climate Change and Impacts (Australia): www.dar.csiro.au/impacts/.

CSIRO Climate Impacts and Adaptation Working Group (Australia): http://www.marine.csiro.au/iawg/.

Earth Simulator, Japan: http://www.es.jamstec.go.jp. This is the world's fastest computer system and is simulating climate at fine spatial resolution.

Global and Planetary Change journal: www.elsevier.com/locate/gloplacha.

Global Change Newsletter: www.igbp.kva.se. Newsletter of the International Geosphere-Biosphere Programme (IGBP).

Hadley Centre, UK: www.metoffice.com/research/hadleycentre. The UK Meteorological Office research arm.

Indian Ocean Climate Initiative (IOCI): http://www.ioci.org.au. Studies the causes and predictability of climate change in Western Australia.

Institute for the Study of International Migration, Georgetown University: http://www.georgetown.edu/sfs/programs/isim. Considers the problem of environmentally and economically forced migration.

International Human Dimensions Programme on Global Environmental Change: www.ihdp.org. Includes a newsletter.

Intergovernmental Panel on Climate Change (IPCC): www.ipcc.ch. Joint body set up by the World Meteorological Organization and the UN Environment Programme. Gives policy-relevant advice on climate change and access to IPCC reports.

International Council for Science (ICSU): www.icsu.org. Association of international non-government science organisations with relevant publications.

IPCC Data Distribution Centre: http://ipcc-ddc.cru.uea.ac.uk. Makes available climate modelling and societal growth projection data.

Methane hydrates: http://gashydrate.nrcan.gc.ca/mallik2002/home.asp. An international initiative re methane gas hydrates, as a potential energy resource.

NASA Earth Observatory: http://earthobservatory.nasa.gov. Observations of Earth showing climate-related phenomena.

National Snow and Ice Data Center: http://nsidc.org. Data sets of hemispheric snow and ice and overview of the 'state of the cryosphere'.

Nuclear energy report: http://www.mit.edu/afs/athena/org/n/nuclearpower.

Oxford Institute for Energy Studies: http://www.oxfordclimatepolicy.org. Topical studies on climate and energy policy.

ProClim: www.proclim.ch. Forum run by the Swiss Academy of Science and its Advisory Body on Climate Change (OcCC).

RAPID project: http://www.soc.soton.ac.uk/rapid/rapid.php. Project studying rapid climate change, especially related to the North Atlantic Ocean circulation.

Sense About Science: www.senseaboutscience.org.uk.

Skeptic magazine: www.skeptic.com. Magazine of the real sceptics, rather than the contrarians who are sceptical of only one side of an argument.

Special Report on Emissions Scenarios (SRES): http://sres.ciesin.org . This site also gives lots of links to global change issues.

Tata Institute for Energy Research (India): www.teriin.org.

Tree Ring Newsletter: www.treeringsociety.org. Annual growth rings in trees provide proxy evidence for climate variations.

Tyndall Centre: www.tyndall.ac.uk/. UK research consortium working on climate change impacts and policy issues. Working Papers available.

UK Climate Impact Programme: www.ukcip.org.uk.

US Global Change Research Program: www.usgcrp.gov.

Woods Hole Institute of Oceanography: www.whoi.edu/institutes/occi/hottopics_climatechange.html. This US laboratory includes work on changes in the North Atlantic circulation.

Index